SEVENTIES RINC
Manchester Airport 19

Part of the 'RINGWAY THROUGH THE DECADES' Series

Written and researched by Mark Williams

Published by RINGWAY PUBLICATIONS
www.ringwaypublications.com

Ringway Publications

First published in Great Britain 2011

A catalogue record of this book is available from the British Library

ISBN No: 978-0-9570826-0-1

Printed and bound in Great Britain by
Beamreach (UK) Ltd
22 Pepper Street
Lymm, Cheshire
WA13 OJB
www.beamreachuk.co.uk

(Extensive data will be made available on our website:
to accompany this and future 'Ringway through the Decades' publications)

www.ringwaypublications.com
Contact: info@ringwaypublications.com

Coming next
EIGHTIES RINGWAY

Coming soon
NINETIES RINGWAY

Contents

Photograph Credits:
Front Cover - 25ʰ July 1971 – See the Airport Diary section for details.
(Geoff Ball)

Back Cover: 30ʰ November 1975 – This early morning shot taken on a frosty Sunday morning, shows a small selection of parked aircraft, with many more parked elsewhere. The majority were diversions into Manchester, on a day that would witness many more.
(Geoff Ball)

Inside - The airport's chandeliers were officially unveiled when Prince Philip opened the new terminal in October 1962. Each chandelier costs £3,000, weighs 2 tonnes and is 17ft long. Containing 1,300 pieces of crystal between them, they were designed by Royal architect Stefan Buzas, hand blown by glass maker Bruno Zanetti and manufactured by the famous Venini factory on the Venetian island of Murano, Italy.
(Geoff Ball)

Acknowledgements

I would like to thank everyone who has contributed, by supplying photographs, data, documents, information and encouragement.

My gratitude goes out to:

MANCHESTER AIRPORT ARCHIVE - Patsy McClements for allowing access to their records, including relevant documents, movement sheets, ATC watch logs and photographs and to Michael Hancock, Business Records Officer, for his helpfulness over the last four years. I would also like to mention his predecessor Paul Isherwood, who sadly passed away in 2007. Without his support over the first twelve years of my research, this book would never have been written and it's dedicated to his memory.

MANCHESTER CENTRAL LIBRARY – in particular the Local Studies Department for arranging access to their archives over the last twenty years, which assisted greatly with missing movements data.

WFEL, Heaton Chapel - to Max Houghton, Sales & Marketing Director, (research and input) and Emmeline Jolley (Fairey Aviation archive access).

RESEARCH/MOVEMENTS - to everyone who helped fill any gaps in my research: Geoff Ball, Ian Barrie, Albert Maycock, Stuart Wardman, John Duffield (1970 movements), Peter Hardy (use of Winged Words/PB Enterprises 1972 - August 1979), David McCartney (supplying Winged Words/PB Enterprises publications for reference), Chris Walkden (ATC logs), Paul Smith (supplying LAAS publications for reference), and TAS (Winged Words for reference September 1979 - December 1979).

PHOTOGRAPH CREDITS – Manchester Airport Archive, WFEL, Ian Barrie, Stuart Wardman and Geoff Ball. Geoff has been taking aviation photographs since the 1960's and continues with as much enthusiasm today, as over the past four decades. His pictures are a delight and Ringway Publications are proud and privileged to present them for everyone's enjoyment.

Foreword

As a teenager I spent many happy hours in the 1950's and early 60's at Manchester Airport watching aircraft come and go. This was in the days before security considerations led to the open viewing terraces being closed.

Although I felt I had a comprehensive knowledge of aircraft movements at the airport, Mark Williams' publication surpasses any previous work to comprehensively record "Seventies Ringway."

To those with a special interest in the history of Manchester Airport this publication will be an invaluable companion.

Lord Glendonbrook of Bowdon

Michael David Bishop, Baron Glendonbrook CBE, was born in Bowdon, near Manchester Airport. He joined the ground handling operation of Manchester-based Mercury Airlines in 1963, which was taken over by British Midland Airways in 1964. After joining British Midland, he became General Manager in 1969, Managing Director in 1972 and Chairman in 1978, after raising the capital to lead a management buy-out.

In memory of Paul Isherwood

1
Introduction

I first noticed aircraft when I was seven years old, whilst living directly under the approach in Cheadle Heath, Stockport. I became intrigued when I saw the boys at school looking up at the planes as they flew over the playground, on their descent into Ringway. They were attempting to read something under the aircraft's left wing, which I soon learnt was the registration, unique to each plane. Later I discovered there were exceptions to this rule, as German or American airlines didn't carry them at all. After a short time I became familiar with the regular pattern of the schedules, by seeing or hearing them and began recognising unscheduled aircraft. My interest solidified between Saturday 2nd and Tuesday 5th January 1971, when I witnessed by sight or sound, at home or at school, an unprecedented amount of aircraft. From my classroom I heard what appeared to be an endless stream overhead, particularly during the afternoon of Monday the 4th, when they kept on coming! From then on I made notes and kept meticulous records.

In February 1971 our family moved to a top floor flat on Lancashire Hill, Stockport, 5-miles out on the main runway approach and the view was fantastic! Aircraft could easily be seen from the lounge and kitchen windows, which were perfect for the approach as they faced south westerly towards the airport. As my bedroom faced the opposite direction, I could see approaching aircraft, although at a further distance away and whenever I saw one approach I would run into the kitchen to positively identify it! One of my favourite memories was seeing Spantax CV-990s from far out, or Coronado's as they were also known. They were easy to spot in advance as they had a reputation for a smoky approach, although they weren't the sole culprits, as older Boeing 707s or Douglas DC-8s were just as likely to leave a trail of smoke as well, in an age seemingly not yet switched onto environmental awareness!

It was an unmistakable sight to see one of these on approach, accompanied by all that smoke! Spantax, with their Coronado's could be seen on a fairly regular basis throughout the 1970's and in their day they were the fastest airliners around. (Manchester Airport Archive)

Despite the great position of our flat, in fog or low cloud anything below 1,500ft could only be heard and as a result good numbers were missed. Also up until Christmas 1975 when I finally got some binoculars, I couldn't read off many registrations, but if anything was missed it was guaranteed the boys at school would have seen them. One airline you didn't need binoculars for was Romania's Tarom, as their under-wing registrations were enormous. During the hot summer of 1975 I remember watching them against the backdrop of a clear blue sky and during this particular summer they sent in a varied selection of aircraft. Apart from the Il-62s, they also used Ilyushin Il-18s, Boeing 707s & BAC 1-11s, all with the massive writing under their wings. Another vivid memory was when aircraft made a 'visual' approach and instead of seeing them on their normal approach course, they would scream directly over the flats, at a seemingly lower altitude and although it was very exciting it was also quite scary! One such occasion was Sunday 30th November 1975, when

JAL B.747 JA-8122 was diverting in from London-Heathrow and made a spectacular visual approach on that cold and frosty morning.

1973 was the year I bought my first Civil Aircraft Markings or 'CAM' as it was referred to and started keeping records This was the bible to any enthusiast, as it listed all British & Irish registered aircraft and any foreign aircraft and airlines likely to be seen in the UK. From my first school Alexandra Park, I could see the approach from the playground and some classrooms, but trying to view aircraft from my next school, Peel Moat Upper in Heaton Moor, wasn't as easy. It was much further away from the approach, but it could be seen from the outside at break or lunchtimes and from most classrooms if you knew where to look, except in low cloud or bad weather when you had no chance!

Saturday 21st June 1975 was the first time I'd made more than a fleeting visit to the airport, spending more than five hours there on a hot, sunny day, one of many that summer. From then on and for the next two years, I visited every two weeks whatever the weather. Most enthusiasts will remember Manchester having excellent spotting facilities in the 1970's, much as they do today with the present day viewing park, which we are very lucky to have, but they were very different. It's a pity the UK's other airports didn't follow Manchester's lead, as many have little or no viewing facilities left.

In 1975 the bus from Stockport to Manchester Airport, the 369, took forty-five minutes and cost 2p for the under-16's. The bus station was an open air row of bus stops, located where the Parachute Regiment Commemoration stone is situated today. Once at the airport we made our way to the booth to the left of the Tower, next to Tower Road and bought entrance tokens to get us through the turnstiles. The man in the booth had the latest Manchester timetables 'hot off the press' at the beginning of each month and if we were lucky he would give us a photocopied sheet of the actual arrivals and departures of the day. To the left of the entrance booth was a long bike shed and handy shelter when waiting for the bus home in bad weather.

Once through the turnstiles and after a short walk to several flights of stairs, we had access to the piers and terraces. From the top, the entrance to the Domestic pier was straight ahead and you could walk its entire length and look down on the aircraft. Another option was to turn right and follow the walkway underneath the northern face of the Tower building, which was another place to shelter from the elements. This led to an open area with benches and a coin-operated telescope and another flight of stairs led to a further open area with more benches and another telescope. Ahead to the left was an indoor viewing area, known as the 'animal-house' or 'glass-house', where everything could be seen through tinted glass. There were lots more benches to sit on, but on a damp day the smell could get a bit much when it was full of spotters drying off!

Ahead out of the covered area was a rinky-dink café on the right, as it opened and closed at irregular times and frequently ran out of stock. At this time it was possible to access the terraces from the main terminal concourse via a door next to the Brabazon Suite, located on the right hand side of the building, when standing at the main concourse windows looking out at the apron. This was the concourse containing the spectacular chandeliers the airport was so famous for. Once through this door, several flights of stairs led to the access to the terraces. From the café more stairs led down to yet another open area with benches, a telescope and a shop selling books, models, timetables and confectionery, which was run by local aviation society PB Enterprises for a time. Our favourite spot was in this area on a strategically placed bench, directly under the staircase. When you walked out of the shop there were three options, the first was ahead and to the right was the entrance to the International pier, which offered the same delights as the Domestic pier, via a turnstile entrance. The second option was to go right after the toilets and make a u-turn to a flight of stairs leading to an elevated covered viewing area, with more seating. From 1974, the third option was another u-turn, eventually leading to what was known as the 'jumbo pier', the third pier to be fully operational that year.

There were lots of stories at the time about friends and relatives throwing various items down from the pier to passengers about to board aircraft. I actually saw this happen, when a woman threw a flight bag to her husband boarding a British Airways BAC 1-11!

Regrettably, these wonderful facilities were temporarily closed for several months in August 1978, due to 'terrorist threats' - sounds familiar? By the late 1980's they had finally succumbed to redevelopment and were lost forever in the early 1990's. Looking back it's hard to believe we had such excellent facilities and as the majestic view from the top of the T1 multi-storey car park will testify, little evidence of those times remains!

For my birthday in February 1976 I received a Kingsonic LW/MW/SW/PB/WB radio, which importantly had an aircraft band. To a thirteen year old it was a fantastic piece of kit and it gave sterling service for ten years, although it became terminally ill during the last three years of its life, when it finally expired and went to air band heaven in 1989! I never knew how much it cost, but I saw one in a shop window a few years later for £10. It was a cracking set and it started my obsession with listening to aircraft and ATC transmission, which I regularly taped on a cassette recorder. I still enjoy listening to the recordings over thirty years later and I've tried to preserve them by transferring them onto CD, but it's difficult due to their age and perilous condition.

Summer 1970 - This quaint morning shot, shows four different BAC 1-11's, awaiting their next flights, witnessed by a small group of spectators. Apart from the BEA, Laker Airways & BUA aircraft is G-AWYS, on lease for the summer to Swissair in their basic colours. (Manchester Airport Archive)

Aircraft in those days were not only individualistic in design, but they also had their own distinctive sound over the airwaves and I could distinguish a 1-11 from a Comet, a Trident or a 747 etc. Every airline type had its own sound too, for example a British Caledonian B.707 would sound different to a British Airways B.707. Aircraft were exciting to listen to back then as they all sound the same nowadays, with no whines, whistles or crackles, just bland unexciting transmission. An Airbus 319 sounds like an Airbus 319 whoever owns it! I still have an aircraft radio and listen in occasionally, but it's just not the same.

My first trip outside of Manchester Airport was an excursion with PB Enterprises to Heathrow & Biggin Hill on Saturday 29th January 1977. The first stop was Heathrow and although there was no snow or ice, Terminal 3 car park at 5am was the coldest and windiest place I'd ever been! We were outside for four hours before the Queens Building opened and we could go inside and eventually thaw out! The coach returned at 1300 to take us from Terminal 1 to Biggin Hill, the aviation equivalent of an antique shop! It was full of curios and antiquities either on show, hidden away in hangars and even parked between trees! The first aircraft in view was IAS Britannia G-AOVP, which had long since been withdrawn from service. The second, vintage type Percival Prince N206UP, formerly G-ALWH, had operated for many years with Decca Navigator and was awaiting its ferry flight to the USA. There were several hangars containing a variety of weird and wonderful aircraft in various stages of disrepair, including the only time I ever saw a gyro-copter. It was also memorable for seeing so many vintage Doves and Herons, mostly derelict and abandoned. I remember being frozen to the bone as we boarded the coach around 5.30pm and hearing Radio 1 playing 'Year of the Cat' by Al Stewart. Whenever I've heard the song since, it's taken me back to that bitterly cold, but very enjoyable day.

Tarom were known for their enormous under-wing registrations. Their Ilyushin Il-18s were often seen at Ringway in the 1970's, particularly during the early part of the decade. They also used BAC 1-11s, Boeing 707s, Ilyushin Il-62s & Tupolev TU-154s throughout this period, which all carried the over-sized registrations. (Geoff Ball)

I was still spotting in May 1979 and Friday the 4th was memorable for many reasons. Firstly it was the day after the General Election when Margaret Thatcher swept to power, secondly it was my last day at school and finally it was the day our family moved to yet another high-rise flat, this time on the other side of Stockport; located on the fourteenth floor of fifteen, around 5-miles from touchdown – and the view was amazing!

Friday 12th June 1981 was the date of my first foreign spotting trip to Paris for the Air Show, with my friend Brian Marshall-Lee. We caught an evening train to Euston on Friday 12th June and a tube to Heathrow, where we spent the night on the floor of Terminal 1 ready for our morning flight to Paris. We boarded L.1011 G-BBAE as BA306 and continued onwards to the show at Le Bourget, where we spent the day before transferring to a hotel near Charles De Gaulle Airport. On Sunday the 14th we made the trip over to Orly Airport and spent the whole day collecting numbers in very hot weather. Paris Orly had a completely different set of flights and aircraft than Charles de Gaulle and the vast amount of traffic by various African-flag carrying airlines was particularly noticeable. We spent the Sunday night on a terminal floor again, this time at Orly, before transferring back to De Gaulle for our Monday morning flight. We flew back to Heathrow on L.1011 G-BBAI as BA307 and spent several hours collecting numbers before catching our train home.

So that's how my passion for aircraft began and forty years later it burns as brightly as ever! Writing this series on Manchester Airport has resurrected many happy memories and it's been a pleasure and a privilege to produce such a labour of love and record these unique and by-gone times for the enjoyment of anyone interested in aviation history.

MARK WILLIAMS

2
Airport Data

Manchester-Ringway Airfield Details
Manchester Airport is located 5321N 0216W, 8-miles south of Manchester City Centre.

Available Runways
Runway 06/24 – 9,000ft x 150ft
Runway 02/20 – 3,282ft x 150ft
Runway 10/28 – 3,273ft x 150ft

Radar Aids
ILS
GCA (Ground Controlled Approach)
PAR (Primary Approach Radar) - also known as Surveillance Radar Approach

Apron
The total area of the apron is approximately 200,000 sq yards. It's served by two piers - the International, 960ft in length with eleven parking stands and the Domestic, 720ft in length with nine parking stands. The stands vary in size, but the biggest on the International pier is capable of handling the largest aircraft. In addition to the pier stands, parking is available for six to eight aircraft on the southern extension to the apron, known as the South Bay. The old apron in front of the hangars covering an area of 30,000sq yards, used by freight and light aircraft, is known as the Freight Apron.

Frequencies
Tower: 118.7
Approach: 119.4
Ground: 121.7
ATIS: 121.95
North/Eastbound departure frequency: 124.2
Southbound (Amber 1) departure frequency: Preston Radar 125.9
Southbound (Amber 25) departure frequency: 127.35
Westbound (Red 3) departure frequency: 125.1

By 1978, the Manchester Airport/Manchester Control frequencies had been revised as follows:
Tower 118.7
Approach 119.4
Director 121.35
Ground 121.7
ATIS 121.95
North/Eastbound departure frequency 126.65
Southeast Bound (Amber 1) departure frequency 124.2 (Secondary 133.4)
Southwest Bound (Amber 25) departure frequency 125.1 (Secondary 133.05)
Westbound departure frequency 125.1 (Secondary 133.05)

3
ATC in the Region

In 1970, UK ATC was divided into three sections, London Airways, Preston Airways & Scottish Airways. Preston Airway's headquarters were located in a large house, Barton Hall, close to Preston and from there a complex network monitored all aircraft in the North West area. The boundaries controlled by Preston were:

NORTH	Deans Cross (near Carlisle)
SOUTH	Stafford/Lichfield
EAST	Dogger Bank
WEST	Point Lynus/Isle of Man

The airways covered by Preston are:

Amber One	The sector North/South between Deans Cross & Stafford/Lichfield
Blue One	The sector East/West between Pole Hill (near Preston) & Dogger Bank
Red Three	The sector East/West between Pole Hill & Point Lynus/Isle of Man
Amber 25	The sector North/South between Pole Hill & Knighton (Shropshire)

Each of the above sectors has its own frequencies:

Amber One	127.45 - Sector north of Pole Hill (North/Southbound)
	125.25 - Sector south of Pole Hill (Southbound)
	125.9 – Sector south of Pole Hill (Northbound)
Blue One	127.45 – Sector east of Oldham, 125.1 – Sector west of Oldham
Red Three	125.1
Amber 25	129.1

All aircraft operating outside controlled airspace broadcast on 125.5 or 126.85 and aircraft in the upper airspace (24,000ft or above) on 132.7. After 2100 on weekdays and all day on winter Saturdays/Sundays, Preston only operates on two frequencies: 127.45 & 132.7 for the upper airspace.

In addition to broadcasting from Barton Hall, Preston Airways also broadcast from Manchester Airport itself and Lindholme (near Doncaster).

By 1978, there had been many changes to the ATC airways structure. One of the main changes was the abolition of the Preston Radar in January 1975, when responsibility was split between Manchester Control and London ATCC at West Drayton. The following information details the changes:

Amber One,	Glasgow (GOW)–Pole Hill (POL)–Honiley (HON)–Midhurst (MID)
Amber One East	Pole Hill (POL)–Lichfield (LIC)–Daventry (DTY)–Woodley (WOD)–Midhurst (MID)
Amber Two	Talla (TLA)–Pole Hill (POL)–Lichfield (LIC)–Daventry (DTY)–Brookman's Park (BPK)
Blue One	Dublin (DUB)–Wallasey (WAL)–Ottringham (OTR)–Dogger
Blue Three	Wallasey (WAL)–Honiley (HON)–Brookman's Park–Dover (DVR)
Green One	Shannon (SNN)–Strumble (STU)–Brecon (BCN)–Woodley (WOD)–Biggin (BIG)
Amber 25	Deans Cross (DCS)–Wallasey (WAL)–Knighton (KNI)–Brecon (BCN)–Exmoor
Red Three	Belfast (BEL)–Isle of Man (IOM)–Wallasey (WAL)–Brookmans Park (BPK) – Lambourne (LAM)
Red Four	Isle of Man (IOM)–Pole Hill (POL)–Ottringham (OTR)

Frequencies:

Pole Hill Sector 132.7	Daventry (Southbound) Sector 133.7
Wallasey Sector 128.05	Daventry (Northbound) Sector 134.75
Brecon (SW) Sector 133.6	North Sea Sector 134.25

January 1970

Since BOAC designated Manchester as the primary diversion airfield for their B.747 Jumbo Jets, they have set aside £80,000 in preparation for receiving diversions from London-Heathrow. The cash, to be spent on specialised ground equipment to handle one B.747, will include passenger steps, luggage and freight loading machinery. This type of equipment would normally be bought by Manchester Corporation, but on this occasion they will only operate and maintain it. Although the first B.747 is expected to be delivered to BOAC this April; it's unlikely it will be used on Manchester's transatlantic services before 1974.

Work to improve the airport's international flight facilities will start at the end of the month. The Control Tower block will be extended and a new six-storey office block will be built by the present Control Cower. Tenants for the new offices include the Preston Air Traffic Control Unit, BEA and Manchester Corporation.

2nd Lloyd International Britannia G-ANCD made the first of many freight flights this month, operating on behalf of BEA Cargo, due to crew shortages.

2nd Privately owned Douglas DC-3 N3179Q night-stopped on a late flight from Amsterdam. It departed the following morning to Bremen, returned late afternoon and stayed for just over an hour before departing back to Bremen.

6th Air Malawi HS.748 7Q-YKB performed a practice ILS and overshoot today, on a test flight out of Woodford. Another exotic HS.748, 9N-AAU of Royal Nepal Airlines, also overshot on two occasions (9th/12th).

12th Iberia operated their final Madrid-Manchester service today, with Douglas DC-9 EC-BIM. Their twice-weekly service operated since 1968 has been withdrawn, but they will return to Manchester in the summer, operating to Barcelona and Palma.

17th Canadian Air Force CC-06 Yukon 15926, the military version of the Canadair CL-44, arrived as CAM560, en route from RAF Valley to Prestwick.

21st German Air Force Noratlas 52+85 arrived into Manchester today and a further flight from RAF Topcliffe to Erding, Bavaria with 52+82 arrived the following day.

22nd The month was devoid of wintry weather up until this evening, when Heathrow was affected by dense fog. Manchester accepted nine diversions between 2034-2217, including two highlights. First was the first visit of a Kuwait Airways B.707 when 9K-ACL arrived at 2115 (KU187 from Kuwait City via Frankfurt) and second, also making its first visit was Air France B.727 F-BPJJ at 2217 from Paris.

22nd Not directly connected with Manchester, but the following news event still makes interesting reading regarding the Boeing 747. Pan American's first fare paying passenger 747 arrived at London-Heathrow today from New York, a day later than originally planned and nearly seven hours later than scheduled, carrying with it a couple of potentially serious problems. The original flight on the 21st, due to take place with N733PA (Clipper Young America), was cancelled due to an overheated engine. It was cancelled again the following day for the same reason, resulting in the passengers having to change planes at Kennedy Airport. The initial delay was caused by the crew spending more than an hour trying to close a faulty door on N733PA. The flight was delayed further when N736PA (Clipper Victor) was brought out of a maintenance hangar and the baggage, freight, food and passengers all had to be transferred onto the replacement aircraft. Once taxiing and ultimately joining the queue for departure, dwarfing the conventional B.707s & DC-8s as it went, it had to return to the gate when the Captain discovered the No. 4 engine was overheating. The runway queue only added to the problem, as it meant Captain Weeks was unable to open up all the engines. Idling at only 4%, there was not enough power to cool the potential hazard of an overheated engine and sure enough, the warning came up on the control-panel. It turned out the conditions outside (icy 15-20 knot crosswinds) had created a partial vacuum across the front of the big jet's fan intake, which stalled the compressor and allowed the rear part of the engine still vigorously sucking in fuel, to overheat. It's a problem the engine manufacturers, Pratt & Whitney, are familiar with but senior officials of the company onboard at the time admitted to have it happen while taxiing, on three occasions so far, was more than a little worrying! The company will be under great pressure to find a quick solution after the earlier trouble, when the engines were sagging into a slightly oval shape. Although the problem may well be a procedural one, such as taxiing on two engines rather than all four, which would have allowed them to develop more thrust and prevent overheating. In spite of the problems, Pan American has no plans to withdraw the aircraft from service. In the meantime the Federal Aviation Agency decided in view of the danger of the 747s turbulent wake, that for the time being following aircraft should stay 10-miles behind on takeoff and landing, instead of the usual 3-miles. The decision has been accepted by the Board of Trade for British Airport's, at least until more is known about the jumbo's turbulence, as the vortices trailing behind an airliner are capable of flipping a light aeroplane onto its back. The new ruling means when the 747 becomes a frequent visitor at Heathrow this summer, ATC will have to stretch the present minimum interval between takeoffs of 1-1½ minutes. This change will neutralise the benefits the 350-seater aircraft would otherwise have had, in easing the congested airways between London and New York. The Chairman of the British Airports Authority said yesterday that the new ruling made it all the more urgent to get a third airport for London.

23rd   Manchester Airport says it will have no difficulty in enforcing the 'jumbo gap', a 10-mile separation between landing jumbo jets and following aircraft. However, the spacing threatens to seriously disrupt airline schedules, especially during peak periods at London Heathrow. It's hoped that before jumbo jets come into service at Ringway, experience will show the safety gap to be over cautious, but in the meantime Ringway's schedules are flexible enough to accept diverted jumbos without trouble. While a minimum gap of 5-miles between landing aircraft is enforced at Ringway, the American FAA ordered that no aircraft should be less than 10-miles behind a landing jumbo, or less than four minutes behind during takeoff. When approaching an airport there must also be a 2,000ft gap in height between the jumbo and other aircraft, when previously the ruling was 3-miles on approach, two minutes on takeoff and a 1,000ft separation gap.

24th   Night flights started again after a three month break for runway strengthening and improvement work, in preparation of B.747 operations. The runway closure has been in effect since last September, when it closed from 0030-0730, Monday-Saturday. Due to a number of hard frosts, the work was completed over two weeks late.

24th   Lufthansa are using Boeing 737s on cargo flights previously operated by Sud-Flug Douglas DC-4s and the last one, D-ACAB, operated yesterday.

27th   Late evening saw more weather diversions from Heathrow, all BEA except for BOAC Boeing 707 G-APFG. The aircraft had been operating a training flight from Stansted to Heathrow when the weather closed in and it eventually diverted into Manchester at 2320.

28th   Last evening's diversions continued sporadically throughout the early hours and the last, at 1232, was BEA Trident 2 G-AVFM (BE285 from Athens). The highlights of this session were TMA DC-6F OD-AEU at 0429 (TL103 from Beirut) & South African AW B.707 ZS-SAH at 1044 (SA234 from Las Palmas). After receiving fourteen weather diversions during the morning, Manchester was unable to take any more by midday, due to staff shortages. BEA was hit particularly hard by staff sickness and uncooperative off-duty workers supposedly participating in voluntary call-out system!

30th   SAS operated SE.210 Caravelle HS-TGF on its SK537/8 Copenhagen service today, which recently returned off-lease from Thai International.

February 1970
Manchester Airport announced a new record was set when they handled 1,552,000 passengers last year, a figure five times greater than fifteen years ago.

Aer Lingus are withdrawing their remaining Viscounts this year. With effect from 1st April most Manchester-Cork/Shannon services, previously operated by Viscounts, will be operated by Boeing 737s, although the occasional Viscount may appear until October.

Cessna distributors, Northair, are relocating part of their fleet to Manchester. The Leeds based air-taxi operator took recent delivery of two Beagle 206s, G-AXZL & G-AWRO, which are expected to take up residency and operate flights on behalf of British Nuclear Fuels to Dounreay.

The airport plays host to a variety of civil and military traffic each month, performing practice approaches for crew training purposes. To all intents and purposes, aircraft give the intention of making a normal approach and landing, but instead at any distance between three to less than a mile from touchdown, they break off the approach. Aircraft seen at Manchester performing such flights were a number of HS.748s on training flights out of Woodford: SAESA XA-SAB (3rd/23rd26th) & XA-SAC (19th) and BFS D-AFSC (23rd). The German HS.748, D-AFSC, due for delivery to Bundesanstalt fuer Flugsicherung (BFS), will operate a similar role to those of our own Civil Aviation Authority, by performing ILS checks and calibration duties at various airports throughout Germany.

4th   SAS used ex-Thai International SE.210 Caravelle HS-TGF again today, operating SK537/8.

4th   Another two German Air Force Noratlas aircraft appeared again this month. 53+31 operated as DCN1300 Alhorn to Bremen today and 53+15 stayed for two hours before departing at 1435 for Oldenburg on the 12th.

12th   The airport was kept busy with another morning rush of weather diversions, mostly British, apart from two Alitalia DC-9s: I-DIKB at 1231 (AZ284 from Rome) & I-DIKV at 1226 (AZ282 from Milan) and KLM DC-9 PH-DNI at 1007 (KL117 from Amsterdam); but the outstanding diversion was private DC-9 N228Z, making its first visit routing Bangor-Heathrow.

15th   Today's visit of Qantas B.707 VH-EAF (QF173 from Tehran) was the first of two this month. The second on the 26th was VH-EAJ, operating from/to Karachi as QF167/8.

17th   BOAC SVC-10 G-ASGI was hit by lightning on its decent into Manchester today, as it positioned in from London as BA2224 to operate the outbound BA537 to Prestwick.

21st   PA-31 D-IGON, arriving at 2030 from Shannon, was on delivery from the Piper factory in Kansas. It departed the following morning for Dusseldorf.

22nd   Another aircraft on delivery was Cessna 185 G-AXVT, arriving from the USA via Dublin, before its departure for Cranfield the following day.

27th   The only visit of a non-British business jet this month was today's arrival of HS.125 D-CAMB, from/to Stuttgart.

March 1970

The airport has benefitted from Heathrow's recent industrial action, as the number of passengers using Manchester's direct European routes has risen steadily for the last three weeks. BEA's seasonal figures were up by 20%, with routes to Paris, Amsterdam & Brussels doing particularly well. Aer Lingus' routes are also up by 20%-30% and business has also increased on BOAC's transatlantic routes.

1st   Just one Qantas flight, B.707 VH-EBP (QF173/4 Tehran-Antalya), operated through Manchester this month. These flights are mainly for families emigrating from the UK to Australia, under an assisted scheme.

2nd   BEA Comet (registration unknown) operating scheduled flight (BE4064) from London, burst its port side tyres on touchdown, when landing in a snowstorm. The runway was blocked for two hours whilst the aircraft was jacked up for a wheel change.

2nd   The latest HS.748 off Woodford's production line appearing at Manchester for a practice ILS was XA-SAF, another aircraft for Mexican-operator SAESA.

3rd   BEA Trident 2 G-AVFA was used to take Manchester City to Oporto, for their European Cup-Winners quarter final first leg match against Portuguese side Academica, the following day.

4th   Dan-Air Comet G-APDN arrived from Gatwick to take more Manchester City fans to Oporto.

4th   Today's newspapers forecasting 'scattered sleet or snow showers with sunny intervals', got it so wrong, as snow came down by the bucket-load over England and Wales!

4th   Arriving on a busy afternoon from Edinburgh was USAF Douglas C-47 51116, making its last visit after being a regular into Manchester during the 1960's. It departed the following morning for RAF Northolt.

4th   HS.125 LN-NPC arrived during the afternoon on diversion from Heathrow, carrying 'Busy Bee of Norway' titles. Sold to McAlpine Aviation in 1972 as G-AVXL, it became a regular visitor to Manchester before being sold on again in 1977 as I-SNAF and withdrawn in 1988.

4th March 1970 – Snow caused chaos in the south and diversions started to arrive during the afternoon. Amongst them was MEA CV-990 OD-AFK as 'Cedar 201' from Beirut and parked either side are Austrian Airlines SE.210 OE-LCO & Alitalia Douglas DC-9 I-DIKO. (Geoff Ball)

4th March 1970 – Also arriving in the afternoon, within an hour of each other, were two Comets from Cairo. SU-ALL & SU-ALM were operated by United Arab, the forerunner of Egyptair and both were taken out of service by 1976. (Geoff Ball)

4th   Although Manchester had a covering of snow; it was nothing compared to the heavy falls affecting the rest of the UK. Ringway received twenty-five diversions, eighteen of which arrived in the afternoon during a two-hour period. Highlights included two United Arab Comets: SU-ALM at 1539 (MS771 from Cairo) & SU-ALL at 1629 (MS779 from Cairo); Aerolineas Argentinas B.707 LV-ISC at 1525 (AR130 from Madrid) which has been the airlines only visit, Austrian Airlines SE.210 OE-LCO at 1612 (OS451 from Vienna) and MEA CV-990 OD-AFK at 1615 (ME201 from Beirut).

5th   Dan-Air Comet G-APDN arrived back from Portugal with Manchester City fans, having seen their team draw 0-0 with Academica.

10th   German Air Force Noratlas 50+06, arriving at 1212 on a training flight from RAF Northolt, was a first visit. It stayed overnight and departed for Birmingham at 0907.

12th   An outstanding military visitor was Swedish Air Force Pembroke 83006, night-stopping on a round trip from Karup.

18th   The influx of Sabena SE.210 Caravelle's, were in connection with Leeds United's game with Standard Liege, in the European Cup Quarter Final second leg tie. SE 210s OO-SRA, OO-SRB & OO-SRF all arrived within twenty minutes of each other at lunchtime. Leeds emerged as the victors, winning the evening match 1-0.

27th Making its first visit to Manchester this afternoon was SAS Douglas DC-9 SE-DBW, operating flight SK537/8, instead of the usual SE.210 Caravelle.

31st Britannia Airways B.737 G-AVRM took Manchester City out to Dusseldorf for their European Cup Winners-Cup semi-final first leg against German team, Schalke. They returned the following evening after City was beaten 1-0.

April 1970

BOAC announced its eighteen-month service linking Manchester with Tel Aviv, has been dropped due to insufficient passengers. The once-weekly flight, via Heathrow had been regularly cancelled after the scheduled VC-10 carried an average of just sixteen passengers. Although the last flight operated on 29th March, the service is still included in their summer timetable. Earlier this year, BOAC cabin crew threatened strike action if they were rostered to transit through their home base at Heathrow on such flights as the Manchester-London-Tel Aviv service; but BOAC denied this was the reason for withdrawing and maintained it was due to lack of passengers.

BOAC took delivery of their first Boeing 747, G-AWNA, at Heathrow this month and although they will be regular visitors to Manchester eventually; they could be idle throughout the summer and possibly longer, due to a pilot dispute over pay and conditions for crewing the type.

Due to BEA experiencing a capacity shortage after losing Trident 1 G-ARPS in a ground fire at Heathrow last year; they are leasing a Cambrian Airways BAC 1-11 and a BKS Viscount.

Several airlines have been changing their operations or increasing flight frequencies through Manchester. Alitalia will still operate from/to Milan, but the evening arrival of AZ288 will continue onwards to Dublin to night-stop, before returning to Manchester the following morning as AZ289, before departing again for Milan. Air France now operates six-times weekly to Paris. KLM have increased frequency on Amsterdam passenger flight KL153/4 to five-times weekly. SAS increased Copenhagen flights from two to three-weekly. BEA will have no scheduled Comet flights during the summer, as all Heathrow flights will be operated by Vanguards & BAC Super 1-11s and Dublin flights will be exclusively operated by Super 1-11s.

ILS traffic included the following from Woodford: Zambia Airways HS.748 9J-ABJ (1st/15th/16th), BFS HS.748 D-AFSD (28th) and RAF Nimrods XV226 (17th), XV238 (17th) & XV236 (23rd). RAF Britannia's noted and identified on training flights were XL635 & XM496 (1st), XL659 (6th/7th), XL660 (15th/27th) and HS.125 G-AXLX overshot on the 8th.

2nd Air Paris Heron F-BGOJ operated a return flight to Paris-Orly.

3rd A total of 350 corporation staff returned to work after a 24-hour unofficial strike over pay parity with British Airport Authority workers. The stoppage, involving firemen and porters, not only brought Manchester Airport to a complete standstill, but it also affected other UK airports including Belfast and Glasgow.

10th Alitalia introduced a new once-weekly cargo service to Milan and Rome with SAM Cargo Douglas DC-6s and the inaugural flight was operated by I-DIMB.

14th Loftleidir CL-44 TF-LLJ arrived early evening on a cargo flight, routing Stockholm-St. Johns as LL301. It was sold in 1975 and saw further service in Belgium and Gabon before crashing in Harare, Zimbabwe in February 1982.

17th Engineers were still repairing the BEA Vanguard, forced to make an emergency landing last night after hydraulic failure. BE5413 was routing Edinburgh-Heathrow, when the pilot reported two of its four hydraulic systems had failed. On touchdown, the remaining two also failed and the pilot said 'he was extremely fortunate, as the complete failure came too late to be of any danger'!

18th Tarom operated several flights during the month, transporting tomatoes from Bucharest. Ilyushin IL-18 YR-IMC, arriving at 1621 today, was the first and the others were YR-IMA (29th), YR-IMC (28th) & YR-IME (24th/29th/30th).

24th Due to the loss of CV-990 HB-ICB in February, BAC 1-11 G-AWYS is being leased to Swissair. It made its first appearance today, operating all flights for the remainder of the month with BUA crews and Swissair cabin staff. As well as Manchester, it's also scheduled on services from Zurich to Nice and Stuttgart.

29th Today saw a mass exodus of flights to Vienna, in conjunction with the European Cup-Winners Cup Final, where Manchester City were taking on Gornik Zabrze. City won 2-1 and the fans returned over the next two days. The victory completed a double for English clubs in Europe, as Arsenal won the Fairs Cup the day earlier, beating Anderlecht 3-0. Aircraft involved were Britannia AW B.737 G-AVRM, Dan-Air BAC 1-11 G-AXCP & Comet G-APDN; Caledonian BAC 1-11 G-AWWY, Donaldson International Britannia G-APNA, Monarch Britannia G-AOVI, Channel Airways Comet G-APYC & Trident G-AVYB and BEA Airtours Comet G-ARGM. There was also another Qantas flight today, when B.707 VH-EBT (QF171/2) arrived from Tehran at 1136 and co-incidentally, it too departed for Vienna at 1811.

15th April 1970 – Schalke football fans are seen disembarking from two of the three LTU SE.210 Caravelle's (D-ABAP, D-ABAV & D-ABAW), which arrived late afternoon from Dusseldorf in connection with the European Cup-Winners Cup second leg with Manchester City. As City won 5-1, it meant they had reached the final on the 29th April against Polish side Gornik Zabrze. Of interest in the background are the striped airport vehicles, used for aircraft requiring Ground Approach Radar. (Geoff Ball)

May 1970
Manchester Airport should be ready to handle Boeing 747s from the end of the month. The main runway's been repaired and upgraded and the installation of flush lighting along the runway length is well in advance. BOAC plan to commence scheduled B.747 flights by early 1974, upon completion of the extension and expansion programme.

BOAC added a second daily service to Montreal (BA605/6) from the end of the month, to complement existing flight BA607/8 to Montreal/Toronto.

Iberia's evening summer flights commenced on the 17th with SE.210 Caravelle's, from/to Palma weekly on Sundays and via Barcelona on Mondays/Thursdays until 28th September.

Summer IT flights commenced with the following airlines: Aviaco (with Iberia SE.210s), Aviogenex, Balair, Balkan, Bavaria & Spantax. UK operators were BEA Airtours, Britannia Airways, British Midland, British United, Caledonian, Channel Airways, Dan-Air & Laker Airways.

The only HS.748 ILS traffic from Woodford was Hawker-Siddeley HS.748 G-11-3 (26th). RAF Britannia's identified were XL636 (12th), XL637 (13th) & XM518 (18th). Other RAF types were C-130 XV298 (22nd) and Nimrod XV226 (29th).

1st   The first regular IT flights direct to Greece commenced today, when Laker Airways operated GK309 to Corfu.

2nd   BUA's new daily Manchester summer service to Jersey (BR050/1), was operated by BAC 1-11 G-ASJH.

4th   BEA's very early Malta flight, BE319/8, operated by Cyprus Airways Trident 5B-DAA, was also making its first visit.

5th   Swissair used BUA BAC 1-11 G-AWYS almost exclusively during the month on passenger flight SR840/1, except for today, when it was operated by Douglas DC-9 HB-IFU.

18th Twin Otter CF-YFT, arriving from Gatwick at 2018, night-stopped before departing the following morning for Dounraey. It returned on the 20th and stayed overnight again, before departing for Brough.

21st CV-440s N14278 & N25278 arrived within five minutes of each other from Stansted, before their departure for Dusseldorf in the afternoon. They are operated by the Armstrong Cork Company, a subsidiary of worldwide floor specialists, Armstrong Corporation.

24th Nigerian registered Cessna 150 5N-AII made a round trip this afternoon, from its current base in Leicester.

27th Belgian Air Force C-119 Boxcar CP-17 arrived at 1326 for a short stay from Brussels, before its departure at 1417 for RAF Leeming.

29th DC-9 PH-DNG positioned in from Amsterdam to operate the outbound KL154 at 1751, after KLM DC-9 PH-DNS went tech on arrival on this morning's KL153.

June 1970

Northern Executive Aviation are considering starting scheduled services between Manchester and other northern cities, after identifying a growing demand for feeder services linking passengers in provincial centre's with international air services from Manchester. They are taking a cautious approach and if their first Islander proves successful on charter work, they will purchase more for their planned services next year.

Horizon Tours announced plans for a huge expansion of holiday charter flights out of Manchester next year, with new routes and extra capacity. They currently use BUA, but as they are about to amalgamate with Caledonian and only operate out of London next year, Horizon have secured the services of a reputable airline, but haven't disclosed who they will be.

New IT destinations to be offered from Manchester next year are Rhodes (Caledonian) & Tangiers (Channel Airways), with all UK charter airlines operating more flights next year.

Transatlantic flights from/to the USA increased this month when the following airlines and aircraft were used: ONA DC-8 N863F (21st), Pan American B.707s N405PA (16th) N454PA (1st) & N491PA (30th); Saturn Airways DC-8s N8008F (27th) & N8956U (6th), TIA DC-8 N4865T (16th/26th), TWA B.707 N28724 (17th) and World Airways B.707s N370WA (28th) & N373WA (11th). Charters from/to Canada included Air Canada DC-8 CF-TJE (18th) and Wardair B.727 CF-FUN (6th/25th). UK airlines operating to the USA & Canada were British United (VC-10), Caledonian (B.707) & Lloyd International (B.707).

It was a very quiet month for ILS traffic, with no HS.748s and the only military aircraft noted were RAF Britannia XM490 (3rd/4th) & Comet XR399 (5th).

1st BEA introduced the BAC Super 1-11 onto the Belfast to Manchester route today, replacing Viscounts. The first flight (BE7504) was flown in a record time of thirty-four minutes.

2nd German Air Force Transall 50+45 arrived at 1212 as DCN2139 on a training flight from Farnborough to Erding. Others were Noratlas 53+38 Oslo/Northolt (18th), Noratlas 53+22 RAF Boscombe Down-Lemwerder & Transall 50+32 Lyneham-Cologne (30th).

5th A warm Friday evening saw the arrival of Mey-Air CV-240 LN-KAP from Oslo. The Norwegian airline started charter operations in 1970 and eventually purchased two Boeing 737s in 1971. Their sole CV-240 served right up until the airlines demise in 1973.

6th Board of Trade officials were investigating a near miss today, after a BEA Vanguard routing London-Edinburgh and a BOAC B.707F from Manchester to New York, came within a mile of each other at 16,000ft over Oldham.

7th Manchester's newest transatlantic air link commenced today. For the summer season only, Chicago is linked as an extension of BOAC's existing flight (BA607/6), to/from Montreal.

9th Itavia Fokker F.28 I-TIDA arrived from/to Milan today, as IH542/3.

24th Dan-Air received the go-ahead to include Manchester in their weekday schedules from Newcastle, serving Bristol and Cardiff. It will be the North East's only air link with Manchester and they plan to operate from 27th July.

29th Dan-Air Comet G-APDN, operating DA1912 to Tenerife, was forced to divert to Las Palmas due to mist and low cloud, before eventually arriving back at Manchester at 1853 the following day.

7th June 1970 – Evening arrival Braathens Douglas DC-6 LN-SUI was on a passenger charter from Stavanger, before positioning out an hour later to Amsterdam. It's seen here parked next to Sabena SE.210 OO-SRE. It was damaged beyond repair in a landing accident at Southend in October 1974, by which time it was operating as OO-VGB for Delta Air Transport. (Geoff Ball)

July 1970

SAS announced a new cargo operation between Copenhagen and Manchester will start in November. Flights will operate five-times a week in conjunction with BEA, using Douglas DC-9s.

A large number of transatlantic flights were operated from/to the USA & Canada by the following: Air Canada DC-8s CF-TJE & CF-TJH (10th); Airlift International B.707 N739AL (1st), American Flyers DC-8 N123AF (23rd), Pacific Western B.707 CF-PWW (3rd/26th), Pan American B.707s N408PA (27th/28th), N412PA (24th), N433PA (25th), N455PA (3rd) & N491PA (6th/13th/15th); Saturn Airways DC-8s N8955U (6th) & N8956U (21st/31st); TIA DC-8s N4866T (10th) & N8960T (18th); TWA B.707 N18711 (11th), Wardair B.727 CF-FUN (14th/18th) and World Airways B.707s N369WA (24th/25th), N370WA (14th/18th), N371WA (28th), N372WA (19th/21st) & N375WA (20th). UK airlines operating to the USA & Canada were British United (VC-10) & Caledonian (B.707) plus Aer Lingus B.707 EI-ASO (19th), B.720 EI-ALA (26th) and Martinair DC-8 PH-MAU (9th), completing a busy month.

HS.748 ILS traffic observed included Zambia Airways HS.748 9J-ABK (9th/17th) and Hawker-Siddeley G-AYFL (14th/17th), which was delivered to Chevron Oil in December 1970 as CF-CSE. Military aircraft were RAF Britannia's XM489 (9th), XM519 (15th) & Nimrod XV236 (16th).

Dan-Air introduced a City-Link service in July 1970, using their sole Nord 262, G-AYFR. The operation linked Manchester with Newcastle, Cardiff & Bristol. The type was replaced by HS.748s in January 1972 and in April the same year the service was extended to include Birmingham & Bournemouth. (Geoff Ball)

1st   Lufthansa commenced a weekday Manchester to Frankfurt passenger service today, using B.737's, which compliments their existing freight operation. Boeing 737 D-ABES operated the inaugural flight LH248/9, landing at 1737. Thirteen different aircraft operated the service during the month and all were first visits.

3rd   Martinair Douglas DC-9 operated the evening BEA BE559 flight from Brussels, due to a Super 1-11 going tech in Brussels.

3rd   Comet G-APDN (flight DA1903 MAN-BCN) departed for Barcelona, but crashed en route killing all 105 passengers and 7 crew onboard. It was the airlines first crash involving passengers. The aircraft's standard routing for Barcelona was VAI, VA34, UB31 with Point Berga as its reporting point, but its actual routing was more of a South Westerly track along VA25-Cognac VOR-Agent VOR-Toulouse VOR to join UB31 for routing into Barcelona. It was the crew's first flight to Barcelona, but both pilots were adequately experienced. The flight departed Manchester at 1608 (Local) and proceeded as normal for ninety minutes, but its final fourteen minutes were recorded as follows:

1753 (GMT)   G-APDN contacted Barcelona ATC and was descending to FL220. After reporting passing the Spanish frontier, he requested further descent clearance and was told to descend to FL90.

1757 (GMT)   G-APDN reported passing the Barcelona FIR boundary and was descending through FL160, giving an ETA of 1801 for Point Berga.

1759 (GMT)   G-APDN was instructed to contact Barcelona approach 119.1. On initial contact a heading of 140° was given and acknowledged by G-APDN. The pilot advised he was descending through FL130 and gave an ETA of 1807 for reporting point (Sabadell).

1800 (GMT)   Barcelona APP requested confirmation of this estimate and the pilot corrected it to 1805. On receiving this information, ATC cancelled the turn to 140° and instructed G-APDN to proceed to Sabadell direct.

1801 (GMT)   G-APDN reported leaving FL100 for FL90 and was further instructed to descend to FL60.

1802 (GMT)   ATC gave G-APDN instruction for a heading of 140°, which was acknowledged and the pilot advised he was descending through FL85 to FL60. Immediately after this transmission, ATC requested confirmation G-APDN was passing Sabadell, to which the pilot replied 'in about thirty seconds' and fifteen seconds later he advised ATC they were passing Sabadell. ATC acknowledged this and confirmed radar contact had been established and G-APDN was given further clearance to 2,800 ft.

1803 (GMT)   G-APDN requested runway information, ATC advised Runway 25, which was acknowledged by the pilot.

1805 (GMT)   Barcelona APP requested G-APDN's altitude, which was reported back at 4,000ft.

1807 (GMT)   ATC called G-APDN for confirmation they were still on course, but G-APDN didn't reply to this, or to any further contacts.

Sometime between 1805 and 1806 (GMT): G-APDN crashed into the north eastern slopes of the Les Agues peak, in the municipal district of Abbacies (Gerona) at about 3,800ft.

In conclusion: The aircraft had been significantly to the east of track since Toulouse VOR. When it reported passing Sabadell, it was actually 52km away. ATC had coincidentally observed an echo of an aircraft over Sabadell on radar, at the same time as G-APDN. G-APDN's continuing displacing to the east could have been caused by defective equipment. It should have reported to ATC it was abeam Point Berga, rather than above. These facts and the incorrect ETA for Sabadell made it difficult for ATC to correctly identify the aircraft on radar.

5th   BEA Airtours Comet G-ARCP, operating inbound KT593 from Gerona, went tech on arrival at Manchester. Substitute Comet G-APMC positioned in from Gatwick in the evening to operate the much delayed KT684 to Palma but this was also delayed, this time by French ATC restrictions. G-APMC finally departed at 2249 and Comet G-ARCP later positioned out to Gatwick.

9th   Fred Olsen operated three flights during the month. Two were freight flights: Curtiss C-46 LN-FOP from/to Oslo today and Douglas DC-6 LN-FOL (10th). The other was their sole Falcon 20 LN-FOE, arriving from Heathrow en route to RAF Leuchars (11th).

9th   German Air Force Noratlas 53+42, arriving at 1404 as DCN2463 from RAF Yeovilton to Erding, was their only training flight through Manchester this month.

23rd   Today saw the last visit of Sterling Douglas DC-6 OY-BAS, operating NB522V from Dublin to Copenhagen, before being withdrawn from service in 1971.

27th   Dan-Air commenced their City-link operation from Manchester today. Nord 262 G-AYFR operated the first flight from Newcastle then departed within ten minutes for Bristol and Cardiff.

30th   Today saw two freight flights operating at similar times, but to different destinations parked together. The first, Belgian-operator Transpommair, was a new airline to Manchester with Douglas DC-6 OO-CTK making a return flight from Ostend. Formerly operated by Sabena and for a time during 1964 by Caledonian as G-ASTS, it operated with the airline until 1973, when it was sold in the USA. The other, Air Fret Douglas DC-7 F-OCOQ from/to Valenciennnes, Northern France, was sold in 1972 and for a short time in 1973 it operated for Aer Turas as EI-AWO.

August 1970

The airport had another bumper month of transatlantic traffic when 290 flights operated to/from the USA & Canada, including 102 charter flights carrying 12,000 extra passengers. These were in addition to the 188 scheduled flights operated by BOAC. The charter flights included Air Canada DC-8 CF-TJH (9th), American Flyers DC-8 N123AF (1st/15th/21st), Capitol DC-8s N4906C (7th) & N4910C (30th); CP Air DC-8 CF-CPT (18th), Pacific Western B.707 CF-PWV (24th/31st), Pan American B.707s N402PA (17th), N403PA (1st), N405PA (25th), N412PA (24th), N416PA (13th/23rd), N420PA (1st/6th27th), N421PA (4th/22nd), N435PA (29th), N491PA (4th) & N702PA (15th); Saturn Airways DC-8 N8956U (21st/26th), TWA B.707s N18711 (10th) & N28724 (1st/25th); Wardair B.707 CF-ZYP (9th/29th), B.727 CF-FUN (5th) and World Airways B.707s N369WA (24th), N370WA (2nd/11th), N371WA (4th/13th/15th), N372WA (6th/26th), N373WA (3rd), N375WA (12th/25th) & N376WA (2nd/9th). UK airlines operating to the USA & Canada were BOAC (B.707), Caledonian (B.707), Laker Airways (B.707), Lloyd International (B.707) and KLM DC-8 PH-DEM (27th).

HS.748 ILS traffic observed included Hawker-Siddeley G-11-5 (5th) & G-11-3 (11th) which later became CS-TAF and was delivered to Sata Air Acores in October 1970 and Zambia Airways 9J-ABW (31st) which left Woodford on delivery to its new owners on 2nd September. The RAF provided a variety of types including Dominie XS726 (11th), Britannia's XM491 (13th/20th), XM519 (21st) & XL659 (26th); C-130 XV195 (18th), Devon WB534 (18th), Nimrods XV226 (19th) & XV242 (25th) and Comet XR395 (19th).

1st August 1970 – With a full complement of crew and passengers onboard, when the pilot of Pan American B.707 N420PA attempted to start the No. 1 engine, a spark within the engine ignited fuel inside the engine cowling, which resulted in the plane being fully evacuated. After being passed as safe to fly later on, it finally left at 2130 bound for New York. (Geoff Ball)

1st   Alaska International C-130 N9263R, in an all-silver scheme, made two visits today. Initially it arrived from Frankfurt at 0036 and departed for Stansted, before returning later from Ostend at 2345 to stay overnight before its departure for Geneva at 1345 the following day.

1st August 1970 – The summer of 1970 saw many transatlantic charters by various American airlines, as well as British ones. In this shot, Pan American Boeing 707s N403PA & N420PA and TWA B.707 N28724 are preparing for their flights to New York. (Geoff Ball)

1st   American Flyers Douglas DC-8-63 N123AF, made five visits this year and today it arrived on Runway 24 from New York, later outbound to Toronto. Their last visit to Manchester was 4th January 1971, when N123AF arrived as a diversion from Gatwick, as they ceased trading in 1971 after being bought by Universal Airlines.

6th   Sterling operated two Fokker F.27s from 1968 to 1973 and today, OY-STN positioned in from Gatwick to operate NB558A to Copenhagen. They were occasional visitors, with OY-STO being the last to visit on 11th December 1971. Both aircraft were sold in Australia in 1973.

7th   TMA Douglas DC-6F operated a freight flight (TL109/110) from Frankfurt to Amsterdam.

9th   German Air Force Noratlas 52+99 arrived at 1005 as DCN2624, on a training flight from RAF West Freugh to Lemwerder. Another on the 25th was Noratlas 53+20, routing from Northolt to Lemwerder as DCN5320.

17th   On a wet Monday morning, Aer Turas Douglas C-54F EI-ARS operated a return cargo flight to Dublin. The airline had been a regular visitor to Manchester since the late 1960's, initially using Douglas DC-4s, as well as their Douglas C-54F. They also used Douglas DC-7s and a sole Argosy for a time before re-equipping again, this time with Bristol Britannia's EI-BAA & EI-BBH from the mid-1970s. C-54F EI-ARS made its last visit on 19th October 1976 diverting from Leeds, before being withdrawn and sold in late 1976.

17th   BOAC B.747 G-AWNA arrived for a seventy-five minute VIP visit today, in a heavy thunderstorm. Strict security was enforced and only airport/airline staff and VIP guests were allowed onboard. It was parked on Stand 28, the end gate of the International pier, where everyone had the opportunity to observe it from close quarters! The aircraft was flown by management pilots, as their regular pilots are still refusing to fly them, even on training flights, due to an ongoing pay dispute. Although the airline has no plans for B.747 scheduled services through Manchester until at least 1974, the airport will be ready to receive any diverted aircraft, as soon as BOAC has the full complement of ground handling equipment.

19th   Aer Lingus flight EI403, a Boeing 737 routing from Heathrow to Dublin, diverted into Manchester due to a bomb scare which turned out to be a hoax!

22nd   A Cambrian Airways Viscount, with forty-seven passengers onboard, had to be evacuated after an electrical fault started a fire in the passenger cabin. Luckily no-one was hurt and the flames were quickly extinguished.

22nd   RAF operated three trooping flights today: Britannia XL659 (RR6405) to Hanover and Britannia XL659 (RR6411) & C-130 XV195 (RR3891) to Gibraltar.

24th   Blue Eagles helicopter display team called in for fuel. The six Sioux's: XT134, XT193, XT206, XT242, XT511 & XW192 were en route from Weeton near Harrogate, to an Air Show at Middle Wallop. They returned on the 29th to participate in the annual Poynton Show the next day.

26th   Dan-Air Ambassador G-AMAH operated this evening's DA401 from Bristol, before departing for Newcastle and the following mornings DA402 (Newcastle-Manchester-Bristol-Cardiff), which was its final visit, as it was withdrawn from service in March 1971. This means the only Ambassadors still flying are G-AMAE & G-ALZO, which are both operated by Dan-Air.

28th   Making its first visit to Manchester this afternoon was SAS Douglas DC-9 OY-KGB, operating flight SK537/8, rather than the usual SE.210 Caravelle.

September 1970

Due to an increase in business, Aer Lingus are hoping to add flights and increase frequencies through Manchester. As a first step with the cooperation of the authorities, they plan to use larger capacity aircraft than the currently used BAC 1-11.

Although transatlantic flights from/to the USA wound down this month, there was still a wide variety. Air Canada DC-8s CF-TJZ (10th) & CF-TJJ (30th); CP Air DC-8 CF-CPQ (21st), ONA DC-8 N864F (25th), Pan American B.707s N412PA (5th), N416PA (26th), N426PA (26th), N435PA (5th) & N454PA (1st/21st/27th); Saturn DC-8 N8955U (10th), Wardair B.707s CF-FAN (10th), CF-ZYP (19th), B.727 CF-FUN (8th) and World Airways B.707s N370WA (1st/21st), N371WA (5th), N372WA (13th/14th), N375WA (9th) & N376WA (2nd/16th). UK airlines operating to the USA & Canada were British United (VC-10), Caledonian (B.707), Laker Airways (B.707) plus KLM DC-8s PH-DCK (29th) & PH-DCN (12th).

HS.748 ILS traffic observed included Ecuadorian Air Force FAE.682 (8th) & FAE.683 (30th). RAF types were Britannia's XM489 (24th) & XM518 (30th); Nimrods XV226 (4th/18th) & XV242 (18th); VC-10 XV108 (18th) and two HS.125s from Hawarden, G-AYIZ (8th) & G-5-18 (24th).

8th   SAS flew an additional Copenhagen flight with DC-9-21 LN-RLO (SK537A/538A).

9th   The only German Air Force training flight through Manchester this month was Noratlas 53+30 at 1005 as DCN2941, on a training flight from Alhorn to Birmingham.

11th   Dan-Air Ambassador G-AMAE made its last visit today, operating from Belfast to Newcastle, before departing at 1934. It was withdrawn in June 1971.

13th   SAS operated an inbound charter from Copenhagen as SK2501 with Douglas DC-9 LN-RLJ, which was making its first visit.

14th   Boeing 707 OO-SJN operated Sabena's evening passenger service, SN623.

22nd   Another regular to Manchester throughout the 1960's, Martinair CV-640 PH-CGD, made its final visit on a round trip from Amsterdam today. After being sold in 1971 as N111TA, it left just one Convair CV-640, PH-MAL, still in service with the airline. They are re-equipping with Douglas DC-8s, DC-9s and a Fokker F.28. Although they operate several DC-6s, their days are numbered too!

24th   USAF T-29 51-17899 arrived at 0849 on a return flight from RAF Northolt. The T-29 is the military version of the Convair CV-240 and this aircraft was based in the UK before being eventually preserved at RAF Duxford in 1973.

24th   Making its first visit today was Air India B.707 VT-DSI (AI507/6 Moscow-Heathrow).

October 1970

A number of scheduled flight changes occurred this month. Air France reduced Paris flights to five-weekly, British United operated their final Jersey service (BR050/1) on the 4th with BAC 1-11 G-ASJE and Swissair reverted to using Douglas DC-9s from the 31st. BOAC no longer operates the Montreal/Chicago flight (BA605/6) and BOAC Cargo are operating three-times weekly to New York via Montreal (BA065) and twice-weekly to Chicago via Montreal (BA067), with inbound flights four-weekly from New York (BA066) and once-weekly from Boston (BA066). They also plan to increase cargo flights to eight a week by early next year and increase available cargo space ex-Manchester on existing and new flights, after their cargo figures slipped from sixth to seventh place in last year's league table of tonnage carried between Europe & USA.

HS.748 ILS traffic was thin on the ground with just two examples, Ecuadorian Air Force FAE.683 (3rd) & FAE.684 (10th/11th/15th). Military traffic fared no better with only the following noted: RAF C-130 XV206 (16th), RAF Comet XR399 (16th) & Nimrod XV245 (23rd).

1st   German Air Force training flights carried out through Manchester were Noratlas 53+09 at 1050 (DCN3161 Alhorn-Filton) today, Noratlas 53+21 at 1214 (DCN3263 Neubiberg-Filton-19th) and Noratlas 53+17 at 1017 (DCN3289 Hatfield-Cologne-24th).

3rd   American Flyers DC-8 N123AF arrived at 2114 from Stansted, before departing at 2243 to Nicosia, under British Midland call-sign BD717.

7th   Early morning fog at Heathrow produced ten diversions, but the only ones of note were Lufthansa B.727F D-ABIX at 0614 (LH930 from Frankfurt) and two QANTAS B.707s - first visitor VH-EAJ at 0717 (QF111 from Karachi) & VH-EBJ at 0953 (QF735 from Bahrain).

7th   Martinair's sole Douglas DC-6, PH-MAM, made its final visit today, operating a freight flight from Bremen, before departing at 0937 the following morning to Amsterdam. It saw further service in Europe, after being sold to Inex Adria of Yugoslavia in April 1971.

9th   In a seemingly repeat performance of last month, another Aer Lingus flight was forced to land at Manchester, because of a bomb scare. EI150 Dublin-Heathrow made an emergency landing at 0853, following an anonymous telephone call, which turned out to be another hoax!

11th   Another bout of early morning fog produced a number of diversions from Gatwick, Heathrow & Stansted, the pick of which was the first visit of Sterling SE.210 OY-SAZ at 0056 (NB753 from Stockholm).

11th October 1970 – A fine shot of a classic aircraft. Vintage 1953 Dove EI-AUK is seen here side-on to the Domestic pier, having just arrived from Coventry, making its one and only visit to Manchester. It was operated by International Air Distributors and although it's Irish-registered, it spends most of its time at Coventry, where it was eventually withdrawn in 1972. (Geoff Ball)

12th   A few more fog diversions arrived this morning, amongst which were British United VC-10 G-ASIX at 0721 (BR102 from Nairobi) & Cyprus Airways Trident 2 5B-DAB at 0729 (CY320 from Nicosia), on its first visit to Manchester.

12th   Following the arrival of last month's Air India B.707, another appeared in the shape of VT-DPM, making its first visit today, operating from Rome to Heathrow as AI121.

13th   Shorts Skyvan G-ASZJ was a first visit of type, operating three flights during the afternoon/early evening between Birmingham, Manchester & Newcastle. It appeared again on the 16th, routing Newcastle-Birmingham.

18th   The last bunch of diversions for the month arrived this morning. They were all BOAC flights from Heathrow, proving how important Manchester was to the airline. In chronological order they were SVC-10 G-ASGK at 0738 (BA032 from Zurich), B.707s G-APFG at 0755 (BA676 from

Miami), G-AWHU at 0832 (BA851 from Anchorage), G-APFI at 0856 (BA670 from Miami), G-APFP at 0947 (BA500 from New York) & G-APFO at 0956 (BA508 from New York).

18th After many years of service, Britannia Airways operated its final Britannia flight out of Manchester. Operated out of Manchester since 1965, they are being phased out in favour of Boeing 737s. Britannia G-ANBE took charge today, positioning up from Luton for an outbound ad hoc flight to Palma, before being withdrawn from service the following month.

18th Viscount EI-APD (EI722/3 from/to Cork) operated the final Aer Lingus Viscount rotation through Manchester. By the following month, the type had been completely phased out of the airlines operations.

18th Another aircraft making its final visit today was Air France SE.210 F-BHRZ, operating its last AF960/1 flight. It was transferred to domestic French-airline Air Inter in March 1971.

19th BEA Viscount (registration unknown), operating BE4834 Birmingham-Manchester, was badly damaged by a lightning strike and landed with a six inch hole in its nose cone.

20th Another Air France SE.210 on its last visit was F-BJTJ, also operating AF960/1. It was sold to fellow French-airline Air Charter International the following month.

25th Spantax have been operating a Saturday summer flight (BX171/0 from/to Palma) with Convair CV-990s and today was the final flight of the season. Due to the unavailability of a CV-990, it was operated by Spantax DC-7s EC-BBT (BX171A/170A) & EC-BDT (BX171/0). These were the last visits of any Spantax DC-7s, as they were assigned to domestic duties only from 1971.

31st The final noteworthy movement of the month was the return to Hawker-Siddeley of the first of three ex-Bahamas Airways HS.748s to be stored at East Midlands, prior to re-sale. VP-BCM arrived from Reykjavik at 1355, before its departure at 1505. The airline had taken delivery of VP-BCK, VP-BCL and VP-BCM back in 1967.

November 1970

Caledonian and BUA have merged, but are still operating with their own separate flight codes and identities, with Caledonian as 'CA' and British United as 'BR'.

Air France further reduced their Paris schedule to three-times weekly from the beginning of the month. Alitalia increased their DC-6 cargo flight to twice-weekly and BEA reinstated the Comet to operate on two Heathrow flights a day, BE4058/61 & BE4086/9.

HS.748 ILS traffic observed was restricted to just two examples again, with Hawker-Siddeley G-AVRR (10th) and Thai Airways HS-THG (17th), which had only just made its first flight on the 11th. The only military aircraft noted was RAF Britannia XM490 (4th).

2nd Having been a regular visitor during the 1960's, Martinair's last Convair CV-640, PH-MAL, made its final appearance today, operating a freight charter from Luxembourg to Belfast.

3rd SAS commenced a five-weekly cargo service from/to Copenhagen, inaugurated by DC-9F SE-DBN. The outbound operates via Prestwick Wed/Fri and via Birmingham Tue/Thu/Sat.

6th The second ex-Bahamas Airways HS.748 for re-sale, VP-BCK, arrived from Reykjavik at 1424. Unlike the previous aircraft, VP-BCM, this one didn't depart until the 9th.

10th Today saw the only visit to Manchester of Norwegian-airline, Trans-Polar, when Boeing 720 LN-TUU operated from/to Oslo as BK701/2. They began operations this year with three Boeing 720s, two of which were ex-Aer Lingus, but by May 1971 they had ceased trading.

11th German Air Force training flights continued through Manchester during the month. Noratlas 53+49 arrived today at 1347 (DCN4016 Alhorn-Northolt) and Noratlas 53+15 at 1417 on the 19th (DCN4064 Northolt-Cologne).

13th The last of the three ex-Bahamas Airways HS.748s for re-sale, VP-BCL, arrived from Reykjavik at 1302, before departing for East Midlands at 1455 for storage.

18th An Aer Lingus B.737, operating mail flight EI9217, flew from Manchester to Dublin in a record twenty-six minutes.

19th Having made its first visit on 18th May, Twin Otter CF-YFT operated two flights this morning from Birmingham to Newcastle, before returning later in the opposite direction.

25th The second BOAC B.747 to visit, G-AWNB, arrived for further staff familiarisation.

26th A total of twenty diversions arrived mainly from Heathrow, but disappointingly most were British. Non-British included TIA DC-8 N4866T at 0907 (TV866 from New York–Frankfurt diversion), East African Airways VC-10 5H-MMT at 0927 (EC710 from Athens) & World Airways B.707 N373WA at 1108 (WO373 from Philadelphia–Gatwick diversion). After the fog had thickened again in the evening, Qantas B.707 arrived at 2339 (QF530 from New York).

30th Manchester's transatlantic passenger flights, BA608/7 & BA538/7, attempted to land but due to fog they ended up diverting back to Prestwick, before returning later in the morning.

December 1970

A plan to avoid the need to tow aircraft across the apron when on mixed International and Domestic flights has been put before Manchester City Council. The sealed-corridor plan, designed for certain passengers to avoid the customs and immigration areas, has been welcomed by customs officials and BEA as it will save time and reduce both staffing levels and walking distances for passengers. The current situation on BEA's Dusseldorf-Manchester-Glasgow flight for example, is that the aircraft arrives on an International stand with the passengers classed as International, but those flying onwards to Glasgow have to disembark for customs clearance as domestic passengers. The plane is then towed across the apron to a domestic stand, where the Glasgow passenger's board it again. The new corridor/separated area would enable aircraft to remain parked on the International pier throughout.

Manchester City Council will be asked to approve the airports £75m plan for the proposed new runway, to be built parallel to the existing 06/24. It's estimated to be 10,000ft long and separated from the existing runway by 800ft. It's predicted when both runways are operational; movements could increase by 30%. However, it's almost certain some houses at the north eastern end in the vicinity of Ringway Road, would have to be acquired for safety reasons. A report being submitted to the Council says if the decision for the new runway is made now, it could be ready towards the end of 1976/77.

Manchester Airport will receive its first automated system for assessment of the runways visual range (RVR), used during bad weather. Currently the procedure is for a human observer to assess the RVR by counting the number of visible runway lights. The new system, already operating at Gatwick and Heathrow, will enable the RVR to be assessed more quickly and accurately.

BEA's first Trident 3B, G-AWZA, was handed over at Hatfield on the 7th and the variant received its Certificate of Airworthiness on 8th February 1971. The inaugural service of the Trident 3 took place on 11th March 1971, with G-AWZC on a scheduled flight from Heathrow to Madrid with regular services commencing on 1st April 1971, initially on routes to Lisbon and Paris.

Dan-Air made an application to extend their City-Link service onwards to Bournemouth.

HS.748 ILS traffic observed were just two examples again: Thai Airways HS-THG (3rd) & Ghana Airways 9G-ABW (9th), which had its career cut short! First flown on the 22nd last month; it was delivered this month and then written-off during a training flight on 22nd January 1971! The only military flights noted were RAF Britannia's XN404 (15th) & XL636 (17th).

11th The second Shorts Skyvan to visit Manchester was G-AXPT, arriving this afternoon from Brussels to clear customs, en route to Sydenham.

11th Braathens Fokker F.28 LN-SUN positioned in from Oslo to operate a return passenger charter, departing at 2116 as BU1658.

12th Gulfstream 1 G-ASXT made its first appearance at Manchester today, operating a flight from its base at Stansted to Turin. It's been recently acquired by the Ford Motor Company (UK) and it's their first aircraft. It returned on the 14th, making the return trip from Turin to Stansted.

12th Qantas operated another assisted-passage flight today, when B.707 VH-EAG operated from/to Karachi as QF167/8.

12th Today saw the last visit of a Sterling Douglas DC-6, when OY-STY operated an inbound charter from Stockholm as NB6157, positioning out later to Copenhagen at 0606 as NB6158E. This aircraft and the airlines remaining DC-6s had all been withdrawn by December 1971.

13th Fog in the London area brought thirty-four diversions into Manchester over a two day period. Of the twenty-one arrivals today, all but two were diverting from Heathrow and it turned into a bit of a 'BOAC-fest' with seven B.707s, two VC-10s and a Super VC-10. Amongst today's highlights were Swissair CV-990 HB-ICF at 1043 (SR800 from Zurich), Alitalia DC-9s I-DIKL at 1220 (AZ268 from Rome) & I-DIKP at 1441 (AZ284 from Milan); two Pan American B.707s:

N455PA at 0735 (PA122 from Seattle) & N473PA at 1232 (PA167 from Brussels); Qantas B.707 VH-EAE at 1237 (QF741 from Rome) and Wardair B.707 CF-FAN at 1020 (WD558 from Vancouver), which was the only Gatwick diversion of note.

13th Air France SE.210 F-BJTM was making it final visit to Manchester today, operating its last AF960/1 flight. It was sold to fellow French-airline Air Charter International in March 1971.

14th German Air Force Noratlas 52+92, arriving at 1624 (DCN4226 Hohn-Northolt) to night-stop, was the sole military training flight this month.

14th Thirteen more diversions arrived between 0928 and 1257, including three Air France Heathrow flights: B.727s F-BOJC (AF804 from Paris) & F-BPJG (AF808 from Paris) and SE.210 Caravelle F-BHRA. These flights would normally return to Paris whenever bad weather delays their arrival at London. Another four BOAC flights arrived plus two Alitalia DC-9s: I-DIKM at 1234 (AZ268 from Rome) & I-DIKY at 1257 (AZ284 from Milan).

18th The morning saw a small, but interesting collection of diversions, with the first two escaping early fog at Dusseldorf. Pacific Western B.707 CF-PWV at 0427 (PW2795 from Montreal), first visitors Transavia B.707 PH-TRV at 0555 (HV370 from Vancouver) & East African Airways VC-10 5X-UVJ at 1039 (EC706 from Entebbe) and finally Olympic Airways B.727 SX-CBE at 1053 (OA281 from Athens), which was also the first visit of an Olympic B.727 to Manchester.

29th The final diversion of 1970 was RAF Comet XR396, arriving at 2053 (RR2862 from RAF Gutersloh).

First/Last Arrivals & Departures 1970

First arrival: PA-23 G-AWIY from Heathrow at 0118
First departure: Lloyd International Britannia BE2100 to Heathrow at 0011
Last arrival: B.727 OO-STE from Brussels at 2308
Last departure: PA-23 G-AWIY to Luton 2309

(+/- % on Previous Year)		
Scheduled Passengers	1,172,000	+ 8.6%
I.T/Charter Passengers	607,000	+28.3%
Transit Passengers	148,000	+94.7%
Total	1,927,000	+18.3%
Freight & Mail (Tonnes)	45,700	+12%
Movements	55,500	+5.5%

Airport Diary 1971

January 1971

HS.748 ILS traffic observed included Air Botswana HS.748 A2-ZFT (14th/25th), South African Airways HS.748s ZS-SBU (19th/21st/22nd) & ZS-SBV (29th) and Zambia Air Force AF602 (29th). RAF traffic noted were RAF Britannia's XN398 (13th), XM498 (14th), Dominie XS709 (19th) and VC-10 XR810 (27th).

1st   BEA clerical staff at Manchester voted in favour of abandoning their two-week strike over pay, as it was having little impact. BEA clerical staff at Heathrow also called off their action, following a warning by their newly appointed Chairman 'that job losses would be unavoidable if the action continued'.

2nd   Today was the first of three when dense fog blanketed the country, particularly over the Midlands and South East, which led to an unprecedented amount of diversions being handled at Manchester. Although only four arrived today, ninety arrived over three days! A short burst this afternoon brought in BOAC SVC-10s G-ASGB at 1347 (BA506 from New York) & G-ASGL at 1446 (BA562 from Detroit); BEA Comet G-APMA at 1640 (BE013 from Paris) and East African Airways VC-10 5H-MMT at 1635 (EC718 from Frankfurt).

3rd   Fog throughout the UK caused the arrival of thirty-four Heathrow and Gatwick diversions into Manchester, which was merely a prelude to the following day's arrivals! In amongst the hoards of BEA & BOAC aircraft were five from Aer Lingus: B.737s EI-ASC, EI-ASE, EI-ASG, EI-ASH & BAC 1-11 EI-ANH; Lufthansa B.737 D-ABEI at 1057 (LH062 from Dusseldorf), Swissair CV-990 HB-ICF at 1006 (SR800 from Zurich) & DC-8 HB-IDB at 1157 (SR165 from Chicago); KLM DC-8 PH-DCD at 1759 (LY1415 from Tel Aviv) & DC-9 PH-DNK at 1155 (KL109 from Rotterdam) and first visit South African Airways B.707 ZS-SAG at 1446 (SA262 from Frankfurt).

4th   Manchester recorded the UK's lowest overnight temperature of -8°c/17°f. Freezing fog and icy conditions were widespread throughout the country again and the regions visibility was reduced to ten yards in places. Trains were halted between Altrincham and Manchester when a diesel train hit a broken cable, which had fallen onto the track under the weight of severe frost. As Ringway was clear of fog, forty-eight weather diversions arrived between 0818 and 1747. It was the writers first day back at school after the Christmas break and I was in a classroom without a view, but I could hear one after another passing overhead. In amongst numerous BEA & BOAC aircraft were the following highlights: Lufthansa B.737 D-ABEI at 1557 (LH058 from Cologne), Caledonian Britannia's G-ATMA (CA774 from Munich) & G-ATNZ (CA1108 from Beauvais) on their final visits to Manchester; Swissair CV-990s HB-ICE at 0954 (SR800 from Zurich) & HB-ICH at 1700 (LY425A from Tel Aviv); Douglas DC-8 HB-IDB at 1034 (SR173 from New York) & Douglas DC-9 HB-IDO at 1613 (SR804A from Zurich); Alitalia DC-8s I-DIWV at 1611 (AZ2668 from Rome) & I-DIWG at 1634 (AZ2610 from Paris) and DC-9 I-DIKP at 1729 (AZ280 from Rome); American Flyers DC-8 N123AF at 1601 (from New York), TWA B.707s N8737 at 1358 (TW6708 from Shannon) & N18706 at 1405 (TW6754 from Shannon); USAF Douglas C-118 53-03303 at 1447 (from Brussels) as a Northolt diversion; three Olympic aircraft originating from Athens: Boeing 727s SX-CBA at 1703 (OA2259) & SX-CBB at 1542 (OA259) and Boeing 707 SX-DBD at 1725 (OA2281) and lastly Qantas B.707 VH-EAF at 1354 (QF743 from Rome). At one point Manchester was the only airport in the country accepting diversions, but even so many were turned away. By the evening Heathrow had over 10,000 stranded passengers and accommodation was sought for them as far afield as Brighton. Prestwick handled thirty diverted aircraft and 3,000 passengers. Stansted was fog bound all day but Gatwick opened briefly, during which time a TWA B.707 got stuck in soft ground after an aborted takeoff, with ninety-two passengers onboard.

5th   Over the last three days, a total of ninety diversions were handled by Manchester and as virtually all were from Heathrow or Gatwick, it seemed unlikely the event would ever be repeated, but it was surpassed at the end of 1972. Even more remarkable was that the majority of arrivals stayed put and by nightfall three days worth were on the ground at once! The following is a summary of aircraft involved, although some may have diverted in more than once:

Aer Lingus	BAC 1-11 EI-ANH, B.737s EI-ASC/ASE/ASF/ASG/ASH
Alitalia	DC-8s I-DIWG/DIWV, DC-9 I-DIKP

American Flyers	DC-8 N123AF
BEA	S1-11s G-AVMM/AVMW, Comet G-APMA,
	Merchantman G-APEL/APEO/APES, Trident 1s G-ARPE/ARPP,
	Trident 2s G-AVFA/AVFC/AVFG/AVFH/AVFK/AVFO, Viscount G-AORD
BOAC	B.707s G-APFM/APFN/AWHU, VC-10s G-ARVH/ARVI,
	SVC-10s ASGB/ASGC/ASGD/ASGG/ASGH/ASGJ/ASGK/ASGL/ASGM
British Midland	B.707 G-AYBJ
Britannia	B.737s G-AVRL/AXNB
Caledonian/BUA	BAC 1-11 G-AWWY, Britannia's G-ATMA/ATNZ,
	B.707s G-ATZC/AVKA/AVTW/AWTK/AWWD/AYEX, VC-10 G-ASIX
Court Line	BAC 1-11 G-AXML
Dan-Air	Comet's G-APDB/APDC/APDJ/APDP, BAC 1-11 G-AXCK
East African AW	VC-10 5H-MMT
KLM	DC-8 PH-DCD, DC-9 PH-DNK
Laker AW	B.707s G-AVZZ/AWDG
Lufthansa	B.737 D-ABEI
Olympic AW	B.707 SX-DBD, B.727s SX-CBA/CBB
Qantas	B.707 VH-EAF
SAM	SE.210 I-DABV
Saturn AW	DC-8 N8955U
South African AW	B.707 ZS-SAG
Swissair	CV-990s HB-ICE/ICF/ICH, DC-8 HB-IDB, DC-9 HB-IDO
Transmeridian	CL-44 G-AXAA
TWA	B.707s N8737/N18706
USAF	C-118 53-03303

5th   The morning after the night before! Even though airport staff had been on duty for up to thirty hours, they were still dealing with the remaining 2,000 stranded passengers, down from a peak of 7,000. They had a six hour wait between touching down and leaving the airport, after collecting their luggage and clearing customs. British Rail estimated 3,000-4,000 passengers travelled to London by rail. Coach firms worked at full stretch ferrying passengers between terminals and railway stations, as well as transporting them onwards to London. The airport's Deputy Director rejected criticism that Manchester had been wrong to accept so many aircraft. He explained that from mid-afternoon onwards, they were the only airport in the country able to accept diversions. Prestwick and Birmingham had been fog free, but were full and although Liverpool was also fog free, it was hindered by technical and handling problems after accepting so many aircraft. The terminal looked like an evacuation area, as every inch was being used by weary and stranded passengers. With so many diversions yesterday, on top of those still on the ground from the day before, every available space on the aprons, bays, disused runways and even light aircraft runway 10/28 was being used for parking. There were even two Boeing 707s and a Douglas DC-8 parked by the South Side hangars. By lunchtime, London was clear of fog for the first time in three days, but with only three de-icing rigs available to de-ice aircraft before departure, the flow back to London was a slow process. By lunchtime the airports official positions were as follows:

HEATHROW – Flights back-log could take up to four days to clear due to aircraft being out of position. Return of diverted aircraft is awaited. Continuing work-to-rule and overtime ban by some workers has added to the problems.

GATWICK - Many passengers still delayed.

LUTON – Fully operational, having been closed for fifty-four hours due to bad weather. More than twelve flights delayed from Sunday and many of yesterday's fifty charter flights are still outstanding.

BIRMINGHAM – Diversions from London stopped as the entire apron and runway are filled with parked aircraft.

6th   Following a late evening deterioration in Heathrow's weather, thirteen more diversions arrived, mainly from BEA and the only one of interest was HS.125 OY-DKP.

7th   British Midland B.707 G-AYBJ (BD702) arrived as a technical diversion, inbound from Seattle via Keflavik. The aircraft had already been delayed for 24-hours due to the UK weather, when it developed a heating failure during its flight. It was on its final descent when the pilot informed ATC his brakes may fail, but in the end he made a safe landing.

7th   German Air Force operated two flights through Manchester this month. Noratlas 53+29 arrived today at 1150 (DCN4319 Alhorn-Northolt) and again at 1535 as DCN5329 on the 18th.

12th   Cambrian Airways Viscount G-AMNZ made its last visit to Manchester today, operating CS502/5 before its withdrawal from service in June.

13th   It was the Midlands turn to be affected by fog, when Coventry, Birmingham & East Midlands were hit with cancellations, delays and diverted flights. Manchester benefitted from twenty diversions, mainly routine apart from the diversion from Coventry of Midland Air Cargo Bristol 170 G-AMLP, arriving from Brussels at 1320.

15th   Manchester announced they'd handled a record of more than 10,000 passengers during the 48-hour shut down of London's airports earlier in the month.

16th February 1971 – Having just arrived from Heathrow as BA065, B.707F G-ASZF is met by ground crew in preparation for the uplift of more cargo. It will eventually depart for Montreal/New York via Prestwick. (Manchester Airport Archive)

17th   PA-23 N6645Y, owned by Formula 1 Racing driver Graham Hill, visited today.

17th   Three Heathrow weather diversions were BOAC B.707 G-APFC at 0840 (BA676 from Miami), first visit TWA B.707 N18702 at 0847 (TW754 from Boston) & BOAC B.707 G-ARRC at 0847 (BA500 from New York).

21st   Aer Lingus BAC 1-11 EI-ANG returned shortly after departure for Dusseldorf as EI630. It was airborne for less than sixty seconds, when a loud bang was heard and the pilot immediately shut down one of the engines. The cause was found to be failure of the compression blades.

27th   Two late evening cargo flights arrived to night-stop. The first, Universal Airlines Argosy N897U from Keflavik to Luxembourg, was sold later in the year to new UK-airline Sagittair as G-APRN. The second was Loftleidir CL-44 TF-LLJ, routing from Rotterdam to Cologne.

28th   SAS Douglas DC-9 LN-RLJ operated today's SK537/8 and again the following day.

28th   Over forty flights were cancelled, due to a two-day strike by BEA engineering and maintenance men. It started at Heathrow on the 25th after the dismissal of twenty-eight men for refusing to prepare a number of jet engines for dispatch to Rolls-Royce for servicing, as they were still operating a seven-week old work-to-rule over a cost of living claim. Ringway's BEA engineers then walked out in sympathy. Even though the strike ended on the 29th, it took several days for flights to return to normal.

February 1971

Having agreed in principal to the building of a second runway, Manchester Council is still waiting for the Government's final decision. Meanwhile, the situation's becoming increasingly divisive between the opposing camps. The supporters want significant expansion, as the current boom in air travel has turned Heathrow into one of the busiest airports in Europe. Those against, including local residents, are unhappy at a 30% increase in traffic and the compulsory purchase of property as when Runway 24 is extended by 900ft to the east towards Moss Nook, it will bring the runway within 1,650ft from housing, which would have to be bought. In addition, the Government's Public Safety Zone Regulations aimed at airports, states obstruction areas may be extended to 4,500ft beyond the end of a runway, meaning that properties right up to the Heald Green border would also be at risk.

Booming business for package tour operators has forced BEA to withdraw their summer scheduled service to Palma, first introduced in 1957, due to mounting losses. Last summer they charged £43 for a return night-tourist fare, yet those paying a similar price for charter flights got two weeks hotel accommodation thrown in as well! Iberia however will continue their summer only service to Palma via Barcelona, commencing 3rd June.

In a move to compensate for the airport's decision to restrict the number of night-flights, British Midland will use Boeing 707s on their IT flights this summer. They planned to use BAC 1-11s for 200 night-flights, but this has been drastically cut. Of the 2,750 allocated night-flights between April and October, 2,050 will be for cargo and the remaining 700 slots will be divided between eleven airlines operating holiday charters.

BOAC Cargo introduced their much-threatened frequency increases this month. They now operate three-times weekly to New York via Montreal (BA065), three-times weekly to Chicago via Montreal (BA067) and inbound flights operate five-times weekly from New York (BA066).

HS.748 ILS traffic observed were Zambia Air Force AF602 (3rd), South African Airways ZS-SBV (15th) & BFS D-AFSD (23rd). RAF traffic were Britannia's XM491 (24th), XM496 (10th), XN395 (4th), XN404 (4th) and Nimrod XV250 (15th).

1st Personal ID for all airport employees was introduced today by recommendation of the Department of Transport, following a spate of bomb scares and aircraft hijackings.

2nd Dan-Air used their sole Airspeed Ambassador, G-ALZO, on DA403 (Newcastle-Bristol) today and the following day, when it returned to operate DA401 (Bristol-Newcastle).

7th Lear Jet 25 N323WA was making its first visit today, arriving at 1943 from Malaga to night-stop, before its departure at 1107 to Keflavik.

11th A dull morning saw the arrival of twenty-seven weather diversions between 0647 and 1256. The first, Caledonian/BUA VC-10 G-ASIX at 0647 (BR106 from Nairobi), was the only Gatwick diversion, the rest were from Heathrow. BEA & BOAC dominated, but there were still some interesting non-British movements including first visit TAP B.707 CS-TBD at 1207 (TP450 from Lisbon). Lufthansa diverted in four flights: B.727s D-ABII at 1035 (LH056 from Cologne), D-ABIU at 1128 (LH030 from Frankfurt) and B.737s D-ABEB at 1042 (LH062 from Dusseldorf) & D-ABEG at 1040 (LH040 from Frankfurt). First time visitors were SAS DC-9 OY-KGH arriving at 1239 (SK505 from Stockholm), South African Airways B.707 ZS-SAH at 1222 (SA256 from Paris) and Zambia Airways with DC-8 9J-ABR at 1151 (QZ802 from Rome).

14th There were no German Air Force training flights through Manchester this month, but the two by the French Air Force were the first for many years. Noratlas No.108 from Villacoublay to Reims as F-RAWM arrived today and Noratlas No.162 from/to Villacoublay as F-RAII on the 20th.

15th A new business jet type appeared today when Gulfstream 2 N7789, owned by Dresser Industries, brought in company executives for a visit to their Manchester factory. An earlier visit of the type to Manchester was made by N902 on 26th September 1969. This was also the day that decimalisation was introduced to the nation. Overnight the old money went out and the new currency came in, which was a massive undertaking for all concerned. The new money was confusing for shopkeepers and customers alike and queues formed all over the country as everyone's change was carefully counted out!

20th There was just one weather diversion when Caledonian/BUA VC-10 G-ATDJ arrived at 0807 (BR666) from Las Palmas. Now the airlines are merged and have four VC-10s between them, these aircraft will be surplus to requirements in a couple years.

21st Air France passenger flight AF960/1 was cancelled today and for the remainder of the month, due to a pilots strike.

22nd   Qantas operated Boeing 707 VH-EBN today as QF173 (Tehran-Heathrow).

March 1971

Work on Manchester Airport's £9m development plan, designed to take the city's airport into the jumbo jet era, will start next month. It includes an extension to the main terminal and a third pier, specially designed to handle wide-bodied aircraft, including the B.747. The new terminal extension, complete with its own multi-storey car park, will enable passengers to drive in, park their cars and join their aircraft whilst remaining completely undercover. The width of the road fronting the present terminal will be substantially reduced and some existing car parks will be taken out of use.

BEA announced the creation of Manchester's own mini airline, the Super 1-11 Division. It will operate domestic and international services and be responsible for BEA's German internal services. It's one of four separate divisions BEA is planning, all with their own aircraft. Other divisions are Mainline based at Heathrow, Scottish Airways and Channel Islands. They will have complete autonomy and the power to introduce or cut routes as appropriate.

Lufthansa will increase frequency on their Frankfurt passenger service from five-weekly to daily from 1st April.

HS.748 ILS traffic observed included Hawker-Siddeley G-11-6 which became Air Gaspe CF-AGI during the month (8th), Hawker-Siddeley G-11-7 which eventually became G-AYVR (24th), BFS D-AFSD (24th/25th), Zambia Airways 9J-ABJ (24th) and newly-registered Air Gaspe CF-AGI (25th/29th). RAF traffic noted were Britannia's XM519 (3rd/4th), XN392 (10th), XN404 (18th/19th/24th), Argosy XR136 (4th/5th) and Nimrod's XV252 (2nd) & XV253 (25th).

1st   Qantas B.707 VH-EAA operated today as QF173/4 (Tehran-Vienna).

3rd   Maersk made occasional appearances throughout the 1970's with their Fokker F.27s. OY-APA arrived today, routing from Dublin to Aarhus via Manchester, in its original blue/white scheme before adopting the blue all-over look in the middle of the decade. The last visit of a Maersk F.27 took place 12th September 1976, also with OY-APA.

4th   BOAC B.747 G-AWND carried out extensive training exercises at Manchester between 1100 and 1257, which included ten landings.

5th   Loftleidir CL-44 TF-LLF positioned in at 0832 to operate an outbound cargo flight to Keflavik, before returning on the 6th with an inbound cargo, again from Keflavik. CL-44 TF-LLH operated further flights from/to Keflavik on the 19th and 21st.

8th   BEA Airtours Comet G-ARGM took Manchester City FC out to Krakow for their Cup-Winners Cup Quarter Final first leg tie against Gornik Zabrze and returned them on the 11th.

9th   Dan-Air Comet G-APDO left with Manchester City fans for the above fixture. The fans returned three days later on the same aircraft, having seen their team beaten 2-0.

21st   After a lengthy pilot's strike, Air Frances' Paris operation finally recommenced today, operated by SE.210 F-BHRP.

26th   Alitalia operated the final freight service with a SAM Douglas DC-6s today, when I-DIMB was used on AZ980/1. They will be replaced by the Douglas DC-9 from next month.

27th   Alitalia SE.210 I-DABA, operating AZ289 inbound from Dublin, burst two tyres on landing.

30th   BEA Airtours Comet G-ARJK left with Manchester City for a play-off match with Gornik Zabrze in Copenhagen. As the second leg played on the 24th was won by City 2-0, it meant the aggregate score was 2-2; extra time was played without conclusion, hence the play-off in Copenhagen. City returned victorious on 1st April, having won 3-1 and their reward was to play Chelsea in the semi-final. Incidentally, one of their full-backs Arthur Mann was left behind due to his fear of flying, but he ultimately agreed to see a hypnotist for a cure!

30th   Dan-Air Comet G-APDD took Manchester City fans to Copenhagen and brought them back the following day.

31st   The final BEA Comet rotation through Manchester took place today with Comet 4B G-ARJN, operating BE4086/91 from/to Heathrow. The airline used the Comet on two Heathrow rotations and the occasional European flight during the winter. A number of aircraft were transferred to holiday-subsidiary BEA Airtours last year, with the remaining making the switch this year. G-APMA however, was retained as a standby and found itself operating on most days throughout the summer, before making its final flight in BEA's service on 31st October 1971 as BE131 Malaga-Heathrow.

27th March 1971 – Newly acquired from Braniff Airlines, TMA Boeing 707F N7096 is seen having positioned up from London to operate a cargo flight to Beirut as TL110. The airline made a second visit on 27th May with Douglas DC-6F OD-AEG. (Geoff Ball)

April 1971

The city's Airport Committee forecast that by 1985, the amount of cargo likely to be handled will reach 400,000 tonnes a year, compared to last year's 40,000. The prediction follows investigations into future freight handling potential and the facilities required to meet the demand.

Scheduled flight changes have seen several airlines tweaking their operations or increasing their frequencies through Manchester. Air France is operating six-times weekly to Paris. Alitalia has replaced the Douglas DC-6 with the DC-9 on its cargo flights and increased frequency to three-times weekly. BOAC replaced the VC-10 with the Super VC-10 on their daily New York flights. BEA will use a mix of BAC 1-11s, Trident's, Vanguard's & Viscount's on their Heathrow flights. KLM has increased frequency on their Amsterdam passenger flight, KL153/4, to five-weekly. Lufthansa's scheduled Frankfurt flight, LH072/3, is operating daily with Boeing 727s and their freight flight, LH4072/3, is operating six-times weekly with Boeing 727Fs.

HS.748 ILS traffic observed included Merpati Nusantara PK-MHD (7th) and Hawker-Siddeley G-AYVR (21st). RAF traffic noted were Britannia's XL660 (7th), XM489 (15th), XM518 (15th), XM519 (21st) & XM520 (22nd); Nimrod's XV253 (19th) & XV254 (22nd) and the best of the month: Valetta WJ491 (28th).

1st   Manchester's newly formed BEA Super 1-11 Division commenced operations today. Apart from looking after the airlines Super 1-11 fleet, it's also responsible for operating the following services with the type from Manchester: Amsterdam, Belfast, Brussels, Copenhagen, Dublin, Dusseldorf, Glasgow, Heathrow & Paris.

1st   Monarch Airlines based a Britannia from today, to operate daily spring charters to Beauvais and Rotterdam. Aircraft used during the month have been G-AOVG, G-AOVH & G-AOVI.

5th   Four HS.125s, G-AXPU/G-AYER/G-AYEP & G-AWMS, descended on Manchester this morning and apart from G-AXPU, they were all were on the ground at the same time.

6th   RAF Vulcan XM611 performed a touch-and-go at 1320 on a round trip from RAF Waddington.

9th   BOAC B.747 G-AWNE, arriving on a New York-Manchester charter flight as BA4008, was witnessed by 3,000 spectators from the viewing terraces. It arrived half full and only specially invited guests and VIP's were allowed onboard. After a lengthy boycotting of the type by BOAC pilots over pay, it will finally enter scheduled service with the airline next month.

12th   Aer Lingus Copenhagen flight EI620/1 was operated by Martinair DC-9 PH-MAX.

14th   Braathens operated two freight flights to Oslo with their Douglas DC-6s. LN-SUB arrived at 0946 and departed at 1222 today and the other, LN-SUI, positioned in from Gatwick at 1622 before departing for Oslo at 1725 on the 18th. Both aircraft were sold the following month.

19th   Qantas operated B.707 VH-EBP today as QF173 (Tehran-Heathrow).

20th   French Air Force operated another training flight when Noratlas No.164 operated from Evereux to Istres today as F-RAIM.

22nd   KLM operated an outbound passenger charter to Amsterdam with Douglas DC-8s. PH-DED operated as KL2263 today and PH-DEM was used on the return flight on the 26th.

May 1971

Due to the airport's £1m shortfall, work on the passenger terminal building extension been rescheduled to start 25th June.

In response to recent hijackings in the Middle East, the airport's installed its first metal detector, to be used primarily on passengers taking transatlantic flights.

BOAC Cargo have amended their Manchester flights to operate three-times weekly to New York via Montreal (BA065) and two-times weekly to Chicago via Montreal (BA067). Inbound flights will be five-weekly from New York (BA066), with an extra Sunday flight direct from Boston (BA066). From the 27th, their daily New York flights will extend onwards to include Birmingham on four days. BEA Cargo began a five-times weekly flight from/to Frankfurt, operated by Invicta Douglas DC-4s. SAS replaced the DC-9F with Fred Olsen DC-6s on their Copenhagen freight flights from the 18th, using LN-FOL/FON until July when the service reverted to Douglas DC-9s again.

Summer IT flights commenced with the following airlines: Aviaco, Aviogenex, Balair, Bavaria, Braathens, Inex-Adria, Sam & Tarom and a variety of UK operators: BEA Airtours, Britannia Airways, British Island Airways, British Midland, Caledonian/BUA, Channel Airways, Court Line, Dan-Air, Donaldson International & Laker Airways.

Transatlantic flights from/to the USA started this month, with the following aircraft/airlines: CP Air DC-8 CF-CPQ (25th), Pan American B.707 N428PA (22nd), Pacific Western B.707 CF-PWV (26th), Wardair B.707 CF-ZYP (16th) & B.727 CF-FUN (3rd). UK flights to the USA & Canada were Caledonian/BUA (B.707), Laker Airways (B.707) plus KLM DC-8s PH-DED (21st) & PH-DEL (25th).

The single HS.748 utilising the ILS was Hawker-Siddeley G-11-9 (12th). RAF traffic noted were Britannia's XL659 (27th), XL660 (20th) & XM496 (12th/26th); C-130 XV291 (20th), Dominie XS727 (26th), HS.125 XW791 (12th) and Nimrod XV226 (12th). HS.125 G-AYRR was on a test flight out of Hawarden (28th).

6th   Monarch Airlines Britannia G-AOVH made its last visit to Manchester today, operating inbound from Rotterdam at 1324 as OM059. After being withdrawn from service in November 1971, the only Britannia's remaining in service with the airline were G-AOVG, G-AOVI, G-AOVN & G-AOVT.

8th   The first BEA Trident 3 paid its first to Manchester this morning, when G-AWZD operated an extra Heathrow service. Twenty-five will be delivered to the airline over the next two years.

11th   First time visitor Malaysia-Singapore B.707 9V-BBB called in at 0852 as ML787, routing from Prestwick to Heathrow.

11th   The second of three Gulfstream 2s to visit this year was PH-FJP, arriving 0905 from Eindhoven on its only visit to Manchester. It was owned by Dutch electronics company Phillips, who operated it for less than twelve months before selling it later in the year.

14th   Monarch Airlines operated the last of their series of Britannia flights to Beauvais and Rotterdam this month, with G-AOVI as OM049/8 from/to Beauvais.

14th   German Air Force operated one training flight through Manchester this month, when Noratlas 53+42 arrived at 1354 as DCN5342 (Birmingham-Nuremberg).

14th   The second military visitor of the day was French Air Force Flamant 304, arriving at 1735 as F-YDAE, routing from Edinburgh to Lorient. The Flamant, a light twin-engined transport aircraft first delivered to the French Air Force in 1949, is designed for pilot/navigation training, light transport and maritime surveillance.

15th   Lloyd International B.707 G-AYRZ made its first visit, operating a trooping flight as LW922B/921B from/to Gutersloh. It returned later in the day, before positioning to Stansted.

20th   BOAC B.707 G-APFG inbound as BA608 from Prestwick, had a three hour delay offloading its passengers, after a set of steps tore a hole in the fuselage. B.707 G-APFI was flown up from London as a replacement, to operate the outbound BA607 to Prestwick.

27th   TMA Douglas DC-6F OD-AEG, operating a freight flight from Gothenburg to Heathrow, was the airlines final visit of the type. They only made the occasional appearance at Manchester and this particular aircraft was sold in 1974.

June 1971
BEA confirmed two new routes will be added three days a week next year. As yet, the destinations are undecided, but Lisbon, Madrid, Geneva & Munich are all being considered. They stressed that the new routes won't result in other loss making routes being dropped.

Air Anglia's go-ahead to start scheduled services to Norwich, Manchester & Liverpool will be the first between East Anglia and the North West.

Transatlantic flights from/to the USA were operated with the following aircraft: CP Air DC-8 CF-CPQ (24th), ONA DC-8 N865F (13th), Pan American B.707s N419PA (4th), N454PA (27th), N495PA (19th); TIA DC-8 N4869T (26th), TWA B.707 N18711 (6th/26th), Wardair B.707 CF-ZYP (6th) & B.727 CF-FUN (4th/12th/18th) and World Airways B.707 N372WA (26th) & DC-8 N803WA (13th). UK airlines operating to the USA & Canada were Caledonian/BUA (B.707), Dan-Air (B.707), Donaldson International (B.707), Laker Airways (B.707), Lloyd International (B.707) and KLM DC-8 PH-DEE (22nd).

HS.748 ILS traffic observed were Mount Cook Airlines ZK-DES (8th/29th) & Merpati Nusantara PK-MHR (29th). RAF Traffic noted were Britannia's XL640 (22nd/24th), XM489 (17th), XM497 (2nd/3rd) & XM518 (30th); VC-10 XR807 (14th), C-130 XV220 (15th) and Nimrod's XV256 (22nd) & XV257 (22nd). HS.125s N58BH (3rd) & G-5-16 (23rd) were on test flights out of Hawarden.

2nd   BOAC B.747 G-AWNE, arriving from Heathrow, carried out crew training flights between 1011 and 1313 before departing later for Prestwick.

3rd   Iberia commenced a summer only twice-weekly service to Palma via Barcelona on 3rd June (IB782/1). The first flight was operated by SE.210 Caravelle EC-BIE.

5th   British Midland B.707 G-AYVE, operating BD537 to Basle, made an emergency landing at Stansted with engine trouble.

6th   Caledonian/BUA sub chartered Air Spain Britannia EC-BSY to operate delayed inbound CA8108 from Palma, after BAC 1-11 G-AWWX went tech at Palma the previous day. This aircraft was sold to the Royal Aircraft Establishment (RAE) at Farnborough as XX367 in November 1971.

7th   Over 5,000 passengers were delayed over the weekend due to a French ATC work-to-rule.

8th   Argentine Air Force C-130 TC-63 was a first time visitor, calling in for customs clearance from Amsterdam, en route to Warton.

8th   Another one-off Britannia visit was this afternoons arrival of African Safari 5Y-ANS, from Gatwick. The former Caledonian example G-ATMA, stayed until the 11th when it departed for Blackpool.

9th   A new military type to visit, the Morane-Saulnier MS.760 Paris No.88, arrived at 1730 as F-YDAG from Glasgow to Lorient. This type of trainer jet has been used by the French Air Force since 1959.

11th   The weekend was affected by major ATC delays and aircraft problems. When Britannia Airways B.707 G-AYSI was unserviceable, Donaldson International B.707 G-AYXR was chartered to operate BY107/8 to/from Palma and then BY313/4 to/from Palma, which was running eleven hours late by then. Dan-Air Comet G-AYWX, operating DA3244, was delayed eight hours due to operational reasons.

11th   German Air Force operated one training flight through Manchester this month, when Noratlas 53+52 arrived at 1512 today as DCN5352 (RAF Marham-Glasgow).

11th   Dan-Air's City-Link flight DA400 was operated by Douglas DC-3 G-APBC, instead of Nord 262 G-AYFR.

12th More than 400 holidaymakers finally flew out today, after weekend delays of four to eleven hours. To pass the time, 140 passengers accepted a free night's entertainment at the Golden Garter nightclub, Wythenshawe, whilst the rest stayed at the Excelsior Hotel or returned home.

17th Iberia SE.210 EC-BBR made its last appearance at Manchester today, although it operated for another two years before being written-off in September 1973.

20th Also making its last visit was Cambrian Airways Viscount G-AMOH, operating CS526/7 before its withdrawal in November.

21st Air France used a Boeing 727, instead of a SE.210 Caravelle twice this month. F-BPJM operated AF960/1 today and F-BPJJ on the 27th.

22nd June 1971 – A new executive jet, the American Grumman Gulfstream 2, is seen here when N397F made its first visit, arriving from Heathrow in the fading light of a summers evening. The last of three to visit Manchester this year, it stayed overnight before returning to Heathrow the following afternoon. (Geoff Ball)

26th June 1971 – TWA B.707 N18711 is seen basking in the afternoon sunshine, after positioning up from Heathrow. It was parked on the Fairey Apron all day so various travel agents could be given a guided tour, before its departure the following morning on a charter to New York. (Geoff Ball)

28th Lloyd International Britannia G-ANCD operated trooping flights from Manchester to Dusseldorf and Gutersloh today.

July 1971

During the first four months of the year 479,733 passengers used Manchester Airport, which was a new record, up 23% on last year. During the same period IT passengers were up 93% and movements were up 15% from 12,864 to 14,744.

September's certification of the airport's £45,000 upgrade of the ILS system will make Manchester one of only three civil airports in the UK with a Category II approach system, which enables suitably equipped aircraft to land in conditions of a minimum 200ft cloud base and 350m runway visibility.

The airport has set up an urgent meeting with the airlines, to halt the drain of cargo from the North West. Businesses are giving Manchester the 'cold-shoulder' by transporting freight to London by road, rather than by air. Officials are particularly concerned by the large drop between March and May; as it's the first fall for several years. During the first five months of the year the cargo figure was 15,250 tons carried, down 4% on the same period last year. If anything, the figures should be up, as SAS commenced cargo operations and BOAC increased flights and allocated more cargo space. Although prices are fixed by the IATA, (International Air Transport Association), Manchester's cargo agents can achieve lower rates by consolidating individual consignments into larger shipments in London. Manchester Airport's aware that even though difficulties existed before, the effects on cargo are far worse because a worldwide recession.

Air Anglia announced the commencement date of their twice-weekly Norwich-Manchester flights was 1st August, but this was later put back to 1st November.

From the 1st, BOAC commenced a second daily B.707 flight, BA605/6, operating to Toronto via Prestwick. Their other flight, BA607/8, operates to Montreal and Chicago via Prestwick.

Transatlantic flights from/to the USA operated with the following: Air Canada DC-8s CF-TJE (18th), CF-TJG (27th) & CF-TJO (6th); CP Air DC-8 CF-CPQ (21st), KLM DC-8 PH-DCI (8th), ONA DC-8 N8760 (14th), Pacific Western B.707 CF-PWV (7th), Pan American B.707s N418PA (28th/29th), N422PA (2nd/23rd) & N428PA (26th); Saturn DC-8s N8955U (28th) & N8956U (24th); TIA DC-8s N8787R (25th) & N8961T (20th); Transavia B.707 PH-TRV (17th), Universal DC-8 N804U (22nd/31st), Wardair B.707 CF-FAN (18th), B.727 CF-FUN (3rd/15th) and World Airways B.707s N368WA (11th/20th), N373WA (17th), N374WA (26th) & DC-8 N801WA (4th/25th). UK airlines operating to the USA & Canada were BOAC (B.707/B.747/SVC-10), Caledonian/BUA (B.707), Dan-Air (B.707), Donaldson International (B.707), Laker Airways (B.707) and Lloyd International (B.707).

HS.748 ILS traffic observed were Mount Cook Airlines ZK-DES (1st), Hawker-Siddeley G-11-1 (8th/15th) & G-AYYH (15th). RAF traffic noted were Britannia's XL640 (22nd), XM489 (8th), XM496 (29th), XM518 (7th/15th), XN392 (19th) and Nimrod XV253 (15th). The following HS.125s were on test flights out of Hawarden: G-AZAF (15th/19th) & 5N-AET (19th).

6th BOAC Heathrow-New York flight BA501, operated by Boeing 747 G-AWNA, called in at Manchester to pick up additional passengers.

6th Dutch Antilles registered HS.125 PJ-SLB, calling in from RAF Yeovilton to Le Bourget, was a first visit and the first PJ- registered aircraft to Manchester.

8th French Air Force operated their first training flight through Manchester for several months today, when Noratlas No.104 operated from/to Evereux as F-RAIS. Noratlas No.174 operated the next day, routing Dijon-Evereux as F-RAIH.

8th Cyprus Airways Trident 5B-DAB operated BEA flight BE4084/7, from/to Heathrow.

9th Kenyan-registered Cessna 182 5Y-KUC arrived at 2115 from its current base, Saffron Waldren and stayed until the 11th. It departed back to base, before returning later and finally departing for Carlisle on the 13th.

12th Nearly 2,000 passengers to/from Manchester suffered delays of up to five hours over the weekend, compared to last week's delays of up to twelve hours, affecting over 3,000 passengers. It was the sixth consecutive weekend of disruption, caused by a combination of French ATC go-slows, bad weather, or technical delays. British Midland had a particularly tricky weekend when B.707 G-AYBJ operating BD706, diverted in from Stansted due to fog on the 10th and B.707 G-AYVE, which was due in on the evening of the 10th operating BD390 from Palma, had to call in at Stansted with technical trouble, before finally arriving at Manchester in the early hours of the 11th. It then needed three tyres changing before going out to Houston on a charter!

12th The second French Air Force Flamant visit this year was No.310, arriving at 1204 as F-YDBE routing from Lorient to Edinburgh. The type saw service with the French Air Force until 1980.

13th German Air Force operated just one training flight through Manchester this month, when Transall 50+45 arrived at 1635 as DCN5706 (Birmingham-Bonn) and night-stopped.

15th   Dan-Air City-link flight DA403 Newcastle-Manchester-Bristol was operated by Ambassador G-ALZO.

20th   In light of recent major ATC delays for traffic overflying France, the Department of Trade in London announced the results of a secret 'spy-brigade' test, carried out on Ringway flights on Sunday 18th. Aircraft due to fly over France were monitored and it was revealed that of the thirty-eight delayed, only three were due to air traffic problems. One unidentified flight supposedly delayed due to 'air traffic congestion', was ninety minutes late because the pilot wouldn't leave until the bar takings cash-box was onboard!

21st   Dan-Air Comet G-APDO, operating DA3262 bound for Alicante, burst a tyre on takeoff and diverted to Gatwick after holding to burn off excess fuel.

22nd   A bomb scare delayed BEA Viscount G-AOJB operating BE3564 to Guernsey, but nothing was found.

23rd   SAS operated two Douglas DC-9s on their SK537/8: OY-KGB today and OY-KGH on the 28th.

25th July 1971 – This shot, taken on a sunny Sunday afternoon, shows bustling activity. Front to back, BEA Viscount G-AOHK (BE3511/2 from/to Jersey), Aer Lingus B.737 EI-ASG (EI631 Dusseldorf-Dublin), BEA Airtours Comet G-APMG (KT591/0 from/to Malaga), TIA DC-8 N8787R from Toronto & Channel Airways Comet G-APZM, newly arrived from Palma. Also note the scores of spectators, enjoying the action at close quarters and Jodrell Bank far in the distance. (Geoff Ball)

August 1971

The airport authorities confirmed Middle East Airlines will commence a Manchester-Beirut service next spring. Full details are yet to be announced, but B.707s will be operated.

This month saw a record 332 transatlantic flights being handled by the airport, compared to 288 for the same month last year. BOAC's scheduled flights accounted for 186 flights and over 8,000 passengers with charter flights accounting for the remaining 146 flights, carrying 15,415 passengers. Aircraft used were Air Canada DC-8s CF-TJE (8th), CF-TJF (28th), CF-TJG (20th), CF-TJT (7th) & CF-TJW (6th); CP Air DC-8 CF-CPQ (17th), KLM DC-8 PH-DED (5th), Martinair DC-8 PH-MAU (8th), ONA DC-8s N864F (6th) & N866F (18th); Pacific Western B.707 CF-PWV (18th), Pan American B.707s N418PA (25th/28th), N419PA (4th/14th/16th/20th), N424PA (28th/30th/31st), N427PA (2nd), N453PA (9th) & N454PA (8th); Saturn DC-8s N8955U (1st/4th/21st/22nd) & N8956U (15th/30th); TIA DC-8 N8788R (24th), TWA B.707 N8737 (2nd), Transavia B.707 PH-TRV (11th), Universal DC-8s N804U (28th) & N8961T (12th/22nd); Wardair B.707s CF-FAN (31st), CF-ZYP (2nd/30th) and World Airways B.707s N368WA (8th), N372WA (8th/15th), N373WA (6th/11th) & DC-8 N801WA (18th). UK airlines operating to the USA & Canada were BOAC

(B.707/SVC-10), Caledonian/BUA (B.707/VC-10), Dan-Air (B.707), Donaldson International (B.707), Laker Airways (B.707) & Lloyd International (B.707).

HS.748 ILS traffic observed was just single example Hawker-Siddeley G-11-2 (25th). RAF traffic noted were Britannia's XM490 (11th), XM517 (26th) & XN398 (4th); Argosy XR136 (27th), Hastings TG500 (4th) and VC-10 XV103 (24th).

3rd   Loftleidir CL-44 TF-LLI positioned in from Luxembourg at 2058 for overnight cargo loading, prior to its onward flight to Tehran as LL081 the following afternoon. It was using a flight number for the first time.

5th   Dan-Air's last Airspeed Ambassador, G-ALZO, made its last visit to Manchester, operating City-link flight DA402. It also made the very last Ambassador flight on 29th September 1971.

5th   Another aircraft making its final visit today was Caledonian/BUA VC-10 G-ATDJ, arriving from Prestwick as CA1110 at 1517, before departing for Gatwick at 1636. Even though the aircraft continued operating right up until its sale to BAC in January 1973, visits to Manchester by the airlines VC-10s were restricted to diversions only.

7th   Caledonian/BUA sub chartered Air Spain Britannia EC-BFJ to operate CA8106/7 from/to Palma, when BAC 1-11 G-AWYU went tech on arrival at Palma.

8th   Due to the unavailability of a Boeing 707, British Midland also sub chartered during the month. Pomair Douglas DC-8 OO-TCP positioned in from Toronto to operate BD615/6 to/from Palma and Douglas DC-6 TF-OAD also operated into Manchester on a round trip from Ostend. They became known as Pomair Ostend and continued operating until October 1974, when financial problems forced them to cease trading.

9th   Iberia SE.210 EC-AVZ made its last appearance at Manchester operating IB782/1, before being withdrawn from service in August 1972.

11th   RAF Puma XW213 was a first visit of type, calling in from/to Heaton Park today. Also operating to/from Heaton Park was RAF Whirlwind XR486 on the 14th.

15th August 1971 – Seen here making its only visit to Manchester is Yugoslav Govt Ilyushin IL-18 YU-AIB, with its clearly visible registration. This aircraft, operating JJ105/6 from/to Pula, was chartered by Aviogenex due to an unserviceable TU-134. (Geoff Ball)

22nd August 1971 – Aviogenex TU-134 YU-AJA is seen being readied for its return to Ljubljana as JJ116. In the background, Adria Airways Douglas DC-6 YU-AFB is seen taxiing to its gate having just arrived as JJ103 from Split, operating on behalf of Aviogenex. (Geoff Ball)

23rd   For the second time in three weeks, British Midland sub-chartered to cover Palma flight BD615/6 when Spanish-airline, Trans Europa, operated the delayed flight in the early of hours, with SE.210 Caravelle EC-BRJ.

30th   Air France SE.210 F-BHRQ made its final visit to Manchester today, before being transferred to Air Inter in March 1972.

31st   Caledonian/BUA B.707 G-AWWD, operating CA1155 from Toronto to Manchester, touched down at 0701, having just flown the route in five hours forty-three minutes. Almost two hours faster than usual, it's thought to be a record for a civilian aircraft.

31st   German Air Force operated Transall 50+81 on a further training flight through Manchester today, arriving at 1635 as DCN5979 (Hamburg-RAF Northolt).

September 1971

Compared to last year, last month's passenger figures of 68,700 were down from 69,200, last month's freight figures were down by 30% and freight traffic for first eight months fell by 15%.

Plans to build a new £8m cargo centre were given final approval by the city's Airport Committee.

Swissair are dropping the Rotterdam sector of their Manchester-Zurich passenger service. From 1st November, it will route direct to/from Zurich.

BOAC terminated Toronto BA605/6 on the 18th, as BA607/8 now operates to Montreal and Toronto via Prestwick. Iberia ceased their summer Palma service on the 30th.

Transatlantic flights from/to the USA & Canada this month were operated by ONA DC-8s N864F (4th) & N865F (8th); Pacific Western B.707 CF-PWV (1st/22nd), Pan American B.707s N424PA (25th), N454PA (1st) & N455PA (4th); TWA B.707 N18711 (2nd), Universal DC-8s N802U (9th) & N804U (3rd); Wardair B.707 CF-FAN (22nd), B.727 CF-FUN (20th) and World Airways B.707s N369WA (11th), N372WA (6th), N374WA (5th) & N801WA (8th). UK airlines operating North Atlantic flights were BOAC (B.707), British Caledonian (B.707), Dan-Air (B.707), Donaldson International (B.707) and Laker Airways (B.707).

1st   From today, Caledonian/BUA are fully integrated, trading as British Caledonian.

7th   Dan-Air B.707 G-AYSL finally left for Toronto, via Gander, thirteen hours late due to technical trouble. To relieve the monotony of their all-day wait, most passengers accepted a coach tour of Cheshire, organised by the airline.

8th   SAS used several Douglas DC-9s on their SK537/8 service this month. First visit SE-DBX operated today and the others were LN-RLJ (15th) & LN-RLK (30th).

8th   Long time resident Heron G-AWDT, based and operated by the Nuclear Power Group since March 1968, made its final flight today for its Knutsford-based owners before its withdrawal and pending sale. Although the aircraft changed ownership eventually and departed on 17th November to Coventry, it was subsequently sold for export to the USA.

11th   Cambrian Airways Viscount G-AMOE made its final visit to Manchester operating CS520/1, before being withdrawn from service in January 1972.

12th   Aer Lingus used Boeing 707 EI-ANV on Amsterdam flight EI602/3 today and B.707 EI-AMW on the 24th.

17th   Canadian Air Force Boeing 707 13705 paid its first visit today. Newly delivered in 1970, it was operating CAM758 (Gatwick-Ottawa).

18th   Air India B.707 VT-DNZ arrived at 1718 (AI131 from Cairo). It departed for Heathrow at 1826, returned as AI130 at 2121 and then left for Tehran at 2218.

23rd   BOAC B.747 G-AWNA, arriving at 1006 (BA506 from New York) as a Heathrow fog diversion, was the first jumbo to divert into Ringway.

23rd   Iberia SE.210 EC-ATV made its last appearance at Manchester operating IB782/1, as it was written-off in January 1972.

24th   Air Spain Britannia EC-BFL operated a one-off charter from/to Palma as JA0120/1 today. It was withdrawn in 1972 with their others, EC-BFJ & EC-BFK, when the airline re-equipped with second-hand Douglas DC-8s.

26ᵗʰ   The fourth Cambrian Airways Viscount to be withdrawn, G-ALWF, made its final visit today operating CS524/5. It was withdrawn 24ᵗʰ December and stored at Cardiff before its final flight to Liverpool on 12ᵗʰ April 1972, via a farewell stop at Heathrow for preservation.

26ᵗʰ   Another aircraft making its final visit today was Channel Airways Comet G-ARDI, arriving at 1517 from Ibiza, before its departure for Alicante at 1710. Although it continued operating right up to the airlines demise in February 1972, it never came into Manchester again and was purchased by Dan-Air for spares.

28ᵗʰ   Today saw the end of regular passenger services by piston aircraft from Manchester. Balair operated the final rotation of their summer IT programme to Basle and the honour of the final flight was bestowed upon Douglas DC-6 HB-IBS as BB700/1.

October 1971

In light of the meeting earlier in the year between the authorities and cargo operators out of Manchester, BEA announced they are restarting freight flights to Heathrow from 1ˢᵗ December, with up to ten flights a week. Manchester Airport estimates 10,000 tonnes of air cargo is being transported by road to Heathrow each year for onward flights and if this trend continues, it could jeopardise plans for the new freight terminal. A memo has been sent to the airlines making it clear that commercial vehicles will be denied access to the airport for the collection of any cargo that could be sent from Manchester by air.

The new Category II ILS underwent CAA checks this month and official certification is expected within the next few weeks.

BEA will operate two new services to Munich and Geneva, three-times weekly from next summer. Since its formation in April, the Super 1-11 Division has undertaken extensive surveys into possible new routes which could show a profit from Manchester and cater for business and leisure traffic. Departure times for the new services will be planned to connect with early morning Glasgow, Edinburgh & Belfast flights. They have no passenger Vanguards scheduled through the winter, but still have a six-weekly Trident rotation from/to Heathrow (BE4054/5).

Due to extensive ongoing checks, ILS traffic was practically non-existent and the only aircraft noted were RAF Britannia XN398 (15ᵗʰ), Merpati Nusantara HS.748 PK-MHR (18ᵗʰ) & Nimrod XV260 (28ᵗʰ).

1ˢᵗ   Aer Lingus Amsterdam flight EI602/3 has seen larger aircraft operating the service on several occasions during the month. B.707 EI-ANV operated today, B.707 EI-ANV (16ᵗʰ), B.707 EI-APG (5ᵗʰ) & Boeing 720 EI-ALA (21ˢᵗ/28ᵗʰ).

2ⁿᵈ   RAF Britannia XL640 (RR6452) & VC-10 XR807 (RR2702) arrived from Brize Norton to operate trooping flights to Akrotiri, Cyprus.

3ʳᵈ October 1971 – Air Spain Bristol Britannia EC-BFJ arrived amidst a morning flurry of diversions, operating another one-off charter as JA144/5 from Gerona to Palma. It was also the final visit of an Air Spain Britannia to Manchester. They operated four aircraft of the type, which were all phased out by 1973 and this particular plane ended its days as a spares source for IAS at Biggin Hill. Any visits from this date would be with their newly-acquired Douglas DC-8-21s and the first to arrive was EC-BZQ on the 6ᵗʰ operating JA112/3 from Luton to Palma. (Geoff Ball)

3rd   Twenty-four diversions arrived into Manchester, including one each from Newcastle and Edinburgh. There were five B.747s on the ground at the same time: Aer Lingus EI-ASJ (IN2140 from New York), BOAC G-AWND (BA500 from New York), Pan American N770PA (PA002 from New York), TWA N53116 (TW770 from Chicago) & N93102 (TW700 from New York). Handling facilities were badly affected by the work-in-progress in the terminal and the only B.747 to offload its passengers (who were transported onwards to London by bus) was the Aer Lingus B.747 arriving from New York via Shannon. Other diversions included the first visit of another Olympic Airways B.727: SX-CBD at 1042 (OA281 from Athens), East African Airways VC-10 5H-MOG at 1031 (EC766 from Nairobi), both Wardair B.707s from Gatwick: CF-FAN & CF-ZYP; Pan American B.707 N497PA at 1048 (PA058 from Chicago) and finally a TWA B.707 making its first visit: N8738 at 1057 (TW760 from Los Angeles).

4th   Manchester received a total of six Heathrow diversions during the morning, which was far less than yesterday. They were all BEA or BOAC aircraft, except for the first visit to Ringway of National Airlines DC-8 N109RD at 0759 (NA002 from Miami).

5th   Air France SE.210 F-BHRC made its final visit to Manchester, before it was sold to Air Senegal as 6V-AAR in December.

7th   Already proving to be a good month for diversions, thirteen more arrived during the morning, including another three Boeing 747s: BOAC examples G-AWNB at 1022 (BA506 from New York) & G-AWND at 0913 (BA500 from New York) and first time visitor TWA N93115 at 0950 (TW700 from New York). Other first time visitors were Lufthansa B.707F D-ABUY at 0637 (LH677 from Anchorage) & Seaboard World DC-8F N8637 at 0419 (SB302 from New York).

7th   German Air Force operated Transall 50+51 on a training flight, arriving at 1045 as DCN6163 (Hohn-Northolt).

8th   Manchester received diversions for the second day running, eight in total, mostly from Gatwick. Amongst them was the second visit of TWA B.747 N53116 at 0624 (TW700 from New York), whose passengers stayed onboard awaiting an improvement in the weather. Also for the second time in a week both Wardair B.707s, CF-FAN & CF-ZYP, diverted in again.

13th   Iberia SE.210 EC-BDC made its last appearance at Manchester, operating AO1026/7 on behalf of Aviaco, before being sold to Aviaco in 1972 as EC-CAE.

15th   The airport announced that so far this month, diversions have netted them an extra £11,500 in landing fees.

17th   RAF Britannia XM490 (RR6479) & VC-10 XR806 (RR2708) arrived from Akrotiri, Cyprus on trooping flights.

18th   Sabena routed New York-Brussels flight SN244 through Manchester this morning, with Boeing 707 OO-SJH.

21st   The first passenger Vanguard leaving the BEA fleet, G-APEF, paid its last visit to Manchester today. It was eventually sold on to Indonesian-airline Merpati Nusantara as PK-MVJ.

24th   Another batch of weather diversions arrived early morning. This time there was only one Boeing 747: first time visitor BOAC B.747 G-AWNG at 0842 (BA500 from New York). Another of interest was the very early arrival of Boeing 720 OY-DSL (OY261 from Copenhagen) diverting in from Stansted. It was the first visit of Danish-airline Conair to Manchester with the second being B.720 OY-DSP, which also diverted in on the 31st. National Airlines DC-8 N109RD diverted in again (NA002 from Miami), first time visitor Seaboard World DC-8F N8642 arrived at 0338 (SB302 from New York), Pan American B.707 N409PA at 0646 (PA054 from Detroit) & KLM DC-8 PH-DEM at 0820 (KL6788 from New York).

November 1971

Cargo figures for September showed a 16% drop and a running total drop of 15%, compared with the UK airports average of an overall drop of 18%. However, there was positive news for passenger traffic, as the year showed an increase of 16% on the same period last year.

      BOAC announced the introduction of B.747s on their daily Manchester-New York service from next May, which will increase capacity from 1,000 to 2,500 seats per week. Cargo carried will also increase as the VC-10 carries up to 5 tonnes of freight and the B.747 up to 20 tonnes.

Manchester recorded its sunniest October since 1959 with 125 hours of sunshine, compared to the average 88 hours.

Air France Paris flight AF960/1 has been reduced to four-weekly this winter. By the end of the month BOAC Cargo will operate four-times weekly to New York via Montreal (BA065) and four-times weekly to Chicago via Montreal (BA067), with inbounds operating four-times weekly from New York (BA066), as well as the new Friday/Sunday service from Chicago via Detroit/Boston (BA068). As usual during the winter, the BOAC VC-10 New York flights extend to Antigua/Bridgetown/Guyana & Port of Spain. BEA Cargo commenced a five-weekly night-flight from/to Heathrow and a four-weekly from Dusseldorf. SAS replaced the DC-9 with Fred Olsen DC-6s on their Copenhagen freight flights from the 18th, aircraft used have been LN-FOL & LN-FON.

HS.748 ILS traffic observed was single example Hawker-Siddeley G-11-6 (10th), the day after its maiden flight. It became Thai Airways HS-THI in January 1972. RAF traffic noted were Britannia's XL639 (4th) & Nimrod XV226 (4th).

1st November 1971 – Dominating this shot are the two Boeing 747s. Morning fog saw seventeen diversions arrive, including first visits EL AL B.747 4X-AXA & Pan American B.747 N732PA. To the right of the Pan American are National DC-8 N109RD and one of the two diverted TWA B.707s. (Geoff Ball)

1st   An unofficial walkout today by Heathrow staff, was centred on Canadian company General Aviation Services (GAS). Operating from Heathrow since 1969, they were the first independent ground handling company at Heathrow. The trouble started when GAS started working with Spanish airline Iberia and airport workers tried to picket an Iberia aircraft during unloading; which led to clashes with the airport's police. Coincidentally, Manchester received a number of weather related Heathrow diversions and those of interest are in order of arrival. National Airlines DC-8 N109RD at 0722 (NA002 from Miami) and the following first visits: Pan American B.747 N732PA at 0951 (PA002 from New York), TWA B.707 N766TW at 0955 (TW708 from New York), EL AL B.747 4X-AXA at 1022 (LY016 from New York), TWA B.707 N775TW at 1046 (TW754 from Boston) & Alitalia DC-9 I-DIKW at 1138 (AZ282 from Rome). Another diversion into Manchester was British Caledonian VC-10 G-ARTA at 1043 (CA101 from Palma), which was also its last visit. After being written-off in a landing accident at Gatwick in January 1972, it left just two VC-10s, G-ASIW & G-ASIX, still in service with the airline.

2nd   BOAC announced the indefinite cancellation of all flights from Heathrow and BEA flights in and out were grounded for a second day. Airport staff voted unanimously to continue their unofficial strike, which escalated when coach drivers and refuellers joined in. BEA is barely functioning and no BOAC flights left today. Pan American were able to operate, but westbound flights had to make fuel stops at Shannon and other airlines refuelled wherever they could. Manchester benefited from a variety of diversions and apart from BOAC flights the following arrived: JAL DC-8 JA8037 at 1909 (JL422 Heathrow-Anchorage), Qantas B.707 VH-EBR at 1211 (QF731 Vienna-Heathrow) & Syrian Arab SE.210 YK-AFC at 2007 (RB403 Rome-Heathrow).

2nd   RAF Britannia XM398 (RR6267) operated an outbound trooping flight to Akrotiri, Cyprus.

3rd   All BEA and BOAC flights remained grounded today, after airport staff voted to remain on strike. Manchester received a quantity of fuel diversions, following a similar pattern to yesterday. A number of BOAC flights called in, as well as another JAL DC-8 with the arrival of JA-8010 at 0908 (JL002A New York-Heathrow) & Qantas B.707 VH-EBW at 1012 (QF731 Rome-Heathrow).

4th   The strike affecting Heathrow since Monday the 1st ended today after lengthy negotiations settled the dispute and workers returned to work, but not before another three fuel diverts descended on Manchester. Qantas B.707s VH-EAF at 1447 (QF755 from Rome) & VH-EAH at 1430 (QF735 from Frankfurt) and Malaysia-Singapore B.707 9M-AOT at 1441 (ML783A from Rome), with the last two being first visits.

5th   A very rare type to Manchester visited today, when Rockwell Thrush Commander N8918Q routing Reykjavik-Birmingham, arrived to night-stop. The type, a 1956-vintage, is principally a crop-spraying aircraft.

8th   One of the six inbound flights arriving from Lourdes during the evening was Monarch Airlines Britannia G-AOVI, making its final visit to Manchester at 2212 as OM443.

8th   Jetstar N3E en route, from Leeds to Heathrow, diverted into Manchester at 1302 with a technical problem and then burst four tyres on landing!

8th   Dan-Airs City-Link service launched on 27th July 1970 has been 'tweaked' so it's possible for passengers to carry out pre-flight formalities, such as check-in and buying a ticket at the gate before boarding. The scheme will be extended to their new service connecting Manchester with Birmingham and Bournemouth next year. They also confirmed the basing of five Comets and a hundred flight crew at Manchester next year. So far this year, the airline has flown more than 100,000 holiday makers from Manchester.

12th   Aer Lingus used Boeing 707s EI-ANV on Amsterdam flight EI602/3 & EI-ALA on the 19th.

15th   RAF Whirlwind XP403 was involved in a search and rescue mission in Glossop, Derbyshire when it dropped in for fuel at 1052 before departing to its home base, RAF Leconfield.

18th   Hansa Jet PH-HFB was only the second of its type to visit Manchester, operating a return flight to Groningen. This particular type is built by German manufacturer Hansa with the co-operation of Dutch company Fokker, who are responsible for the wings and the Spanish aeronautical concern, CASA, provides the rear fuselage and tail. The prototype made its first flight in 1964 and PH-HFB was one of three delivered to the RLS, the Dutch equivalent of the CAA. The others were PH-HFA & PH-HFC, which were all used until 1976, when they were sold in the USA.

20th November 1971 – Czech national airline CSA operated two freight flights from/to Prague today and both were first visits. CSA Avia 14 OK-LCA arrived via Amsterdam (OK6655) & CSA IL-18 OK-WAJ (OK6649) on a grim Saturday lunchtime. The Avia 14 is essentially the Russian Ilyushin IL-14, but built under licence in Czechoslovakia. (Geoff Ball)

21ˢᵗ November 1971 – Air Centrafrique DC-8 -55 TL-AAK made three visits to Manchester towards the end of 1971. By this date, it had already visited once and its last was Tuesday 7ᵗʰ December. It was repossessed in April 1972 and between then and 1982, it was used by a variety of American operators as well as French airline UTA as F-BOLK. (Geoff Ball)

22ⁿᵈ   The unique Aerospatiale Super Guppy made the first of many visits today, when F-BTGV positioned in from Paris Le-Bourget to take the first set of Airbus wings for onward transport and assembly at Toulouse. The wings had been roaded in from the factory at Broughton, near Chester, early on Sunday morning, to keep road disruption to a minimum. At the time the following saying was coined 'Every Airbus is delivered by the wings of a Boeing!' The Guppy is basically a converted Boeing 377 Stratocruiser, with up-rated engines.

23ʳᵈ   Hawker-Siddeley HS.748 G-ATAM, arriving at 1007 on a return flight to Hatfield, made a further visit on the 3ʳᵈ December, before departing 5ᵗʰ December to Malmo.

24ᵗʰ   Israeli Air Force Noratlas 4X-FAV performed a touch-and-go at 1237, whilst on a training flight from Copenhagen to Birmingham.

29ᵗʰ   Patchy fog at Heathrow brought in six diversions in thirty minutes. BOAC B.707s G-APFI at 1104 (BA925 from Rome) & G-APFJ at 1114 (BA680 from Bermuda); BOAC VC-10 G-ARVE at 1111 (BA522 from Philadelphia), BOAC B.747 G-AWNB at 1101 (BA506 from New York), Lufthansa B.727 D-ABIA at 1108 (LH030 from Frankfurt) and first visit Alitalia DC-9 I-DIKA at 1129 (AZ282 from Rome).

December 1971

BEA plans to expand next year by adding and increasing frequencies on existing routes, equates to an overall seating capacity rise of 44% and new routes to Geneva and Munich are confirmed for next April. Brussels will increase from three to six-times a week, Amsterdam from three to four a week, Copenhagen from two to three a week and other new services will be introduced over the next two to three years. They hope the changes will help redress the balance, as currently more than 50% of Manchester's passengers are travelling to London for onward flights.

    ILS traffic noted during the month was confined to the RAF with Britannia's XL639 (9ᵗʰ), XL659 (15ᵗʰ), XM489 (30ᵗʰ), XM491 (21ˢᵗ) & XM520 (8ᵗʰ).

1ˢᵗ   Fog at Heathrow sent in a number of morning diversions, including BOAC B.707 G-ARRA at 0911 (BA562 from New York). Amongst its passengers was the Prime Minister, Harold Wilson. His American visit had been cut short, so he could attend a debate on Rhodesia at the House of Commons. Another diversion, HS.125 G-AYLI, was particularly unlucky having to divert twice from East Midlands. A further twenty-four diversions arriving between 1805 and 2211 were all from Heathrow, except for one. Included in this batch were BOAC Boeing 747 G-AWND at 2003 (BA4037 from Athens), a football charter returning England football fans from Athens and Nigeria Airways B.707 5N-ABJ at 1957 (WT906 from Rome), making the airlines first visit to Manchester.

5ᵗʰ   Deterioration in Heathrow's late evening weather gave Manchester five diversions. Alitalia DC-9 I-DIKS at 2056 (AZ266 from Milan), first visit TWA B.707 N788TW at 2145 (TW702 from

New York), BOAC VC-10 G-ARVE at 2151 (Air Ceylon 117 from Rome), Air France SE.210 F-BHRT at 2156 (AF945 from Lyon) & BOAC SVC-10 at 2159 (BA592 from New York).

7th Air Centrafrique DC-8 TL-AAK made the last of its three visits, night-stopping after arriving from Luanda at 1110.

7th An afternoon deterioration in Heathrow's weather brought in another twenty-three diversions. The first two from Brize Norton were RAF VC-10 XR810 at 1552 (RR2758 from Akrotiri) & RAF Britannia XN404 at 1629 (RR6286 from Akrotiri). Most arrivals were from British or European airlines, but Alitalia DC-9 I-DIBO at 1931 (AZ246 from Rome) was a first visit.

9th German Air Force operated Transall 50+61 on a training flight, arriving at 0801 as DCN6696 (Wunsdorf-Northolt).

10th Qantas operated their first flight through Manchester since April today, with Boeing 707 VH-EAA as QF176 (Heathrow-Bahrain).

10th The fortunate two millionth passenger to pass through Manchester was presented with a silver fruit bowl!

12th From today, BOAC are operating B.707s on their New York/Caribbean flights.

21st Douglas DC-3 N655GP arrived at 0623 from Inverness and departed at 0739 for Cologne. The owners of the pre-war aircraft, VAPF Airwise, planned to use it for transporting prospective buyers to view timeshare properties in Spain, but the business never got going!

23rd The foundation stone for the new International terminal was laid today. The work started in June and the first phase should be ready by July next year and the rest by April 1974.

28th Aeroflot made their first visit to Manchester when TU-104 CCCP-42456 night-stopped on a flight from Moscow via Berlin, in preparation for transporting 1,600 rabbits to Russia. The New Zealand Whites and Californian Black Ears left their breeding centre near Northwich early on the 29th in wooden crates and the flight departed for Moscow at 1213.

31st BOAC undertook extensive crew training today with B.747 G-AWNF & SVC-10 G-ASGG. Another crew training flight was BEA Airtours recently acquired B.707 G-APFK.

First/Last Arrivals & Departures 1971

First arrival:	Merchantman G-APEK/BE2101 from Frankfurt at 07.12
First departure:	B.737 EI-ASF/EI9217 to Dublin at 00.16
Last arrival:	B.727 OO-STB from Brussels at 23.31
Last departure:	Merchantman G-APEL/BE2100 to Heathrow at 23.19

(+/- % on Previous Year)		
Scheduled Passengers	1,180,000	+ 0.7%
I.T/Charter Passengers	908,000	+49.6%
Transit Passengers	192,000	+29.7%
Total	2,280,000	+18.3%
Freight & Mail (Tonnes)	39,800	+12.9%
Movements	60,800	+9.7%

Airport Diary 1972

January 1972

HS.748 ILS traffic observed included Thai Airways HS-THI (4th/5th), Polynesian Airways 5W-FAN (6th) & Air Botswana A2-ZGF (14th/20th). RAF traffic noted were Britannia's XM489 (7th) & XN392 (5th). Crew training flights noted were BEA Airtours G-APFK (1st/2nd/3rd/8th), BOAC B.707s G-ASZF (13th), G-AXGX (10th) & G-AYLT (11th). Crew training flights differ slightly from ILS training flights, as they actually land, rather than overshoot.

There was a 13% drop in freight and mail last year, when an estimated total of 39,800 tonnes of cargo passed through, compared with 45,700 tonnes the previous year. However, the downward trend was offset by an 18% increase in passengers last year, when more than 2,276,000 passed through compared with 1,927,000 in 1970.

Runway 24 received full CAA certification and is upgraded to CAT II operations. Improvements were also made to the approach, threshold and runway lighting.

1st BEA Airtours operated further training flights today with their newly acquired Boeing 707 G-APFK. As the first of several aircraft transferred from BOAC, it undertook further flights on 2nd/3rd/8th.

2nd Universal Airlines DC-8 N804U operating Frankfurt-Keflavik, made their last visit to Manchester today, as they ceased trading during the year. This aircraft was sold to Canadian airline Nordair as C-GNDA in 1974 and then to Evergreen International as N810EV in December 1978.

8th Martinair DC-8 PH-MAU (CA1496 from Toronto/Prestwick), operated an inbound transatlantic charter on behalf of British Caledonian.

12th Fairey Aviation DC-3 G-AHCT operated its last flight before being withdrawn and left parked outside the hangar. It was eventually moved to the fire dump, before disappearing completely in November 1975.

14th British Midland Viscount G-AVJB landed amidst a full emergency. It was routing from East Midlands to Glasgow, when a fire warning indicator necessitated the pilot to close down of one the engines. After landing safely, it was discovered a faulty warning circuit was to blame, so Viscount G-APNE positioned in from Heathrow to transport the passengers onwards to Glasgow.

14th Aer Lingus utilised Boeing 720 EI-ALC on today's Amsterdam flight EI602/3 and again on the 21st. B.720 EI-ALA was used on Dusseldorf flight EI630/1 on the 29th.

19th Today's arrival of B.707 N373WA (WO373 from Los Angeles) was the last scheduled visit of a World Airways B.707 to Manchester, but its final appearance was as a diversion on 22nd September 1973. It was sold to Saudia in late-1973 and World Airways gradually phased out the type in favour of the Douglas DC-8.

26th Dan-Air's sole Nord 262, G-AYFR, made its final visit into Manchester today. It was operating the regular City-Link flight, routing Newcastle-Bristol before its final departure at 0838. It was sold the following month and the service is now operated by HS.748s.

30th Gulfstream 2 N1000 night-stopped en route to Rotterdam and although the executive type is still relatively new, it was sold later in the year as N100AC.

31st Qantas operated Boeing 707 VH-EAI through Manchester today as QF173 (Tehran-Heathrow), which was also a first visit.

31st Freezing fog at London-Heathrow provided Manchester with a short burst of three BOAC diversions, including B.747 G-AWNA at 0914 (BA034 from Rome).

February 1972

HS.748 ILS traffic observed were Hawker-Siddeley G-11-7 (10th) & Colombian Air Force FAC-1101 (16th). RAF traffic noted were Britannia's XM491 (23rd) & XN392 (10th) and VC-10 XV104 (17th). Two crew training flights were BOAC B.707s G-APFL (18th) & G-ARRC (22nd).

Passenger figures rose by 24% in January, compared to the same month last year, but freight saw a 5% drop for the same period.

BOAC reversed last November's decision to introduce the B.747 on Manchester's New York service this summer. Last year's announcement had taken the airport by surprise, as they weren't expecting the airline to introduce the aircraft until 1974. BOAC says the increase in capacity provided by the new aircraft 'would be too greater a step for them to take', even though the lower transatlantic fares they are introducing for this summer will increase demand. As they are just about breaking even this financial year, they won't run the risk of introducing a larger plane they may not be able fill. This means the Manchester-New York summer service will be operated daily by SVC-10s, with four flights direct and the other three operating via Prestwick.

1st Aer Lingus used Boeing 720s EI-ALA on Amsterdam flight EI602/3 today and EI-ALC on the 4th.

3rd Alitalia passenger service AZ288/9 was cancelled, due to an industrial dispute in Rome.

7th BEA flew fourteen Merchantman flights from Dusseldorf this month. The first this evening was G-APEJ, organised by LEP Cargo on behalf a wholesaler bringing in 18 tonnes of candles. Each flight carried 500,000 candles for onward distribution throughout the UK.

9th Heron G-APMV, owned by local firm Ferranti, made its last visit today. Although its Edinburgh based, it spends a lot of time at Manchester transporting personnel between the two points. First registered in 1958, it's to be sold during the month and exported to Puerto Rico.

11th Dan-Air bought the last four Comet 4s operated by Aerolineas Argentinas. Two will be used for spares and the others, LV-AHU & LV-AIB, have been re-registered as G-AZIY & G-AROV respectively. G-AROV has yet to visit, but G-AZIY made its first visit to Manchester today, operating an inbound charter from Rome.

14th Comet G-APYC with 119 passengers, operated the final Channel Airways flight into Manchester today (CW114 from Palma), the same day the airline went into receivership. Although it was impounded on arrival, it was allowed to leave for Stansted on the 18th. With the exception of G-ARDI which was withdrawn and used for spares, all their Comets were sold to Dan-Air: G-APMB, G-APYC, G-APYD & G-APZM.

21st AZ288/9 was cancelled again today and for the rest of the month, due to strike action by Alitalia staff. Freight flight AZ900/1 was also cancelled from the 25th.

22nd February 1972 – Air Commerz Viscount D-ADAN, one of two Viscounts purchased from Aer Lingus in 1970, is seen parked on the South Bay on a grey and overcast morning, next to Dan-Air Comet G-APDG. This German airline was short lived, as it ceased trading in September 1972, when both Viscounts were repossessed. (Geoff Ball)

26th Dan-Air Comet G-AZIY returned to Manchester within ten minutes of departure, due to fumes in the cabin. Although the fault was known to be electrical, engineers were unable to find the source.

27th Early morning fog brought in a varied collection of diversions from London-Heathrow and produced no less than four first visits. Alitalia DC9 I-DIZF at 1050 (AZ282 from Rome), Seaboard World DC-8F N8633 at 0435 (SB306 from New York) and two JAL DC-8s: JA8012 at 0933 (JL002A from New York) & JA8014 at 0813 (JL423 from Anchorage).

27th February 1972 – Two JAL Douglas DC-8-55s diverted in from Heathrow during the morning. JA8014 in the foreground served the airline until 1982 and JA8012 in the background, crashed at Delhi, India in June 1972. (Geoff Ball)

28th   Qantas operated B.707 VH-EAB as QF173/4 (Tehran-Belgrade) today.

March 1972

HS.748 ILS traffic observed was single example Hawker-Siddeley G-11-8 (2nd), on its maiden flight. RAF traffic were Britannia's XL637 (30th), XL639 (16th), XL659 (15th), XN392 (2nd/9th) & XN404 (20th) and Belfast XR368 (29th). The only crew training flight was BOAC B.707 G-APFC (13th).

Even though last month's cargo figures of 3,500 tonnes handled showed an increase of 13% on the same month last year, the airport authorities have commissioned a report to forecast how much accommodation is likely to be needed in the new freight village, following the uncertainty after last year's fall in cargo traffic.

1st   Maersk Fokker F.27 OY-APF made two visits during the month, operating from/to Copenhagen today and from/to Stockholm on the 6th.

2nd   RAF operated three flights today, which all night-stopped. Bassett XS767 arrived at 1747 from RAF Cranwell, Pembroke WV748 at 1749 from RAF Upavon and Devon VP958 at 1841 from RAF Wyton.

2nd   Fog at Heathrow provided two more first visits. National Airlines DC-8 N108RD arrived at 0712 (NA002 from Miami) and TWA B.707 N763TW at 0952 (TW754 from Boston).

3rd   Aer Lingus used Boeing 720 EI-ALA on Amsterdam flight EI602/3 and again on Dusseldorf flight EI630/1 on the 23rd.

5th   Dan-Air Comet G-AROV was their latest second-hand aircraft making its first visit to Manchester, arriving at 1725 (DA3411 from Malaga).

12th   US Navy operated a return flight to Stuttgart with T-29 Sabreliner '165518', which arrived at 1438 and stayed for nearly an hour. This was the first military version of the aircraft to visit and the first civil registered visit was N701NC on 23rd May.

14th   Another US military visitor was USAF Convair VC-131D 54-2822, arriving at 0935 from RAF Mildenhall to night-stop. Delivered in 1955 and based on the Convair CV-440, it has improved sound-proofing and can carry up to forty-four passengers. Assigned to carry Government officials and dignitaries, it's currently based in Germany, but from 1973 it was based in Iran before returning to the States in 1978 and finally retired in 1989.

15th   Ringway witnessed the remarkable sight of six Belgian Air Force aircraft diverting in from Leeming today, all within an hour of each other! Two were DC-6s (KY-3 & KY-4) and four were C-119 Boxcars (CP-16/CP-34/CP-35/CP-39).

15th   French Air Force operated a training flight through Manchester today with first-timer SE.210 Caravelle No.141, routing Benbecula-Le Bourget as F-RAFG.

15th   As if six Belgian Air Force aircraft weren't enough, the day also saw the arrival of Moroccan light aircraft Cessna 421 CN-TEN operating from/to Toussos, which is also uncommon to Manchester.

15th Portuguese national carrier TAP operated Boeing 727 CS-TBO during the evening, from/to Lisbon.

22nd During lunchtime at school, the writer and his friends witnessed the wonderful sight and noise of Israeli Air Force Noratlas 4X-FAH on a practice ILS approach and touch-and-go. It was the second to appear at Manchester.

22nd Another USAF Convair VC-131D arrived, this time 52-5788 at 1328, operating from/to its base at RAF Mildenhall.

23rd Not to be outdone, the German Air Force also showed up with Noratlas 50+09. It was on a training flight routing Northolt-Edinburgh and stayed on the ground for seventy minutes.

30th Resident Dove G-AMZN, owned by Manchester wire manufacturers Richard Johnson & Nephew, arrived from Hatfield at 1807 operating the last revenue flight for its local owners. Based since 1965, it left Manchester the following month, after being sold and exported to Sweden.

30th Air France produced first visit Boeing 727 F-BPJR on today's AF960/1.

April 1972

No ILS traffic was observed, but the crew training flights were BOAC B.707s G-APFG (24th), G-ARRB (8th) & G-AXXY (24th).

There were several scheduled flight changes by the airlines this month. Air France will operate Paris-flight AF960/1 as a daily service for the first time. BEA will commence new services to Geneva and Munich, with Heathrow flights being operated by Super 1-11s except for BE4054/63, which is scheduled for a Trident. BOAC Cargo will operate twice-weekly to New York (BA065) and four-weekly to Chicago via Montreal (BA067). Lufthansa will extend their weekday Frankfurt flights onward to Glasgow (LH074/5), with the weekend service extending to Dublin (LH076/7) and the type reverting back to Boeing 737s. Lufthansa introduced a twice-weekly cargo service from Chicago with Boeing 707s, but reduced their night-time Frankfurt cargo flight (LH4070/1) to twice-weekly. Sabena increased frequency on Brussels passenger flight (SN623/4) to five-weekly, which is re-timed to mornings rather than staying overnight. SAS freight flights are now three-weekly to Copenhagen via Birmingham and twice-weekly to Copenhagen via Oslo.

3rd RAF VC-10s XR809 & XR810 operated trooping flights from/to Gutersloh today and VC-10 XV101 (RR2862 from Gutersloh) operated a further flight on the 21st.

4th Invicta Airlines based a Vanguard at Manchester from today, for the daily spring charters to Beauvais and Rotterdam operated by Monarch Airlines last year. Aircraft used during the month were G-AXOO, G-AXOP & G-AZRE.

5th KLM operated Douglas DC-8 PH-DCU on this morning's Amsterdam passenger KL153/4. Other DC-8s used on the flight this month were PH-DCD (7th), PH-DCS (12th), PH-DCW (16th) & PH-DCB (24th).

6th German Air Force Noratlas 50+39 arrived as DCN7310 on a training flight from Cologne to Northolt. Another operated on the 19th, when Noratlas 50+10 arrived at 1249 as DCN7387 (Cologne to RAF Wattisham).

10th Dan-Air extended their City-Link service today, by adding Bournemouth operating via Birmingham.

12th A new airline to Manchester, Swiss operator SATA, operated former Swissair SE.210 HB-ICO today as VS1110/1 from/to Zurich.

15th Another new airline to the UK is East Midlands based Sagittair. They are operating three former Universal Airlines Argosies and G-APWW paid its first visit today, on a freight flight from Cologne at 0604 as SS1262.

18th HS.125 PJ-SLB arrived from Le Bourget at 1136 for customs clearance, en route to Hawarden for maintenance, before returning at 1637 for its flight back to Le Bourget.

27th Saturn C-130 N12ST arrived on an inbound freight flight from Keflavik, before departing later for East Midlands.

May 1972

ILS traffic observed were all RAF aircraft: Britannia's XL637 (24th), XL660 (3rd) & XM520 (19th); Argosy XP448 (10th), Dominie XS734 (15th) and C-130 XV292 19th). The only crew training flight was BOAC B.707 G-AXGX (5th).

This month's scheduled news is: BOAC's Caribbean flights (BA538/7), operated with a mix of VC-10s & SVC-10s, have ended for the winter and will terminate at New York. KLM are operating a Douglas DC-8 on Wednesday's KL153/4. After last winter's frequency increase BOAC Cargo made reductions during the summer: New York is served twice-weekly via Montreal (BA065) as is Chicago (BA067), but inbound flights maintain a healthy frequency with five a week (BA066).

Summer IT flights are in full swing and the following have programmes from Manchester: Air Spain, Aviaco operated by Iberia SE.210s, Aviogenex, Balair, Balkan (from July), Bavaria, Braathens, Inex-Adria, Phoenix Airlines, Sam, Spantax & Tarom as well as a variety of UK operators: BEA, BEA Airtours, Britannia Airways, British Caledonian, British Midland, Court Line, Dan-Air, Invicta Airlines & Laker Airways.

Transatlantic flights from/to the USA & Canada started this month. Pacific Western B.707 CF-PWV (21st), Wardair B.707s CF-FAN (13th) & CF-ZYP (27th) and UK airlines BOAC (B.707), British Caledonian (B.707), British Midland (B.707) & Laker Airways (B.707).

Manchester's BEA Super 1-11 Division carried out its plan and went head-to-head with other tour operators, when BAC 1-11 G-AVMP operated the first charter flight to Palma on the 6th. Their summer IT programme is as follows: Saturday BE9016/5 0900/1445 to/from Palma, Saturday BE9006/5 1320/1935 to/from Palma, Saturday BE9022/1 1530/2110 to/from Gerona, Saturday BE9012/1 1700/2330 to/from Ibiza and Sunday BE9004/3 0930/1540 to/from Palma.

2nd Cambrian Airways leased BKS Viscount G-APEY for the summer, which paid its first visit today operating CS522/3.

4th German Air Force Noratlas 50+63 arrived at 1245 as DCN7647 (Bremen-RAF Northolt).

10th Invicta Airlines flew the last of their Beauvais and Rotterdam flights today, when G-AXOO operated IM322/3 from/to Beauvais. From the 14th, the airline will operate a weekly flight from/to Munich (IM106/7), previously operated by Donaldson International last year.

10th Braathens Fokker F.27 LN-SUF operated an inbound charter from Oslo today, before positioning out later to Stavanger. This aircraft was delivered to the airline in September 1966 and served the airline for ten years before being transferred to Busy Bee of Norway.

13th Sabena's Brussels flight SN623/4 is now operated by SE.210 Caravelle's, but today the airline used Boeing 727 OO-STA.

13th Royal Navy Wessex XT764 called in for fuel during a search and rescue detail in the Hayfield area and stayed for forty minutes, before departing in the direction of Buxton.

13th May 1972 – Air Spain Douglas DC-8-21 EC-CAD, is seen amidst the backdrop of the continuing construction work on the International pier. One of the most colourful airlines ever to grace the Manchester aprons sadly went into liquidation in 1975. (Geoff Ball)

19th Air France sub-chartered other aircraft to operate AF960/1 during the month. Spantax CV-990 EC-BJC was used today and Finnair SE.210 OH-LSD on the 26th.

26th New Swiss-based airline, Phoenix Aviation, operated the first of their summer flights to Basle today. Operating with former TWA Boeing 707 N732TW initially, they added a second aircraft, BAC 1-11 HB-ITL, which first operated from Manchester on 9th June.

22nd May 1972 – Remembering the sight of six Belgian Air Force aircraft on the ground in March - another group of military movements arrived late afternoon, this time three Bolivian Air Force CV-340s: TAM-41, TAM-43 & TAM-46. They were on delivery to the Bolivian Air Force, having been recently purchased from Spanish charter airline Aviaco, who had operated them since 1959. They were routing from Mildenhall to Keflavik when one developed a fault in-flight and as a result all three diverted in. The first, TAM-41, is seen here taxiing to its parking spot, adjacent to Fairey Aviation. (Geoff Ball)

29th Air France SE.210 F-BHRR made its final visit to Manchester, before being transferred to Air Inter early next year.

31st Jetstar N516WC was making its first visit to Manchester, arriving at 0918 from Edinburgh, before departing at 1137 for Luton.

June 1972

ILS traffic observed was confined to military examples again and RAF aircraft noted were Britannia's XL637 (7th), XN398 (28th) & XN404 (8th/14th/15th); Varsity WF417 (12th), Argosies XP448 (27th) & XN816 (28th) and Israeli Air Force Noratlas 4X-FAJ (7th). The only crew training flight was BOAC VC-10 G-ARVK (8th).

This year's transatlantic flights from/to the USA & Canada are showing much less variety and frequency than the previous two years. Most are operated by UK airlines, particularly British Caledonian, with two flights on some days. BOAC, British Midland, Laker Airways & Lloyd International all operated during the month, as did North American carriers - Pacific Western B.707 CF-PWV (24th), Pan American B.707s N433PA (26th) & N425PA (30th); TWA B.707s N28724 (24th), N8735 (30th) & N8737 (30th) and Wardair B.707 CF-FAN (4th/17th).

The airport is running a free minibus service, transporting passengers between the car parks and the terminal building. The three buses can carry up to twelve passengers, but luggage space is limited.

1st Iberia commenced their summer only twice-weekly service to Palma, via Barcelona (IB782/1) and the first flight was operated by SE.210 EC-ARJ.

4th Former British Midland Viscount G-AVJB has been bought by new UK-airline Kestrel Aviation, who already operates Douglas DC-3 G-AMFV. It made the first of several visits this year today operating from Deauville, but its last visit on 9th October was just before they ceased trading and the aircraft was repossessed by British Midland in November 1972.

6th The first stage of the new terminal extension was finished today, when the enlargement of the departure lounge was completed.

7th RAF Britannia's XM496 (RR6715) & XM497 (RR6716) operated trooping flights from/to Gutersloh.

9th Royal Saudi Air Force operated their second flight into Manchester today, when C-130E 1608 arrived from/to Jeddah via Milan as RSF879, before departing on the 11th. Incidentally the first visit was back in 1970.

13th Another new French Air Force training aircraft to Manchester, the Falcon 20, appeared when No.154 arrived at 2212 from Stornaway, en route back to its base at Villacoublay.

14th   The second of Sagittair's three Argosies, G-APRN, paid its first visit to Manchester today at 0535, operating a freight flight from Belfast as SS1376. Their last Argosy to visit was G-APWW on the 22nd June, as they ceased trading in September.

17th   Lloyd International's Britannia G-AOVP arrived to operate a freight flight to Istanbul on behalf of Donaldson International (who disposed of their remaining Britannia's in 1971). This aircraft wasn't long for this world either, as it too was withdrawn following the collapse of Lloyd International two days later on the 19th. By the end of the month, it was left parked at Stansted until July 1973, when it was flown to Biggin Hill and broken up for scrap in 1977.

17th   Monarch Airline's replaced their ageing Bristol Britannia's with three second-hand Boeing 720s. G-AZFB was the first to visit Manchester, operating OM496 from Luton to Bourgas today and the others, G-AZKM & G-AZNX, are yet to visit.

20th   Aer Lingus used Boeing 720 EI-ALA on Amsterdam flight EI602/3 and B.720 EI-ALC was used on Dusseldorf flight EI630/1 on the 22nd.

20th   Scheduled flights operated by foreign carriers, including Aer Lingus and most BEA Domestic and European flights, were cancelled at Manchester today due to a pilots strike over the growing problem of hi-jacking. They wanted an international convention and a worldwide strike, but this was watered down by a combination of legal injunctions, management appeals, Government pressure and the withdrawal of support from the British Airline Pilots Association (BALPA). Frankfurt and Amsterdam were shut down completely and Heathrow's Terminal 2, which handles foreign European airline services, was virtually closed after twenty European airlines cancelled their flights. Although BEA cancelled their entire domestic network in and out of Heathrow, their domestic operations from other airports were unaffected.

22nd   This month's German Air Force training flight, operated by Transall 50+92, arrived at 1217 as DCN8026 (RAF Northolt-Cologne).

30th   Sabena's evening freighter SN197/8, normally scheduled for Boeing 727's, was operated by Boeing 707F OO-SJH.

July 1972

HS.748 ILS traffic was confined to Hawker-Siddeley G-11-1, making its maiden flight (10th). RAF traffic noted were RAF Britannia's XL639 (19th), XM518 (26th), XN398 (27th) & XN404 (5th); Dominie XS727 (5th) and Argosy XR143 (24th).

Scheduled changes worthy of note include the introduction by BOAC of a second summer Canadian service, BA603/4, five-times-weekly to Montreal via Prestwick. The existing BA607/8 will be daily to Toronto via Prestwick, but Chicago will not be operated this year. SAS cargo flights will operate five-weekly to Copenhagen via Oslo.

For the first time in ten years, from 1st November a winter programme will operate from Manchester to Jersey (via Birmingham), when BEA commence a three-times-weekly operation. They are also considering a once-weekly service to Cyprus next summer.

There was a considerable increase in transatlantic flights this month. Aircraft used were Air Canada DC-8 CF-TIP (31st), KLM DC-8s PH-DCK (8th), PH-DEB (4th), PH-DEC (20th) & PH-DEE (1st); Martinair DC-8 PH-MAU (16th/24th), Pacific Western CF-PWV (4th/23rd/25th/26th), Pan American B.707s N404PA (29th) & N421PA (2nd/30th); Saturn DC-8 N8956U (16th), TIA DC-8 N8786R (18th), Transavia B.707 PH-TVA (17th), TWA B.707s N8735 (22nd), N8737 (17th), N28724 (10th/16th/23rd/24th) & N28728 (10th/18th/25th); Wardair B.707 CF-ZYP (9th/24th) and World Airways DC-8 N802WA (27th). UK airlines were BOAC, British Caledonian, Dan-Air, Donaldson International & Laker Airways, all with Boeing 707s.

1st   A new Russian airliner, the Tupolev TU-154, made its first visit to Manchester today, when Balkan launched a fortnightly IT flight to the Black Sea resort of Varna. The first of this summer series of flights was operated by LZ-BTA (LZ903/4). The following week (8th) another fortnightly IT flight to Bourgas, also on the Black Sea commenced with LZ-BTB making its first visit (LZ907/8). It's loosely based on the Hawker-Siddeley Trident and Boeing 727 in terms of the design being a tri-jet layout, with two engines at the rear and a third through the tail. It first flew in 1970, but didn't enter passenger service until February 1972, with Russian state airline Aeroflot. Balkan Airlines became the launch export customer of the TU-154, with an initial order of two aircraft.

5th   Royal Saudi Air Force operated another flight into Manchester, when C-130E 1609 operated from/to Jeddah via Milan as RSF880, before its departure on the 7th.

6th   Aer Turas Bristol 170 EI-APC, the last example in Europe still flying, positioned in from Nantes to operate a cargo flight the following day to Bordeaux.

8th   Aer Lingus Boeing 720 EI-ALC made its final visit to Manchester, operating Amsterdam flight EI602/3, before being sold to Trans European as OO-TEB the following month.

9th   The evening Aer Lingus freighter EI9212/3, operated by Aer Turas Argosy EI-AVJ, returned in the early hours the next day to operate EI9216/7. These were the aircraft's only visits to Manchester, as after operating for the airline for less than a year, they were found unsuitable for their operations and this particular aircraft was sold later in the year in November.

11th   Aer Lingus used Boeing 720 EI-ALA on Amsterdam flight EI602/3 and also on the 27th.

12th   The new UK-airline Air Bridge Carriers, set up this year, made their first visit to Manchester today operating Viscount G-APPX from Newcastle to their East Midlands base. They were formed initially to transport fresh produce from the Channel Islands to the UK and operate ad-hoc charters. By the end of the year they had acquired all of Sagittair's Argosies, following their demise.

13th   German Air Force Transall 50+92 arrived at 1103 as DCN8251 on a training flight (Hohn-Hatfield) and a second, 50+90, operated on the 21st as DCN8436 (from/to Alhorn).

17th   The first of Dan-Air's batch of ex-BOAC Comets to be withdrawn from service was G-APDD. Only delivered to Dan-Air in October 1969, it made its last visit to Manchester today, operating DA3874 to Rimini before being withdrawn from service on 26th August.

18th   Hansa Jet D-CITO made its first visit today on a return flight from Munich, before returning on the 20th from/to Munich. It was operated by German aerospace company, Messerschmitt-Bolkow-Blohm (MBB) until 1978, when it was sold in the USA.

19th   Royal Aircraft Establishment (RAE) Comet XV814 arriving at 1045 as MPDXA, stayed until 1604, before departing for Farnborough. This aircraft is used as a test-bed for navigation equipment/avionics and continued development of the RAF Nimrod.

31st   Swedish cargo-airline Air Traders, made the first of three visits to Manchester this year during their brief existence, when Vanguard SE-FTI positioned in from Stansted to operate an outbound charter to Oslo as WE652. Vanguards SE-FTH, SE-FTI & SE-FTK were all converted to freight operations, but by the end of the year the airline had ceased trading.

August 1972

The only HS.748 observed on the ILS was Polynesian Airlines 5W-FAO (2nd/9th). RAF traffic noted were RAF Britannia's XL659 (12th/16th), XM497 (2nd); C-130 XV291 (11th) and Argosies XR137 (21st), XR143 (15th) & XN855 (31st). Crew training flights noted were BOAC B.707 G-ARWD (8th) & BOAC B.747 G-AWNI (30th).

Amidst the continuing uncertainty on the size of the new cargo village, a 9% increase in freight carried between January-July was announced, compared to same period last year. The original plan was for a complex costing £8.6m, capable of taking the forecasted figure of 400,000 tonnes of cargo per year by 1985. The Airport Authority wanted airlines, larger freight firms and groups of smaller cargo agencies, to invest in the new facilities by paying the construction costs of the sections they wished to occupy, on new thirty-five year leases from Manchester Corporation. However, last April it was decided to halve the expenditure to £4m and build a village capable of handling between 175,000-200,000 tonnes per year. The airport suffered a further blow when the airlines and freight companies said they wouldn't pay for the new building. It was then agreed that Manchester Corporation would build the village and charge a rental for its use. The city's Airport Committee has called for an updated consultants report to forecast future cargo levels and have asked airlines and freight companies to estimate how much freight they are likely to handle. Once they have the information, it will be included in a new report, which is not expected to be out for several months. In the meantime, the final size and shape of the freight village remains unknown.

British Caledonian will commence nonstop scheduled services to New York from 1st June next year, in direct competition with BOAC. It's the first time BOAC has faced competition on its transatlantic services out of Manchester, since Sabena were forced off the New York route in March

1964. The new flights will originate from Gatwick and operate via Manchester on Mon/Tue/Thu/Sat.

The month saw another varied selection of transatlantic flights. UK airlines operating were BOAC (B.707/SVC-10), British Caledonian (B.707), Dan-Air (B.707), Donaldson International (B.707), Laker Airways (B.707), Air Canada DC-8 CF-TJH (28th), KLM DC-8s PH-DCK (6th), PH-DEC (15th), PH-DEF (12th) & PH-DEM (12th); Martinair DC-8s PH-MAS (21st) & PH-MAU (16th); ONA DC-8 N864F (6th), Pacific Western B.707 CF-PWV (9th/10th/20th/25th/30th), Pan American B.707s N421PA (21st), N426PA (4th) & N454PA (26th); Saturn DC-8 N8955U (16th), TWA B.707s N8737 (17th), N28724 (16th), N18709 (21st/27th), N28726 (6th/27th) & N28728 (17th); Wardair B.707s CF-FAN (8th/13th), CF-ZYP (27th) and World Airways DC-8s N801WA (20th) & N802WA (26th).

1st   SAS Douglas DC-8 LN-MOC, operating a return flight from Billund, Denmark, was a first visit and the first SAS DC-8 to arrive at Manchester since OY-KTC on 10th August 1969.

2nd   The first Finnair Douglas DC-9 into Manchester arrived today, when OH-LYG operated an outbound flight to Helsinki as AY5873. The return flight on the 9th was operated by SE.210 Caravelle OH-LSC (AY5874).

4th   CL-44 G-ATZI, currently leased by British Air Ferries from Transmeridian, made its first visit today operating an inbound freight flight from Tarbes, before departing later for Ostend. It was later purchased by new Swiss-airline Transvalair in 1974.

6th   SAS operated Douglas DC-9s on their SK537/8 service this month. OY-KGI was used today, OY-KGC on the 13th and both were first visits.

8th   Royal Saudi Air Force operated another flight into Manchester today, when C-130E 453 arrived from/to Jeddah via Milan as RSF881, before departing on the 10th.

9th   The Army Air Corps operated three flights this month through Manchester, all with DeHavilland Beavers. Today, XP805 as Army 583 (Netheravon-Dunkeswell) and XV271 operated Army 324, (Belfast-Blackbushe). Beaver XV271 also came in again the following day as Army 324 (Woodvale –Belfast).

11th   Air Anglia let their passengers fly on a real aircraft today, when they used Douglas DC-3 G-ANTD on their Norwich-Liverpool service, rather than Islander G-AXVP. The DC-3 appeared again on the 19th, bringing Norwich City FC up for the third League match of the season against Manchester City. It wasn't a good day for Norwich, as they were comprehensively beaten by City 3-0

12th   Sabena's evening freighter, SN195/6, was operated by Boeing 707 OO-SJH.

13th   Aer Lingus used Boeing 720 EI-ALA on Amsterdam flight EI602/3.

16th August 1972 – This shot was taken on the day the L.1011 Tristar arrived at Manchester. It shows N305EA about to land for the first time, in bright sunshine on a demonstration flight from Luton before departing to Amsterdam with various travel press and travel agency staff onboard. It's in basic Eastern Airlines colours, with Court titles on the forward fuselage, due to their order for two aircraft. (Geoff Ball)

13th Aer Lingus B.737 EI-ASA was seen at Manchester today, operating Cork flight EI762/3 in a curious colour scheme after completing a lease with Air Cameroon. It had an all-white tail with a red stripe along the fuselage tapering towards the nose, flanked with a thin green stripe above and a thin yellow stripe below.

16th Saturn Airways DC-8-61 N8955U arrived on an inbound charter from New York via Gander, before positioning out later to Stansted. This was the last year the airlines DC-8s were seen on a regular basis at Manchester.

22nd Dan-Air are using flight numbers as opposed to their registration for ATC purposes, but the exception to this rule is the City-Link HS.748 operation, which still uses its registration as the ATC identifier.

22nd RAF Britannia XL658 made two return trips, ferrying troops out to Dusseldorf.

27th Single Heathrow weather diversion, TWA B.707F N765TW, made its first visit arriving at 0750 (TW790 from Detroit).

28th Zambian-registered Beech 55 Baron 9J-ACS arrived at 1102 from Aberdeen, before departing for Oxford at 1630.

28th The monthly visits of German Air Force aircraft continued with the arrival of Transall 50+81 at 1518 today, as DCN8816 (Glasgow-Northolt).

30th BOAC Boeing 747 G-AWNI made its first visit to Manchester today, arriving for crew training exercises, which included four ILS approaches.

30th Israeli Air Force Noratlas 4X-FAH also visited today, performing a touch-and-go en route from Alconbury to Leeds.

September 1972

Another lean month for ILS traffic, when the only aircraft observed were RAF Britannia XL659 (13th) & C-130 XV204 (19th) and the only crew training flight was BOAC B.707 G-ATWV (26th).

Transatlantic flights wound down again this month, with the following UK airlines operating flights: BOAC (B.707), British Caledonian (B.707), Dan-Air (B.707) & Laker Airways (B.707) and the following aircraft: KLM DC-8s PH-DCD (30th) & PI-C804 (20th); ONA DC-8 N867F (4th), Pacific Western B.707 CF-PWV (10th), Pan American B.707 N495PA (27th) and Wardair B.707 CF-ZYP (3rd/4th/5th/17th/23rd).

Work on a second multi-storey car park to accommodate 2,000 cars, costing nearly £1.25m and planned for land north of the terminal extension, is not expected to start before 1975. An Airport Committee report forecasts that by mid-1970, there will be insufficient parking spaces, even when the first multi-storey car park is completed next year.

A feasibility study for the first direct link between Manchester and Athens, planned for 1974 by Olympic Airways, has been described as very favourable and a final decision's expected in the next few months.

The first visit of the McDonnell-Douglas DC10 to Manchester is expected to take place in November, when a Laker Airways example will arrive for demonstration purposes. The airline has also received CAA approval for their Skytrain 'low fare, no reservation' transatlantic service from Stansted, following rejection of their application to operate from their base at Gatwick.

Dan-Air will base a Boeing 727 at Manchester next year, after the recent acquisition of three second-hand aircraft from Japan Airlines.

1st Phoenix Aviation B.707 N732TW made its final visit today, operating HP800/1 from/to Basle. It was subsequently sold to Trans European as OO-TEC.

1st RAF VC-10 XR807 (RR2861) operated a trooping flight from/to Gutersloh. Others during the month were VC-10 XV102 (RR2851 from Gutersloh-23rd) & VC-10 XV105 (RR2860 outbound to Gutersloh-25th).

1st Aer Turas Bristol 170 EI-APC operated extra cargo flight EI9206/7, from/to Dublin on behalf of Aer Lingus and another the following day, which turned out to be the last visit of the type until 1985. Delivered to Aer Lingus new in 1952 as EI-AFR, it saw further service with Skyways, Middle East Airlines, BOAC & BKS, before being sold to Aer Turas in 1966. It was sold again later this year in December, to french cargo operator Transportes Aeriens Reunis as F-BTYO.

2nd   German leisure-airline Condor were the first to order and operate the Boeing 747 and when Boeing 727 D-ABIM (Bavaria flight BV608/9) arrived from/to Munich, it was a first visit to Manchester of both the airline and the aircraft.

3rd   Ford Motor Company's Gulfstream 1 N304K, arriving at 2133, was bringing in personnel from Rome. It also operated inbound from Salzburg on the 17th.

3rd September 1972 – Moormanair Douglas DC-3 PH-MAG arrived late Sunday evening on a return flight from/to Amsterdam. This Dutch company operated three Douglas DC-3s between 1968 -1973, but one of these, PH-MOA, was lost in a landing accident at Southend in June 1971. (Geoff Ball)

4th   The remaining Aer Lingus Boeing 720, EI-ALA, made its final visit today operating evening freighter EI9216/7, before being sold in October to Club International as N734T.

5th   Royal Saudi Air Force operated their fourth flight into Manchester this year, when C-130E 1609 arrived at 1033 from/to Jeddah via Milan as RSF882, before its departure on the 7th.

7th   Royal Navy operated two flights today out to RAF Yeovilton: Sea Heron XM286 at 1041 (Navy827) & Sea Devon XJ319 at 1107 (Navy819). Two more operated the following day returning personnel from RAF Yeovilton: Sea Devon XJ324 at 1526 (Navy709 & Sea Heron XM296 at 1532 (Navy824), which formerly operated with the Queens Flight.

7th   BOAC diverted four flights into Manchester: B.707 G-AWHU at 0759 (BA686 from New York) and three B.747s - G-AWNB at 0629 (BA610 from Montreal), G-AWNF at 0755 (BA500 from New York) & B.747 G-AWNG at 0814 (BA600 from Toronto). Also arriving was TWA B.707 N772TW at 0808 (TW754 from Boston), making its first visit.

9th   Having operated a summer programme from Manchester since 1963, Braathens will not be returning next year. Their final flight today was BU725/6, operated by F.28 LN-SUN.

10th   Two British Caledonian B.707s made their last visits to Manchester this month. The first, G-AVTW, arrived at 0944 today (CA2565 from Toronto) and was sold to Portuguese national carrier TAP as CS-TBI in April 1973. The second, G-AZPW, arrived at 0612 (CA2065 from Toronto) on the 26th, returning to PIA, from whom it was leased the following month.

10th   1958-vintage Fairchild F.27 N4305F operated a return flight to Gatwick today and again on the 11th.

17th   A first visit of type was company demonstrator Mitsubishi MU-2 N184MA. It stayed for several days and made further visits throughout the rest of the month.

20th   The monthly German Air Force training flight was operated by Transall 50+78 today, arriving at 1311 as DCN9063 from Cologne to Northolt.

20th   KLM operated Philippine Airlines Douglas DC-8 PI-C804 (KL6399 Amsterdam-New York) in full Philippine colours.

21st   Early morning fog at London-Heathrow brought in two B.747 first visits: Pan American N750PA at 0726 (PA002 from New York) & TWA N93117 at 0957 (TW716 from New York).

28th   Only the second RAF Puma to land at Manchester so far was XW233 today, making a brief stop from Odiham, on its way to Northern Ireland.

October 1972

HS.748 ILS traffic observed included Hawker-Siddeley examples G-11-2 (4th) & G-AYVR in full Bouraq of Indonesia colours, which later became PK-IHD (6th) and Air Gabon TR-LQY (4th). RAF traffic noted were Britannia's XL636 (11th), XL639 (18th), XL657 (25th), XM520 (4th) & XN398 (19th); Belfast XR365 (6th) and Argosy XP413 (25th). Crew training flights were BOAC B.707 G-ARWD (8th) & B.747 G-AWNI (30th).

From the 14th, BOAC reverted to a daily New York via Prestwick flight (BA538/7) and Montreal (BA603/4) was terminated. After operating the route since 1968, Alitalia ceased their Milan/Rome passenger service on 30th. Iberia operated the last Barcelona/Palma service on the 28th last month and will return next year with Douglas DC-9s. The following SE.210 Caravelle's have made their last visits, although some may continue operating on behalf of Aviaco:

EC-ARJ   Last visit 04/09/72, sold to Far Eastern Air Transport as B-2501 08/73.

EC-ARK   Last visit 21/09/72, transferred to Aviaco in 01/73.

EC-AVY   Last visit 17/08/72, withdrawn 10/72.

EC-AYD   Last visit 31/08/72, transferred to Aviaco in 04/73.

EC-AYE   Last visit 15/06/72, withdrawn 12/73.

EC-BIA   Last visit 28/09/72, written-off 11/73.

EC-BIC   Last visit 13/09/72, written-off 08/73.

EC-BID   Last visit 11/10/72, written-off 03/73.

BEA announced their largest ever winter programme out of Manchester. From 1st November, nearly fifty flights a week will operate to the following eight European cities: Brussels, Copenhagen, Paris, Munich, Dublin, Malta, Amsterdam & Geneva. Another seventy-five flights a week will operate to London, Glasgow, Edinburgh & Belfast, including increased frequencies to Paris, Brussels & Copenhagen. Services to Munich and Geneva introduced in April will maintain their three-times weekly service throughout the winter. There are two Trident rotations from/to Heathrow and Jersey will be served throughout the winter. There are no Vanguard passenger schedules, as the type is being withdrawn from service by the airline.

BEA Airtours operated their last summer programme from Manchester with Comets, as they are being replaced with surplus ex-BOAC Boeing 707s, the first two being G-APFH & G-APFK. The following Comets made their last visits to Manchester as BEA Airtours aircraft, as by early 1973 they had been transferred to Dan-Air: G-APMG (24th June), G-ARJN (30th September) & G-APMF (21st October).

BOAC announced their Manchester-New York flights will operate as a daily non-stop service next summer, following a record breaking period when passenger numbers were up 40% between April and September, compared to last year. However, they are mindful that British Caledonian will be commencing a direct service on the route next year.

Following recent talks with the Republic of Ireland, Britain has expressed its concern over the level of Aer Lingus fifth-freedom rights between Manchester and the Continent and warns they may have to reduce or withdraw the services. Flights currently operating from Manchester to Amsterdam, Copenhagen, Dusseldorf, Frankfurt & Zurich are generating £800,000 a year and continue to show a healthy growth. Although they've operated the flights from Manchester since 1947, the most important European destination, Brussels, was withdrawn in 1966 due to a British protest. BEA's Manchester based Super 1-11 Division currently operates to three of these European points, but the remaining two to Frankfurt and Zurich are only operated from Heathrow. The division responsible for BEA's German domestic services is suffering from a slump in West Berlin traffic, but they expect to increase their share of traffic out of Manchester.

Due to the Italian government's restriction on flights per hour at Rome and Milan, Alitalia announced their intention to withdraw passenger services from Manchester, but continue with their cargo operation.

Air Anglia also withdrew flights from Manchester this month. Their service, linking Norwich with Manchester and Liverpool, had barely existed a year when the last flight operated on the 30th. Regularly operated by Islander G-AXVP, PA-23 Aztec's also made frequent appearances and even a Douglas DC-3 operated once on the 11th August.

1st   Having operated an IT programme from Manchester since 1967, Bavaria is the second airline not returning next year. Their final flight today, was operated by BAC 1-11 D-ALLI (BV708/9).

3rd   Royal Saudi Air Force C-130E 1607 is the latest making its first visit, operating from/to Jeddah via Milan as RSF889, before its departure on the 5th.

5th   In a week already memorable for its sunshine, Manchester received the welcome sight of Loganair Beech 18 G-ASUG, arriving from Blackpool at 1946.

8th BEA operated two inbound charter flights from today, with Vanguards G-APEA & G-APED, which both positioned out to Heathrow later. Co-incidentally they were also making their last visits as G-APEA was withdrawn from service in November and G-APED in January 1973.

10th Royal Aircraft Establishment (RAE) Devon XA880, used for communication duties, made two return flights from/to its base at Llanbedr, North Wales.

12th Evening visitor USAF C-130 64-0532, was from/to Frankfurt Rhein Main AFB.

14th RAF VC-10 XR806 made two return flights from Gutersloh (RR2881) today. Another took place on the 30th, with VC-10 XR808 (RR2885).

15th BEA operated a £2 return flight to Blackpool today, when Super 1-11 G-AVMW took out eighty passengers, before flying another planeload to Majorca. The day-trippers were picked up from Blackpool late evening, for their return flight to Manchester.

17th Having been the backbone of the airlines services to Europe, Wardair's sole Boeing 727, CF-FUN, operated its last flight out of Manchester today. Its early-morning arrival at 0632 (WD104 from Winnipeg), was due to fog at Amsterdam. Although this aircraft didn't leave the fleet until 1973, it's not been used on UK services this year.

18th The monthly German Air Force training flight continued with Transall 50+81, arriving at 1303 as DCN6012 (Cologne-RAF Northolt).

26th The first nose-in parking procedure took place today, when VC-10 G-ARVB (BA538) arrived at 0745 on Stand 8. The first pushback departure was also today, when B.707 G-APFM (BA607) left Stand 6. Nose-in parking, replacing traditional side-on parking, will be fully operational on the west side of the International pier (Pier B) from the 1st of next month.

27th French Air Force Falcon 20 No.154 arrived at 1021, on a training flight from Prestwick to Villacoublay.

27th Pacific Western's second B.707, CF-PWZ, acquired in August this year, made its first visit operating a flight from Budapest to Sondre-Stromfjord, Greenland. Unfortunately, this was its only visit to Manchester, as it was written-off in January 1973.

29th Sterling operated two charters from Copenhagen, which were both first visits. SE.210 OY-SAH arrived at 1545 (NB3033) today and OY-SBZ at 2103 (NB3035) on the 30th.

30th SE.210 I-DAXI operated the final Alitalia scheduled passenger flight from Manchester, departing at 0938 for Milan-Linate. It's the last time any of their SE.210s would visit, although some were transferred to their charter subsidiary, SAM, to compliment their existing aircraft. By February 1977, the SE.210 had been phased out completely by the airline.

November 1972

HS.748 ILS traffic observed were Hawker-Siddeley G-AZJH (10th) & G-BAFY (10th) and Bouraq PK-IHD (10th). RAF traffic noted were Argosies XN816 (2nd), XP448 (27th) & XR137 (13th/20th); Victor XL231 (10th) plus Israeli Air Force Stratocruiser 4X-FPY (28th), which overshot late morning. Crew training flights were: BOAC B.707s G-APFM (14th/16th/20th) & G-APFP (1st); B.747 G-AWNE (25th) and Laker Airways DC-10 G-AZZC (24th).

Scheduled flight changes during the month were: Air France to operate six-weekly through the winter. Air Anglia and Alitalia no longer operate passenger services. BOAC's VC-10 New York flights (BA538/7) will extend to Antigua/Bridgetown/Guyana & Port of Spain. SAS are using Fred Olsen DC-6s again on their Copenhagen freight flights, but will no longer operate via Oslo. Winter IT flights are being operated by Air Spain, Britannia Airways, British Caledonian, British Midland, Dan-Air, Laker Airways & Spantax.

1st Of the twenty-one weather diversions today, most were from Heathrow. The first diversion arriving at 0455 was BOAC Cargo B.707F G-ASZG (BA066 from Prestwick) and as the morning gave way to a warm sunny day, more arrived, though few were foreign. Another B.747, G-AWNK, arrived at 0625 (BA024 from Nairobi) and out of the twenty arrivals by lunchtime, only the following were noteworthy: Lufthansa B.727F at 0539 (LH4060 form Frankfurt), Gatwick diversion SAM SE.210 I-DABV at 1055 (MQ224 from Milan), first visit Alitalia DC-9 I-DIBJ at 1155 (AZ282 from Rome), East African Airways VC-10 5X-UVJ at 1145 (EC724 from Rome) and lastly RAF VC-10 XR807 at 1253 (RR2340 from Akrotiri).

1st Aer Turas Douglas C-54F EI-ARS operated extra cargo flight (EI9218/9) for Aer Lingus.

2nd Manchester received nine arrivals after fog descended on Heathrow again in the early hours. They were mainly BEA aircraft and included five Vanguards/Merchantman: G-APEG at 0033 (BE2833 from Glasgow), G-APEH at 0024 (BE209 from Gibraltar), G-APEO at 0016 (BE2885 from Belfast), G-APES (BE'ES from Milan) & G-APEU at 0257 (BE2883 from Belfast).

4th Fog at Haydock Racecourse prevented three light aircraft from landing there for today's meet, so PA-30 Twin Comanche G-AVHW arrived at Manchester at 1104, as did PA-23 Aztec's G-AZMG at 1109 & G-AYWG at 1148.

6th Rousseau Aviation HS.748 F-BSRU diverted in at 1618, due to the weather at Leeds.

7th Following today's cancellation of BOAC Montreal/Toronto BA608/7, Scottish-based BOAC Viscount G-AMOG arrived to ferry passengers from/to Prestwick.

9th Now that Aviaco no longer operates Iberia SE.210s, today was a sign of times to come, when Iberia Douglas DC-8 EC-ARB operated outbound flight (AO1071 to Palma).

10th Three different HS.748s; G-AZJH, G-BAFY and Bouraq example PK-IHD, were on test flights from Woodford today, as was RAF Victor XL231 which overshot in the afternoon.

11th Comets are still in regular use in the UK with operators such as BEA Airtours, Dan-Air & Royal Air Force, but the last international airline still operating schedules with the type is Sudan Airways; who operated their final Comet service into Heathrow today, as they are being replaced with Boeing 707s.

14th Another Hansa Jet to visit Manchester this year was D-CASU, diverting in due to fog at Warton. This aircraft is also operated by the German aerospace company, Messerschmitt-Bolkow-Blohm (MBB) and it served with them until 1974.

14th This month's Royal Saudi Air Force flight was operated by C-130E 455 today, from/to Jeddah via Milan as RSF890, before departing on the 16th.

15th RAF VC-10 XV102 (RR2757) & Britannia XL637 (RR6752) operated inbound trooping flights from Hanover and Gatow respectively. On the 16th, Britannia XM518 arrived as RR6753 from Gutersloh.

22nd HS.125 PJ-SLB arrived from Calais at 1817, before departing for Le Bourget at 1848. It was sold in February 1973 as F-BSSL.

23rd Today was the first visit to Manchester of a McDonnell-Douglas DC-10, when Laker Airways G-AZZC arrived from Gatwick. Delivered eleven days earlier, it was on a demonstration flight to local travel agents, before departing to Glasgow the next day for further flights. They also took delivery of their second aircraft, G-AZZD, today and will be operating a weekly charter flight to Toronto from next April.

24th The second of Dan-Air's batch of ex-BOAC Comets to leave the fleet was G-APDJ. It made its last visit to Manchester today (DA1034 to Tunis), before being withdrawn later in the month.

26th Southend and Luton received more than twenty diversions this evening, after Heathrow and Gatwick were affected by fog, but Manchester only received five. Two were from Gatwick: SAM SE.210 I-DABP at 2320 (MQ532 from Milan) & Dan-Air Comet G-APZM at 2344 (DA1110 from Rome) and three were from Heathrow: BEA Trident 1 G-ARPP at 2207 (BE207 from Gibraltar), BOAC B.747 G-AWNB at 2219 (BA594 from New York) and Swissair DC-9 HB-IFN at 2308 (SR860 from Zurich).

27th German Air Force Transall 50+97 arrived at 0914 as DCN6273, routing Hohn-St. Athan.

29th The first and only ever visit of a Laos registered aircraft occurred today. Skyvan XW-PGL was returning to Shorts at Sydenham from Marseilles, when it was forced to divert into Manchester due to high winds.

December 1972

The only ILS traffic observed were RAF Britannia XL660 (13th) & RAF Victor XL231 (19th). Crew training flights were: BOAC B.707s G-APFG (5th) & G-AYLT (21st) and Laker Airways DC-10 G-AZZD (11th).

Aer Lingus announced the gradual phasing out of their European services out of Manchester, following an agreement between British and Irish Civil Aviation Authorities. The details are as follows:

1st April 1973 - The Zurich service will cease (EI660/1) / currently once a week.
1st April 1974 - The Dusseldorf service will cease (EI630/1) / currently three times a week.
1st April 1975 – The Frankfurt service will cease (EI650/1) / currently three times a week.
1st April 1977 – The Amsterdam service will cease (EI602/3) / currently four times a week.
1st April 1978 – The Copenhagen service will cease (EI620/1) / currently three times a week.

Another batch of Boeing 707s will be transferred from BOAC to BEA Airtours over the coming months and their last visits as BOAC aircraft are as follows: G-APFD & G-APFG (18th December), G-APFL (21st September), G-APFO (31st August) & G-ARWD (9th November).

4th French Air Force Noratlas 205/62-KS arrived at 1130 as F-RBKS, on a training flight from Reims to Istres.

4th RAF operated numerous trooping flights during the month, all with Britannia's. XM497 (RR6802 from Gatow-4th), XL657 (RR6804 from Gatow-5th), XM491 (RR6806 from Gatow-7th), XL637 (RR6808 from Gatow-7th), XL658 (RR6846 to Hanover-8th), XL637 (RR6811 from Gutersloh-8th) and XL659 (RR6810 from Gatow-9th).

5th Royal Saudi Air Force C-130E 1610 operated from/to Jeddah via Milan as RSF891, before departing on the 7th.

8th Air France SE.210 F-BJTA made its final visit today, as it was sold as XU-JTB in April 1973.

9th BEA Trident 3 G-AWZW made its first visit to Manchester today, on its inaugural flight since being delivered only ten days earlier.

11th The second DC-10 to visit was Laker Airway's second aircraft, G-AZZD, operating a crew training flight.

11th Jet Commander/Westwind 24 F-BPIB was a new executive jet to visit Manchester. It's effectively an Israeli IAI Westwind 24 and the first 150 were built under licence by Aero Commander of the US, before licence production was passed to Israeli Aircraft Industries.

12th Pan American operated a couple of charters this month. B.707 N450PA arrived at 0919 today (PA1450 from New York) and B.707 N474PA at 0646 (PA1474 from New York) on the 13th and were both first visits, having been delivered new in 1967 and 1968 respectively.

14th The first French-registered SE.210 Caravelle to visit that wasn't operated by Air France arrived today, although it used to be! F-BJTE was transferred to Air Charter in May 1971 and flew a return charter to Le Bourget today.

17th There were few diversions this month up until today, when seventeen arrived. The busiest period was between 0613 and 0931, when twelve came in. Amongst them was the first visit of Bahamas World, when B.707 VP-BDE arrived at 0756 from Nassau and it diverted in again on the 19th. Others were British Caledonian VC-10 G-ASIX at 0613 (BR106 from Entebbe) making its last visit to Manchester, East African Airways VC-10 5H-MMT at 0645 (EC664 from Entebbe), Qantas B.707 VH-EAI at 0804 (QF580 from Bermuda), KLM DC-8 PH-DEM at 0825 (KL6868 from New York) and lastly an early Pan American B.707, N762PA at 0931 (PA102 from New York) - but the best diversion days were still to come!

19th In amongst a very busy day of movements was RAF Victor XL231, carrying out ILS approaches, possibly two. Also today was a rare visit to Manchester of an RAF Pembroke, when XL929 operated from/to Northolt during the morning.

19th Having been woken up earlier than usual by unscheduled aircraft, the writer realised a weather situation was going on, but it seemed to stop after VC-10 G-ARVJ arrived around 0630. Apart from RAF Comet XR397 around 0830, which I assumed was a diversion, all was quiet until Heathrow's visibility deteriorated again mid-morning. This change brought in eight diversions, in just over sixty minutes, with most arriving during school break times. The scream of East African Airways VC-10 5Y-ADA (EC614 from Rome) overhead was fantastic and by lunchtime the diversions were more varied and from different airports. Amidst the backdrop of a clear blue sky, I saw the Bahamas World B.707, VP-BDE, arrive again. Although most southern airports were fog-bound, the diversions had all but stopped due to ground congestion, except for the arrival of Mey-Air Boeing 737 LN-MTC at 1356 (MT257 from Roros). Manchester's weather had been relatively mild, 9°c with six hours of sunshine and parts of North Wales saw temperatures of 18°c! The next wave started just after

1530, with BEA Trident 3 G-AWZC (BE745 from Zurich). Another sixteen followed in the space of ninety minutes, including two first visits: MEA B.720 OD-AFW at 1608 (ME201 from Beirut) & Zambia Airways DC-8 9J-ABR at 1601 (QZ802 from Prestwick), having diverted there earlier in the day and Braathens B.737 LN-SUP at 1620 (BU721 from Gothenburg). I saw most arrivals and MEA B.720 was observed with its trailing smoke, as I waited for my bus home from school. The last to arrive was BEA BAC 1-11 G-AVMM at 1816 (BE615 from Berlin), as the airport refused to take anymore due to severe congestion, on a day when Manchester received fifty-two in total!

19th Widespread fog affected twenty-three counties during the day. It also meant that a crucial and long-awaited Government decision on the future of the nationalised steel industry was postponed, when key Ministers were unable to travel to London.

20th Another batch of fifteen diversions arriving early morning and evening, were all British except for one, but two were first visits. Alitalia DC-9 I-DIZA at 2025 (AZ278 from Rome) and British Caledonian's newly-acquired Boeing 707F G-AYZZ at 1545 (BR5002 from Las Palmas). The B.707F made only one more visit to Manchester, when it diverted in two days later. It was on lease from American Airlines between June 1972 and December 1973.

24th Seaboard World DC-8F N8632 (SB306 from New York/Gander) arrived operating a flight originally intended for Heathrow. Technically, as the flight plan was changed to operate into Manchester, it wasn't a diversion, but it was a first visit!

29th Today was the start of a chaotic four days of freezing fog and black ice, similar to the events of January 1971. Manchester received twenty-seven diversions, but apart from five Aer Lingus flights and a Swissair, they were mostly mundane. The airports affected were varied and included Birmingham, Liverpool, Heathrow, Gatwick, Blackpool, East Midlands & Luton.

30th Over 4,000 diverted passengers arrived at Manchester over the weekend of the 30th/31st, on sixty-four aircraft, from a variety of southern airports. Of the forty-seven arriving today, the bulk included twelve BEA flights, seven Britannia Airways, six Dan-Air, four Aer Lingus, three Laker Airways and three BOAC. Non-British diversions included Qantas B.707 VH-EBR at 1213 (QF739 from Frankfurt), Malaysian-Singapore B.707 9V-BBA at 1216 (SQ785A from Frankfurt) & Qantas B.747 VH-EBE at 1219 (QF737 from Rome), which all arrived within six minutes of each other. The Qantas B.747 had to wait several hours before its passengers could be offloaded and transported onwards to London by surface transport. Airports not affected by the weather, such as Stansted, Gatwick, Liverpool & Prestwick also had large quantities of diversions thrust upon them.

31st A further seventeen diversions arriving today, brought the total number over the last three days to ninety-one, which equalled the number set in early January 1971. Even though Heathrow and Luton were closed to most aircraft all day, the only diversions of interest were SAS SE.210 OY-KRE at 1828 (SK509A from Copenhagen) and first time visitors Alitalia DC-9 I-DIKJ at 2043 (AZ290 from Milan), Kuwait Airways B.707 9K-ACK at 2137 (KU183 from Paris) & Pan American B.707 N404PA at 2302 (PA054 from Boston) – with more to come tomorrow!

First/Last Arrivals & Departures 1972

First arrival:	B.737 EI-ASC/EI9216 from Dublin at 00.15
First departure:	B.727 OO-STB to Brussels at 00.53
Last arrival:	B.737 EI-ASE/EI9216 from Dublin at 23.44
Last departure:	PA-23 G-AWXW to Heathrow at 23.51

(+/- % on Previous Year)		
Scheduled Passengers	1,236,000	+ 4.7%
I.T/Charter Passengers	1,087,000	+19.7%
Transit Passengers	215,000	+11.9%
Total	2,538,000	+11.3%
Freight & Mail (Tonnes)	45,200	+13.5%
Movements	64,800	+6.5%

Airport Diary 1973

January 1973

Sabena will terminate their passenger flight to Brussels (SN623/4) at the end of March, even though the service was increased to five-weekly and retimed to mornings only last April. The say the withdrawal is temporary, due to an interim shortage of suitable aircraft since phasing out the SE.210. The loss of these flights will be offset by BEA, who will increase frequency to Brussels by up to eight flights a week from 1st April. Sabena will also terminate services to Budapest, Hamburg, Istanbul, Palma, Liege, Jeddah & Alicante.

SAS replaced the SE.210 Caravelle with the Douglas DC-9 on their Copenhagen passenger service (SK537/8), with effect from 14th. The Caravelle has operated the service since its inauguration in 1966 and although the type made the occasional visit on the service over the next eighteen months, they had all been sold or withdrawn by the end of 1974. The final SAS SE.210 visit was SE-DAB on 8th May 1974 operating SK537/8 and the remainder made their last visits as follows: 1972 - OY-KRF (04/11), SE-DAF (12/11) & LN-KLI (10/12); 1973 - LN-KLP (12/01), LN-KLR (27/03), OY-KRA (25/11), OY-KRC (10/01), OY-KRD (07/01), OY-KRE (08/06), SE-DAA (26/05) & SE-DAE (22/11); 1974 - LN-KLH (22/02) & SE-DAB (08/05).

HS.748 ILS traffic observed were Royal Thai Air Force HS-TAF (2nd/5th), Hawker-Siddeley G-BAFY (8th) & G-AYYG (18th) and Australian Navy N15-709 (18th/25th/31st). RAF traffic noted were Britannia's XL637 (10th) & XM520 (10th); Nimrod's XW666 (2nd) & XV226 (8th); C-130 XV176 (10th) and Argosy XP448 (26th/29th). Crew training flights were: BEA Airtours G-APFK (1st/2nd/3rd/8th), BOAC SVC-10 G-ASGI (10th) and B.707's G-APFJ (17th), G-ATZD (17th) & G-AYLT (11th).

1st January 1973 – The year started with a further thirty-two diversions arriving on top of the ninety-one received in the last three days of 1972. Seen here are Olympic Boeing 720s SX-DBG & SX-DBK, having diverted from Heathrow as OA259 & OA281 respectively. Amongst the aircraft in the background are Pan American B.707 N404PA, which arrived as 'Clipper 054' the previous evening and JAL Douglas DC-8 JA-8037, which arrived late morning as JL423 from Anchorage. (Geoff Ball)

1st   This was the day the UK joined the EEC, or Common Market. It was also another weather affected day when freezing fog blanketed the country and Heathrow was fogbound all day. Manchester received thirty-two diversions, carrying 3,000 extra passengers. Other airports also benefitted, including Liverpool, Bournemouth, Birmingham & Gatwick. It wasn't a great start when 'Ascot 1073' from Ottawa attempted a diversion into Manchester, only to overshoot, due to the visibility being below the aircrafts limit. The RAF VC-10, carrying VIP passenger the Prime Minister Edward Heath, then headed south to make an approach at Heathrow, where it overshot again before eventually landing at Gatwick. British Airways B.747 G-AWNI, operating BA437 held for over four hours in the south, awaiting a clearance in the Heathrow weather, before eventually diverting to Manchester. The day had similarities to two years earlier on 4th January 1971, when Manchester was the only major airport open and under great pressure to handle vast amounts of diversions. However, this time round the airport showed more restraint by turning away at least thirty diversions, including 'Beeline 747V' from Copenhagen, operated by a Sterling SE.210. Having said that, the airport handled 123 diversions over the last four days! It was the fourth consecutive day of fog at Heathrow, where passengers slept on coaches due to lack of floor space at the airport. Hotel rooms were in short supply, but even if there had been availability, most people had run out of money by then. Facilities were also stretched at Gatwick, after receiving more than thirty diversions from Heathrow and it took more than four hours to clear 400 passengers through customs from a diverted B.747 flight. BEA reported ninety of its services from Heathrow had been cancelled and half its fleet grounded. Amongst the thirty-two diversions arriving at Manchester were KLM DC-8 PH-DEE at 1105 (KL3528 from New York), JAL DC-8 JA-8037 at 1115 (JL423 from Anchorage), National Airlines DC-8 N108RD at 1402 (NA002 from Miami), two Olympic Airways Boeing 720s from Athens - SX-DBK at 1405 (OA281) & SX-DBG at 1517 (OA259), which were both first visits; Pan American B.747 N754PA at 1427 (PA106 from Washington), the second visit of MEA B.720 OD-AFW (ME201 from Beirut), Swissair CV-990 HB-ICH at 1621 (SR806 from Zurich), first visit Alitalia DC-8 I-DIWA at 1625 (AZ280 from Rome), Syrian Arab SE.210 YK-AFC at 2301 (RB405 from Rome) and seven BEA Tridents!

2nd   Fog affected Heathrow for the fifth day running, but Manchester was unable to accept any more diversions, due to of lack of parking space and handling facilities. The old Runway 02/20, Runway 10/28 and various taxiways were still accommodating yesterday's diverted aircraft. By lunchtime the situation was improving and aircraft started to leave for Heathrow. The inbound BA537 from Heathrow was cancelled due to the amount of BOAC aircraft being out of position. 'Swissair 800' operated by CV-990 HB-ICB inbound to Manchester, would have been a Heathrow diversion from Zurich, but it was turned away and set course for Gatwick instead, which played host to a further twenty-three diversions.

2nd   Royal Saudi Air Force C-130E 1606 operated from/to Jeddah via Milan as RSF800, before departing on the 4th.

3rd   After accepting numerous diversions over the past few days, it was Manchester's turn to be affected by bad weather. Twenty-eight flights were diverted to other airports, including AF960 (Paris-MAN) to Heathrow, EI650 (Dublin-MAN) to Liverpool, EI651 (Frankfurt-MAN) to Dublin, KL153 (Amsterdam-MAN) to Liverpool, LH075 (Glasgow-MAN) to Frankfurt and SR840 (Zurich-MAN) to Birmingham.

4th   Two Heathrow diversions in the early hours - BOAC B.747 G-AWNB at 0017 (BA506A from New York) & BEA Merchantman G-APER at 0048 (BE2882 from Belfast), arrived before Manchester was affected by bad weather again, when a further eighteen flights were lost. Included were AF960 (Paris-MAN) which diverted back to Paris and British Caledonian B.707 CA2104 (Toronto-MAN) & Aer Lingus EI9212 (Dublin-MAN), which both diverted to Liverpool.

5th   Another weather affected day when more flights were lost, including Aer Lingus EI651 & EI602, HS.125 G-AYRY and SAS SK538 (Dublin-MAN), which all diverted to Liverpool, while Lufthansa LH075 (Glasgow-MAN) diverted onwards to Frankfurt.

6th   On the fourth and final day of fog, Manchester saw only thirteen arrivals all day and an abundance of cancellations. Twenty-five aircraft were diverted away, including Spantax BX587 (Tenerife-MAN) to Birmingham, Court Line 1-11 G-AXMH, Aer Lingus EI603 (Amsterdam-MAN) & EI621 (Copenhagen-MAN) and Swissair SR840 (Zurich-MAN), which all diverted to Liverpool. Aer Lingus EI620 (Dublin-MAN) diverted to Heathrow, Air Spain JA144 (Tenerife-MAN) to Gatwick and finally Lufthansa LH076 (Frankfurt-MAN) diverted to Dublin.

8th   German Air Force Transall 51+08 arrived at 1239 as DCN6407 (Hohn-RAF Northolt). Another training flight passed through on the 17th, when Transall 50+36 arrived at 1115 as DCN6468 (Cologne to RAF Northolt).

9th   Sabena SE.210 OO-SRK was the first aircraft to visit in their new colour scheme.

12th   SAS SK537/8 was flown by a SE.210 Caravelle for the final time today, as this flight is now scheduled to be operated by DC-9s. LN-KLP operated the last sector as SK538 (Dublin-MAN-Copenhagen) departing at 1652, although its destination today was actually Stockholm!

14th   Braathens B.737 LN-SUG, operating a charter from Gatwick to Oslo, was also making a first visit.

14th Sabena operated two extra passenger flights - Boeing 727 OO-STD (SN3623/4 from/to Brussels) this evening and Boeing 707 OO-SJN (SN611A/612A) on the 22nd.

16th BEA BAC 1-11 G-AVMM, operating the Manchester-Dusseldorf (BE824), made it in fifty-eight minutes, more than thirty minutes quicker than the regular flying time!

17th It was Liverpool's turn to be affected by bad weather today, when eleven diversions arrived at Manchester, including eight Cambrian Airways flights.

18th Fourteen flights diverted away today due to weather, including Air France AF960 (Paris-MAN) to Heathrow, Aer Lingus EI602 (Dublin-MAN) to Leeds and EI603 (Amsterdam-MAN) to Liverpool. Lufthansa's evening cargo flight LH475 (Chicago-MAN) diverted onto Frankfurt and RAF HS.125 RR3522 diverted to Liverpool.

22nd N30RP arriving at 1043, was operating from/to Heathrow, where it's a regular visitor. It was the sixth different Gulfstream 2 to visit Manchester and the first this year.

24th Yakolev YAK-40 SP-GEA, arriving from Heathrow to pick up a Polish trade delegation visiting the Ferranti plant in Hollinwood, departed later for Newcastle. It was a first visit of type by the Russian-built, small three-engined airliner, which first flew in 1966 and entered service with the state airline, Aeroflot, in 1968.

February 1973

Figures released showed Ringway maintained fourth place in last year's UK airport passenger league table. First was Heathrow with 18,681,464, second was Gatwick with 5,362,001 and third was Luton with 3,112,654. Manchester saw a 13.8% increase in freight handled, but lost the second spot to Gatwick.

Iberia confirmed they will operate their seasonal service to Barcelona/Palma again, twice weekly from 1st June with Douglas DC-9s, which are replacing their SE.210s.

No HS.748 ILS traffic was noted. RAF traffic noted were Britannia's XL659 (22nd) & XM520 (28th); Victor XL231 (8th/13th/14th), Belfast XR365 (16th), Argosy XP413 (27th) and RAE Britannia XX367 (22nd/26th).

2nd German Air Force Transall 50+86 arrived at 1338, on a training flight from Hohn to Northolt. Another passed through on the 17th when Transall 50+36 arrived at 1115, as DCN6468 (Cologne-Northolt).

4th February 1973 – Swissair CV-990 HB-ICE is seen having arrived as Heathrow diversion 'Swissair 800'. Other morning diversions in the background, parked on disused Runway 02/20, are BCAL B.707 G-AZRO flanked by two BOAC B.707s. (Stuart Wardman)

4th Fifteen fog diversions arrived between 0036 and 1221, all from Heathrow apart from diverted Air Spain DC-8 flights EC-BXR at 0036 (JA117 from Alicante) & EC-BZQ at 1123 (JA1448 from Palma) from Luton and single Gatwick diversion British Caledonian B.707 G-AZRO at 0448 (BR106 from Entebbe). Of the Heathrow diversions, eight were BOAC flights and the others were Olympic Airways B.720 SX-DBG at 0859 (OA285 from Thessaloniki), Swissair CV-990 HB-ICE at

0938 (SR800 from Zurich), National Airlines DC-8 N108RD at 1005 (NA002 from Nairobi), the first visit of a South African Airways B.747, ZS-SAO at 1134 (SA234 from Frankfurt) and the last visit of a JAL DC-8, JA-8014 at 1227 (JL411 from Copenhagen).

5th RAF Britannia's XM491 (RR6567) & XL660 (RR6568) operated outbound trooping flights to Gibraltar. The return flights on the 17th were operated by Britannia's XL640 (RR6579) & XL639 (RR6580).

5th Lear Jet D-IOGE was the first of four executive aircraft making their first visits during the month. Others were RAF HS.125 XX505 (16th), Leeds diversion HS.125 I-BOGI (21st) and Lego Citation 500 OY-DVL (26th).

6th Royal Saudi Air Force C-130E 453 operated from/to Jeddah via Milan as RSF802, before departing on the 8th.

14th One flight due into Manchester, but re-routed through Gatwick instead, was TIA DC-8 N4869T inbound from Budapest.

16th Today was the first visit of a French Air Force Nord 262, when 66/118-IT operated as F-SDIT from Warton to Villacoublay.

20th Itavia Fokker F.28 I-TIDA from Bergamo was destined for Leeds, but by the time it reached UK airspace, the airport was closed, so it diverted into Manchester instead. Out of the six Fokker F.28s operated by the airline in the 1970's, two were lost in air crashes, including I-TIDA which came to grief at Bergamo in April 1975.

25th Mey-Air Boeing 737 LN-MTC made its second visit to Manchester, diverting in en route from Gothenburg to Lisbon with a technical problem.

26th Pan American B.747 N736PA made its first and only visit to Manchester, arriving from Heathrow to operate an outbound charter to Malaga, on behalf of BEA. This particular aircraft was noteworthy for two reasons; firstly it was the first Boeing 747 seen in the UK, when it landed at Heathrow in January 1970 and secondly it will be remembered as the unfortunate plane involved in the Tenerife air disaster in March 1977.

28th Sabena's evening freighter, SN197/8, was operated by Boeing 707 OO-SJH rather than the regular B.727.

March 1973

The Manchester-Amsterdam route will be the first to benefit from a three-times-daily operation from 1st April, when BEA and Aer Lingus increase their frequencies and complement KLM's operation. This was Manchester's first international air route, shortly after the airport opened in 1938.

The only HS.748 ILS traffic observed was Australian Navy N15-709 (14th). RAF traffic were Argosy XN855 (1st), Belfast XR362 (8th), Nimrod XV228 (21st/29th), Britannia XN404 (28th), Andover's XS599 (28th) & XS644 (29th). Others were RAE Comet XS235 (26th) & Israeli Air Force Noratlas 4X-FAC (27th).

3rd KLM DC-8F PH-DCT arrived at 1423 (KL9174 from New York), with a consignment of textiles.

11th Manchester received eight weather diversions during the morning, but the only ones of interest were Swissair DC-8 HB-IDB at 0731 (SR2163 from New York) & BOAC B.747 G-AWNK at 1130 (BA032 from Zurich), arriving amid the chaos of air traffic congestion over France, which caused delays of up to eighteen hours at the weekend.

12th Dan-Air Comet G-APDP made its final visit today, arriving at 0256 (DA1006 from Palma). It departed at 1325 for the airlines engineering base at Lasham, where it was withdrawn from use.

13th BEA Merchantman G-APEO had the indignity of tipping onto its rear, with its nose pointing up in the air, when the tail steady became detached!

15th TMA B.707F OD-AFX arrived from Heathrow today and left for Bombay via Beirut the following day. Onboard was 34 tonnes of drilling equipment, the heaviest single freight load ever carried ex-MAN.

17th British Caledonian B.707 G-AVKA paid its last visit to Manchester, arriving at 0612 (BR2112 Gatwick-Winnipeg). After serving the airline for only six years, it was sold to TAP as CS-TBH in April.

21st   French Air Force Falcon No.93 operated a training flight as F-RAFN, from Shannon to Villacoublay.

27th   Israeli Air Force Noratlas 4X-FAC completed two ILS approaches, before setting course for Copenhagen.

27th   Fred Olsen Falcon 20 LN-FOE made its first visit, night-stopping on a flight from Leeds. This aircraft replaces Falcon 20 LN-FOD, which was sold to the French Air Force.

27th   Court Line L.1011 Tristar G-BAAA arrived at 0943 in a distinct yellow/gold/orange colour scheme, on a crew training detail from Luton to Glasgow. It's the first of two to be delivered to the airline, to be based at Luton and it's the first of its type based in Europe.

27th   Visits by SAS SE.210 Caravelle's are at a premium nowadays, however LN-KLR paid a visit at 1108 today, diverting in from Heathrow (SK521 from Gothenburg), along with first visit B.747s BOAC G-AWNH at 1012 (BA570 from Chicago) & Pan American N742PA at 1056 (PA106 from Washington).

28th   TAP B.727 CS-TBO operated a flight from Heathrow to Lisbon and the return on the 31st.

29th   Sabena operated their final passenger flight rotation, SN623/4, from/to Brussels with SE.210 OO-SRG.

30th   Lunchtime arrival Icelandair B.727 TF-FIA was carrying a cargo of stainless steel rings packed in polythene bags. It left for Frankfurt, ultimately bound for Doha.

31st   East Midlands based airline Alidair operates with two Viscounts, G-AVIW & G-AVJL and G-AVIW was the first to visit Manchester today, operating an inbound charter (QA905 from Beauvais).

April 1973

The current 5p admission charge for the spectator terraces will be doubled later in the year, but will include full access to the piers. The Airport Authorities are also proposing issuing permits for schoolchildren, at a cost of £3 per year.

Following BOAC's opposition to British Caledonian's application to serve Atlanta, Houston & Dallas from Manchester, the CAA will hold a public enquiry on 5th June. The airline also announced a twice-daily service connecting Manchester and London-Gatwick, operated by BIA Heralds, would commence 1st November.

Scheduled flight changes this month included Air France increasing frequency of Paris-flight AF960/1 up to daily in the summer. Alitalia's cargo flights to Milan-Rome to remain three-weekly. BEA commenced a new four-weekly service to Milan. All Heathrow flights will be operated by Super 1-11s, apart from BE4084/7 which is scheduled for a Trident and there are no Viscounts based during the summer. They will also operate various IT flights with Super 1-11s & Trident's on behalf of BEA Airtours. BOAC Cargo operates twice-weekly to New York, via Montreal (BA065), twice-weekly to Detroit via Montreal (BA067) and five-weekly from New York (BA066). From the 29th, BOAC will swap their VC-10 operation from Caribbean flights to a daily direct New York service. Cyprus Airways began operations from Manchester from the 6th, with a weekly Trident flight from/to Larnaca, via Brussels. KLM added a weekly Sunday service, (KL155/6). Lufthansa's twice-weekly freight flights from Chicago will operate via Toronto. Sabena will continue their cargo flights but passenger services have now ceased. Northeast Airlines are operating a twice-weekly service to Paris Le Bourget until 3rd June. SAS freight flights are operating four-weekly to Copenhagen, with Fred Olsen Douglas DC-6s.

HS.748 ILS traffic observed were: Australian Navy N15-709 (10th/25th) & SATA CS-TAH (19th). RAF traffic noted were Belfast's XR365 (12th) & XR367 (3rd); Britannia's XL657 (4th), XM490 (26th), XM517 (5th/11th/18th/19th), XN392 (12th) and Argosy XN817 (25th). Civil ILS traffic observed were HS.125 G-AVRF (6th) & Dove G-ARHW (17th/18th).

1st   Nose-in parking was introduced on the eastern side of the International pier today, with the western side following in due course. There will be fourteen stands, compared to ten when they were self-manoeuvring. Nose-in parking for the Domestic and new Long-haul pier will be introduced on 1st January 1974, when the reallocation of stand numbers takes place. The Domestic pier will be numbered from Stand 41 upwards and the Long-haul from Stands 21-27, providing a total of thirty-two nose-in stands. In addition, a further fourteen parking positions will still be available for airliners on various parts of the airfield, such as the South Bay and Fairey and another eleven stands on taxiways can also be used during emergency and diversionary periods. As the re-concreting work on the new apron on the north side of the long-haul pier nears completion, it's hoped it can be used during peak Autumn periods for aircraft parking, especially on the South Side of the pier, although it's unlikely any passengers would be offloaded there.

2nd Late evening arrival, Aeromexico DC-8 XA-SIA, had the President of Mexico onboard for the first leg of his official state visit to Britain. He stayed overnight in Manchester and although the aircraft positioned out to Stansted, it returned the next morning before eventually departing for Heathrow with the President and his entourage.

2nd Laker Airways began the first of a series of weekly charter flights from/to Toronto and today's departure at 1143 of DC-10 G-AZZC as GK6201, was the first ever transatlantic 'advance booking charter'. ABC flights have been introduced by the airline industry and aviation authorities in Europe and North America, to replace the complicated, unworkable 'affinity group' charter rules with a more rational set of conditions, easier to implement and less open to abuse. In the late 1960's, an obscure rule crafted by IATA (International Air Transport Association), allowed so-called 'affinity groups' to charter aircraft to fly across the North Atlantic at fares below the IATA's minimum. This loophole came to the attention of a determined group of mainly non-IATA airlines, seeking to exploit it. They included leading independent British airlines such as Britannia Airways, Caledonian, Dan-Air & Laker Airways and some privately owned independent airlines, notably British United, who were IATA members themselves! At the time, the IATA was dominated by state-owned flag-carriers, using the organisation for the creation of rules to protect them from what they considered to be excessive and unwarranted competition by the independent airlines. The relevant rule stipulated transatlantic charter flights were permissible, provided they transported groups of passengers from the same club, on the same aircraft and not unconnected individuals securing cheap flights. Tickets for 'affinity group' charters had to be booked at least three months in advance and all passengers had to be fully paid-up members of an officially recognised organisation. Although some were genuine, the overwhelming majority were fakes, set up for the sole purpose of signing up as many "members" as were required to profitably fill a transatlantic charter flight. Prospective passengers were issued with back-dated, bogus membership cards of non-existent organisations, sometimes on the day of departure itself. In some cases this was done openly, in specialist travel agencies that sprang up on both sides of the Atlantic, ready to cash in on the cheap flights bonanza. They unscrupulously sold thousands of tickets to people falsely representing themselves to the aviation authorities in Britain, US & Canada, as members of imaginary 'affinity groups'. When the scam came to the relevant authority's attention, departure areas at the main airports on both sides of the Atlantic were policed, with the aim of catching bogus "members" and preventing them from boarding flights. Gatwick's departure lounge was one of the more prominent places where unannounced raids took place, with increasing regularity and as a result large numbers of "members" were denied boarding. Some flights even left without a single passenger! There were also reports of raids on airlines, after being tipped off by IATA members, or fellow independent competitors. Airlines were fined several thousand pounds, for each bogus passenger listed on an 'affinity group' charter. In the end, the authorities and the airline industry agreed the absurd system worked to nobody's satisfaction and admitted the real purpose of most 'affinity group' travellers was to fly the Atlantic at an affordable price. They decided to scrap the entire system and replace it with one recognising the growing demand for cheap flights, below the official IATA minimum. The resulting compromise led to a set of new rules covering 'advanced booking charters' or ABC, stipulating flights had to be booked at least four weeks in advance, which was subsequently changed to two weeks.

2nd BOAC New York flight BA538, operated by SVC-10 G-ASGG, never made it to Manchester as crosswinds forced its diversion into Heathrow.

2nd Falcon 20 F-BIHY, arriving at 0947 from Le Bourget as a Leeds diversion, was one of three biz-jets making their first visits during the month. The others, both on the 25th, were RAF HS.125 XW789 & Lear Jet 24 D-ICAR.

2nd BEA began a four-times-weekly service to Milan, operating as a code-share with Alitalia.

3rd   Today should have seen the first visit to Manchester of the new Airbus A.300, but after F-WUAC developed a technical fault en route from Hamburg, it diverted to Toulouse.

3rd   Royal Saudi Air Force C-130E 456 operated from/to Jeddah via Milan as RSF806, before departing on the 5th.

3rd April 1973 – Air Anglia operated a Norwich-Manchester-Liverpool service between November 1971 and October 1972, mainly with the company's Islander G-AXVP, although Douglas DC-3 G-AOBN occasionally operated the flight. Today it was carrying Norwich City supporters for their match with Manchester Utd. (Geoff Ball)

4th   Inbound Lufthansa cargo-flight LH473 from Chicago overflew Manchester and proceeded direct to Frankfurt with technical trouble. Coincidentally, so did LH475 the following day, when it too reported technical trouble and carried onto Frankfurt.

4th   Invicta Airlines based a Vanguard at Manchester from today, to operate daily spring charters to Beauvais and Rotterdam. G-AXOY positioned in from Manston to operate the following morning's IM327 to Rotterdam. The only other Vanguard used this month was G-AYFN, a former Air Traders machine, carrying no titles but still sporting their blue colours.

6th April 1973 – Early this month, SAS sub-charted Nordic Air Electra's to operate their Copenhagen freight service and LN-MOI is seen here being loaded. They operated two Electra's until November, when they were sold to Fred Olsen, which in turn replaced their Douglas DC-6s. (Geoff Ball)

6th   The airports new multi-storey car park was officially opened today and on schedule, despite last years building strike. Although the ultimate capacity is for 2,500 spaces, only 750 are available now and a further 200 will be ready in May.

6th   Cyprus Airways commenced a new service to Nicosia today, routing via Brussels. Operating as a code-share flight with British Airways, Trident 2 5B-DAC made the inaugural flight.

6th   RAF VC-10 XV104 (RR2480) arrived on a trooping flight from RAF Gutersloh. Others during the month were VC-10 XV104 RR2482 & VC-10 XR807 RR2483 (8th); VC-10 XV102 RR2484 & VC-10 RR2485 (9th); Britannia XL660 RR6708B (18th), VC-10 XV109 RR2501 & VC-10 XV103 RR2502 (26th) and VC-10 XV109 RR2503 (29th).

6th   The bulk of BEA Airtours summer programme will be operated by BEA Trident's, but a weekly Boeing 707 flight commenced today, operating on alternate weeks to Athens (KT986/7) & Corfu (KT988/9) via Gatwick, with G-APFG being used on today's Athens flight.

7th   Air Anglia arrivals, DC-3 G-AOBN & F.27 G-BAKL, were in connection with the bottom of the first division clash between Manchester Utd and Norwich. United won 1-0, which guaranteed them a place in the top division again next season.

7th   PA-23 Aztec N14253, arriving at 1510 from Keflavik, entered the South Side for work at NEA and re-emerged as G-BAUW, before departing to Coventry on the 12th.

8th   British Midland operated their final IT flight into Manchester today with BAC 1-11 G-AXLM (BD476 from Trieste via Gatwick). Due to financial difficulties, they have withdrawn from the IT market and are selling their three BAC 1-11s, as they are unable to sell the B.707s due to legal reasons. Their B.707s, G-AYBJ & G-AYVE, were bought in 1971 so they could enter the lucrative transatlantic charter market and be utilised on European ITs, but after heavy losses they were withdrawn from transatlantic operations the following year. In a bid to recover some of their losses, they are being leased out along with other Boeing 707s recently purchased, which is proving a great success. The last visits of the BAC 1-11s to Manchester were:

G-AXLL	07/01/73	Sold 05/73 to Transbrasil as PP-SDT.
G-AXLM	08/04/73	Sold 1974 to Transbrasil as PP SDV.
G-AXLN	02/10/72	Sold 1974 to Transbrasil as PP-SDU.

8th   Fairflight Charter Doves G-APZU & G-AZPG arrived late evening from Biggin Hill to operate flights to Amsterdam. They had short careers with the Biggin Hill based operator, as G-APZU served from 1973-1975 and G-AZPG from 1972-1974.

9th   JAT B.707 YU-AGE operated from/to Split, carrying the Hadjuk Split team for a European Cup game with Leeds United, who won the tie 1-0.

9th   Tarom IL-18 YR-IMK arrived at Manchester today, carrying a consignment of vegetables for our shops. Further flights were operated by YR-IMI (16th) & YR-IMZ (25th).

9th   KLM DC-8F PH-DCW arrived at 0838 (KL9191 from New York), with a further consignment of textiles.

9th   Seaboard World DC-8F N8783R, arriving at 2037 (SB1310 from Frankfurt), departed the following day with a record load of fertiliser bound for Nairobi via Athens.

9th   Dan-Air Comet G-APDC flew its final passenger flight, arriving at 1746 operating DA1305 from Tunis. It sat around until the 16th, when it was flown to Lasham on its final flight, before withdrawal from service. It was ultimately broken up, an unfortunate end for this record breaking aircraft. Delivered new to BOAC in September 1958, it had achieved a number of firsts. It beat America's Boeing 707 into transatlantic service by three weeks, operating the very first jet service across the North Atlantic from London to New York on 4th October 1958, although it had to refuel at Gander due to headwinds. On 19th December 1958 it inaugurated BOAC jet services to Canada, operating to Montreal and on 21st January 1959, it operated a proving flight to Tokyo. After all this, it made its sad departure from Manchester at 1801 without fuss or fanfare, to meet its ultimate challenge at the hands of the scrap man!

10th   BEA Trident 1 G-ARPD (BE5034 Heathrow–Glasgow), diverted in with its fire warning indicator light on.

12th   Aer Turas Douglas DC-7F EI-AWG made its first visit today, operating an inbound charter. It was one of six operated by the airline from 1969-1974, but by 1973 there were only two left. The first, EI-AWG, would visit Manchester on two more occasions before being written-off in a landing accident at Luton in March 1974. The second, EI-AWO, only operated from May 1973-December 1973 and never visited Manchester.

13th   Transmeridian CL-44-0 N447T made its first visit today. It's a standard CL-44 that's been converted by the Conroy Aircraft Company to an oversized transporter, which later became known as the 'Skymonster'.

13th   Dan-Air B.727 G-BAFZ operated the first revenue service of the type on the UK register. It positioned in yesterday and departed for Alicante at 0830 today as DA1035.

16th   Dan-Air Comet G-APDK made its last visit today (DA1215 from/to Alicante), before its withdrawal from service the following month.

17th   German Air Force Transall 51+02 arrived at 1432 as DCN6949 to night-stop, during a training flight from Glasgow to Cologne.

18th   French Navy PA-31 '914' called in to clear customs, en route RAF Kinloss-Brest.

22nd   The Hunting-Percival Pembroke was never a common RAF type to visit Manchester, but XL954 arrived at 0231 today, operating a flight from/to RAF Wildenrath.

24th   World Airways DC-8-63 N802WA arrived at 2359 from Bangor, USA. It was parked on the South Bay, before finally departing to Malaga on the 26th. This particular aircraft was to visit Manchester one more time on the 18th July, before `coming to grief' after an accident in Alaska in September 1973.

25th April 1973 – One of the highlights of the year was the arrival of Alitalia Boeing 747 I-DEMU at 1449 as AZ8208, to take Juventus FC fans home after their European Cup tie with Derby County at the Baseball Ground, Derby later that evening. The game finished 0-0, but having already lost the first leg 3-1, it meant Derby was out of the tournament. Incidentally, the inbound flight with Italian fans operated into Heathrow, before positioning up to Manchester. (Geoff Ball)

29th   BOAC VC-10 G-ARVJ inaugurated their new daily non-stop service from Manchester to New York (BA533) today, brought about by increased demand from passengers taking advantage of cheaper North Atlantic fares. It wasn't the first time they had operated a Manchester-New York direct service, as in 1969 they ran a three-weekly service during the summer months.

29th   Dan-Air Comet G-APDG made its last visit to Manchester, arriving at 1811 (DA1304 from Malaga). It positioned out to Lasham on 2nd May and was withdrawn from service.

29th   Aer Lingus Boeing 707 EI-ASN operated evening freight flight EI9212/3.

May 1973

There were more scheduled changes during the month. BOAC introduced a daily Toronto service via Prestwick (BA603/4), whilst the existing BA607/8 continued to Montreal via Prestwick. They also introduced two-weekly Tuesday SVC-10 flights from 5th June; BA538/7 now operates via Prestwick from/to New York/Antigua/Bridgetown/Port of Spain & Guyana, while BA536/5 operates from/to New York via Prestwick. British Midland introduced a Saturday summer service to Newquay (BD034/3) from the 19th and two flights to Ostend, BD254/3 & BD256/5, on Sundays from the 20th. Cyprus Airways began a fortnightly flight to Nicosia, via Athens, from the 14th (CY724/5).

The following airlines have summer programmes from Manchester: Air Spain, Aviaco, Aviogenex, Balkan, Inex-Adria, JAT, Phoenix Aviation, SAM & Spantax, plus UK operators: BEA Airtours, Britannia Airways, British Caledonian, British Island Airways, Court Line, Dan-Air & Laker Airways.

Transatlantic flights from/to the USA & Canada began this month with the following; Pan American B.707s N407PA (11th), N412PA (18th), N891PA (10th/19th) and TWA B.707s N8731 (4th), N18709 (25th/30th) & N28724 (23rd). UK airlines were BOAC (B.707), British Caledonian (B.707), Dan-Air (B.707) and Laker Airways operating a weekly DC-10 from/to Toronto.

RAF traffic noted were Britannia's XL637 (10th), XM517 (24th), & XN398 (4th); C-130 XV178 (4th/7th), Argosies XN855 (4th), XP439 (7th) & XR137 (9th/10th); Belfast's XR368 (31st) & XR371 (15th) and Nimrod XV228 (31st). Civil ILS traffic observed was just HS.125 G-5-17 (15th). Crew training flights were operated by BEA Trident 3 G-AWZA (9th), BOAC VC-10 G-ARVI (14th/20th) and BOAC B.707 G-APFM (25th/26th).

2nd   There were numerous biz-jet first visits during the month, starting with today's arrival of French Air Force Falcon 20 No.167 from Shannon to Villacoublay. Others were Belgian Air Force Falcon 20 CM-01 from/to Northolt (15th), Falcon 20 F-BTCY (15th), HS.125 G-AZVS (24th), Warton diversion Hansa Jet D-COSA (24th) & Gulfstream 2 N902 routing Edinburgh-Gatwick (29th).

4th   Fourteen diversions arrived in the early hours, mainly from Heathrow, eleven of which arrived within an hour of each other just after midnight. Amongst them was first time visitor Air France Boeing 727 F-BPJI at 0054 (AF832 from Paris).

5th   Two RAF flights operating from/to Gutersloh today were Britannia XN404 (RR6500/1) & VC-10 XV102 (RR2527). A further flight on the 13th was Britannia XN398 (RR6509 to Gutersloh).

6th   British Caledonian's 'new' Boeing 707 G-BAWP, formerly EI-ASO with Aer Lingus, made its first visit today (BR2224 Toronto-Gatwick).

7th   Sterling SE.210 OY-SBZ, arriving at 1550 (NB3691 Billund-Cambridge), returned the following day from Cambridge. Other SE.210 flights during the month were French Air Force No.141 Shannon-Orly (23rd) & SAS SE-DAA as SK1520 from Copenhagen (26th).

8th   Royal Saudi Air Force C-130E 1608 operated from/to Jeddah via Milan as RSF808, before departing on the 10th.

12th   Invicta Airlines operated the last of their Beauvais and Rotterdam flights, with G-AXOY (IM323 from Beauvais). From the 27th, they have a weekly flight from/to Basle as IM136/7 and the first was operated by G-AYFN.

19th   JAT's introduction of a once-weekly summer only scheduled service to Pula and Dubrovnik was the first scheduled service between Manchester and Yugoslavia.

21st   Britannia Airways used flight-numbers as their ATC identifier, rather than their registrations, from today.

30th   Laker flight GK323 to Rhodes was delayed for over eleven hours today, after BAC 1-11 G-AVBW developed a hydraulic fault before takeoff. G-AVBY was brought off a training flight to cover, but this too went tech with a pressurisation fault and faulty radio cable, so G-AVBX was flown in from Berlin-Tegel and the flight finally left at 2148!

30th   French Navy Nord 262 No.75 operated a training flight from Lorient to RAF Kinloss.

30th   A varied selection of airlines brought delegates into Manchester to attend the Golden Products Conference, including Pan American B.727 N327PA, Trans European B.720 OO-TEA & B.707 OO-TEC; WDL Fokker F.27 D-BAKI and Condor B.727 D-ABIR, twice.

31st   Queens Flight HS.748 XS793 brought Princess Alexandra into Manchester, for a series of local engagements.

June 1973

Once British Airways has become a combined operation next April, they plan to launch at least two new European routes from Manchester. They also said that further reorganisation of their charter operation will result in expansion of resorts and increased frequencies. Extra capacity will also be offered on holiday routes, with the introduction of more B.707 and Trident aircraft next summer.

Flights from/to the USA & Canada continued with ONA DC-8s N865F (6th/27th) & N866F (17th); Pan American B.707s N407PA (9th), N412PA (3rd), N884PA (18th) & N893PA (17th); TWA B.707s N8731 (7th), N18701 (20th), N18709 (21st), N28724 (6th), N28726 (27th), N28728 (24th) and Wardair B.707s CF-FAN (2nd) & CF-ZYP (20th/22nd). UK airlines operating to USA/Canada were BOAC (B.707), British Caledonian (B.707) & Dan-Air (B.707).

The only HS.748 ILS traffic observed was SATA CS-TAH (4th). RAF traffic noted were Argosies XN855 (6th), XP413 (4th/5th) & Britannia XL639 (6th).

2nd   The inaugural flight of British Caledonian's new service to New York took place today, operated by B.707 G-AZJM, departing at 1242. The interiors of their B707s have been refurbished and now include in-flight entertainment.

2nd   Another Comet made its last visit today when G-APDO arrived at 0206 (DA822 from Palma), before positioning out to Gatwick. It first flew in 1953 and was withdrawn from service later in the month.

2nd   There were more trooping movements today when VC-10s XR806 & XV109 made round trips to Hanover, before departing for RAF Gutersloh. Others were Britannia's XN404 (RR6600) &

XM398 (RR6601) and VC-10 XV106 (RR2680) operating two round trips to Hanover; Britannia XL639 (RR6521) operating two round trips to RAF Gutersloh (16th) and finally VC-10 XV10 (RR2686/7) & Britannia XM491 (RR6609/10) also made two round trips to RAF Gutersloh (30th).

3rd   The end of the Golden Products Conference in Manchester brought in another selection of airliners, similar to those used on the 30th May: Trans European B.707 OO-TEC twice & B.720 OO-TEA; Pan American B.727 N314PA and Condor B.727 D-ABIN.

4th   Iberia commenced their summer Barcelona/Palma service today with DC-9s. EC-BYD operated the first flight, which was also a first visit.

4th   Another French military training flight this month was operated by Nord 262 No.73, routing Lossiemouth-Lorient.

5th   Royal Saudi Air Force C-130E 452 operated from/to Jeddah via Milan as RSF810, before departing on the 7th.

6th   The latest BOAC Boeing 747 making its first visit was Heathrow diversion G-AWNJ, arriving at 1107 (BA570 from Chicago).

7th   Dove G-ARJB arrived at 1240 from Amsterdam, before departing for Birmingham. Operated by JC Bamford (JCB Excavators) since 1960, it was making the last of three visits this year. It was withdrawn in 1974, when the company replaced it with brand new HS.125 G-BJCB.

7th   One of three Prestwick diversions this morning was vintage Pan American B.707 N762PA at 0801 (PA076 from New York). This aircraft was delivered new to the airline in 1962.

8th   Aerospatiale Puma F-OCNS is the company's current demonstrator. It was making a tour of the UK when it arrived at 1720 from Bournemouth, before departing for Battersea Heliport at 1816.

10th   BOAC B.747 G-AWNI called in en route Toronto-Heathrow as BA600 carrying passengers from Manchester's cancelled flight, BA604.

11th   Operators started to resume normal service today, after a weekend of major ATC disruption, caused by an explosion at the Barcelona Communication Centre on the 9th. Traffic routing via France or Spain was badly affected and as delays built up traffic routed via other alternatives, namely Germany, which soon suffered long delays as well! The hornet's-nest was aggravated further by the crews going 'out of hours'. Lufthansa outbound Frankfurt flight (LH075) was delayed for more than three hours, until a replacement crew was located.

19th   Italian Air Force Douglas C-118 MM-61965, arriving on a Medivac flight from Pisa at 1158, was the only ever visit of an Italian Air Force DC-6 variant.

20th   Phillips Electronics latest Falcon 20, PH-ILY, made its first visit at 1931 from Eindhoven.

21st   Pan American B.747 N733PA diverted in at 1600, (PA124 Seattle-Heathrow) with technical trouble.

22nd   This morning's KLM KL153/4, operated by DC-8 PI-C801, was in full Philippine Airline colours.

27th   Six early morning diversions from Luton were one each from Britannia Airways & Court Line and four from Monarch Airlines: Britannia G-AOVT and all three Boeing 720s - G-AZFB, G-AZKM & G-AZNX.

28th   Aer Lingus Boeing 707 flight IN2114 routing Boston-Dublin, was diverting into Manchester due to bad weather, but it eventually made it to Dublin.

29th   Sabena Boeing 707 OO-SJG arrived 0903 (SN'JG from New York) and departed onwards for Brussels at 0954.

July 1973

After completion of the departure lounge extension in April 1972, the newly extended International Arrivals Hall was also open for business. The next phase will be the new long-haul pier (Pier C) and associated aprons, scheduled to open 1st January 1974. The final phase, consisting of the extension to the existing concourse, a new check-in hall and completion of the multi-storey car park block, is scheduled to be open by July 1974. Future projects may include the much discussed cargo terminal, to the north west of the present terminal building and the proposed second runway.

The airport announced its intention to be operating the proposed second runway by late 1979. The City Council has agreed in principal to the funding and the next stage is the submission of a planning application to Cheshire County Council by the end of the year. The corporation will then submit a Compulsory Purchase Order to the Ministry of the Environment for the required land. It's almost certain a public enquiry will be held, probably in the middle of next year, with a decision by the end of next year. If the go-aheads given, it's expected the following two years will be spent on design work and the three years thereafter on building work, which would start in 1976.

Although it never landed at Manchester, the Good Year Airship N2A, overflew the area on many occasions during the summer, notably the 2nd performing a low flypast.

Transatlantic flights from/to the USA & Canada have been numerous: Air Canada DC-8s CF-TIM (16th) & CF-TIU (24th); Capitol DC-8 N867F (2nd), CP Air DC-8s CF-CPG (28th), CF-CPO (22nd), CF-CPP (7th) & CF-CPS (25th); ONA DC-8s N865F (20th/27th), N866F (9th) & N8971U (6th/17th); Pacific Western B.707 CF-PWV (5th), Pan American B.707s N409PA (2nd/7th), N410PA (30th), N425PA (26th/30th), N495PA (24th), N496PA (29th), N884PA (19th) & N887PA (11th/16th); Sabena B.707 OO-SJG (20th), TIA DC-8s N797FT (10th), N4867T (20th) & N4868T (2nd/7th/28th); TWA B.707s N18709 (26th), N28724 (18th/24th) & N28728 (3rd/4th); Wardair B.707s CF-FAN (18th/19th/27th/28th/30th), CF-ZYP (16th/17th) and World Airways DC-8 N802WA (18th). UK airlines operating USA/Canada flights were BOAC (B.707), British Caledonian (B.707), Dan-Air (B.707), Donaldson International (B.707) and Laker Airways (B.707).

HS.748 ILS traffic observed were BFS D-AFSE (16th) & Australian Navy N15-710 (26th). RAF traffic noted were Britannia's XL637 (12th), XL655 (11th), XL657 (20th), XN392 (27th) & XN404 (26th); Argosies XN816 (13th), XN817 (9th), XN855 (3rd), XR140 (10th) & XR143 (4th); Varsity WF371 (4th), Nimrod XW665 (12th), French Air Force Falcon 20 ·No.260 (2nd) and RAE Comet XS235 (3rd).

2nd   Manchester's porters and airport staff, protesting over the French Government's decision to continue with nuclear testing, are boycotting Air France flight (AF960/1), which was cancelled until the 9th.

3rd   Royal Saudi Air Force C-130E 1609 operated from/to Jeddah via Milan as RSF812, before departing on the 5th.

4th   Cessna Citation D-INHH was the only biz-jet first visit this month, arriving at 1513 from Saarbrucken.

6th   RAF VC-10 XV108 arrived as RR2405 on a trooping flight from Gutersloh.

6th July 1973 – Seaboard World DC-8-63 N8641 is seen here on a wet and gloomy Friday evening, still in basic Loftleidir colours, as it was previously leased to them. It's in passenger configuration and due to operate an outbound transatlantic charter on behalf of Overseas National. (Geoff Ball)

10th   Pilatus Porter OO-AER, inbound from Antwerp around 1215, had to return there due to technical trouble. Had it have landed, it would have been a first visit of type, although it did finally arrive later in the year on the 27th September.

10th   New French-airline to Manchester, Catair, operated a flight from/to Le Bourget with SE.210 Caravelle F-BUFF, arriving on a humid afternoon at 1525. The aircraft, which served the airline until 1978, was white with a broad blue cheatline and blue Catair titles. The word 'cheatline' signifies a horizontal stripe, originated from the idea that a horizontal stripe would cheat the observer into thinking it was longer, or faster, than it actually was! A further flight operated from/to Le Bourget on the 31st, with SE.210 F-BUFC.

13th Northern Executive Aviation reported a 40% increase in private charters for the first six months of the year, compared to the same period last year.

14th RAF VC-10s XV101 (RR2408) & XV105 (RR2409) arrived from Hanover and Brussels respectively.

16th A record 2½ inches of rain fell at the airport in a 24-hour period up to 0900 today, making it the wettest day at Ringway since August 1942!

16th Today was the last visit of Dan-Air Comet G-APDM, when it arrived at 0951 (DA834 from Alicante), substituting for the usual B.707. It positioned back to Gatwick at 1222 and was withdrawn from service later in the year.

18th German Air Force Transall 50+87 arrived at 1259 as DCN7402, on a training flight from Cologne to Northolt.

19th RAF Britannia XL658, inbound during the morning on a trooping charter, was forced to return to Brize Norton due to technical trouble. It finally made it at 1346 as RR6652.

20th Overseas National DC-8 N865F was operating over ten hours late and rather than leave the passengers in the terminal, they were offered the choice of a cabaret show at the Golden Garter, Wythenshawe, or being put up at the Excelsior Hotel until the flight left at 0321.

20th Hawker-Siddeley HS.748 G-AZJH arrived from Woodford in two-tone grey colours. The aircraft stayed overnight, before departing to Ostend the following morning.

26th TWA flight TW8367 inbound from New York diverted to Heathrow due to Manchester's weather, so B.707 N28724 arrived from Gatwick (TW8366) in the afternoon to operate the return flight to New York.

27th Scottish-based airline, Loganair, operated two outbound charters to Glasgow with Skyvan G-AWYG & Islander G-BANL. The return flights operated on the 29th with Skyvan G-AWYG and vintage Beech 18 G-ASUG.

August 1973

BEA broke their own record last month, when over 27,000 passengers were carried on international flights by their Super 1-11 Division. This represents a 35% increase on July last year, following on from a 41% rise in June.

The month saw a varied selection of transatlantic flights with the following: Air Canada DC-8 CF-TJV (8th), Airlift International DC-8 N6164A (8th), CP Air DC-8s CF-CPO (26th) & CF-CPS (29th); ONA DC-8s N863F (14th/20th/21st/28th), N864F (21st), N866F (10th), N8971U (5th) & DC-10 N1031F (4th/10th); Pan American B.707s N410PA (14th), N419PA (7th/8th), N435PA (18th/19th), N887PA (21st), N891PA (12th), N893PA (21st/27th) & N897PA (20th/21st); TIA DC-8s N4868T (10th) & N4869T (8th); TWA B.707s N8735 (29th) & N8737 (16th) and Wardair B.707s CF-FAN (9th/15th/25th), CF-ZYP (7th/28th) & B.747 CF-DJC (14th/23rd/30th). UK airlines were BOAC (B.707), British Caledonian (B.707), Dan-Air (B.707) & Laker Airways (B.707).

HS.748 ILS traffic observed were Mount Cook ZK-MCA (22nd) & BFS D-AFSE (29th/31st).

1st RAF VC-10 XV108 arrived as RR2438 on a trooping flight from Dusseldorf. Others were Britannia XN404 RR6673/4 Dusseldorf-Brussels (4th), VC-10 XV106 RR2445 Brussels-Brize Norton (18th) & VC-10 XR810 RR2448 Brize Norton-Dusseldorf (22nd).

2nd British Caledonian B.707 G-AYSI, operating BR2068 to Toronto, had the notoriety of being involved in an overbooking fiasco. A tour operator booked 239 names for the flight, a surplus of 51 passengers, although the airline was notified of 187. At check-in, 119 people turned up and a further 120 arrived without tickets. The B.707 eventually departed with a full load of 188 passengers and the remaining 51 left two days later.

4th Overseas National is operating two brand new Douglas DC-10s, N1031F & N1032F, as well as their fleet of Douglas DC-8s. The first, N1031F, paid its first visit to Manchester in the early hours from Cologne.

8th Airlift International, an airline rarely seen at Manchester, paid a visit with DC-8 N6164A operating a delayed charter from Toronto, on behalf of CP Air.

9th French Air Force Falcon No.49 operated a training flight as F-RAFJ from Shannon to Villacoublay.

12th Dan-Air sub-charted Sabena B.707 OO-SJC to operate flight DA827/8 to/from Tunis.

14th British Midland flight BD068 (Heathrow–Teeside) was diverting into Ringway around 2110, but it eventually ended up at RAF Leeming instead.

15th BEA Vanguard G-APEI positioned in from Heathrow to operate Amsterdam flight BE526/7.

15th The second Mitsubishi MU-2 to visit was N291MA, operating from/to Leavesden.

20th Maersk HS.125 OY-APM, made its first visit at 1317 from Lille.

20th Air Anglia Fokker F-27 arrived from Leeds at 1131 to operate to Stavanger.

21st Anyone on the terraces today would have been treated to the remarkable sight of three Pan American B.707s. N887PA, N893PA & N897PA had recently arrived from New York and were parked up next to each other on the International pier.

21st French-airline Catair operated a further flight from/to Le Bourget, this time with SE.210 Caravelle F-BUFC.

23rd Early production Dove OO-BPL, built in 1949 and operated by Belgian International Air Services, flew a return flight to Brussels, arriving at 1024.

25th PA-34 Seneca N55583 arrived on a delivery flight, routing Shannon-Gatwick.

27th Cessna 210 D-ECYE was due in today, but it went to Liverpool instead.

27th Dan-Air Comet G-APDB made its last visit today, substituting for a B.707. It arrived at 1832 (DA834A from Alicante), before positioning out to Gatwick at 1923. Its final revenue flight was 12th November (DA1048 Alicante-Teeside), before positioning down to Lasham the following day for eventual preservation, having carried over 800,000 passengers and flown 36,828 hours.

27th The first Iberia Boeing 727 to visit Manchester arrived today, when EC-CBL operated delayed Aviaco flight AO1518/9.

29th Persistent morning fog in the South East saw nineteen diverted aircraft arrive at Manchester, carrying over 2,000 passengers and a new record was set when five wide-bodied aircraft were on the ground at once. BOAC B.747 G-AWNK arrived at 0747 (BA024 from Nairobi), BOAC B.747 G-AWNC at 0906 (BA500 from New York), first visitors Pan American B.747 N747PA at 0738 (PA120 from Los Angeles), TWA B.747 N53110 at 0826 (TW700 from New York) and one of Manchester's own flights, Laker DC-10 G-AZZC. Another first visit was TWA B.707 N762TW at 0814 (TW754 from Boston).

September 1973

A fourteen week, £50,000 programme to carry out major resurfacing work on the main runway 06/24 started on the 3rd. The airport will be closed each night between 0230 and 0730 during September and October. During the closures, three IT night flights will be diverted to Liverpool, but Manchester cargo flights will be rescheduled to operate before the closure and others should be unaffected. The work's due for completion on 15th December.

There's a revived, but cautious optimism, that declining freight figures can be reversed. BEA Cargo is on a major sales drive to attract goods from Yorkshire and the North East, with the aim of doubling their freight revenue at Ringway by the middle of next year. This follows the drop in freight figures in 1971 when, for the first time in several years, traffic fell significantly. So great were the shockwaves from being 6,000 tonnes down on 1970, that by the middle of 1972 it was questioned whether this was the end of Manchester's freight boom. It was asked if the downturn was due to the general economic state of the country and the world slump in trade, or was it something more permanent. Perhaps it was due to the increasing amount of cargo being roaded to London and flown out of Heathrow to overseas destinations, because it was cheaper for business to do it that way. Having said this, the decline proved to be temporary, when end of year figures for last year showed a 13% increase. There were two main reasons for the upturn, firstly was the reduction in differential cargo rates between London and Manchester, which made Manchester more competitive and secondly because trucking air freight to London had become more expensive, due to recent increases in haulage costs. In view of the upturn, the future of Manchester's planned cargo village, which has been shelved, is likely to be reconsidered and decided upon by the end of the year.

Transatlantic flights were operated by the following UK airlines: BOAC (B.707), British Caledonian (B.707), Dan-Air (B.707), Laker Airways (B.707) and the following aircraft: CP Air DC-8 CF-CPO (26th), ONA DC-8 N863F (2nd/3rd) & DC-10 N1031F (17th); Pacific Western B.707

CF-PWJ (20th), Pan American B.707s N407PA (10th), N412PA (3rd), N427PA (5th), N428PA (18th), N883PA (5th/25th) & N897PA (24th); Transavia B.707 PH-TVA (9th/11th/13th/14th), TWA B.707s N18709 (3rd/16th) & N28728 (6th/19th/21st); Wardair B.707 CF-FAN (21st/22nd) and World Airways DC-8 N801WA (15th).

HS.748 ILS traffic observed were Mount Cook ZK-MCA (22nd) & BFS D-AFSE (29th/31st). RAF traffic noted were Britannia's XM496 (17th), XN392 (27th) & XN404 (24th); Argosy XR137 (6th), Belfast XR364 (7th) and Andover XS600 (10th). Others were RAE Comet XW626 (11th), French Air Force Falcon 20s No.238 (18th) & No.49 (21st); Israeli Air Force Stratocruiser 4X-FPY (19th) and HS.125 G-BAZB (20th).

4th   Royal Saudi Air Force C-130E 1606 operated from/to Jeddah via Milan as RSF816, before departing on the 6th.

7th   Lear Jet 25 OY-BFC, operated by Business Jet Flight Centre based at Copenhagen, made its first visit today. Other biz-jets making their first visits were HS.125's G-BBGU (8th), G-BAXL (18th) & RAF XX507 operating RR1643 Northolt-Edinburgh (30th), Falcon 20 F-BSTR (18th) and Gulfstream 2 N227G from/to Luton (28th).

8th   Five aircraft diverted away from Manchester today, due to the weather. Included were Aviogenex flights JJ103 (Split-MAN) & JJ105 (Pula-MAN) which diverted to Gatwick and SVC-10 G-ASGD (BA534 from New York), which elected to divert to Prestwick.

9th   Transavia B.707 PH-TVA operated the first of several sub-charters for Dan-Air and British Caledonian during the month.

9th   Six aircraft diverted in, including TMA B.707F OD-AFX at 0735 (TL301 from New York) from Shannon, which had previously visited as PH-TRV with Transavia. Three of Manchester's own flights were also lost to the weather: Dan-Air B.707 G-AZTG (DA6107 from Toronto) diverted to Gatwick, BOAC VC-10 G-ARVH (BA534 from New York) diverted to Prestwick and for the second day running, Aviogenex flight JJ105 (Pula-MAN) diverted to Gatwick.

18th   A near miss was reported to the CAA when BA604 (SVC-10 G-ASGF) inbound from Toronto and a BEA Viscount en route London Heathrow-Aberdeen, travelling in opposite directions, came close enough for both pilots to report a near miss about 20-miles north of Manchester and 18,000ft over the Pennines. No avoiding action was necessary, but international law requires aircraft flying below FL290 (29,000ft) to be at least 1,000ft apart.

18th   Another Air France SE.210 leaving the fleet was F-BHRS, making its final visit to Manchester today, before being transferred to Air Inter early next year.

19th   Israeli Air Force Stratocruiser 4X-FPY, arriving from Aalborg, Denmark via Newcastle, carried out three ILS approaches.

19th   British Caledonian B.707 G-AZRO paid its last visit (BR2126 to Toronto), before it returned to PIA eventually, from whom it was leased.

20th September 1973 – Dan-Air HS.748 G-ARMX is seen on a pleasant evening, having just arrived as DA115 from Bournemouth/Birmingham. The spectators above however, are far more interested in the BEA BAC 1-11 next door! (Manchester Airport Archive)

20th Pacific Western B.707F CF-PWJ arrived at 1328 (PW3868 from Tehran), operating a freight charter.

21st Aircraft substitutions on Aer Lingus flights were commonplace in 1972, particularly on Amsterdam flights when upgrades to larger aircraft, such as B.707/720s, regularly took place. However, the only upgrade this year was today, when B.707 EI-ANO operated EI602/3.

22nd This month's trooping flights were RAF Britannia XN398, outbound to Gutersloh as RR6533 today and VC-10 XV104 as RR2488, outbound to Hanover on the 23rd.

22nd RAF Belfast XR371, operating from/to Brize Norton as RR706, arrived in the evening and stayed for less than twenty minutes.

23rd Royal Navy Whirlwind XK969 called in at 2244 from Lancaster, before departing for Leconfield.

24th British Caledonian BR237 from Gatwick didn't make it with the planned B.707, as it returned with technical trouble. Second aircraft, G-ATZC, made it later in the day but on its return the following day as BR238, it too suffered technical trouble and operated direct into Gatwick.

25th First time visitor Citation 500 ZS-RCC, arriving at 1649 from Prestwick, promptly took refuge in the Servisair Hangar until its departure on the 28th.

26th German Air Force Transall 50+56 arrived at 1329 as DCN7804, on a training flight from Cologne to Northolt.

27th Air France flight AF960/1 diverted to Heathrow, due to the Manchester weather.

27th Afternoon Heathrow flight BE4064/9, operated by BEA Airtours Comet G-ARCP, was also the aircrafts final visit as such, as it was sold in November to Dan-Air. It was re-registered as G-BBUV in order to avoid r/t confusion with BAC 1-11 G-AXCP.

28th Court Line HS.125 G-AVRG arrived at 1501 from RAF Leuchars, in its colourful yellow, gold and orange scheme.

October 1973

More than two million passengers passed through the airport during the first nine months, an increase of 14% on the same period last year.

Scheduled flight changes included the termination of BOAC Toronto flight (BA603/4) on the 14th and the direct New York flight (BA534/3) on the 27th, when it reverted to the New York/Caribbean operation the following day. Others finishing were British Caledonian's New York flight, which effectively terminated on the 14th except for one-offs on the 21st & 28th. Cyprus Airways operated the last Larnaca flight on the 26th and the last Nicosia flight on the 1st.

BEA Airtours disposed of their remaining Comets at the end of the summer and G-ARJL flew the final flight from Paris to Gatwick on the 31st. Since operations began in March 1970, their Comets have flown twenty-one million miles and carried two million passengers. There was no summer service from Manchester with the type this year, although they made the occasional appearance up until this month and their last visits were as follows:

G-APMC	01/05/73	Withdrawn by 10/73, sold to Dan-Air for spares.
G-ARCP	27/09/73	Sold to Dan-Air 11/73 as G-BBUV.
G-ARGM	31/05/73	Withdrawn by 10/73, sold to Dan-Air for spares.
G-ARJK	17/04/73	Sold to Dan-Air 10/73.
G-ARJL	04/05/73	Withdrawn by 10/73, sold to Dan-Air for spares.

1st Pan American B.747 N731PA made its first visit, arriving at 1126 on a charter flight from New York.

1st Today was the final visit of a BEA passenger Vanguard, when G-APEN operated Heathrow flight BE4084/7.

2nd Royal Saudi Air Force C-130E 1607 operated from/to Jeddah via Milan as RSF818, before departing on the 4th.

6th German operator WDL operated two Fokker F.27 flights today, which night-stopped from/to Dusseldorf. D-BAKI arrived at 1050 as IP773 and D-BEKU at 1322 as IP672.

6th Spanish-airline Trans Europa made its first visit to Manchester since September 1971, when SE.210 EC-BRJ arrived as TR264 from Gerona as a Belfast diversion, operating as a British Midland sub-charter.

7th   Hungarian state-airline Malev IL-18 HA-MOA brought in the Hungarian State Puppet Theatre as part of Hungarian Week and IL-18 HA-MOI, arriving on the 14th, returned them to Budapest. Both were first visits and it was the first visit of the airline since 1967.

9th   KLM Amsterdam flight KL153/4 was operated by NLM Fokker F.27 PH-KFE today, when the DC-9 due to operate it was forced to return to Amsterdam with technical trouble.

10th   Braathens B.737 LN-SUP arrived at 1753 (BU1577E from Stansted) to operate a charter to Oslo the following day. It was one of three different Braathens to visit this year, although this one had been in before on the 19th December 1972. The others, LN-SUG (14th January) and LN-SUS (16th December), were both first visits.

12th   US Army Beech U-21 66-18037 is basically a military version of the Beech 65 Queen Air. Arriving at 1633 from Farnborough, it stayed until the 14th when it departed for Hanover.

13th   RAF VC-10 XV108 operated from/to Hanover today as RR2526. The only other trooping flight during the month was VC-10 XR807 as RR2488 from Hanover (14th).

15th   RAF Pumas XW207 arriving today and XW205 on the 29th, called in to uplift fuel whilst helping with the erection of a bridge in the Bollin Valley, behind the South Side hangars.

17th   Newly-registered HS.125 G-BAYT made its first visit today, from Heathrow to Edinburgh.

20th   Incredibly, Dan-Air Comet G-AZIY was the eighth aircraft to be withdrawn by the airline this year. It made its final visit to Manchester today, positioning in from Gatwick at 0803 and departed at 0929 as DA9415 to Gerona, before being withdrawn the following month.

21st   Monarch Britannia's G-AOVG (OM745 at 2147) & G-AOVN (OM827 at 2205), operated inbound flights from/to Tarbes and were both making their final visits to Manchester. The withdrawal of G-AOVG in January 1974 and G-AOVN in November 1973 left just one Bristol Britannia, G-AOVT, in service with the airline.

23rd   Transavia SE.210 PH-TRP, arriving from Luton at 1406 as HV2615, had the Osmond's onboard for their concert at the Free Trade Hall; even though the airport had released a press statement saying the aircraft would not be allowed to land at Manchester. It had been issued to deter fans from arriving at airport, following an incident at Heathrow a few days earlier, when the weight of large numbers of hysterical female fans had caused a wall to collapse on the terraces of the Queens Building, resulting in several fans being injured.

25th   Pacific Western B.707F CF-PWJ arrived two days late as PW3878, on another freight charter from Tehran.

26th   A flurry of morning diversions, mainly from Heathrow, weren't of much interest except for Boeing 707 G-AXXY arriving at 0820 (BA688 from Bermuda). This was the first aircraft to appear at Manchester in full British Airways colours.

27th   British Caledonian operated their final New York flight (BR237/8), with Boeing 707 G-ATZC. Following heavy losses on the four-times weekly service, the frequency had been wound down during the month, particularly after the 14th.

28th   Another short burst of Heathrow diversions produced four BOAC flights and Alitalia DC-9F I-DIBK at 1057 (AZ978 from Milan). In amongst them was Boeing 707 G-AXXZ at 1014 (BA692 from Bridgetown), in a hybrid scheme of full BOAC colours and British Airways titles.

30th Due to fog, there were no movements between 0130 and 1315, with most flights being either diverted or cancelled. However, once the fog had cleared the airport was hit by a deluge of twenty Heathrow diversions during the evening, all British apart from Nigeria Airways B.707 5N-ABJ at 1815 (WT904 from Kano) and first visit Alitalia DC-9 I-DIZE at 1834 (AZ460 from Milan).

30th Yet to be delivered Rousseau Aviation HS.748 F-BUTR, arrived during the evening on demonstration for British Airways.

31st Fred Olsen operated the SAS freight flight for the final time this month, which have been operated almost exclusively by their two Douglas DC-6s, LN-FOL & LN-FON during the year. LN-FOL, which operated today's final flight, was sold to Iscargo as TF-IUB in April 1974 and LN-FON, which last visited on the 27th, operated for Fred Olsen until 1976 when it was sold in Zaire.

31st Lufthansa's twice-weekly freight flights from Chicago operated for the final time today, when B.707F D-ABUY was in charge of the last LH473 Chicago-Toronto-Manchester service.

November 1973

Work on the new long-haul pier and apron is progressing well and should be completed by January. The air bridges are assembled and under test and the stands on the new pier will be numbered 21-27 inclusive, with the even numbers on the north side. As from 1st January 1974, the Domestic pier stands will be renumbered 41-51 and nose-in parking will be introduced, except on Stands 42 & 44 (the present 22 & 24). The piers will be allocated letters, so the Domestic will be 'Pier A', the existing International 'Pier B' and the new one will be 'Pier C', making a total of thirty-two stands available.

The Super 1-11 Division of BEA announced a forecast profit of £300,000 for the financial year, on top of a further expansion plan. It's now part of the British Airways group and when it was formed in 1971, it inherited an annual loss of £1.5m. The profit is due to expansion of their direct flights to Europe and the cutback of uneconomical domestic services. New routes planned, but not yet confirmed, will be Rome (1974), Frankfurt (1975) & Zurich (1976). Others being seriously considered include Hamburg, Lisbon, Stockholm & Nice. The division currently operates to twelve European destinations and four domestic cities, in addition to operating German internal services linking Berlin with other West German cities, with around fifty daily return flights.

The winter schedules show that BEA will not be operating any passenger Vanguard flights, but have increased the use of Tridents on their Heathrow schedules. They are also basing a Viscount to operate scheduled flights to Dublin and Jersey. BEA will also operate a number of IT flights from/to Palma, with Tridents. Other changes include Air France operating six-weekly through the winter. BOAC Cargo amended their Detroit flight via Montreal (BA067) back to four-weekly. British Caledonian has commenced a twice-daily service to Gatwick, operated by British Island Airways Herald's. KLM now operate KL153/4 on weekdays and lunchtime flight KL155/6 on Saturday/Sunday. SAS has reverted to Douglas DC-9s for Copenhagen freight flights. Winter IT flights are being operated by Air Spain, Britannia Airways, British Caledonian, Court Line, Dan-Air, & Laker Airways.

HS.748 ILS traffic observed were BFS D-AFSE (1st/2nd) & Hawker-Siddeley G-BBPT (12th/14th). RAF traffic noted were RAF Britannia's XM489 (29th), XM491 (19th/21st) and Belfast's XR363 (19th), XR370 (21st) & XR371 (28th). Crew training flights were operated by BOAC B.707s G-ARRA (21st) & G-ARRC (17th).**1st** Another short-lived UK airline, Silver City Airways, was set up earlier in the year in February, operating with ex-Air Traders Vanguard G-AYLD. It diverted into Manchester in their basic colours at 0738 today due to fog at Stansted, but by the end of the month they were gone and G-AYLD was sold to French-airline Europe Air Service, as F-BUFT.

1st Vegetable charters were Tarom IL-18s YR-IME today and YR-IMF on the 11th.

1st Falcon 20 OH-FFV was a first visit, operating from/to Helsinki. Other biz-jets making their first visits were Green Shield Stamps HS.125 G-BART (6th), HS.125 HB-VBZ (7th), IAI Westwind D-CGLS, Citation 500 N512CC (8th) and Lear Jet 25s I-TAKY (18th) & OO-LFZ (26th).

2nd Rousseau Aviation HS.748 F-BUTR arrived from Woodford at 1604 whilst on delivery to the airline, before departing on the 5th.

4th RAF Britannia XL660 (RR6608 from/to Dusseldorf) was operating a trooping flight.

5th   Moscow has become a regular destination for the first time and a series of flights commenced today when Dan-Air B.727 G-BAEF departed Manchester, on behalf of Thomson Holidays. DA707 departs on Mondays at 1530 and returns on Fridays at 1630 as DA708.

6th   Royal Saudi Air Force C-130E 1607 operated from/to Jeddah via Milan as RSF820, before departing on the 8th.

8th   Canadair T-33 Silver Star CF-IHB arrived at 1737 to night-stop, before departing at 1330 on its very last flight to Southend for preservation.

17th   When Electra N42FM arrived with Santana for a concert in Manchester it was observed 'that the pilot would not look out of place as a member of the group'!

19th   PA-23 Aztec N6610Y, arriving from East Midlands at 1651, was destined for work with NEA. It was re-registered as G-BBSR and departed for Glasgow on 17th January 1974.

21st November 1973 – Saturn Airways Electra N852U arrived on a freight charter on behalf of Shell, bringing in a 10-tonne generator in anticipation of power shortages. Having acquired Universal Airlines in 1972, Saturn themselves were absorbed into TIA during 1976. (Geoff Ball)

22nd   The day produced twenty-five fog diversions, mainly from Heathrow and although it was predominantly a British affair again, it did produce the first visit of Nigeria Airways newest Boeing 707, 5N-ABK, at 2233 (WT908 from Rome) which was only delivered in January. By far the busiest period was late evening, when Manchester received fourteen Heathrow diversions from 2217-2349. In amongst these were SAS SE.210 SE-DAE at 2233 (SK519 from Copenhagen) and Alitalia DC-9 I-DIBO at 2241 (AZ290 from Milan). Incidentally, Birmingham received at least twenty-five BEA diversions this evening, including sixteen Tridents!

22nd   The fuel crisis has forced British Airways to take the drastic action and cut flights. Frequent service routes are most likely to be affected, as they should have less impact for passengers, although Malta's weekly service will be dropped and Jersey's frequencies reduced.

24th   Air Anglia arrivals DC-3 G-AOBN & Fokker F.27 G-BAUR were in connection with the first division match between Manchester Utd v Norwich. Nearly 37,000 spectators witnessed one of the last games by George Best in a red shirt, but even he was unable to inspire or turn the game around, which ended as a dour 0-0- stalemate!

25th   Another PA-23 Aztec, N6525Y, arrived for work with NEA and eventually became G-BBTL. The aircrafts first flight was 20th December and ultimately it became a Manchester resident.

30th   Due to dense, freezing fog there were no arrivals between 0829 and 1731. Amongst the flights diverted and lost were British Caledonian BR981 (Gatwick-MAN) to Blackpool, BOAC Cargo BA067 (Heathrow-MAN) & KL153 (Amsterdam-MAN) both to Birmingham, BOAC BA537 (Heathrow-MAN) to Prestwick, Lufthansa LH074 (Frankfurt-MAN) to Heathrow; Air France AF960 (Paris-MAN), Aer Lingus EI650 (Dublin-MAN) EI602 & (Dublin-MAN) all to Liverpool and EI767 (Birmingham-MAN) which overflew direct to Cork.

December 1973

The Government declared a state of emergency, which lasted into next year. Central heating oil was rationed and the supply of petrol was reduced and then rationed. Power cuts and no warning blackouts were a regular occurrence from mid-November. Sporting fixtures were cancelled, as were concerts, as the organisers had no way of knowing if or when the lights would go out! Road and street lighting was drastically reduced and a voluntary speed limit of 50mph on Britain's major roads and motorways became compulsory. The catalyst was the Arab-Israeli war flaring up again in October. Even though a peace deal was signed last month, it wasn't fully resolved until the Americans brokered a further peace accord between Egypt and Israel in 1977. The repercussions of the 1973 spat were far reaching when the Arab oil producing countries, Saudi Arabia in particular, drastically reduced supplies to any country seen to be siding with Israel. As we were considered to be one of those countries, we suffered greatly. As if that wasn't enough, there was also an overtime ban by miners and rail workers, freezing temperatures, terrorist bombings, kidnappings and hijackings! It's no wonder visitors to Manchester were scarce this month, especially towards the end, due to the combination of fuel problems and the seasonal decline in traffic. The fall in the airport's movements was a good indicator of the UK's uninspiring economic situation!

Due to County Council boundary changes, a new joint committee will be formed to run the airport from 1st April 1974. It will contain equal members from both sides and the Chairman will alternate between the two. The Airport Authority will be served by the Chief Executive of both councils and any surpluses or deficits will be shared by both authorities.

A familiar sight to aviation enthusiasts and travellers is the airport's Ground Controlled Approach Radar (GCA) or Precision Approach Radar (PAR). The system takes control of an aircraft around 8-miles from the runway, although its distance to touchdown would be much greater. The controller monitors the aircraft's position on radar, which shows the angle of descent and direction in relation to the runway; while at the same time issuing instructions to bring the aircraft down for the landing, known as talk-down. However, the ILS (Instrument Landing System) is now the preferred method for aircraft, although in its earlier days it wasn't always reliable or accurate in poor visibility, so in those conditions PAR was used for monitoring the approaches instead. The PAR vehicles, easily identified by their orange and white stripes, were usually located at the side of the runway. The truck contained a standby generator and the attached trailer held the PAR equipment and there was also a separate rest caravan. The unit could be moved to either end of the runway, depending on the landing direction, but as PAR is rarely used these days it's to be withdrawn from service on 28th February next year.

HS.748 ILS traffic observed were Hawker-Siddeley G-AZJH (12th) & G-BBTA (7th) and CAA HS.748 G-AVXI, which operated checks on the ILS itself (19th). The only crew training flight was BOAC B.707 G-ASZF (28th).

2nd December 1973 – BAC 1-11 N44R, owned by Rockwell industries, is seen here parked on the Fairey Apron. Arriving on 25th November from Reykjavik, it remained there until today's departure to Blackpool. (Geoff Ball)

2nd   The only biz-jet this month was RAF HS.125 XX508, arriving at 1535 (RR1469 from RAF Northolt).

3rd   RAF VC-10 XV105 (RR2601 from/to Hanover) was operating a trooping flight.

4th   Royal Saudi Air Force C-130E 1611 operated from/to Jeddah via Milan as RSF822, before departing on the 8th. Another, C-130E 455, arrived on the 19th as RSF940 from Milan and departed two days later.

4th   Freight charters for Shell during the month were Saturn Airways DC-8 N8955U today and C-130 N12ST on the 6th.

7th   First time visitor Sterling SE.210 OY-STK operated BE831/2 from/to Copenhagen, in lieu of BAC 1-11 G-AVMU, which had gone tech in Copenhagen.

8th   Aeromaritime Guppy's F-BBPA & F-BTGV have been transporting Airbus wings throughout the year at the rate of around one every two months and F-BPPA arrived today from Bristol-Filton, before departing for Bremen the following day.

11th   Following a Government directive to reduce fuel use, BEA finalised further reductions in services today and cuts of 23% to their Manchester services are also expected.

11th There were two German Air Force training flights this month. The first, Transall 50+38 as DCN8278 (Glasgow-Landsberg) was today and Transall 50+78 as DCN8342 (Cologne-RAF Northolt) was on the 19th.

12th Pacific Western B.707F CF-PWJ arrived at 0914, operating a freight flight from Tel Aviv to Ottawa as PW3806.

11th Sabena's evening freighter, SN127/8, was operated by Boeing 707 OO-SJL.

14th World Airways DC-8 N801WA arrived at 0752 to operate an outbound Toronto charter, on behalf of Dan-Air.

14th Super 1-11 G-AVMW (BE824 from Glasgow), with ninety-six passengers onboard, burst a tyre on landing.

14th Due to a 25% reduction in aviation fuel, British Airways have made further cuts from Manchester this month, in addition to the Christmas Day and Boxing Day cancellations, bringing the number of flights axed to forty-two. Shelved until further notice are all services to Geneva (BE818/9) and Malta (BE848/9), the daily New York (BA538/7) from the 15th, daily morning Edinburgh (BE4576/802), Mon morning Brussels (BE814/5), the Wed Amsterdam (BE808/9) & Copenhagen (BE832/3) flights, the Thurs Paris (BE802/3) and Sat Milan (BE806/7). From the 17th there will only be three return services to London Heathrow: MAN-LHR (BE4057) 0800/0845 daily, (BE4065) 1050/1135 Sat, (BE4079) 1605/1650 Mon-Fri and LHR-MAN (BE4054) 0825/0910 Mon-Fri, (BE4092) 1945/2030 Sun and (BE4094) 2005/2050 daily.

15th Night flights from Manchester were resumed today, following completion of the resurfacing of the main runway. The airport authorities say it's the last major resurfacing that can be carried out before the centre has to be completely reconstructed, because of inadequate foundations. Despite the cutback in flights caused by the fuel crisis, the airport's set for a record breaking year and while provisional figures aren't available as yet, it's understood that last year's record of 2.6 million passengers has already been bettered.

15th The new £9m terminal and jumbo pier will be opened officially on 25th March 1974.

19th British Airways are restoring half the services cut earlier in the month for fuel economy reasons and hope to run a near normal service in the New Year.

23rd Air France flight AF960/1 was operated by Air France/TAT Fokker F.27 F-BUFO today.

24th After receiving eleven fog diversions from various airports between 0134 and 1144, Manchester became fog-bound itself, when nothing arrived after 1503 or departed after 1602. Amongst those diverting away was Air France AF960, which ended up at Luton.

27th The Maule M-4, an American four-seat monoplane that first flew in 1957, made a first visit of type to Manchester, when UK-based ZK-DON arrived at 1023 from Hawarden, before departing at 1144 for Exeter.

First/Last Arrivals & Departures 1973

First arrival: BAC 1-11 G-AWYS/CA1290 from Malaga at 00.31(diversion)
First departure: B.737 EI-ASE/EI9217 to Dublin at 01.44
Last arrival: B.737 G-BADR/BY640 from Gerona at 23.50
Last departure: B.737 EI-ASE/EI9213 to Dublin at 22.06

(+/- % on Previous Year)		
Scheduled Passengers	1,371,000	+10.9%
I.T/Charter Passengers	1,215,000	+11.7%
Transit Passengers	141,000	-35.5%
Total	**2,727,000**	**+7.4%**
Freight & Mail (Tonnes)	45,300	+0.2%
Movements	66,500	+2.6%

Airport Diary 1974

January 1974

The year began where the previous one left off, with oil in short supply, only now it cost four times more than six months ago! Coal was also scarce, particularly towards the end of the month and as the miners were still striking over pay, the power cuts continued and candle sales soared! No advance warning of the blackouts was given, but it was made known through local evening newspapers when there was a risk; for example the North West was split into zones, each with a risk rating of high, medium, or low. The risk was also broken down into time zones, so areas had different risks at different times, although the writer remembers the blackouts were usually late afternoon to early evening. Oil and coal shortages occupied the people's thoughts and they were unimpressed by the Government's inability to deal with the problem. In response to the mood of the country the Conservative Prime Minister, Edward Heath, announced a General Election the following month, which Labour won. Even though Harold Wilson was returned to power, he called another election in September, which he also won but with a greater majority, giving him a stronger mandate on which to govern and implement his policies.

On the positive side, the aviation scene saw the delivery of many new Tridents and not just to BEA, as China started receiving their own as part of a trade deal finalised in 1971. On the negative side, most British types were declining in numbers, such as Comets, Vanguards, Britannia's, VC-10s & Viscounts. This year also saw the withdrawal of the first Trident 1, even though BEA had only taken delivery of their last Trident 3 two years ago. The only new British type on the horizon was the Avro 146, but this was still in the early stages of development. All this had paved the way for the Americans to dominate the aviation industry. During the sixties the only American jet airliners being used in large numbers were Boeing 707s and Douglas DC-8s, but after getting their act together, Boeing for example were producing the 727, 737 & 747, which were all increasing in very large numbers following worldwide orders. Also increasing were McDonnell-Douglas aircraft, with their DC-9 and DC-10 types. Lockheed was producing the L.1011-Tristar, which BEA and other airlines ordered. Despite the American domination, Europeans were also launching new aircraft. The Airbus A300 was still undergoing test flights, but was due to enter service with Air France between London and Paris by next May. Propliners were also in slow decline, as the trend towards jet domination continued, but due to Eastern Europe opening up as a holiday destination, Russian types became more prominent at Manchester and the rest of the UK. Luckily for enthusiasts, they used jets and propliners, which were none too common previously. Smaller British aircraft, such as Doves and Herons also dwindled, when executive jets became the new mode of transport for companies and the rich and famous.

The month was quiet, with a distinct lack of interesting visitors for two reasons. Firstly was the UK's mild and windy weather, which resulted in very few diversions and secondly was the fuel crisis and impending 3-day week, which came later in the month. Fuel availability for private aircraft was reduced by 50% and although Lufthansa were still operating passenger flights from/to Frankfurt, the Glasgow and Dublin extensions had ceased.

Military traffic noted were Britannia's XN392 (24th) & XN404 (17th); C-130 XV175 (25th), RAE Comet XW626 (24th) and Israeli Air Force Stratocruiser 4X-FPN (29th). Crew training flights were operated by BOAC VC-10 G-ARVB (2nd), BOAC B.707s G-AXXY (12th) & G-AXXZ (4th) and Cambrian Airways Viscount G-AOYP (15th).

3rd Today's unusual aircraft substitution was Rousseau Aviation/TAT HS.748 F-BSRA, operating AF960/1 as replacement for the regular SE.210 Caravelle.

5th BEA/BOAC flights were returning to normal and for the first time since the fuel strike began, full services on the Manchester-Heathrow route were restored. Most axed international services were reinstated and the only flights still not operating were to Malta and Geneva. Dan-Air however, had sufficient fuel stocks to operate a full schedule this month.

5th RAF VC-10 XV103 operated a trooping flight from/to Hanover as RR2633/4.

5th Following warnings for strong winds in North West, two Dan-Air Comets from Gatwick to Liverpool, G-ARJN (DA7509) & G-APMG (DA7511), diverted to Manchester.

7th   Aer Turas Douglas DC-7F EI-AWG, arriving at 1256 operating extra freight flight EI9206/7 on behalf of Aer Lingus, was the last visit of a Douglas DC-7.

8th   Royal Saudi Air Force C-130E 1610 operated from/to Jeddah via Milan as RSF800, before departing on the 10th.

9th   Fourteen diversions, including eleven from Heathrow, arrived on a busy evening starting with BOAC VC-10 G-ARVL at 2024 (BA'VL from Prestwick). Amongst those of interest was the first visit of the pure-cargo UK airline, IAS, operating out of Gatwick and Luton, when Britannia G-ANCF arrived at 2137 (FF9467 from Palma). Although it was predominantly a British affair, other diversions included SAS SE.210 SE-DAB at 2124 (SK519 from Copenhagen), Alitalia DC-9 I-DIKP at 2130 (AZ6278 from Milan), Cyprus Airways Trident 1 5B-DAC at 2200 (BE523 from Amsterdam) and East African VC-10 5H-MOG at 2354 (EC736 from Rome).

10th   The last visit of a British Caledonian VC-10 occurred today when G-ASIW diverted in from Gatwick at 0536 (BR810 from Ascension). It was sold to Air Malawi as 7Q-YKH later in the year in November.

11th   Aer Lingus utilised Boeing 707 EI-ASN to operate Amsterdam flight EI602/3.

18th   HS.125 G-BAZA made its first visit today, arriving at 1741 on a flight from Stockholm to Gatwick. Another biz-jet first visit this month was Falcon 20 I-RIF (28th).

20th   KLM flight KL153/4 was operated by DC-8 PH-DCS.

29th   Israeli Air Force Boeing Stratocruiser 4X-FPN overshot around 1600, on a training detail out of Upper Heyford. It had already made two approaches at Prestwick, prior to its ILS approach at Manchester.

30th   German Air Force Transall 51+07 arrived at 1301 as DCN8499, on a training flight from Cologne to Landsberg.

February 1974

British Airways Overseas Division will retire eleven VC-10s by the end of July. All will be sold and it's suggested that some maybe used by an unnamed Manchester based charter operator and others on some of the European Division's longer routes. The decision to retire the VC-10 follows re-examination of the Overseas Division's traffic prospects, which predicts falls between 15%-20%. The European Division will also retire their remaining passenger Vanguards by April.

British Airways will commence once-weekly flights from Manchester to Rome on 7th April, but a new Saturday morning service to Glasgow is on hold, due to continuing fuel restrictions. BOAC Cargo's inbound New York flight (BA066) is down to once-weekly.

Cyprus Airways flights to Nicosia from Manchester (CY358/9) will re-commence on the 6th April.

HS.748 ILS traffic was solitary Hawker-Siddeley example G-BBGY (25th/26th). RAF traffic noted were Andover's XS600 (26th), XS601 (19th) & Britannia XM496 (1st).

1st   Today's first visit of Air Bridge Carriers Argosy G-AZHN, was one of only two visits by the airline this year. The other was Argosy G-APRN on the 28th June.

4th   Another rare visit to Manchester by Airlift International occurred today, when DC-8 N6162A operated an outbound charter to Toronto, which was missed by most due to its unearthly arrival time of 0151!

5th   World Airways B.747F N747WA arrived with ten diesel generators for onward transport to an engineering company in Ludlow, Shropshire, in readiness for the blackouts. Due to the urgency of the cargo, it was flown rather than shipped from Oakland, via New Orleans and New York.

5th   Royal Saudi Air Force C-130E 455 operated from/to Jeddah via Milan as RSF802, before departing on the 7th.

9th   A major uplift of schoolchildren to join a cruise ship at Naples included two flights today by Italian airline SAM, with SE.210 I-DABM (MQ9905) and I-DABV (MQ9907). SE.210 I-DABT (MQ9907) and I-DABZ (MQ9905) were utilised the following day.

11th   Two Seaboard World DC-8s were on the ground at the same time today, after appearing on a dull and grey Monday. They were Heathrow diversions from Shannon, N8632 at 1438 (SB306) and N8641 at 1747 (SB300) and the last visits of any Seaboard DC-8s in their own striking gold-livery.

12th   Today's Canadian Air Force training flight routing through Manchester, was only the second since B.707 13705 arrived on the 17th September 1971. B.707 13701 made its first visit today, arriving at 1412 as CAM720A (Kinloss-Mildenhall) and stayed for twenty minutes.

13th   Noratlas No.166, arriving at 1030 as F-RABV on training flight from RAF Leuchars to Valkenburg, was the first French Air Force Noratlas to visit since December 1972.

13th   Today's arrival of Falcon 20 D-CORF, was one of three biz-jet first visits during the month. The others were Falcon 20 F-BUYI (18th) and Citation 500 HB-VDC (21st).

15th February 1974 – Air Executive Norway Skyvan LN-NPA is shown having just arrived from Kristiansand, operating a late evening freight flight. Built in 1972 and delivered to the airline in July 1973, it operated until 1979, when it was sold to AMA-Flyg as SE-GEX. (Geoff Ball)

16th   TAT Fokker F.27 F-BUTA & Beech 90 F-BTCA night-stopped, after bringing in French Rugby fans. Touraine Air Transport (TAT) was a French regional airline formed in 1968, based at Tours. F-BUTA operated with the airline until 1978, when it was sold to Air Guadeloupe as F-OGIB, but in 1980 it became G-BHMW with Air UK and served them for nearly twenty years.

17th   World Airways B.747F N747WA arrived with a further consignment of diesel generators. The total weight of the cargo, 95 tonnes, broke the record for the heaviest commercial load ever flown into the UK!

19th   Another two Boeing 707s, G-APFB & G-APFF, were transferred from BOAC to British Airtours this year. Boeing 707 G-APFB made its last visit to Manchester today as a BOAC aircraft and G-APFF made its last visit on 1st April 1974.

19th   Martinair DC-9F PH-MAR arrived from Amsterdam at 1456 to operate a freight flight to Monrovia, via Las Palmas.

23rd   SAM SE.210s I-DABL & I-DABZ returned school-children from their winter cruise, as did I-DABT the following day.

25th   Lufthansa B.747F D-ABYE called in en route New York-Frankfurt, to offload 34 tonnes of aluminium. They still hold transatlantic traffic rights between Manchester and the USA, since operating a scheduled cargo service between Chicago and Manchester, which ceased last October.

27th   Today was the third visit of World Airways B.747F N747WA, with another cargo of diesel generators.

March 1974

The construction of a 113 acre freight terminal has been approved by Greater Manchester Council's Planning Committee. The entire site is within the north Cheshire green belt, so a public enquiry will be held on the 14th May. The proposed terminal involves a substantial departure from the plan approved by the Department of the Environment. It would be located between Hasty Lane and Yew Tree Lane, close to the M56 and linked to the airport by a direct road, at an estimated cost of £4m.

The planned growth in air freight means the current hangars would be inadequate, as they can only handle 120,000 tonnes per year, compared to the estimated flow of 400,000 tonnes by 1985.

Lufthansa's commencement of a Manchester-Dusseldorf service from 1st April will increase flights between the two cities to twelve a week (including BEA's current services) and coincide with the termination of the Aer Lingus service to Dusseldorf at the end of the month.

The month saw an increase in RAF liaison flights stopping off at Manchester, en route from London to Belfast, with HS.125 and HS.748 aircraft.

HS.748 ILS traffic identified were Hawker-Siddeley G-BABJ which is destined for the South Korean Air Force (20th/21st) and Tanzanian Govt 5H-MPG (25th/26th). RAF traffic noted were C-130s XV189 (11th) & XV200 (14th); Argosy XR137 (1st), Dominie XS732 (15th), Victor XH672 on a test flight out of Woodford (20th/21st) and Canadian Air Force B.707 13705 (12th).

1st   French Air Force Nord 262 No 83 arrived from Warton, operating under a new French AF call-sign system 'FM'.

2nd   Saturn C-130 N17ST, arriving in a half-white/half-silver colour scheme, brought in two more diesel generators and also PA-24 N5092P which was roaded to Shobdon.

5th   Royal Saudi Air Force C-130E 452 operated from/to Jeddah via Milan as RSF804, before departing on the 9th.

7th   German Air Force Transall 50+77 arrived at 1447 as DCN8663, on a training flight from Southend to Northolt.

8th   Queens Flight Wessex XV732, arriving at 1426 from Lancaster University, was operating a proving flight.

12th   Canadian Air Force B.707 13705 made an ILS approach on a training flight today, but this time it didn't land. Another that nearly made it onto the tarmac was B.707 13703 on the 25th, which would have been a weather diversion from Gatwick.

14th   Sterling SE.210 OY-SBY arrived at 1025 on a charter from Gothenburg as NB2697, before leaving for Le Bourget later in the day.

18th   Another Air France SE.210 leaving the fleet was F-BKGZ, making its final visit to Manchester today, before being sold in September to Royal Air Lao as XW-PNH.

19th   HS.125 G-BBAS, operated by Hawker Siddeley, made its first visit today from Hawarden to Frankfurt and HS.125 G-BACI also made a first visit on the 26th.

21st March 1974 – Aircraft were parking nose-in to the pier by now and this scene includes a number of Heathrow fog diversions: British Caledonian B.707 G-AZJM (BR222), Zambia DC-8 9J-ABR (QZ802) and newly arrived BOAC B.707 G-APFM (BA556 from Chicago). Also parked on Pier B is Manchester's own services VC-10 G-ARVJ (BA538/7) & B.707 G-APFJ (BA648/9). (Geoff Ball)

19th   Rockwell 690 N57057, the current company demonstrator, visited at 1844 on a flight from Dublin, before taking up British registry the following month as G-BCAY.

20th   Queens Flight Wessex XV732 arrived from Eaton Hall, Cheshire, the country house of the Duke of Westminster, with Princess Alexandra who was attending a local engagement.

21st   There had only been one day of bad weather in the south so far this year, but today saw the arrival of twelve diversions between 0743 and 1043 and all but one were from Heathrow. The first arrival, TWA B.747 N93104 at 0743 (TW700 from New York) was also the only first visit. Others included the second visit of Zambia Airways DC-8 9J-ABR at 0945 (QZ802 from Rome) and the last visit of a Swissair CV-990 to Manchester when HB-ICE arrived at 1043 (SR800 from Zurich), as they had disposed of their fleet of eight by 1975, with most being bought by Spanish-airline, Spantax.

22nd March 1974 – HS.748 A2-ABA (left) is seen displaying its super small registration, having arrived from Woodford to clear customs prior to its delivery flight to its new owners, Protea Airways of South Africa. Although the airline's South African, the aircrafts to be based in Botswana for the summer, hence the A2-markings. It returned to its Canadian owners in October this year, under its former registration of C-FINE. 18th April 1974 - Copa Panama HS.748 HP-484 (right) also arrived to clear customs en route to Woodford. (Geoff Ball)

25th   The city's Lord Mayor officially opened the airport's £8.3m extension. The average time from design to completion of a building this size is seven years, but it was completed in a record time of less than five, despite builder's strikes and a shortage of materials. Also, the final cost was close to the original estimate. It's Britain's first drive-in airport, almost double its original size, capable of taking the biggest airliners with loads of up to 400 passengers. It has capacity for 5 million passengers a year and in peak times will be able to cope with 4,000 passengers an hour, a figure equal to the total number using Ringway annually before the Second World War! The extension includes the doubling of the Control Tower administration block, housing departments such as ATC, telecommunications and meteorology/aeronautical information services. A new 13-level multi-storey car park building, a check-in hall with fifty desks, a baggage handling system, immigration and customs hall and an International Arrivals area. A new pier for long-haul passengers, Intercontinental Pier C, is now connected to the terminal building by moving walkways, equipped with air bridges linking directly to the aircraft. It's capable of taking up to four B.747s and one B.707 or VC-10, or seven B.707/VC-10s. The airside frontage of the existing terminal building has been extended outward by 30ft and International Departures now has a transit lounge restaurant, cocktail bar, private dining suite and roof terraces. The old customs hall has been converted into an extension of the main concourse area, giving an additional waiting area and the western half of the booking hall has been adapted as a Domestic baggage claims area. The Domestic and International piers are now known as Pier A and Pier B respectively.

25th   Police marksmen and army bomb disposal experts were called in, after special branch detectives uncovered a suspected IRA bomb plot. The security operation, involving more than 200 police, was ordered after detectives found plans of the new extension, with drawings and maps with comments scribbled on them, during a swoop on an IRA suspect's home. While the security operation was taking place, King Hussein of Jordan arrived unexpectedly at 0941 after his aircraft, Boeing 707 JY-ADP (RJ001 from Washington), diverted into Manchester due to fog at RAF Brize Norton. The King, flying into Britain for a brief visit, remained on the aircraft until security had cleared the way for him and twenty minutes later he was hustled away by detectives and his fifteen bodyguards, to a private suite for refreshments. He stayed for ninety minutes, before leaving for London for talks with his Ambassador.

25th British Airways B.747 G-AWNN diverted in as 'Speedbird 506' from New York, with more than 250 passengers. This too had to wait on the apron, until the security operation was over.

26th A morning diversion from Stansted, Pacific Western B.707 C-FPWJ (PW523 from Montreal), was noted in the airlines new colours. It was registered C- rather than CF-, as Canada has adopted the C- prefix. Another morning arrival was Heathrow diversion TWA B.707F N15713 at 0720 (TW609 from Frankfurt), which was also a first visit.

31st Alidair commenced a six-times-weekly newspaper flight to Kinloss/Lossiemouth.

April 1974

Following an Airport Authority report, it was announced that the ban on house building near the airport had been extended to commercial development. The large area of land to the north of the airport will be kept available for expansion for the next twenty years. It's bounded by the Wilmslow to Altrincham Road, the M56, its airport link and the proposed extension eastwards towards Styal Road and Styal. Assurances were given that in the event of any further expansion, an open space would be left between the airport and the Wythenshawe estate and that preservation of the surrounding greenbelt area would supported. The Planning Committee also recommended opposition to a plan to develop a fifty acre site as a hotel, exhibition centre and office/car parking complex, between Outwood Lane and the M56 link road, close to the airport.

BEA operations at Manchester are in the black for the first time in twenty years. Manchester's Super 1-11 Division made a profit of £593,000 in the financial year up to March 1974, despite a major loss being predicted. It also carried over 875,000 passengers from Ringway, an increase of 12% over the previous twelve months. BEA will also introduce a Manchester-Frankfurt service next year.

The following airlines made changes this month: Aer Lingus terminated their Dusseldorf service on 30th March. Air Malta commenced a once-weekly service from the 7th. British Airways commenced a once-weekly Rome service from 7th, but terminated flights to Antigua/Bridgetown/Port of Spain & Guyana, known as the 'Caribbean Connection', which first operated in 1969. Their Heathrow schedules are operated exclusively by Super 1-11s and no Viscounts are based, although they will operate schedules to Guernsey, Jersey & Isle of Man. Cargo schedules show three-weekly flights to New York, with one via Montreal (BA461) and twice-weekly to Montreal/Detroit (BA469). Merchantman flights are unchanged, two-weekly from/to Amsterdam (BE2023/18), once-weekly from Brussels (BE2037), four-weekly from Dusseldorf (BE2083) and five-weekly from/to Heathrow (BE2282/2102). Cyprus Airways recommenced on the 6th with a weekly flight to Nicosia, via Brussels. KLM flight KL153/4 operates daily with the KL155/6 being dropped. Lufthansa introduced a five-weekly service to Dusseldorf; Frankfurt remains daily but extends to Dublin at weekends and the Frankfurt freight flights operate three-weekly. Sabena maintains a five-weekly cargo service to Brussels. SAS will operate passenger flight SK537/8 three-weekly, with cargo flights increasing to five-weekly during the month. Swissair maintains daily passenger flights to Zurich, while cargo flights operate via Glasgow on the inbound leg, with frequency remaining at four-weekly.

HS.748 ILS traffic observed was sole example Hawker-Siddeley G-BBGY (10th). RAF traffic included the outstanding arrival of Shackleton WL757, inbound to Woodford for attention (17th) and RAE Comet XS235 (22nd).

1st British Airways officially came into full operation today, following the merger between BEA, BEA Airtours, BOAC, Cambrian Airways & Northeast. Since the announcement of the amalgamation in 1972, they've been slow to repaint aircraft in the new corporate colours, with many still operating in a hybrid style of new titles and old colours.

1st British Airways started operating a curious alpha-numeric system on their Manchester-Heathrow flight numbers. For example, BE4058 inbound from Heathrow, would have the number '0' removed and the letter 'L' inserted on the end (BE458L). The return flight, BE4059, would follow the same format but instead of the letter 'L' there would be a 'Y' (BE459Y). However, for whatever reason, the system had been ditched by November.

2nd Royal Saudi Air Force C-130E 1610 operated from/to Jeddah via Milan as RSF806, before departing on the 9th.

7th Air Malta commenced scheduled operations between Manchester and Malta with two Boeing 720s, AP-AMG & AP-AMJ, leased from PIA and AP-AMG operated today's inaugural flight.

8th RAF VC-10 XV107 arrived at 1203 (RR2294 from Gutersloh) on a trooping flight.

8th Amongst the modern jets was this morning's arrival of 1953-vintage DH.Dove G-AMZY, from/to East Midlands. It's been in service since 1959, firstly with Bristol Siddeley Engines and then Rolls-Royce. Sadly it wasn't long for this world, as it was withdrawn from service in July.

11th HS.748 G-BBGY, arriving at 1625 from Woodford, was on delivery to the South Korean Air Force. It departed for Nice in the 13th and eventually became No.1713.

13th Transavia SE.210 PH-TRY, arriving from Cologne at 0301 as HV2960, operated a further flight from Cologne on the 18th.

15th Two Aviaco SE.210s made their last visits to Manchester this month. EC-ATX operated from/to Palma as AO1066/7 today and EC-AXU from/to Palma as AO1068/9 on the 19th. Both were sold in February 1976, to TAC Colombia.

17th French Air Force Falcon 20 No.154 made a brief stop, en route from Prestwick to Villacoublay.

23rd Aer Lingus utilised Boeing 707 EI-ANV to operate Amsterdam flight EI602/3.

25th French Air Force Noratlas No.138/64-BK arrived at 1123 as FM4005, on training flight from RAF Leuchars to Valkenburg.

27th Following the announcement earlier in the year regarding the phasing out of the VC-10, the final scheduled VC-10 operation through Manchester took place today. G-ARVJ operated BA538 0924/1027 (Prestwick-Manchester-Heathrow) and G-ARVH operated BA539 1305/1347 (Heathrow-Manchester-Prestwick) and the last visit details of the rest are as follows:

G-ARVB 25/04/74, Withdrawn from service by 07/74, scrapped at Heathrow in 10/76.
G-ARVC 09/04/74, Sold to Gulf Air 07/74 eventually becoming A4O-VC.
G-ARVE 22/05/74, Withdrawn from service by 10/74, scrapped at Heathrow in 10/76.
G-ARVF 13/04/74, Leased to a private Arab operator 07/74.
G-ARVG 22/04/74, Sold to Gulf Air 07/74 eventually becoming A4O-VG.
G-ARVI 28/01/74, Sold to Gulf Air 03/74 eventually becoming A4O-VI.
G-ARVK 19/07/74, (ILS), Sold to Gulf Air 01/75 eventually becoming A4O-VK.
G-ARVL 11/02/74, Sold to Gulf Air 07/74 eventually becoming A4O-VL.

The remaining three: G-ARVH, G-ARVJ & G-ARVM, continued in service with British Airways.

27th April 1974 – This aerial shot, taken from departing Alidair Viscount G-AVIW, shows three BEA/British Airways BAC 1-11's & BOAC Cargo Boeing 707 G-ASZG operating BA469. It's clear that nose-in parking is yet to be introduced on Pier A, while Pier C is still not in use. (Geoff Ball)

29th   Eight diversions arrived during the morning due to fog, including the final visit of a Qantas B.707, when VH-EAB arrived at 0908 (QF007 from Bombay). The Boeing 707 is gradually being phased out on their London services and replaced with the B.747. All diverted passengers were kept onboard, pending an improvement in the weather. The last to arrive, BAC 1-11 G-AVMR at 1125 (BE619 from Bremen), was due to ATC delays into London. Another Heathrow diversion was TWA B.707 N770TW at 0838 (TW754 from Boston), making its first visit.

May 1974

British Airways Manchester transatlantic flights, BA538/9 & BA648/9, were cancelled from the 8th - 22nd inclusive, due to a cabin crew strike by the Overseas Division.

The following airlines have summer programmes from Manchester: Air Spain, Aviaco, Aviogenex, Balkan, Inex-Adria, JAT, SAM, Spantax & Tarom, as well as a variety of UK operators: BEA, Britannia Airways, British Airtours, British Caledonian, British Island Airways, British Midland, Court Line, Dan-Air & Laker Airways. UK airlines operating USA/Canada flights this summer are British Caledonian (B.707), Dan-Air (B.707) and Laker Airways (DC-10). American airlines operating from/to the USA & Canada were ONA DC-10 N1032F (29th), TWA B.707s N8737 (20th), N18709 (6th/23rd) and World Airways B.747 N748WA (19th).

The only two aircraft noted and identified on the ILS were RAF Dominie XS734 (14th) & RAF Comet XR399 (29th).

2nd   Cessna 206 5Y-ALY, arriving at 2046 from Reykjavik, departed on the 6th to Gatwick on delivery to Kenya. Remarkably another Kenyan registered aircraft visited on the 16th, when Cessna 172 5Y-ATN arrived from Reims and stayed until the 24th.

4th   RAF Britannia XM520, arriving at 2055 (RR6383 from Gutersloh), was on a trooping flight.

7th   Royal Saudi Air Force C-130E 1607 operated from/to Jeddah via Milan as RSF808, before departing on the 9th.

8th   Although SAS SK537/8 has operated with Douglas DC-9s since January 1973; the SE.210 still made the occasional appearance and today saw the very final visit of an SAS SE.210, when SE-DAB operated the flight.

13th   RAF Comet XK659 arrived at 1056 from Wyton, on its final flight and when it taxied to the South Side it was greeted by packs of press! It was eventually dismantled by NEA and then transported to Pomona Dock at Salford on the 13th June, where it became a restaurant and nightclub, joining a ship restaurant 'Westward Ho' already stationed there.

14th May 1974 – Belgian Air Force Douglas DC-6 OT-CDG/KY-4 is seen here having just arrived at Manchester en route Woodford-Brussels as a technical diversion. The Belgian Air Force operated into Manchester using a variety of aircraft between 1974 and1977. (Geoff Ball)

16th   Passengers were finally checking in at the new terminal today, two months after it officially opened. The delay had been caused by teething-trouble with the baggage handling conveyors.

18th   Copa Panama HS.748 HP-484 arrived at 1305 from Reykjavik to clear customs, en route to Woodford. It was purchased by Hawker Siddeley and re-registered as G-AZJH for onward sale to the King of Nepal. In 1977 it was re-registered, again as G-BCDZ, when it was converted into a prototype Coastguarder version.

19th   The second Iberia Boeing 727 to visit was EC-CFB, diverting in at 1506 as IB742 en route Madrid-Dublin, due to a bomb scare.

20th   Sobelair SE.210 OO-SRI arrived at 2106, operating a delayed Court Line flight from Gerona.

24th   Aer Lingus B.737 EI-ASH, leased during the winter to Canadian airline Transair, is back and it operated this evenings Amsterdam flight EI602. It's still in Transair colours with Aer Lingus titling, but as it's due to return to Transair on lease this winter, it was uneconomical to restore it to full Aer Lingus colours.

25th   Hayward's Aviation Dove G-ASDD made the first of many visits during the summer, ferrying crews between Manchester and Gatwick, on behalf of British Airtours and its last visit was the 2nd November.

29th   Monarch Airlines remaining Bristol Britannia, G-AOVT, made its last visit to Manchester today, operating a pilgrimage flight from Tarbes as OM1135. It was withdrawn from service in June 1975 and put on permanent display at RAF Duxford.

29th   Overseas National's second DC-10, N1032F, finally made its first visit to Manchester today, arriving from Gatwick at 1150 to operate a flight to Toronto via Bangor.

29th   Phillips Electronics Fokker F.27 PH-LIP operated a return flight to Eindhoven and again on the 31st.

31st   Five pieces of an engine cowling fell from Dan-Air B.727 G-BAJW, ten minutes after takeoff. It was outbound for Malaga as DA2086, with 115 passengers onboard. One piece, measuring 15ft x 6ft, landed on a golf course near Congleton. ATC informed the pilot and he eventually diverted to Gatwick, where the passengers boarded replacement aircraft, Comet G-AYVS, two hours later.

June 1974

British Airways withdrew their last passenger Vanguards during the month, but the nine Merchantman freighters continued in service. The last visit of a passenger version to Manchester was G-APEN on 1st October 1973. By November 1973, the four passenger aircraft remaining in service: G-APEH, G-APEN, G-APER & G-APEU were rostered to operate just three scheduled flights a week. One to Gibraltar and two to Edinburgh and the rest of the time they were either acting as back-up aircraft for the Trident fleet, or operating charter flights. The final Vanguard passenger service took place on the 16th June, when G-APEU flew a round trip between Heathrow and Jersey. Complete listings, including last visits/fates, are as follows:

G-APEA	08/10/72	Withdrawn 11/72.
G-APEB	30/12/72	Withdrawn 06/73.
G-APEC	16/09/71	Crashed in Ghent, Belgium 02/10/71.
G-APED	08/10/72	Withdrawn 01/73.
G-APEF	21/10/71	Sold to Merpati Nusantara as PK-MVJ in 05/72.
G-APEH	01/08/73	Sold to Merpati Nusantara as PK-MVF.
G-APEI	15/08/73	Sold to Merpati Nusantara as PK-MVG.
G-APEN	01/10/73	Sold to Merpati Nusantara as PK-MVE.
G-APER	27/09/73	Withdrawn by 03/74.
G-APEU	15/07/73	Withdrawn 06/74.

     American airlines operating from/to the USA & Canada were ONA DC-10s N1031F (21st) & N1032F (19th); Pan American B.707s N493PA (6th) & N885PA (16th/17th); TWA B.707s N8729 (3rd), N8731 (10th), N28724 (24th), N28726 (17th) and Wardair B.747 C-FDJC (12th).

     The only aircraft noted and identified on the ILS were RAF Argosies XN814 (14th), XN816 (10th) and XR143 (26th).

1st   Mitsubishi MU-2 EI-AWY arrived from Castlebar at 1823 to night-stop and unusually, it was parked inside the Servisair hangar.

3rd   Aer Lingus B.737 EI-ASK (EI602 from Dublin), has recently returned off lease with United Airlines. It's in full Aer Lingus colours, but with a blue fuselage stripe instead of a green one.

4th   Royal Saudi Air Force C-130E 452 operated from/to Jeddah via Milan as RSF810, before departing on the 6th.

4th   French Air Force Falcon 20 No.238 made a touch-and-go at 1326, en route from Shannon to Villacoublay.

6th   HS.125 HB-VAG, arriving at 1455 from Gatwick, was one of several biz-jets making first visits this month. Others were Falcon 20 I-EDIM (7th), Lear Jet OH-GLB (20th) & Gulfstream 2 N677S (20th).

7th   SAS operated Douglas DC-8Fs SE-DBI & LN-MOC on several of their Copenhagen freight flights during the month, starting with SE-DBI today.

8th   RAF VC-10 XR810 arrived at 1521 (RR2330/1 from/to Hanover).

9th   KLM Douglas DC-8 PH-DCK arrived from Amsterdam to operate a round trip to Hanover.

9th   Aviogenex TU-134 YU-AJD, operating JJ109 from Rijeka with fifty-five passengers onboard, burst four tyres on landing. TU-134 YU-AJA arrived the following morning to take the outbound passengers on the return leg.

17th   Lufthansa Boeing 707F D-ABUA stopped off at Manchester, en route Chicago-Frankfurt as LH471.

17th   Irish-operator Aer Turas have used various types in their short twelve year history. They began with a single Dragon Rapide in 1962, but soon changed their focus from passenger to freight, operating aircraft as diverse as the Bristol 170 and Douglas DC-3s & DC-4s. They then upgraded to Douglas DC-7s, the last of which was written-off this year, but they still operate Douglas DC-4 EI-ARS. After a brief flirtation with an Argosy, they soon realised it was unsuitable for their operation, which brings the story up to date with their latest acquisition - Britannia EI-BAA, arriving at 2248 from Luton.

19th   Air France SE.210 F-BJTM made its last visit to Manchester, operating AF960/1. It was sold to Air Burundi in 1975 as 9U-BTA.

19th   German Air Force Transall 50+68 arrived at 1525 as DCN9201, on a training flight from/to Northolt.

26th   Canadian Air Force routed another training flight through Manchester today. B.707 13703 was the third to visit, operating Prestwick-Mildenhall as CAM720A.

27th   British Airways Jersey flight BE3511/2 was operated by Alidair Viscount G-AVIW.

29th   Today saw four Irish registered light aircraft on the ground at the same time - PA-28 Cherokee's EI-ASV & EI-AWL, AA-5 EI-AYD and PA-39 Twin Comanche EI-AYG.

July 1974

An Airport Consultative Committee was informed that properly equipped aircraft could make automatic landings at Manchester, if it wasn't for the airports infamous hump! The airport's Director, Gordon Sweetapple said the new ILS installed on the main 06/24 runway last month, has proved to be the best in Britain according to the CAA, but automatic landings were not possible because of the runway's hump. The elimination of the hump is one of the reasons the airport wants a second runway. They plan to dig up the present runway, level it and rebuild it with stronger foundations.

American airlines operating from/to the USA & Canada were Air Canada DC-8s C-FTIL (23rd), C-FTIN (29th) & C-FTIS (21st); ONA DC-10s N1031F (19th/26th) & N1032F (10th/31st); Pacific Western B.707 C-FPWV (27th), Pan American B.707s N492PA (22nd), N493PA (21st), N883PA (7th/9th/16th/19th/28th), N897PA (20th) & B.747 N652PA (24th/27th); TWA B.707s N8731 (1st/5th/20th), N28724 (8th/22nd), N28726 (2nd/15th/26th/29th) and Wardair B.747 C-FDJC (3rd/23rd/25th).

HS.748 ILS traffic observed was Hawker-Siddeley G-BABJ (3rd/5th). RAF traffic noted was just Andover XS599 (25th/26th). Other ILS traffic included Dove's G-AREA (10th) & G-ASMG (9th); British Airways Trident 1 G-ARPP (12th) and VC-10 G-ARVK (19th).

1st   German Air Force excelled themselves with three training flights this month. Transall 50+35 arrived at 1201 today as DCN9297 from RAF Bentwaters to Alhorn. Transall 50+48 arrived at 1327 as DCN9299 (RAF Northolt-Alhorn) to night-stop (4th) and Transall 50+92 at 1300 as DCN9355 (Cologne-RAF Northolt) (17th).

1st   Rockwell 685 N9243N spent two nights in the Servisair hangar, before leaving for Oxford on the 3rd for radio work, then flying back to the USA via Stornaway & Keflavik.

2nd   Royal Saudi Air Force C-130E 452 operated from/to Jeddah via Milan as RSF812, before departing on the 4th.

6th   RAF Britannia XL658 arrived today at 1521 (RR6573 Fairford-RAF Akrotiri). Others included RAF Britannia XM489 (RR6571 Leuchars-Fairford-8th), VC-10 XV104 (RR2343 Glasgow-Fairford-11th) and XM518 Britannia (RR6578 Leuchars-Fairford-21st).

6th   A walkout by more than a hundred Air Catering Services staff meant there was no in-flight food, drinks or duty free. They were demanding backdated cost of living increases and the airlines worst affected were British Airways, Dan-Air & Aer Lingus.

10th   An unidentified RAF Canberra was noted carrying out two runs 2000ft over the airport, whilst undertaking an aerial photography mission, using call up sign 'BLP 94'.

12th   British Airways Trident G-ARPP was carrying out Autoland trials. The system was pioneered by BEA and the Trident was designed to have Autoland fitted as standard, so their Trident fleet could land in dense fog. At 2,000ft the Trident locked onto a beam transmitted from the runway, known as the glidepath, which tells the aircraft whether it's to the left or right of the runway and by how much. When the aircraft reaches around 1,000ft, the pilot switches to Autoland and the Trident follows a second beam, which points it at the correct angle to the runway. During this time the controls function automatically, while the pilot monitors the instruments. The landing commences at 65ft and at this point the throttles close. Prior to May 1972 the aircraft's limits in poor weather were 400m RVR, with a 100ft decision height, which would have been categorised as a CAT.2 landing capability. But from May 1972, it was categorised as a CAT.3 aircraft, which meant it could land in an RVR of 75m and with a 0ft decision height. Despite this, weather diversions by Trident's were still commonplace, as many crews were yet to be trained. It should always be remembered that Autoland led the way towards the 'fly by wire' system, now adopted by all modern aircraft, which means that visibility of almost zero would not be a problem, but this would take many years. Trident G-ARPP was specifically testing Autoland for its compatibility with Manchester's ILS system and its effectiveness with the runway's hump.

13th   Cyprus Airways operated their final flight (CY358/9) today with Trident 1 5B-DAE. After many years of tension between Greek and Turkish Cypriots, the situation came to a head on the 20th, when Turkish forces invaded the island and subsequently split it into two autonomous regions. International air services were immediately suspended and of the four Tridents the airline operated, two made it back to the UK to see further service with British Airways, the third was completely destroyed and the fourth was left abandoned at Nicosia Airport, where it remains today still bearing the scars of war! Their last visits to Manchester are as follows:

5B-DAB   29/06   Badly damaged, remains abandoned at Nicosia airport.
5B-DAC   06/07   Damaged, eventually sold to British Airways as G-AVFB.
5B-DAD   01/04   Damaged, sold to British Airways as G-ASWU.
5B-DAE   13/07   Completely destroyed at Nicosia airport on 22/07/74.

14th   Spitfire G-ASJV, arriving at 1707 and operated by the Battle of Britain Memorial Flight, had just participated in the Barton Air Show.

14th   B.707 G-AYVE operating BR3909 to Ottawa today, made the first of several visits this summer, while on lease to British Caledonian until September.

15th   HS.125 D-CJET made its first visit, arriving for customs clearance today, en route to Hawarden for maintenance. It routed through Manchester again on the 19th for the same reason, prior to its return to Germany.

19th   HS.748 G-BCDM arrived at 1209 from Woodford, with Dove G-ARHW not far behind to take the crew back to Woodford. The HS.748 finally departed for Ajaccio on the 26th for delivery to the Indonesian-airline, Bouraq, where it eventually became PK-KHL.

20th   Polish national airline LOT had not appeared at Manchester for many years, but they operated a charter from/to Warsaw today, with first time visitor Ilyushin IL-18 SP-LSF (LO1563/4). The same aircraft also operated the return flight on the 10th August (LO1565/6).

22nd   HS.125 F-BSSL arrived for customs clearance, en route to Hawarden for maintenance and again on the 25th for the same reason, prior to its return to base at Le-Bourget.

23rd   British Airways Trident 1 G-ARPM diverted into Manchester with a suspected bomb and eighty-six passengers onboard, including the RUC's Chief Constable. On touch-down, it was met by the emergency services and evacuated via the chutes. The bomb, wrapped in brown paper, was found under a rear passenger seat by a British Airways employee, even though nothing had been found during the routine search prior to takeoff! It's understood that the bomb was primed to explode once the jet had levelled at around 20,000ft.

24th   Forty-eight passengers were taken off a British Airways 1-11 bound for Belfast after another bomb scare, but this one turned out to be a hoax.

24th   Pan American had operated numerous charters to the USA so far this year, but today was the first time they used a Boeing 747, when N652PA positioned in from Heathrow at 1723, before departing at 1850 for New York.

26th   Transvalair CL-44 HB-IEN positioned in from Jeddah to operate an outbound freight charter to Tripoli, on behalf of Fairey.

26th July 1974 – This shot perfectly illustrates the popularity of Manchester Airport with the general public and aviation enthusiasts alike. Many make the trip to watch aircraft from some of the best airport spotting facilities around. This Friday evening's photograph shows RAF HS.748 XS794 calling in at Manchester to clear customs, operating a flight from Northolt to Edinburgh as 'Ascot 1739'. (Geoff Ball)

28th   Leased British Caledonian B.707 G-BAWP paid its last visit to Manchester today, operating outbound to Montreal as BR2845, before returning to Aer Lingus as EI-ASO.

August 1974

Due to steep oil prices, the state of the economy, three-day-week and loss of consumer purchasing power, the IT market has dropped considerably this year. By mid-month some tour companies were in a critical state, culminating in the collapse of Clarkson's and its parent airline Court Line on the 15th. When the airline fell, they had been operating eighteen IT flights a week from Manchester, to thirteen destinations.

The airport recorded 172,000 fewer passengers between January and July, compared with the same period last year. The 11% decrease was in contrast to the freight figures, which had increased by 6%.

Pensioners will now be given free admission to the spectator terraces, except for Sundays and Bank Holidays from 1200-2000, when the normal charge of 10p will apply.

American airlines operating from/to the USA & Canada were Air Canada DC-8s C-FTIL (11th), C-FTIR (28th) & C-FTJU (25th); ONA DC-10 N1031F (21st/23rd), Pan American B.707s N408PA (28th), N419PA (7th), N426PA (9th/10th), N491PA (23rd), N492PA (21st), N493PA (6th/10th), N881PA (17th/21st), N883PA (27th), N897PA (10th) & B.747 N733PA (17th); TWA B.707s N8729 (3rd/5th/23rd/27th), N8731 (20th), N28724 (21st), N28726 (2nd/9th) & N28728 (12th/16th); World Airways DC-8 N801WA (10th) and Wardair B.747 C-FDJC (13th/14th). Pan American put in an astonishing performance with thirteen flights this month, operated by ten different aircraft, including a Boeing 747 and four Boeing 707s making their first visits!

The only ILS traffic noted was RAF Dominie XS730 (8th) and RAF Victor XL193 (27th).

3rd Aeroflot TU-104 CCCP-42403 arrived at 0953 to take passengers to Manchester's newly twinned city, Leningrad. The return flight took place on the 17th, with TU-104 CCCP-42456.

5th RAF trooping flights were numerous again this month. XV105 VC-10 (RR2400 from/to Hanover) & (RR2401 Hanover-Brize Norton) operated today; XV105 VC-10 (RR2402 Brize Norton-Gutersloh) on the 6th, Britannia's XL635 (RR6730 from/to Gutersloh) & XL659 (RR6731 Hanover-Brize Norton) on the 7th and VC-10s XV101 (RR2413 Brize Norton-Hanover) & XR806 (RR2411/2 Dusseldorf-Hanover) on the 23rd.

6th Royal Saudi Air Force C-130E 1611 operated from/to Jeddah via Milan as RSF814, before departing on the 8th.

7th French Air Force Falcon 20 No.238 made a touch-and-go at 1728, en route from Shannon to Villacoublay.

8th Donaldson International ceased trading today, after being in business since 1968. Their existing four Boeing 707s: G-AYXR, G-AYVG, G-AZWA & G-BAEL, were repossessed and flown out to Miami. G-BAEL was the final aircraft to visit Manchester on the 23rd July.

10th The only World Airways Douglas DC-8 to visit Manchester this year was today, when N801WA called in en route Chicago-Geneva.

11th Invicta Airlines new Vanguard, G-BAFK, made the first of two visits this year, operating from/to Tarbes as IM960/1.

12th RAF Devon VP952, based at RAF Northolt with 21 Squadron, arrived from Northolt to operate a return trip to RAF Leconfield.

14th Coventry-based Rockwell 690 N57091 made the first of numerous visits today, arriving to operate a return flight to Hamburg. It remained American-registered until late 1976, when it finally took up British marks and became G-BEJN.

15th The second airline to fail within seven days, but with considerably more backlash, was Court Line, who ceased trading today. Shortly before last year's oil crisis they took delivery of two brand new Lockheed L.1011 Tristars, believing the current trend of soaring package holiday sales would continue. They had also recently bought two major UK tour operators, Clarkson's and Horizon to help consolidate their business, but it had the opposite effect! The airline was under great financial strain after buying high priced oil in advance and acquiring tour operators who ended up struggling for survival. With thousands of holidays unsold, the airline and their tour operators went into liquidation and as a result, large numbers of holidaymakers stranded overseas had to finance their own way home. To prevent this from happening again, ABTA, the Association of British Travel Agents, introduced a bonded-scheme to protect customers against failed tour operators and guarantee their money back or travel home. The final Court Line flight into Manchester was pink BAC 1-11 G-AXMF (OU682 from Malta). It was impounded on arrival, but eventually positioned out to Bournemouth on the 29th.

16th HS.125 G-AVPE made its first visit to Manchester, arriving at 2053 from Bristol-Filton. Delivered new to BAC in 1967, it operated for them until 1989.

16th French Air Force Nord 262 56/312-GE arrived at Manchester as F-TEBK for customs clearance. It was providing support for the French display team, Patrouille Magisters, taking part in the Woodford Air Show. Incidentally the Magisters arrived at Woodford via Lyneham, where they cleared customs using the call-sign F-TFVK.

18th Italian operator Aeropa made their first visit today when B.707 N716HH arrived at 0112 (VZ1602 from Rimini), with stranded Court Line passengers.

18th Aviaco SE.210 EC-ARI made its last visit to Manchester today, operating AO1212/1605 Mahon-Malaga & AO1604/1213 Malaga-Mahon. It was withdrawn from service in January 1977.

21st Cessna 340 N69449 was carrying out demonstration flights.

21st USAF VT-39 Sabreliner 61-0667 called in for fuel whilst on a training mission, en route Stuttgart-Mildenhall.

17th August 1974 – Aeroflot Tupolev TU-104 CCCP-41419 is seen here arriving on stand, operating as SU42419 from Leningrad. In those days they used their registration as the ATC flight identifier and this aircraft was the last of three Aeroflot TU-104s to visit Manchester. (Geoff Ball)

21st   The German Air Force returned to sanity this month, after going mad with three training flights last month! Transall 50+67 arrived at 1341 today (DCN9503 Cologne-Northolt).

22nd   Aeropa operated a second flight from Manchester within a week when their second B.707, I-SAVA, positioned up from Luton today to operate Dan-Air flight DA2709 to Malta, due to an unserviceable Boeing 727. Unfortunately, on its return it also went tech and ended up staying for a further thirty-three hours before springing to life again!

23rd   Overseas National DC-10 N1031F made the airlines final transatlantic charter visit to Manchester, inbound from Los Angeles, following the announcement they were ceasing ABC flights. This particular aircraft was involved in a fatal crash in January 1976.

25th   The Blue Eagles display team called in en route from Mottram Hall, Cheshire to Nottingham and again on the 31st from Wigan to Birmingham. The team, belonging to the Army Air Corps, consists of five Sioux helicopters.

25th   Philippine Air Transport C-130 RP-C97, arriving on a cargo flight routing Gander-Shannon, was observed to be operating with a very young crew!

26th   Cessna 172 N1423V arrived at 2037 on a delivery flight from Reykjavik to Biggin Hill.

September 1974

The airport experienced a 12% drop in passengers for the first eight months of the year, compared with the same period last year. The biggest fall was a 22% decrease in the IT market, mainly due to the collapse of Clarkson's.

Work in progress at the north east end of the main runway means that approaches to Runway 24 are localiser only, with no glidepath; which would account for there being just one ILS visitor this month, when RAF Dominie XS712 appeared on the 26th.

British Airway's new Manchester-Rome service has been so successful; it's to continue through the winter. The Alidair newspaper flights to Kinloss/Lossiemouth that started in March continue with the same two Viscounts, G-AVIW & G-AVJL. SAS continue using Douglas DC-8s, their two Douglas DC-9s and even a couple of Fred Olsen Electra's on their cargo flights.

American airlines operating from/to the USA & Canada were Air Canada DC-8 C-FTIP (15th), Pan American B.707s N408PA (17th/28th/29th), N419PA (8th), N491PA (11th/17th), N492PA (10th), N880PA (4th), N883PA (25th) & N885PA (7th); TWA B.707s N8731 (2nd/6th/23rd), N18709 (24th), N28726 (16th), N28728 (8th/10th/16th/30th) and Wardair B.747 C-FDJC (3rd/24th). Pan American gave another impressive performance this month with ten flights, seven aircraft and one first visit (N880PA)!

2nd   RAF trooping flights were plentiful this month, with VC-10 XV101 (RR2474 Brize Norton-Hanover-today), RAF VC-10 XR806 (RR2475 Brize Norton-Gutersloh-4th); Britannia XM496 (RR6353 Gutersloh-Brize Norton-5th) and VC-10 XV107 (RR2483 Brize Norton-Hanover -21st).

3ʳᵈ   Royal Saudi Air Force C-130E 1607 operated from Lyneham to Jeddah via Milan as RSF816, before departing on the 5ᵗʰ.

3ʳᵈ   Lear Jet EC-CJA was the first Spanish-registered biz-jet to visit Manchester, arriving at 1115 from Gerona.

4ᵗʰ   PA-34 Seneca PH-NAZ arrived from Brough at 1034, having declared a full emergency with throttle cable trouble.

10ᵗʰ   Dublin based Lear Jet G-BBEE made its first visit today. Owned by Irish paper and packaging company, Jefferson Smurfit, it's the first of its type onto the British register.

12ᵗʰ   German Air Force Transall 50+69 arrived at 1859 (DCN5069 flight from/to Wunsdorf). Unusually it was using its serial as its call-sign, rather than a random flight number.

15ᵗʰ   Transavia SE.210s, PH-TRY & PH-TRU, arrived from Amsterdam to cover Dan-Air flight DA2309/10 to/from Naples, after the B.727 went tech.

16ᵗʰ September 1974 - British Midland was mainly involved in leasing out Boeing 707s to third-world operators, having left the fiercely competitive IT and transatlantic market completely by 1973. B.707 G-AYBJ is seen here operating a charter for British Caledonian. Also of note is the ex-Fairey Dakota, G-AHCT, rotting away in the background! (Geoff Ball)

18ᵗʰ   The last of three Lear Jet's making their first visits was SE-DFA, calling in for customs clearance at 0715, en route to Humberside. It returned the following day, again to clear customs, before departing for Amsterdam.

18ᵗʰ   German Air Force Transall 50+50 arrived at 1633 as DCN9681, on another training flight. It was a last minute substitution, as the aircraft originally planned was 50+88.

19ᵗʰ   Cessna 172 G-AYAO, routing from/to Cranfield, was notable for having a STOL conversion (short takeoff and landing).

21ˢᵗ   Stellair FH.227 LN-KAA, the stretched version of the Fokker F.27, was taking an outbound load of fifty passengers to Billund. It was a first visit of type and of the airline.

25ᵗʰ   Mitsubishi MU-2 SE-GHX arrived from Barrow at 1751 to clear customs. It continued onwards to Karlstad, which claims to be the sunniest city in Sweden.

26ᵗʰ   British Caledonian B.707 G-AWTK (BR2920 from Vancouver as BR2920) paid its last visit as such today. Although it remained with the airline, it was re-registered as G-BDCN.

27ᵗʰ   Single Heathrow diversion this morning was British Airways B.707 G-APFJ, arriving with the curious call-sign - 'Speedbird Malaysian 894'.

28ᵗʰ   Tarom produced a first visit of type today, when IL-62 YR-IRA arrived on the last charter of their summer programme. Although the type was scheduled to operate a Saturday service throughout the summer, it was almost exclusively operated by a Boeing 707. The Ilyushin IL-62 was another Russian airliner loosely based on another western type, this time the VC-10. It first flew in 1963 and entered service with state-airline Aeroflot in 1967. Tarom ordered two of these aircraft, YR-IRA & YR-IRB, which were delivered in April last year.

29ᵗʰ   Cessna 310 4X-CAE was the first visit of an Israeli registered light aircraft. It arrived from Gatwick at 1737 and departed to Amsterdam on the 1ˢᵗ October.

29ᵗʰ   The first of BOAC's original batch of sixteen Boeing 707s delivered in 1960, had been withdrawn by the end of the year. G-APFH, having been transferred to BEA Airtours in 1971, made its last visit arriving at 2204 (BE9223 from Ibiza), before later positioning to Gatwick. It was eventually sold in the USA in 1975 and ultimately broken up. Its final flight was Heathrow-Tucson on 11th May 1975, carrying 5 tonnes of spares and a spare engine.

October 1974

The full length of the runway was available from mid-month, but remedial work on the 24 glidepath was still in progress. Once completed, the ILS will need to be flight checked, so until then if the cloud base falls below 600ft, approaches must use the 06ILS as the only aid available on Runway 24 is an SRA approach (Surveillance Radar Approach), which terminates at 2-nautical miles, when the aircraft is at 600ft and from then on its up to the pilot to do the rest!

A new twice-daily weekday service linking Manchester, Birmingham & Aberdeen will be launched by British Airways next month. It's in response to the demand from business and industry in the North and the Midlands following the development of North Sea oil projects. Initially, Birmingham and Manchester will share the traffic, but separate services may be introduced later.

ILS traffic noted and identified were RAF Andover XS644 (17th), Israeli Air Force Boeing 707 4X-JYA (21st) and Royal Navy Canberra WK142 (22nd).

1st   HS.125 G-BAYT brought the Prime Minister, Harold Wilson in for a flying visit!

1st   Dan-Air Comet G-APMF made its last visit to Manchester, arriving at 1826 (DA8436 from Cologne), before positioning out to Birmingham at 1908. It was withdrawn in November, having only been in service with the airline for eighteen months.

1st   RAF Trooping flights during the month were Britannia XM489 RR6520 Brize Norton-Gutersloh today and VC-10 XV103 RR2616 Hanover-Brize Norton on the 5th.

2nd   The first aircraft to visit in out of sequence marks was JC Bamford's new executive aircraft, HS.125 G-BJCB, operating to Copenhagen before its return on the 4th.

3rd   Dan-Air flights DA114 & DA115, were operated by Alidair Viscount G-AVIW.

4th   Making a quick visit to Fairey from RAF Benson was the company's Islander, G-BCJY, which is Britten-Norman's long-nose demonstrator.

5th   JAT's Saturday service from/to Dubrovnik has been operated by a variety of aircraft this summer: SE.210 Caravelle's, Douglas DC-9s & Boeing 707s, but from the 17th August it's been operated exclusively by SE.210s. The last flight of the season was today, when YU-AHB visited Manchester for the last time and was also the last visit of any JAT SE.210.

8th   Royal Saudi Air Force C-130E 453 operated from RAF Lyneham to Jeddah via Milan as RSF818, before departing on the 10th.

10th   German Air Force Transall 50+79 arrived at 1543 as DCN9797 (Lyneham-Bonn).

17th   RAF Andover XS644 was noted in a new colour scheme of green and grey camouflage, as it performed ILS approaches on Runway 06.

18th   The second Dan-Air Comet to be withdrawn this year was G-APMD. It made its last visit today, arriving at 0140 (DA4822 from Malta), before departing at 2255 (DA2745 to Athens). It had been withdrawn from service by January 1975.

18th   PA-28 Cherokee EI-ASV arrived at 1535 from Dublin for an extensive overhaul with NEA, before finally departing on the 10th December.

21st   Having used the Noratlas & Stratocruiser on training flights, the Israeli Air Force are using Boeing 707s and today, 4X-JYA overshot on a flight from RAF Mildenhall to Furstenfeldbruck, Germany. It was seen using Runway 06 in a colour scheme of green/blue tail with a white circle and emblem, white roof and a green/blue cheatline.

21st   Wardair B.707 C-FFAN (WD501 from Vancouver), was the only visit this year by one of the airlines B.707s.

22nd   Royal Navy Canberra WK142 overshot today as Tarnish 09, on a test flight out of Salmesbury. Also today, Royal Navy Sea Devon XJ324 arrived at 1657 from Yeovilton, with a Vice Admiral onboard.

23rd   Maersk Fokker F.27 OY-APD arrived at 2155 to transport car parts to Gothenburg, on behalf of SAAB.

23rd   British Airways VC-10 G-ARVJ appeared on a crew training flight from/to Heathrow.

24th Bergen Air Transport DC-4F LN-MOJ positioned in from Ostend to operate another outbound flight transporting car parts to Gothenburg, on behalf of SAAB.

24th SAS returned to Douglas DC-9 operations on their cargo flights this month, apart from a couple of times when Fred Olsen Electra's were used. LN-FOI operated today and LN-FOG on the 31st.

26th Three Heathrow flights called into Manchester due to an ESSO fuel strike at Heathrow, so technically they were diversions: British Airways BAC 1-11 G-AVMJ at 1206 (BE616 Heathrow-Berlin), Trident 1 G-ARPN at 1502 (BE6536 Heathrow-Belfast) and Pan American B.747 N656PA at 1241 (PA101 Heathrow-New York).

27th Loganair Trislander G-BAXD called in for a fuel stop, en route Norwich-Glasgow. The type, based on the successful Britten-Norman Islander, has a third engine through the tail and a longer fuselage. It was delivered new to the airline in April 1973.

November 1974

Bad weather at this time of year normally produces a quantity of unexpected airliners, but this month there were just two Heathrow weather diversions. Rain, wind and mild temperatures were the overall trend, but fog affecting Manchester caused Swissair SR840 to divert to Liverpool three times in six days (17th, 18th & 22nd).

Ongoing work on the 24 glidepath proved problematic for the CAA this month, when several flight-checks were carried out.

In addition to disposing of their surplus VC-10s, British Airways has begun the withdrawal of some of their Trident 1s, starting with G-ARPU. Delivered new in August 1965, it made its last visit on 19th February this year, operating Heathrow flight BE4084/7.

The following airlines made changes this month: British Airways commenced a twice weekday service to Aberdeen with Viscounts. Apart from a night-stopping Trident (BE4086/4053), all other Heathrow flights are operated by Super 1-11s and Jersey flights now operate with a Jersey based aircraft. Transatlantic passenger flights remain daily to New York (BA538/9) & Montreal/Toronto (BA648/9) with Boeing 707s. Cargo services show a once-weekly inbound flight from New York (BA468) with outbounds twice-weekly to New York (BA469) and once-weekly to Boston (BA479), operating via Montreal. KLM flight KL153/4 operates Monday-Saturday with lunchtime flight KL155/6 on Sundays and cargo flights three-weekly. Lufthansa Frankfurt passenger flight LH074/5 now operates via Dusseldorf, the separate flights have been dropped and the Frankfurt freight flight (LH4072/3) operates five-weekly. Sabena operates a four-weekly cargo service to Brussels. SAS operates passenger flight SK537/8 three-weekly and cargo flights increased to five-weekly during the month. Swissair maintain their daily passenger flights to Zurich (SR840/1) and cargo flights operate via Glasgow on the outbound leg with frequency remaining at four-weekly. Winter IT flights are operated by Britannia Airways, British Airways, British Caledonian, Dan-Air & Laker Airways, who also have weekly ABC flights to New York and Toronto.

The only ILS traffic noted and identified was RAF Andover XS600 (27th).

1st RAF Trooping flights have been numerous: VC-10 XR810 (RR2651 from/to Gutersloh-5th) and the following Britannia's all from Gutersloh: XL660 (RR6661-today), XL660 (RR6668-21st), XM491 (RR6669-22nd), XM491 (RR6670-23rd), XM517 (RR6671-26th), XM517 (RR6672-27th) and XL637 (RR667529th).

1st The new Domestic passenger baggage reclaim hall was opened today. Converted from the former check-in area, it was the final major stage of the development scheme.

1st Three more fuel diversions were British Airways Trident's G-ARPO at 1754 (BA6554 Heathrow-Belfast) & G-ARPG at 1822 (BE5056 Heathrow-Glasgow) and first visit Pan American B.707 N896PA at 2047 (Heathrow-Atlanta).

1st Air Spain began irregular operations from Manchester in the 1960's with Britannia's and became regular operators in 1972, with Douglas DC-8s. 1974 was particularly hard for the airline, when rising fuel prices and the soaring cost of living resulted in consumers taking fewer holidays than the year before. These factors severely cut into their operating costs and they ceased operations on 30th January 1975. They flew their final flight from Manchester today, with Douglas DC-8 EC-CAD operating JA134/5 from/to Palma, arriving 2131 and departing 2258. For the record their final visits to Manchester are detailed below:

EC-BXR   13/10/74   Withdrawn 01/75, sold as N48CA in 1976.
EC-BZQ   03/12/73   Sold as N8605 in 02/74.
EC-CAM   12/10/74   Withdrawn 01/75, sold as N8606 in 1976.
EC-CAD   01/11/74   Withdrawn 01/75, sold as N8602 in 1976.
EC-CDA   19/10/74   Withdrawn 01/75, sold as N8608 in 1976.
EC-CDB   29/09/74   Withdrawn 01/75, sold as N8603 in 1976.

5th   Today's visit of British Airways L.1011 G-BBAE, was the first of an extensive crew training programme with the new type. It was also the first visit of a L.1011 Tristar, since the inaugural flight by G-BAAA in March 1973.

5th   TIA Douglas DC-8 N4865T arrived 0703 (TV865 from Gander), before departing for Frankfurt. The next day saw the first visit of one of their new Douglas DC-10s, N102TV (Nice-Shannon and a second DC-10, N103TV (Miami-Malaga), also called in on the 16th.

5th   Royal Saudi Air Force C-130E 1610 operated from RAF Lyneham to Jeddah via Milan as RSF820, before departing on the 7th.

5th   Balair Douglas DC-6 HB-IBS, now an all-freight aircraft, operated a flight from Basle at 1049, before departing the following morning to Belfast.

6th   BAF Carvair G-AXAI, operating a cargo flight from/to Belfast, was the first Carvair to visit since 18th July 1971.

9th   Air Charter's B.727 F-BPJV & SE.210 F-BJTG brought school-children in from Nice. The flight was originally planned for an A.300, but too many passengers put paid to that!

9th   Sabena Cessna 310s have been regular visitors to Manchester on crew training flights since their first visits in 1971. OO-SEE arrived at lunchtime today routing Gatwick-Brussels and Cessna 310 OO-SED, arriving from Birmingham at 1247 on the 19th, made a full emergency landing with loss of oil in the starboard engine.

12th   Bergen Air Transport's Douglas DC-4s, LN-MOB & LN-MOJ, made frequent visits to Manchester this month, transporting car components to Gothenburg on behalf of SAAB. LN-MOB operated 13th/15th/26th/27th/28th/29th and LN-MOJ on the 19th/20th/21st.

14th   Air Freight Douglas DC-3, arriving at 1453 from Lydd, was also involved in shipping car parts to Gothenburg.

21st   German Air Force Transall 50+88 arrived at 1206 as DCN9899, on a training flight from Cologne to Northolt.

22nd   The month was very lean for weather diversions and the only two from Heathrow arrived this morning: East African Airways VC-10 5X-UVJ at 0944 (EC644 from Frankfurt) and British Airways SVC-10 G-ASGD at 0952 (BA128 from Bermuda).

25th   Flights from Manchester to Ireland returned to normal today, after a 48-hour protest ban by porters over the Birmingham bombings.

28th   The only biz-jet making its first visit this month was G-BCII, operating from Coventry to Frankfurt. It was also the first Citation 500 on the British register.

29th   For eleven minutes during the evening, a Tristar and a DC-10 could be seen on the ground simultaneously. L.1011 G-BBAE was on a crew training flight and Laker DC-10 G-BBSZ was operating an outbound flight to Toronto.

December 1974

Car parking, meals, drinks and other items are to rise following the drop in revenue caused by a slump in passenger numbers. A new 50p passenger tax will be introduced on domestic flights, the current 50p surcharge on international flights will be doubled and aircraft landing fees will also go up. Multi-storey parking for 24-hours will increase from 78p to 90p; the daily charge from 39p to 60p and the thirty minutes free-parking on the perimeter will be replaced with a 10p charge.

Rebates could be offered to airlines operating newer and quieter aircraft, such as the L.1011 Tristar, DC-10 & Airbus A.300. Manchester is in favour of the scheme, but it's not been welcomed by some of the other airports and as yet, no firm decision's been made on the matter. Meanwhile work on sound-proofing 1,500 homes in the airport's vicinity is well under way, which includes double glazing, sound deadening doors and roof insulation. A public enquiry into the proposed second runway will be held towards the end of next summer and it could be another year after that when the Government makes its decision.

December 1974 was remarkable for its unusually mild weather and as a result, Manchester received just one weather diversion! Ironically it was Manchester's own New York BA538, operated by B.707 G-APFP that overflew Prestwick straight to Manchester. The second irony is that it was diverting away from an airport that's rarely affected by bad weather!

The only aircraft using the ILS for training was RAF Britannia XN392 (20th), as both the 24ILS and the 06ILS were unavailable from the 11th to 20th inclusive. Crew training flights were dominated by British Airways L.1011 Tristar G-BBAE on 3rd/4th/5th/16th/18th/19th/30th & 31st.

3rd   Royal Saudi Air Force C-130E 1610 operated from RAF Lyneham to Jeddah via Milan as RSF822, before departing on the 5th.

4th   RAF Trooping flights were Britannia's XL636 RR6732 Hanover-Brize Norton today, XL635 RR6476 Brize Norton-Hanover (29th) and VC-10 XR806 RR2706/7 from/to Hanover (30th).

10th   The morning produced another Gulfstream 2, when N7789 arrived at 0831 from Brussels. Although it was the fourth different aircraft to visit this year, it had been in before.

13th   Aer Lingus operated Boeing 707 EI-ANV on today's Amsterdam flight EI602/3.

16th   Pan American B.747 N653PA arrived at 1531 to operate an outbound charter to New York. It was deputising for a Boeing 707 that had been damaged at Heathrow the week before and was showing the scars to prove it!

17th   BAF Carvair G-ASKN arrived from Southend to operate another car parts flight on behalf of SAAB.

18th   German Air Force Transall 50+17 arrived at 1222 as DCN8044, on a training flight from Cologne to Northolt.

21st   British Airways' Montreal/Toronto flight BA648/9 was terminated at Prestwick, so Scottish-based Viscounts, G-AMOG & AMON, ferried passengers from/to Prestwick.

22nd   Braathens F.27 LN-SUL, a seaman's charter from Bergen, night-stopped before departing to Stavanger the next day.

22nd   LOT operated a Christmas charter from/to Warsaw, with first time visitor Ilyushin IL-18 SP-LSC (LO2141/2). It also operated the return flight on 5th January (LO2147/8).

27th   In a slow month with regards to news concerning Manchester, a devastating cyclone hit the Darwin region of Australia. An evacuation took place and incredibly a Boeing 747, with a normal configuration of 333 economy and 32 first-class, carried 674 passengers and 23 crew on the six-hour flight from Darwin to Sydney! The extra passengers were accommodated by strapping five people into three seats and sitting children on the laps of able bodied adults.

First/Last Arrivals & Departures 1974

First arrival: B.720 G-AZFB/OM089 from Monastir at 00.54 (diversion)
First departure: BAC 1-11 G-AVMP/BE4057 to Heathrow at 08.05
Last arrival: BAC 1-11 G-AVMU/BE845 from Dublin at 21.30
Last departure: L.1011 G-BBAE to Prestwick at 21.45

(+/- % on Previous Year)		
Scheduled Passengers	1,361,000	-0.8%
I.T/Charter Passengers	958,000	-21.2%
Transit Passengers	99,000	-29.8%
Total	2,418,000	-11.4%
Freight & Mail (Tonnes)	46,300	+2.2%
Movements	65,100	-2.2%

Airport Diary 1975

January 1975

The final figures for 1974 made grim reading. Scheduled passengers were stagnant, transit passengers were down and alarmingly, package holiday sales were down 21% on 1973. The economic situation and collapse of Court Line were two major contributing factors.

British Airways continued its L.1011 Tristar crew training programme, using the three aircraft delivered so far, which are currently based at Prestwick due to a boycott of the plane by BA engineers and ground staff at Heathrow. Details of their Manchester training flights are as follows:

G-BBAE (2nd/3rd/6th/7th/8th/9th/10th/15th/17th/25th/26th)
G-BBAF (4th/5th/11th/16th/19th/20th/21st/22nd/23rd/27th/28th/29th/30th/31st)
G-BBAG (26th/27th/28th/29th/31st)

Runway 24ILS was fully available from 9th January, after being unserviceable since 2nd September last year. The only HS.748 observed on the ILS was Brazilian Air Force C91-2507 (21st/29th). RAF traffic noted and identified were Dominie XS732 (23rd) and Nimrod XZ280 (31st).

2nd Bristow's Whirlwind G-AODA arrived at Manchester Docks from Trinidad over the New Year as 9Y-TDA. After being unloaded from the ship, its British marks were applied to the doors with tape and the 9Y- registration was masked out. It was then transported to Manchester to night-stop, before flying on to Bristow's HQ at Redhill.

6th Falcon 20 F-BTCY arrived on a hospital flight from Oran, Algeria.

7th British Airways 1-11 G-AVMP/BE4069 was hijacked bound for Heathrow and the timetable of events was as follows:

1410 BE4069/G-AVMP departed Manchester with forty-six passengers and five crew.

1440 BE4069/G-AVMP arrived at Heathrow, but during the flight a hijacker had taken control of the plane, armed with a pistol and explosive canister. He demanded to be flown to Paris, or he would blow up the plane. Negotiations took place at Heathrow, after the hijacker allowed the aircraft to land to refuel. He continued with his demand to be flown to Paris-Orly, but the French authorities refused permission. He then demanded £100,000 and a parachute and threatened to blow up the plane if his demands weren't met, giving a deadline of 1730.

1600 The aircraft was refuelled.

1730 The hijacker extended his deadline to 1800.

1800 The deadline passed and the hijacker gave a further extension of fifteen minutes.

1814 A parachute was brought to the aircraft.

1815 The deadline passed yet again and the hijacker was still at the back of the plane, holding a stewardess as hostage and clutching a grenade to his chest.

1900 The pilot contacted ATC to advise he couldn't stall the hijacker much longer.

2030 The Metropolitan Police Commissioner arrived at Heathrow to take charge.

2200 The ransom money was taken onboard.

2217 G-AVMP departed Heathrow, with the hijacker unaware of the plan to fly over the English Channel, before returning north and landing at Stansted, to be met by a group of Metropolitan police officers, flown in from Heathrow to join up with the Essex force.

2330 BE4069/G-AVMP landed at Stansted. The terminal's lighting had been reduced and the signs blanked out, but the hijacker sensed it was a trick and tried to make a getaway down the aircraft steps onto the tarmac with his hostage, but he was soon overpowered. It was later discovered the pistol was a replica and the canister was harmless.

Conclusion: Several days later the airport was cleared of any blame, after the Trade Secretary arrived at Manchester to discuss development and security with airport's managers, council officials and union leaders. Afterwards he confirmed the airport had conformed to the rules laid down for such events and that no blame could be attached to the airport.

7th Lufthansa used three Boeing 727s: D-ABRI (7th), D-ABLI (10th) & D-ABIG (12th) on their Frankfurt service LH072/3 this month, due to the annual Frankfurt Trade Fair.

7th Royal Saudi Air Force C-130E 1612 operated from/to Jeddah via Milan as RSF801, before departing on the 9th.

12th   British Airways introduced a 'no reservations walk-on' shuttle service between Heathrow and Glasgow, using a fleet of Trident 1Cs modified to a 100-seat layout. It's the first type of service in Europe to offer a guaranteed seat!

14th   British-based Beech 90 N14CP operated by the footwear company Scholl, made the first of numerous visits throughout the 1970's, arriving at 1354 from Glasgow.

15th   USAF Convair VT-29 60-33468, arrived at 1233 as 'Clue 94E' from Bristol-Filton to Stuttgart. Delivered new to the United States Air Force in 1954, it was withdrawn in May.

23rd   French Air Force Falcon 20 No.238 was unusual as it stayed on the ground for an hour, rather than performing the usual touch-and-go training detail.

23rd   Icelandair Boeing 727 TF-FIE called in at 2119 for fuel, en route Las Palmas-Keflavik.

28th   Boeing 707F D-ABUE (LH4072 from Frankfurt), was making its first visit.

30th   Preston Radar & Airways closed today and was replaced by Manchester Control. The radar centre was on the first floor of the Tower block at Manchester, while the airways part was at Broughton Hall near Preston. The last aircraft handled by Preston was Aer Lingus flight EI9216 Dublin-Manchester, operated by Boeing 737 EI-ASE. The unit controlled the aircraft flying below 13,000ft in the Manchester Terminal Area. Radar information was provided from two transmitters, one at Clee Hill, Shropshire and one at St. Anne's, as well as the airports own scanners. Preston's work is now divided between Manchester Sub Centre, based at the Tower at Manchester and London ATCC at West Drayton. The first aircraft under the control of Manchester Sub Centre was Alidair Viscount G-AVJL QA433 Manchester-Lossiemouth.

February 1975

Last summer's collapse of Court Line placed Manchester Airport third in the passenger movement's league, above Luton, whose passenger numbers had dropped by 37% to 2,030,860. Although both airports were affected, Luton suffered the greatest as Court Line was based there, operating substantially.

The 24ILS was unavailable again for most of the month. It had a habit of being unreliable when it was too cold or foggy, which affected not only regular traffic, but also the number of aircraft using it purely for practice. The only HS.748 ILS traffic observed was Brazilian Air Force C91-2507 (3rd/4th). RAF traffic noted and identified were Nimrod XZ280 (13th) and Victor XL513 (17th).

Increased traffic on the Manchester-Heathrow route has led to British Airways adding an extra daily flight in each direction. From 1st April, there will be eight daily and six at weekends and they are expecting to carry 370,000 passengers this year. In the 1960's, they were forced to cut capacity following British Rail's introduction of a more frequent and much faster service on the upgraded, electrified, Manchester-London Euston route, which enticed away business commuters previously travelling by air.

British Airways BAC Super 1-11s G-AVMH, G-AVMR, G-AVMS, G-AVMT, G-AVMW, G-AVMY & AVMZ, have all been noted in the airlines new colours. Their L.1011 Tristar crew training sorties continued throughout the month, with more than twenty landings. Manchester was used almost daily, with as many as five visits on some days and full details are as follows:

G-BBAE   (3rd/4th/5th/6th/7th/8th/13th/14th/15th/16th)
G-BBAF   (1st/3rd/5th/6th/7th/8th/12th/13th/14th/15th/17th)
G-BBAG   (1st/2nd/4th/9th/10th/11th/12th/13th/17th/18th/19th/20th/22nd/23rd/27th/28th)
G-BBAH   (4th/19th/20th/23rd/24th/26th/27th/28th)
G-BBAI   (21st/22nd/28th)

2nd   KLM used Douglas DC-8 PH-DCK on this morning's KL153/4, in full Affretair colours with KLM stickers.

2nd   Pan American B.747 N652PA, arriving at 0648 (PA120 from New York), was the only aircraft of interest amongst this morning's five Heathrow diversions.

3rd   Even though the UK was experiencing a mild spell and Manchester saw temperatures of 12°c, fog has been a problem. Heathrow was affected yesterday and East Midlands today, which resulted in a couple of interesting diversions. The first at 1145 was Rolls-Royce HS.125 G-BARR, making its first visit, even though it had been delivered brand new in March 1973. The second was Frankfurt-based FAA Convair ET-29C N94, arriving at 1136, making its one and only visit.

3rd RAF liaison flights between Northolt and Belfast continued into this year. Aircraft passing through this month included Andover XS597 (8th), HS.748 XS794 (3rd/24th/28th) and HS.125s XW789 (21st), XW790 (15th), XW791 (21st) & XX508 (28th).

4th Standard British Airways VC-10 G-ARVJ operated this morning's New York service BA538/9. It was also making its final visit to Manchester, as it was sold to the Qatar Government later this year in October.

4th British Airways L.1011 Tristar, G-BBAH, made its first visit today having only been delivered to Heathrow on the 24th January.

4th Royal Saudi Air Force C-130E 458 operated from/to Jeddah via Milan as RSAF802, before departing on the 6th.

4th HS.125 9Q-CCF arrived at 1313 from Brussels for customs clearance, en route to Hawarden for maintenance. It returned from Hawarden 12th February, before its departure to Zaire.

4th The first interesting executive visitor of the year was Dresser Industries BAC 1-11 N5037, routing Brussels-Luton. Formerly operated by American Airlines and delivered new in 1966, it only saw service for seven years, before being sold privately.

6th RAF Whirlwind XJ726, used for helicopter training, called in at 1108 from RAF Ternhill before departing later for Crewe.

6th Industrial action forced British Airways to cancel more than sixty flights today, affecting 2,500 passengers. Other flights operated by Aer Lingus, Air France & Lufthansa, who use British Airways facilities, weren't affected due to their own staff facilitating operations by carrying out their own checking-in and ticketing. British Caledonian, KLM, BIA, Dan-Air, Britannia & Laker were also unaffected, as they are handled by Servisair. The action started on the 3rd, when British Airways clerical staff blocked some flights, but by the 5th the ban had been extended to all flights. The strike affected members of APEX (The Association of Professional, Clerical, Executive & Computer Staff), who are concerned about the introduction of the company's new 'walk on, walk off', shuttle service between London-Glasgow, which doesn't require a ticket reservation. Normal operations were finally resumed at Manchester on the 8th.

7th Alaska International C-130 N9232R bound for Cambridge, arrived at 0645 from Thule, Northern Canada as a technical diversion.

8th February 1975 – RAF Andover XS597 was making a short stop at Manchester to clear customs, en route from Belfast to Northolt as RR1655. There were many of these flights, particularly in 1975 and other aircraft used were HS.125s and standard HS.748s. (Geoff Ball)

9th Visits by Douglas DC-3 aircraft are slowly dwindling and the second to Manchester so far this year was Air Freight G-APBC, on a flight from Gatwick to Prestwick.

9th KLM Douglas DC-9 PH-DNA, the first DC-9 to be delivered to the airline in March 1966, made its last appearance at Manchester today, operating afternoon flight KL155/6. It was leased to Italian airline Itavia, before they purchased it in May 1977 as I-TIGU.

10th   Today was the best for diversions for quite a while. Thirty-one arrived, mainly from the S South East, including British Airways latest B.747, G-AWNP, which made its first visit arriving at 1118 (BA510 from New York). It was one of nineteen from British Airways throughout the day. Sterling SE.210 OY-SAC (NB195 from Copenhagen) arriving at 1858, departed back to Copenhagen as NB196, once the outbound passengers had been brought up from Stansted.

12th   The first German Air Force training flight this year was Transall 50+84, arriving at 1157 as DCN8213 from Cologne to Northolt.

15th   IAS Cargo's second operational Bristol Britannia, G-AOVF, arrived today on a freight flight to Saarbrucken.

21st   Mention should be made of Beagle Terrier D-EBMU, arriving by road from Shobdon, with its wings removed and nose severely damaged, after crashing last September. It was stored inside the British Airways export warehouse and eventually air freighted to Germany.

21st   British Airways L.1011 Tristar G-BBAI made its first visit today, carrying out more training flights, having been delivered to Heathrow two weeks earlier on the 7th.

21st   A second dispute in as many months, this time by Servisair who handle most IT operators as well as KLM and Air Malta, affected operations today. Clerical workers belonging to the APEX union, seeking parity with their British Airways counterparts, walked out over pay. Even though some members carried on working, the Servisair engineers refused to handle outbound aircraft and although airlines such as Dan-Air could handle themselves, flights still couldn't operate! Consequently Dan-Air and Laker operated from Liverpool, Britannia and Air Malta from Birmingham and KLM suspended passenger flights until the strike ended on the 5th March, after arbitration was accepted.

23rd   A number of Heathrow diversions arrived this morning, due to snow. They were mainly British, except for Lufthansa B.737s D-ABEF at 1054 (LH068 from Munich), D-ABEM at 1022 (LH040 from Hamburg) and Alitalia DC-9 I-DIZU at 1146 (AZ282 from Rome) on its first visit. One that didn't make it was Air India B.747 VT-EBE, routing New York-Heathrow as AI112. Had it arrived, it would have been the first visit of Air India since B.707 VT-DNZ on 18th September 1971.

24th   Company demonstrator Cessna 206 N1630U arrived from Brussels at 1305 to nightstop.

28th   Due to continuing industrial action by Servisair staff, more than a hundred passengers expecting to board a Laker Airways flight to Alicante, had the surreal situation of seeing their plane, BAC 1-1 G-ATPK, on the tarmac at Manchester and then having to take a thirty minute bus ride to Liverpool Airport in order to catch it, after the aircraft eventually positioned over!

28th   Fairey Aviation Dove G-AKSS made its final flight, arriving at 1704 from White Waltham. It remained at the Fairey hangar until January 1976, when it was broken up.

28th   The only RAF trooping flight so far this year was Britannia XM489, arriving at 1734 as RR6375 (Belfast-Brize Norton).

March 1975

Manchester will be the first airport in Britain to give rebates on landing fees for quieter aircraft. Although the 20% reductions will cost the airport around £22,000, it's believed the scheme would increase revenue by encouraging airlines to introduce quieter aircraft sooner rather than later. British Airways in particular have been approached about a Boeing 747 service from Manchester. The reduction could also attract new services into Manchester rather than Heathrow, as it would be cheaper. It's been stressed that the principal objective of the scheme is to speed up the introduction of quieter aircraft out of Manchester, as presently only the A300 Airbus, Boeing 747, Douglas DC-10 and the L.1011 Tristar meet the new requirements.

Charges for the multi-storey car park will increase by between 25%-50% this May, but the first thirty minutes will remain free after all. A request to install a number of coin-operated amusement machines in the main concourse was rejected by the Airport Committee.

The airport's Director, Mr Gordon Sweetapple, revealed that opposition from British Airways has prevented three international airlines from starting operations at Manchester. He also discussed with the joint committee, ways to increase traffic and how to make greater efforts to interest more tour operators, particularly from the USA into using Manchester rather than the London airports. One of the Councillors was concerned as to why Manchester wasn't used more, especially as recent reports stated Heathrow and Gatwick were increasingly overcrowded. Manchester handled just short of 2.5 million passengers, while Heathrow and Gatwick combined handled around 25 million.

Traffic fell sharply during February, compared with last year. Passenger figures decreased by 16% and cargo fell by 20%, which was probably due to the recent strikes.

British Airways continued their crew training programme, with flights virtually daily between the 1st and 19th. They even pitched in with a B.747, when G-AWNM appeared almost daily between the 7th and 16th. The airline will have six L.1011s ready for revenue service by the end of the month, to be used on flights from Heathrow to Brussels, Madrid, Malaga, Palma & Paris. Aircraft used for training flights were:

B.707s: G-ASZF (13th), G-AXGW (12th) & G-AXGX (2nd/5th)
B.747:   G-AWNM (7th/8th/10th/11th/12th/13th/15th/16th)
Tristars: G-BBAG (1st/2nd/3rd/4th/5th/6th/8th/9th/10th/18th/19th)
          G-BBAH (1st/2nd/3rd/4th/5th/10th/11th/13th/15th/19th/20th)
          G-BBAI (12th/16th/17th/18th)

The 06 & 24ILS were out of service again for long periods during the month and the only ILS traffic observed was Brazilian Air Force HS.748 C91-2508 (21st).

4th   Royal Saudi Air Force C-130E 453 operated from/to Jeddah via Milan as RSF803, before departing on the 6th.

4th   German Air Force Hansa Jet 16+07 arriving at 0916, was a Warton diversion.

5th   Trans European Airbus A.300 OO-TEF and Boeing 720 OO-TEB arrived during the morning with Anderlecht fans for this evenings match at Leeds. It was the first visit of an A.300, although the team had arrived the previous day on Sobelair SE.210 OO-SRC. The match, played in swirling fog, had to be abandoned for seventeen minutes during the first half, but it did finish with Leeds Utd winning 3-0.

6th   Fairey Aviation's last remaining Dove, G-AWFM, made its final flight arriving from White Waltham at 0927. It remained withdrawn at the Fairey hangar until 11th June, when it was sold to Biggin Hill-based Fairflight Charter.

12th   German Air Force Transall 50+73 arrived at 1151 as DCN8345, on a training flight from Cologne to Northolt.

14th   The airport was hit by a one-day strike, when 400 ground staff walked out over pay. Today's scheduled services were either cancelled or diverted to other airports, affecting 5,000 passengers. The strikers, employed by Manchester City Council and Greater Manchester Council, included porters, baggage handlers, maintenance workers, car park attendants and firemen. A skeleton fire service was maintained on a standby basis, in case of emergencies. Private aircraft were unaffected and continued operating. A further one-day strike took place on the 20th.

15th March 1975 – Europe Air Service Vanguard F-BTOV is seen arriving from Perpignan, bringing in French fans for the England v France Rugby League match in Leeds. By this time EAS were one of only three airlines worldwide operating Vanguards in a passenger configuration. (Geoff Ball)

16th   Beech 90 F-BTCA arrived from Leeds at 1547 to clear customs, before its return to Le Bourget. This flight was in connection with the England v France rugby match.

17th   HS.125 PK-PJR was the first Indonesian registered aircraft to land at Manchester, arriving from Luton at 1535. Delivered new in November 1968 to Pelita Air Services, it was bound for a maintenance check at Hawarden.

21st Two of BOAC's original batch of sixteen Boeing 707s, were withdrawn this year. G-APFP made its last visit today, operating New York flight BA538/9. In May, it was flown from Heathrow to Philadelphia for display at the Franklin Institute, Pennsylvania.

23rd Today saw the first visit of a Sabena B.737, when OO-SDJ operated the evening freight service. The B.737 will permanently replace the B.727 on freight flights from the 28th.

24th Philippine Air Transport C-130 RP-C100 arrived from Athens to export more bridge sections on behalf of Fairey.

26th The airport was closed for the third time in two weeks, due to industrial action lasting for twenty hours. Flights were either cancelled or diverted and only private aircraft could operate. The continuing action by 400 ground staff was over demands for enhanced premium payments for shift work. Previously the strikers had given eight hour warnings, enough time for airlines to make alternative arrangements, but their union the TGWU warned that only four hours notice would be given for the next stoppage.

27th After many years the BNFL flights to/from Dounraey, will no longer be operated by Northair Beagle 206s. Of the four utilised by the airline, three left for Leeds - G-ASOF (21st), G-ATYW (27th) & G-AXZL (25th). The fourth, G-AWRO, made the final flight today, arriving at 1226 (NT107 from Dounraey), before being stored in the South Side hangars. The BNFL flights have been transferred to Vernair and their first will operate on 1st April next month.

28th French-airline TAT operated Twin Otter F-BTAU through Manchester today. It was due in on the 26th, but it went to Leeds-Bradford instead because of the ongoing strike action.

28th British Caledonian's latest Boeing 707, G-BCLZ, (BR212 from Las Palmas) diverted into Manchester today at 0743.

29th The second British Airways B.707 to leave the fleet this year was G-APFC, which operated New York flight BA538/9 for the last time today. On the 22nd May, it was flown to the USA for preservation at a museum in Wichita. Only three of the original sixteen (G-APFJ, APFM & APFN) still operate for British Airways.

31st Aer Lingus had to relinquish another European service out of Manchester today, when BAC 1-11 EI-ANH operated the final Frankfurt flight, EI650/1.

31st Aer Lingus evening freighter service, EI9212/3, was operated by Boeing 707 EI-ANV.

April 1975

A major report produced by the CAA recommending Manchester as the country's premier international airport outside of London, is seen as a green-light for the second runway. It promotes Manchester and Birmingham as the chief airports, serving central England. Manchester will be the primary airport, handling all long-haul services, although the report concludes it could be years before long-haul flights are profitable. The report goes a long way in assisting the airport's application for the new runway, which is crucial if the prediction of 13 million passengers by 1980 is to be achieved.

The following have made changes from this month: Aer Lingus terminated their Frankfurt service on 31st March. Air France will operate a mix of SE.210s and B.727s on their Paris flights. British Airways changed back to SVC-10s on New York flights (BA538/9). KLM KL153/4 is operating daily and the lunchtime KL155/6 has been dropped. Lufthansa's Frankfurt freight flights continue five-weekly, but with Boeing 727s. Sabena reintroduced a passenger service to Brussels - SN617/8 operates lunchtimes Mon-Fri with Boeing 737s and cargo flights also operate with Boeing 737s. SAS are operating Fred Olsen Electra's on their five-weekly cargo flights until July.

Alidair had a busy month, operating the numerous charter flights to Rotterdam and Beauvais previously flown by Invicta and Monarch Airlines. They also operated a nightly newspaper flight to Lossiemouth with G-AVJL, G-AZNH and F-BOEC, which is ex-Air Inter.

ILS traffic observed included Brazilian Air Force HS.748 C91-2508 (11th/17th), RAE Comet XS235 (2nd), RAF Victor XM715 (10th) and HS.125 9Q-CFW (16th).

1st Sabena returned to the Manchester-Brussels route today after a two year gap, when B.737 OO-SDJ operated the first flight. After twenty-five years of continuous operation, the airline withdrew its passenger service in March 1973, but continued with the cargo flights, which coincided with the phasing out of their SE.210 Caravelle's. The Boeing 727 is no longer scheduled through Manchester and their last visits were OO-STD (14th March), OO-STB (19th March) and OO-STE substituting for a B.737 on passenger service SN617/8 (11th September).

3rd   Aer Lingus Boeing 737 EI-ASH made its first visit since 31st October 1974, operating EI602 (Dublin-Amsterdam). It had only returned from Canada at the end of March, after being on lease to Transair. Operating in their basic colours, but with Aer Lingus titles, it remained in this livery all summer before returning to Transair again in December.

4th   Today was the latest in a series of stoppages by airport staff. This one commenced at 0200 and as only four hours notice was given, it was not enough time for airlines to make contingency plans, so aircraft had to position out to other airports with the passengers following in fleets of coaches! As the strikes were due to last until 0600 tomorrow, all scheduled flights were cancelled and charter flights flew from other airports. Passengers for London were taken by rail and transatlantic passengers were offered rail travel to London to catch their flights from there. The airlines are losing confidence in Manchester, after six strikes so far this year and they warned that unless ground staff can guarantee there will be no more stoppages, they will use other airports. Figures for the financial year 1974-1975, revealed that the airport had made a loss for the first time in eighteen years!

7th   French Air Force SE.210 Caravelle No.141 performed a touch-and-go at 1551, on a training flight from Shannon to Villacoublay.

7th   Iberia DC-9 EC-BIN arrived at 1522 (IB1216 from Santiago) with Barcelona FC for their European Semi-Final with Leeds Utd (won by Leeds Utd 2-1). On the 9th, the team returned to Barcelona on DC-9 EC-BYH.

8th   Royal Saudi Air Force C-130E 1606 operated from/to Jeddah via Milan as RSF804, before departing on the 9th.

9th   German Air Force Transall 50+50 arrived at 1247 as DCN8455, on a training flight from Cologne to RAF Northolt. Another operated on the 24th, when Transall 50+48 arrived at 1305 as DCN8567, from/to Landsberg.

11th   Withdrawn Beagle 206 G-AWRO was joined by a second example, G-ATYW, arriving from Leeds at 1221. Both aircraft now sit in the western end of the South Side hangars.

14th   RAF trooping flights during the month were VC-10 XR810 RR2875 from/to RAF Gutersloh today and VC-10 XV103 RR2877 RAF Brize Norton-Hanover on the 16th.

15th   Saturn International operated C-130 N11ST on a freight flight from Milan to Sofia.

16th   Merchantman G-APES made its last visit to Manchester as a British Airways aircraft (BE2282 from Heathrow). It was withdrawn the following month and remained at Prestwick for over a year. After being sold and flown to Heathrow on 27th August 1976, it became the first Merchantman for Air Bridge Carriers.

16th   Monarch Airlines added BAC 1-11s to their operating fleet and the first to visit Manchester was today, when ex-Court Line G-BCWG operated OM929/30 from/to Rotterdam. A second, G-BCXR, arrived on the 19th operating another Rotterdam return flight, OM931/0.

16th   Bergen Air Transport Douglas DC-4F LN-MOJ arrived on a cargo flight from Newcastle to Stavanger, showing clear signs of its previous owner, Greenlandair. Bergen AT operated two Douglas DC-4s until 1977, when they were both sold in Zaire.

17th   Royal Saudi Air Force C-130E 453 arrived today, operating a westbound flight (RSF904), bound for the Lockheed factory in Georgia. It was one of three visits by RSAF Hercules during the month, passing through Manchester rather than Shannon due to the fuel strike in Ireland. Other visits were 453 returning east-bound (24th) and 1608 (26th).

18th   The fuel strike in Ireland brought Aer Lingus B.747 EI-ASI into Manchester on a 'crew training' flight, but its real purpose was the uplifting of 25,000 gallons of fuel. It had Aer Lingus fuselage colours and an Air Siam tail.

18th   British Airways Viscount G-AOHG made its final visit to Manchester (BEBE3679 from Guernsey). After loyal and continuous service since 1957, Viscounts were starting to be withdrawn, partly because of their age and partly because the merger had duplicated routes and aircraft. After G-AOHG, others followed and their last visits are as follows:

G-AOHG 18/04   Last flight 01/05/75, stored at Cardiff.

G-AOHH 01/12   Last flight 13/12/75, stored at Leeds.
G-AOHN 02/07   Last flight 01/08/75, stored at Cardiff.
G-AOHR 19/08   Last flight 26/08/75, stored at Cardiff.
G-AOHS 18/06   Last flight 20/06/75, stored at Cardiff.
G-AOHW 30/10   Last flight 05/11/75, stored at Newcastle.
G-AOJC 02/10   Last flight 14/10/75, stored at Cardiff.
G-AORD 21/12   Last flight 31/12/75, stored at Birmingham.

22nd   Two biz-jets making their first visits today were Falcon F-BSBU from/to Eindhoven and Gulfstream 2 N100WK, which night-stopped before departing the following morning for Oslo.

23rd   PA-28 N33850 arrived at Manchester on its delivery flight, due to the Irish fuel strike.

28th   Wardair B.747 C-FDJC (WD816 from Toronto), with 432 adults and 30 minors onboard, was the largest single inbound load into Manchester.

29th   British Airways Merchantman G-APEO made its last visit to Manchester, operating BE2037 from Brussels. It was withdrawn the following month and remained at Prestwick for over a year. It was flown to Heathrow during September 1976 and broken up a year later.

30th   Today saw the first ever visit of a Potez 840. It's a four-engined 18-seat executive turboprop, which first flew in 1961 and only eight were ever built. F-BMCY operated from/to Paris Le Bourget and again the following day.

30th   British Airways has terminated all but one of their Merchantman services, consisting of the five-times weekly Heathrow flight, the four-times weekly Dusseldorf and the once-weekly Brussels. The only flight that remains is the twice-weekly Amsterdam operation.

May 1975

Since the creation of British Airways, the airline has undertaken a drastic review of its aircraft and operations. First to go were passenger Vanguards and recently a few Merchantman also left the fleet. Next was the standard VC-10s, which were gradually phased out and some of the remaining original B.707s were also sold and ultimately withdrawn. Viscount withdrawals have already started and next in the firing line were Trident 1s. A number of these were converted for shuttle service operations, but the remainder weren't so lucky. G-ARPU was the first to be withdrawn from service and the withdrawals continued into this year. The following Tridents made their last visits to Manchester during 1974/1975 as follows:

G-ARPA   08/10/74   Withdrawn 02/75
G-ARPB   27/12/74   Withdrawn early 1975
G-ARPC   08/09/75   Destroyed by cabin-fire 28/12/75
G-ARPE   09/12/74   Withdrawn early 1975
G-ARPF   10/02/75   Withdrawn by 04/75
G-ARPG   02/11/74   Withdrawn during 1975
G-ARPJ   22/03/75   Withdrawn early 1975
G-ARPM   08/11/74   Withdrawn early 1975

With the exception of G-ARPC, all were scrapped at Prestwick by October 1976.

British Airways reverted back to operating Boeing 707s on New York service (BA538/9) from the 23rd. Lufthansa operated Boeing 727s on its passenger flights this month with D-ABKC (7th/23rd) making its first visit and D-ABCI (11th).

The following airlines have summer IT programmes from Manchester: Air Malta, Aviaco, Aviogenex, Balkan, Inex-Adria, JAT, Spantax & Tarom, as well as a variety of UK operators: Britannia Airways, British Airtours, British Airways, British Caledonian, Dan-Air & Laker Airways. Airlines operating regular flights to the USA/Canada this summer are Air Canada, British Caledonian (B.707), CP Air (DC-8), Dan-Air (B.707), Laker Airways (B.707 & DC-10) and Wardair (B.707 & B.747). Other USA/Canada flights operated this month were Pacific Western B.707 C-FPWV (8th), Pan American B.707s N403PA (23rd), N406PA (26th) plus first visit B.747 N741PA (5th) and TWA B.707s N762TW (31st), N8729 (18th), N18712 (23rd/30th), N28724 (24th) & N28726 (6th/9th),

ILS traffic observed and identified included Brazilian Air Force HS.748 C91-2508 (2nd/14th) and RAF types Nimrod XV227 (2nd), Bulldog XX617 (2nd) & Dominie XS712 (7th).

2ⁿᵈ JAT commenced their weekly summer programme today with B.727 YU-AKF. They planned to use DC-9s, but after operating a B.727 for the first two rotations, it became a regular Boeing 707 operation from the 16ᵗʰ.

3ʳᵈ May 1975 – Just about to cross the threshold of Runway 24, is Dan-Air Comet 4B G-APYD, arriving at 1746 (DA1631 from Alicante). This aircraft was one of the few still in the old colours and the last but one Comet 4B to be withdrawn in 1978. (Geoff Ball)

5ᵗʰ RAF operated numerous trooping flights during the month including VC-10 XV108 (RR2181 to Hanover-today) & (RR2186 from/to Gutersloh-13ᵗʰ), Comet XR396 (RR5285/6 from/to Gutersloh-13ᵗʰ), VC-10 XV101 (RR2187 from/to Gutersloh-14ᵗʰ), VC-10 XV108 (RR2188 from/to Gutersloh-14ᵗʰ), VC-10 XV108 (RR2189 from/to Gutersloh-15ᵗʰ), VC-10 XV101 (RR2190 from/to Gutersloh-16ᵗʰ), Britannia XL640 (RR6672 to Gutersloh-16ᵗʰ), Britannia XL640 (RR6689/90 from/to Hanover-20ᵗʰ) and finally C-130 XV207 (RR4119 from/to Gutersloh-20ᵗʰ),

6ᵗʰ Royal Saudi Air Force C-130E 1614 operated from/to Jeddah via Milan as RSF805, before departing on the 9ᵗʰ.

7ᵗʰ The month also saw a quantity of Royal Navy flights, including Sea Heron's XR442 (19ᵗʰ/20ᵗʰ), XR443 (23ʳᵈ) & XR445 (7ᵗʰ/16ᵗʰ) and Sea Devon XK896 (13ᵗʰ/21ˢᵗ).

10ᵗʰ Diversion sessions during the summer due to fog are rare, but not uncommon and tend not to last long, before the strength of the sun burns it away. However, Zambia Airways Boeing 707 9J-ADY arriving at 0851 (QZ'DY from Lusaka), was one of four weather diversions this morning. This aircraft is relatively new to the airline, having been purchased from Aer Lingus (ex-EI-ASN).

11ᵗʰ Stellair FH-227 LN-KAA night-stopped from Oslo to Genoa on behalf of Braathens.

12ᵗʰ Alidair purchased another ex-Air Inter Viscount, F-BGNT, which made its first visit early this morning, positioning in from East Midlands to operate newspaper flight QA433 to Lossiemouth. It also operated on various other dates during the month.

13ᵗʰ During the afternoon, RAF Comet XR396, Royal Navy Sea Devon XK896 and Army Air Corps Sioux XT814 were all on the ground together. Other British military visits during the day were VC-10 XV108 (twice) and HS.125 XX508.

16ᵗʰ Queens Flight Wessex XV732 called in with the Duke of Edinburgh onboard. He was opening a Fleet Air Arm Exhibition in Manchester, which accounted for all the Sea Heron and Devon movements.

18ᵗʰ Having been occasional visitors to Manchester this year, Air Canada are operating a series of summer flights to Canada, on behalf of North American tour operator, Jetsave. The first flight, operated by DC-8 C-FTIL, departed at 1108 (AC089 to Toronto).

31ˢᵗ A new type to visit Manchester was business jet Aerospatiale SN601 Corvette, when F-BVPS arrived at 0732 from Le Bourget. The type developed in the late 1960's, first flew in December 1972, but disappointing sales ceased production in 1976, after only twenty-seven were sold.

June 1975

The month began with snow falling on the Pennines, due to a vigorous low pressure system, bringing in Arctic northerly winds from the Arctic Circle. The 2ⁿᵈ saw overnight temperatures in Manchester fall to 2°c, while the daytime maximum only reached 10°c. Snow delayed a county championship cricket match in Buxton with Lancashire, yet less than a week later the region saw temperatures of 27°c and up to fifteen hours of sunshine! Over the month there was 273 hours of sunshine, compared to only 137 hours last June.

A third terminal, primarily for charter traffic, is amongst the long-term plans for the airport and a report for its development will be presented to the Airports Consultative Committee this month. Although it's difficult to forecast a time scale, it's unlikely to be needed before the 1980's and as no design work has been carried out, the cost cannot be pre-determined. Other plans for the next few years include a second runway, dedicated cargo terminal, second multi-storey car park, aircraft maintenance area and extensive alterations to the existing piers.

The airport's new quiet jet rebate scheme, mentioned earlier in the year, is being backdated to 1st April and will run on a trial basis for twelve months.

British Airways maintenance staff at Heathrow were on strike for more than a week during the first part of the month, over working practices on the new L.1011 Tristar; which continues to be the cause of various industrial disputes.

Apart from the airlines previously mentioned operating summer programmes, other USA/Canada flights this month were Pan American B.707s N406PA (30th), N409PA (17th) & N422PA (13th/14th/16th) and TWA B.707s N8729 (28th), N8731 (7th), N763TW (10th), N772TW (16th) & N18709 (21st).

HS.748 ILS traffic observed and identified included Brazilian Air Force HS.748 C91-2509 (10th/17th/18th). RAF types were Comet XR399 (5th), Dominies XS713 (26th) & XS729 (5th); Victor's XL232 (10th/19th), XL511 (20th), XL512 (24th) and Nimrod XZ281 (19th). Civil aircraft were HS.125s RP-C111 (17th) & G-AVRG (24th) and Beech 90 N35KA (23rd).

2nd Philippine HS.125 RP-C111 arrived at 1227 for customs clearance, en route to Hawarden.

3rd Air Freight Douglas DC-3 G-AGYZ operated an extra flight on behalf of Sabena, arriving at 0442 (SN133 from Brussels) and positioning out to Lydd at 0649. Further flights were operated by DC-3 G-APBC (10th/24th).

3rd Lufthansa Boeing 727 D-ABKC, operating today's Frankfurt LH074/5, was a first visit.

3rd There were two Royal Saudi Air Force flights during the month. Today, C-130E 1609 operated from/to Jeddah via Milan (RSF806), before departing on the 5th and C-130E 1612 arrived on the 20th operating Rome-Jeddah (RSF883), before departing on the 22nd.

3rd German Air Force Transall 51+08 arrived at 1348 as DCN8713, on a training flight from Northolt to Landsberg. Another operated on the 11th, when Transall 50+60 arrived at 1246 as DCN8843 from Cologne to Northolt.

4th Morning Amsterdam KLM flight KL153/4, operated today by Garuda Indonesia DC-8 PK-GEB, was only the second Indonesian registered aircraft to visit Manchester.

5th Comet XR399 turned up today for a practice ILS and overshoot, marking the last appearance of type at Manchester in RAF service. These aircraft operated for Transport Command 216 Squadron based at Lyneham, but due to defence cuts, the squadron was disbanded this year. The interiors were frequently changed, sometimes between one leg of a journey and the next. They went from the general transportation of troops or other personnel with rear-facing seats, to a V.I.P configuration when carrying royalty, government ministers and other important dignitaries, or to an evacuation aircraft, with bunks and medical facilities. They were polished until they gleamed for any V.I.P flights and were generally maintained to a very high standard. Having said this, the original aluminium wings/lower fuselages were quickly changed to pale grey paint, to protect against corrosion. Five of these aircraft were sold to Dan-Air, who found they were significantly better kept and more economical than aircraft bought from other airlines, but unfortunately they only saw four more year's service with the airline, before being permanently retired.

5th A 'call of nature' can be a costly affair! Inbound Aberdeen flight BE7907 was less than 2-miles out, when the pilot was informed that a passenger had locked himself in one of the toilets. He had to abort the approach and go round, all because the passenger had enjoyed the in-flight refreshments a little too much! British Airways were less than amused, as the incident wasted expensive fuel and made the aircraft late. This was also the day the nation went to the polls to reaffirm the UK's commitment to their EEC membership, with 70% voting in favour of remaining.

6th ONA DC-8 N868F was an early morning diversion from Mildenhall and a first visit.

10th Belgian Air Force DC-6 KY-3 arrived at 1422 as a support flight, in connection with three Belgian Air Force HS.748s, currently being assembled at Woodford. It also operated on the 11th from RAF Lyneham, arriving at 1031, before departing for Woodford.

11th Another new type to Manchester was an Australian twin-engine turboprop, when GAF Nomad VH-AUI arrived from Dublin to operate various demonstration flights.

15th Aer Lingus leased B.737 EI-ASK again for the summer. It made its first appearance at Manchester today operating EI767 (Birmingham-Cork) and its final visit on 17th October, operating EI603 (Amsterdam-Dublin). It was white, with a United Airlines cheatline and Aer Lingus titling.

16th Two withdrawn Northair Beagle 206s, G-ATYW & G-AWRO, were joined by a third when G-BCJA arrived at 1612 from Leeds.

18th French Air Force Falcon 20 No.238 made a touch-and-go at 1357, en route from Shannon to Villacoublay. Other flights were Falcon No.238 (19th) and No.167 (27th).

20th Today was the only visit of an Irish Air Corps DH.Dove to Manchester, when Dove No.201 arrived at 1111 from Baldonnel. It was the last of four delivered to the IAC in 1970.

20th UNI-Air DC-3 F-BCYX arrived at 1338 on a tech stop, en route Kirkwall-Morlaix.

21st June 1975 – Pakistan International Boeing 720 AP-ATQ, leased to Air Malta between 1974 and 1978, is seen here on a warm Saturday morning, keeping TWA Boeing 707 N18709 company. Remaining in service until 1986, it was broken up in April of that year. (Geoff Ball)

21st A reported collision between an Air India Boeing 747 and an Alitalia DC-9 happened when they were taxiing out for departure at Heathrow. The first Cricket World Cup was inaugurated this year, with Australia and the West Indies contesting today's final.

23rd The newest HS.125 on the UK register was G-BCXF. Operated by Marconi Electronics, it arrived at 0931 today, on a return flight from Luton.

25th Sterling operated the first of a series of weekly charters to/from Copenhagen via Dublin. SE.210 Caravelle's were used on alternate Wednesdays or Thursdays, depending on the route - (Wednesday: NB548 Dublin-Copenhagen & Thursday: NB547 Copenhagen-Dublin). SE.210 OY-SAJ arrived at 1543 today as NB548 and the last flight operated on 28th August with SE.210 OY-SAM (NB547).

July 1975

The month didn't see as much sunshine as June, with 173 hours recorded. However, it did see consistently high temperatures, culminating in some violent overnight thunderstorms on the 14th, when the temperature got no lower than 21°c.

In a bid to wipe out part of a looming deficit due to various developments at the airport, big price rises are on the way for operators, motorists and the general public using airport services. Domestic passenger load supplements and aircraft parking charges will be increased by 15% and by 10% for baggage and cargo handling. Multi-storey car parking will increase by 22% to £1.10 for 24-hours and admission to the spectator terraces has been raised to 15p.

Not directly to do with Manchester Airport, but relevant nonetheless, was the news that British Airways Trident 2Es and 3Bs have been granted CAA clearance to land in Category 3B weather conditions, equating to landing in zero visibility. This means Trident diversions due to fog should be a thing of the past, although it will take time to train their pilots.

USA/Canada flights were operated by Pan American B.707s N422PA (8th/25th), N424PA (26th), N497PA (21st) & N886PA (15th/22nd) and TWA B.707s N8729 (19th), N771TW (5th), N18709 (12th/26th), N28727 (12th/22nd/26th) & N28728 (19th).

HS.748 ILS traffic noted was British Airways HS.748 G-BCOE (7th/8th/9th/10th). RAF types observed and identified were Dominies XS727 (29th) & XS731 (2nd). British Airways operated crew training flights again with B.707s G-ARRA (29th) & G-ARRC (24th) and VC-10 G-ARVM (28th).

1st Sabena continued operating Air Freight Douglas DC-3s on additional freight flights. DC-3 G-AMWW was used on this morning's (SN133 from Brussels), arriving at 0405 before positioning out to Lydd at 0649.

2nd Another Air France SE.210 Caravelle leaving the fleet was F-BHRA. It made its final visit to Manchester today, before being withdrawn from service in November. Delivered new in April 1959, it was the airlines second SE.210.

3rd British Airways Viscounts, G-AMOG & G-AMON, normally confined to internal Scottish operations, had an away-day to Manchester transferring passengers from/to Prestwick due to the cancelled Manchester sector of BA648/9.

7th RAF operated the following trooping flights: Britannia XL636 (RR6388 from Gutersloh-today), VC-10 XV105 (RR2283 from Gutersloh-29th) and VC-10 XV108 (RR2284/5 from/to Gutersloh-31st).

7th Ford Motor Company's HS.125 G-AYFM operated a return flight from Stansted as FD703/4.

8th Royal Saudi Air Force operated three flights through Manchester during the month: C-130E 1609 from/to Jeddah via Milan as RSF807 operated today before departing on the 10th; C-130E 453 at 1600 Rome-Jeddah as RSF1047 (18th) and C-130E at 1608 as RSF884 Rome-Jeddah (21st).

9th German Air Force Transall 50+90 arrived at 1348 as DCN8972, on a training flight from Hohn to RAF Northolt. Another operated on the 31st, when Transall 50+66 arrived at 0951 as DCN9050 from Glasgow to Cologne.

12th The Red Arrows landed at Manchester and for the first time all ten Gnats night-stopped, before participating in the Barton Air Show the following afternoon. After performing their display, they returned briefly to Manchester, before leaving for Cranwell.

12th LOT operated charter flight LO3131/2 from/to Warsaw today, with Ilyushin IL-18 SP-LSF. A further flight was operated by IL-18 SP-LSG as LO3135/6 on the 26th.

13th Yakolev YAK-11 G-AYAK, built in Russia in 1956 and new to the UK register in 1970, is believed to have been rebuilt. Used extensively for training by the Soviet Air Force, it's now privately owned and based at Booker. It's a frequent visitor on the air show circuit, hence today's arrival at 1541, after its appearance at the Barton Air Show.

14th Cessna 500 Citation N5268J arrived at 2249 on a delivery flight routing Reykjavik-Seville, before departing on the 16th.

15th Lufthansa Boeing 727 D-ABKJ, operating Frankfurt flight LH074/5, was making its first visit.

18th Four RAF Pumas - XW221, XW225, XW228 & XW229, arrived in connection with a Grand Parachuting Spectacular at Tatton Park.

18th Aer Lingus operated Boeing 707 EI-ASM on Amsterdam flight EI602/3. It was the aircrafts one and only visit, as it was only on short-term lease from Zambia Airways and returned to them in January 1976.

23rd French Air Force Falcon 20 No.238 made a touch-and-go at 1842, en route from Shannon to Villacoublay.

23rd   Royal Navy Sea Devon XJ350 declared an emergency with oil leak problems, en route from Lee-on-Solent to Lossiemouth. It was parked at Faireys until the 30th, during which time the following aircraft came and went with spares and labour: Sea Heron XR443 (24th/25th/29th/30th) and Sea Devon's XJ317 (29th), XJ347 (25th) & XJ348 (26th).

24th   British Airways Merchantman G-APEL made its last visit to Manchester, operating BE3023/18. It was withdrawn later in the year and remained at Prestwick until it was flown to Heathrow on 20th July 1976, when it was sold to Europe Air Service as F-BYCF.

25th   The airport officially became MIA today (Manchester International Airport).

26th July 1975 – Tarom's fortnightly flight from/to Constanta (RO775/6) is normally operated by Ilyushin Il-62s, but today it was operated by BAC 1-11 YR-BCF (RO775/6) & Ilyushin Il-18 YR-IMD (RO775A/776A). (Geoff Ball)

August 1975

The excellent summer weather continued and the month saw consistently warm temperatures and 216 hours of sunshine.

Philippine Air Transport operated a number of C-130s flights this month, transporting girder bridge sections made by Fairey. RP-C99 & RP-C100 made appearances and additional flights carrying the same cargo were made by Tradewinds, who have taken over from Transvalair.

USA/Canada flights this month were Pan American B.707s N419PA (2nd), N453PA (24th), N881PA (15th), N886PA (18th) & N887PA (24th); Transair B.707 C-GTAI (17th), DC-8 C-GNDA (29th) and TWA B.707s N8731 (16th/30th), N18709 (11th/23rd), N18712 (9th), N28727 (2nd) & N28728 (13th/16th).

HS.748 ILS traffic observed were; British Airways G-BCOF (14th/15th) & Brazilian Air Force C91-2510 (25th). RAF types were Andover XS607 (26th) & Victor XL160 (27th/28th). British Airways crew training flights noted were B.707s G-APFN (22nd/23rd), G-ARRA (3rd/4th/6th) & G-ARRC (16th/17th).

2nd   The Blue Eagles display team, with their six Sioux helicopters, called in at 1641 en route from Nottingham to Preston.

2nd   RAF operated numerous trooping flights again during the month: VC-10's XR810 (RR2301 to Gutersloh-today) & XV103 (RR2319 from/to RAF Gutersloh-27th), Britannia's XL640 (RR6369 to Gander-11th), XM518 (RR6371 to Gander-22nd), XM489 (RR6374 to Gander-24th) and XM496 RR6376 RAF Brize Norton-Gander-26th).

3rd   PA-31 PH-TVB operated by Dutch-airline Transavia, arrived from Millom, Cumbria at 2125 to clear customs en route to Amsterdam, in the airlines full colours.

5th   Beagle 206 G-BCJD, arriving at 0905 from Leeds, joined G-AWRO & G-BCJA on the South Side for storage. In 1976, G-AWRO departed for Leeds on 5th May, G-BCJD for Staverton on 23rd March and G-BCJA for Biggin Hill on 7th November, with the last two being sold in the USA.

Another, G-ATYW, which arrived in April for storage, has been operating BNFL flights on behalf of Northern Executive since the end of last month, but it left for Leeds on the 13th.

5th Royal Saudi Air Force C-130E 1609 operated from/to Jeddah via Milan today as RSF808, before departing on the 8th. On the 20th, C-130E 463 operated Rome-Jeddah as RSF885, before departing on the 22nd.

5th The last visit by an Invicta Airlines Vanguard to Manchester took place today, when G-AXOY arrived at 1938 as IM147 from Tarbes. The airlines owners, European Ferries, announced earlier in the year they would cease operations by October and this aircraft operated the very final flight; a one-hour pleasure flight from Luton on 26th October.

7th UNI-Air DC-3 F-BCYX called in at Manchester again, arriving at 1345 on a flight from Benbecula to Quimper. It continued operating for the airline until 1977.

9th Lufthansa operated Boeing 727 D-ABIA on today's Frankfurt LH076/7. Others were D-ABKD (21st), D-ABKA (25th) & D-ABGI (29th), which were all first visits.

12th American-airline TIA made its only appearance this year, when Douglas DC-8 N4866T called in at 1448 from Philadelphia, en route to Amsterdam.

16th LOT operated two more charter flights this month from/to Warsaw, using Ilyushin Il-18s and both were first visits. SP-LSH LO3137/8 was today and SP-LSD LO3133/4 on the 23rd.

17th Canadian operator Transair can trace its roots back to 1947 and until 1965 it was purely a domestic carrier. In 1974 they purchased Boeing 707 C-GTAI, which made its first visit to Manchester today, operating from/to Toronto on behalf of Dan-Air.

23rd The Blue Eagles display team called in today, after participating in the annual Poynton Show, before departing for nearby Mottram Hall later.

25th Iscargo DC-6F TF-IUB (formerly LN-FOL with Fred Olsen) positioned in from Rotterdam to operate an outbound cattle charter to Venice.

27th Israeli Air Force C-130 4X-FBA carried out three ILS runs, en route Frankfurt-Alconbury, having already completed three ILS approaches at Brussels.

28th RAF Britannia XM519 (RR6374 from Brize Norton) ultimately bound for Gander, went tech on arrival. Another Britannia, XL660, was dispatched from Brize Norton to operate the flight.

29th Transair operated another sub-charter for Dan-Air today, when Douglas DC-8 C-GNDA made its first visit, arriving at 1428 as ND539 from Gatwick bound for Toronto.

29th August 1975 – Nordair Douglas DC-8-61 C-GNDA is about to depart on an ad-hoc flight for Toronto, on its only visit in this guise. It made frequent visits during 1971 as N8961T with Universal Airlines, before it was purchased by Nordair in 1974, before being finally sold to Evergreen International in December 1978 as N810EV. (Geoff Ball)

30th G-BCYF, the first Falcon 20 onto the UK register, arrived at 0827 on a round trip from Heathrow where it's currently based.

30th British Caledonian B.707 G-BCLZ (BR2108 from Toronto) made the last of its five visits to Manchester. Leased from China Airlines since September 1974, it was due to return next month.

September 1975

USA/Canada flights were operated by Capitol DC-8 N900CL (6th), Pan American B.707s N410PA (5th), N419PA (7th), N428PA (16th), N880PA (28th), N886PA (22nd) & B.747 N754PA (20th) and TWA B.707s N8731 (5th), N763TW (20th), N18712 (15th/22nd), N28726 (27th/29th) & N28728 (12th).

HS.748 ILS traffic observed were Brazilian Air Force C91-2510 (15th) & BFS D-AFSG (30th). RAF types were Victor XL160 (3rd/9th) & Whirlwind XR458 (18th). British Airways crew training flights noted were B.707s G-APFM (17th), G-APFN (30th), G-ARRC (19th) & G-AXXY (16th).

1st   Lufthansa operated Boeing 727 D-ABGI on today's Frankfurt LH074/5.

2nd   Royal Saudi Air Force C-130E 452 operated from/to Jeddah via Milan today as RSF809, before departing on the 4th. C-130E 1610 also operated from/to Jeddah on the 22nd as RSF886, before departing on 24th.

5th   Belgian Air Force DC-3 K-10/OT-CWE from Yeovilton arrived on its first visit today.

6th   American-airline Capitol made its only appearance this year, when first time visitor Douglas DC-8 N900CL arrived, operating an inbound flight from New York. It appeared again later in the day from Gatwick, operating a flight for Dan-Air to Toronto.

6th   Loganair began operating an Islander flight routing Birmingham-Glasgow, through Manchester on Saturday evenings. G-AXVR arrived at 1739 today and others during the month were G-AXVR (13th), G-BANL (20th) & G-BDDV (27th).

8th   Today was the writers first day back at school, after a long hot summer break. It was also the day when ten Heathrow diversions arrived early in the morning. All were British Airways flights, except for Aer Lingus B.737 EI-ASD at 0731 (EI9160 from Dublin) and Ghana Airways VC-10 9G-ABO at 0819 (GH700X from Accra). Apart from Boeing 707 G-ATZD at 0917 (BA150 from Port of Spain), I saw them all before leaving for school. It was cloudy and breezy by the afternoon when Trident 1 G-ARPC arrived, still in BEA colours, on its last visit operating Heathrow flight BE4064/3 before being withdrawn from service in December.

11th   PA-23 Aztec's F-BNFU & F-BUUJ arrived from Morlaix to clear customs at Manchester, before carrying onwards to their eventual destination, Leeds.

14th   RAF trooping flights during the month were C-130s XV188 (RR4221) & XV209 (RR4222) routing Lyneham-Wildenrath today and Britannia XL637 (RR6428/9) from/to Hanover on the 27th.

18th   Another biz-jet type making its first appearance this year, the French-manufactured Falcon 10, is basically a smaller version of the already successful Falcon 20. F-BVPR was the first example to Manchester, arriving at 1649 today on a return trip from Le Bourget.

20th   The writer witnessed the arrival of Pan American Boeing 747 N754PA around teatime on his way home, after spending the day at the airport. Its visit was the result of a Heathrow charter and a Manchester charter combined, as both flights were to be operated by separate B.707s.

21st   Pacific Western B.707F C-FPWJ arrived at 1329, operating a freight flight from Tehran to St. Johns.

25th   Air Charter SE.210 F-BJTG operated from/to Paris-Orly as SF435/6.

27th   TWA B.707 N28726 (TW5128 from Heathrow), was the first TWA aircraft to visit Manchester in their new colour scheme.

October 1975

British Airways announced their intention to start a scheduled service to Nice from next April, bringing the total number of destinations served by the airline to twenty-three. It's being launched as a joint venture with Air France and further expansion of routes from Manchester are planned, with the possibility of Frankfurt and Zurich being added to the network within the next few years.

HS.748 ILS traffic observed were BFS D-AFSG (21st/30th), Ecuadorian Air Force FAE-738 (28th) and Brazilian Air Force C91-2510 (29th). RAF types were Whirlwind's XR453 (8th) & XP331 (8th/10th) and Sioux XT801 (17th). British Airways crew training flights noted were B.707s G-ARRA (1st), G-AXGX (31st) & B.747 G-AWNC (17th/21st).

4th   Loganair continued their Saturday evening Birmingham-Glasgow flight through Manchester and today's was operated by G-AXKB. Others during the month were G-BDDV (11th), G-BANL (18th) & G-AWNR (25th).

10th The arrival of British Airways VC-10 G-ARVH, operating a charter for Ingersoll-Rand, was the last passenger visit of one of their standard VC-10s. After being withdrawn from service in early 1976, G-ARVM became the last standard VC-10 still operating for the airline.

10th Belgian Air Force DC-3 K-08/OT-CND arrived at 1134, from/to Brussels.

14th Royal Saudi Air Force operated two flights during the month: C-130E 1601 from/to Jeddah via Milan as RSF810 today and C-130E 461 from/to Jeddah as RSF887 on the 20th.

17th Of the ninety-nine weather diversions this month, Alitalia B.747 I-DEMO was one of the highlights. After operating a charter from Rome to Dublin it was due to position out to Prestwick to pick up more passengers, but by the time it was due to leave, Prestwick's visibility had also fallen below limits. It was then decided to send the aircraft to Manchester and coach the passengers down from Prestwick to continue their flight to Dublin and it arrived using an Aer Lingus Dublin-Manchester flight number. Today's diversions also included first visit TWA B.707 N774TW at 0854 (TW876 from New York) and Aer Lingus B.747 EI-ASJ at 0925 (IN104 from New York), both diverting from Dublin.

18th RAF VC-10s XV101 (RR2406) & XR810 (RR2404), were operating outbound trooping flights to Hanover and strangely they were parked on the Domestic pier. The flights were part of 'Exercise Inside Right', a nationwide mobilisation exercise.

20th Royal Navy Wessex XT764 had been carrying out demonstrations at various local schools during the day, when it arrived at 1333 from Sale, Cheshire.

24th The next six days saw seventy-one weather diversions into Manchester. Six Britannia Airways B.737s were present on the pier on the 29th and ten different Britannia B.737s diverted in during a 24-hour period over 28th/29th.

24th The day started with one early morning diversion, British Airways BAC 1-11 G-BBME, arriving at 0812 (BE883 from Rome). Although it was missed by the writer, the flood gates had opened by 0930 and numerous diversions followed. I saw all the arrivals from various classrooms and the next diversion, Wardair B.707 C-FFAN at 0924 (WD591 from Edmonton), didn't arouse too much suspicion but the following British Airways Boeing 747, G-AWNH at 0935 (BA660 from Miami), certainly did! There was a total of twenty arrivals between 0949 and 1108, fifteen of which were diversions and included East African Airways VC-10 5Y-ADA at 1031 (EC644 from Nairobi), Lufthansa B.737 D-ABCE at 1039 (LH056 from Cologne), KLM DC-8 PH-DEA at 1043 (KL119 from Amsterdam), Lufthansa B.737 D-ABEI at 1045 (LH040 from Hamburg) and first visitor Luxair SE.210 Caravelle LX-LGF at 1049 (LG401 from Luxembourg), which I couldn't identify having never seen the airline before. I also saw and recorded my first Gulfstream 2, when N580RA arrived at 1137. Two more first time visitors also arrived: Pan American B.727 N326PA at 1113 (PA055A from Hanover) and Lufthansa B.727 D-ABKI at 1118 (LH030 from Frankfurt). While I was home for lunch, three more diversions arrived: Alitalia DC-9 I-DIZF at 1209 (AZ282 from Rome), British Airways Merchantman G-APEG at 1223 (BE2183 from Zurich) and Alitalia DC-8 I-DIWG at 1249 (AZ458 from Milan) and an hour later the last diversion arrived, British Airways B.707 G-ATZD (BA110 from Nassau).

28th After the arrival of six diversions late last night and more this morning, the writer and a couple of friends made a trip to the airport. We caught the 9am 369 bus from Stockport and on the journey we saw the arrivals of Caribbean B.707 G-AVZZ (IQ804 from Bridgetown) and a new airline to Manchester, BWIA B.707 9Y-TEJ (BW900 from Port of Spain). At first I was unsure whose Boeing 707 it was, but it was very colourful! Once at the airport we immediately noticed there were more diversions than anticipated and as we made our way towards the international and jumbo pier we saw numerous airliners scattered around the aprons, taxiways and disused runway. One of my personal highlights was South African Airways B.747 ZS-SAM (SA234 from Sal Island), which arrived whilst we were on the bus. It was parked on stand 23 and looked unusual because of its five engines; although it wasn't uncommon at this time for Boeing 747s to carry a spare. Other highlights were Pacific Western Hercules C-FPWK and hybrid British Caledonian/Qantas Boeing 707 G-BDKE, making its only visit to Manchester while on a short term lease to British Caledonian. The diversions had stopped by the time we got to the airport, but we did see Ecuadorian Air Force

HS.748 FAE-738 perform an ILS and overshoot around lunchtime, although we thought it was a RAF HS.748 at first. We left around 2pm, after realising there wouldn't be any more diversions.

28ᵗʰ October 1975 – The month saw many weather diversions and following dense fog in the south late on the 27ᵗʰ, Pacific Western C-130 CF-PWK made its first visit (PW386 from Ankara), operating a freight flight originally bound for Stansted. This particular aircraft was written-off in April 1982. (Geoff Ball)

28ᵗʰ October 1975 – Another diversion was B.707 G-BDKE (BR6478 from Lagos). In basic Qantas colours and British Caledonian titles, it's seen here parked on disused runway 02/20. It was leased to BCAL from this October for three months only before returning to Qantas as VH-EAC. (Stuart Wardman)

28ᵗʰ Today saw the final visit of a RAF Britannia to Manchester, when XM498 diverted inbound with tech trouble (RR6471 Belfast-Gutersloh). It was announced earlier in the year that their last two Britannia Squadrons, No.99 and No.111, based at Brize Norton, would be disbanded and all aircraft would be withdrawn by February 1976.

29ᵗʰ Gulfstream 1 N720G arrived at 0936 from Brussels and departed for Heathrow at 1738, but the highlight of today's sixteen diversions was the first visit of Boeing 707 N309EL, operated by the Eli Lilly Corporation, diverting in from Liverpool where it was a regular visitor.

November 1975

The Airport Joint Committee gave Dan-Air approval to establish a maintenance base at Ringway. Their plan to transfer the maintenance of BAC 1-11 and HS.748 aircraft from Lasham to Manchester means the number of engineering staff will increase from forty to two-hundred!

1ˢᵗ The month saw a wide variety of RAF flights, starting with trooping flights VC-10s XR810 (RR2487 from Hanover), XV107 (RR2488 from/to Hanover & (RR2489 from Hanover) today and VC-10 XV107 (RR2191 from Lossiemouth) on the 19ᵗʰ. Other RAF visits were Devon's VP958 (6ᵗʰ/19ᵗʰ), VP981 (30ᵗʰ) & WB533 (19ᵗʰ); Andover's XS597 (17ᵗʰ) & XS639 (10ᵗʰ); HS.125s XW789 (7ᵗʰ), XX507 (9ᵗʰ/28ᵗʰ) & XX508 (13ᵗʰ) and Pembroke WV740 (19ᵗʰ).

4ᵗʰ The arrival of LOT IL-18 SP-LSE (LO4195/6) was to transport Wrexham FC to Poland, in conjunction with a Cup-Winners Cup game with Stal Rzeszow. The team returned on the 6ᵗʰ, onboard IL-18 SP-LSA (LO4200/1). The match itself ended in a 1-1 draw, but having already won at home, it meant Wrexham had qualified for the next round.

4th   Royal Saudi Air Force operated four flights this month: C-130E 452 from/to Jeddah via Milan as RSF810 today, C-130E 463 from/to Jeddah as RSF1158 (12th), C-130E 465 from/to Jeddah via Rome as RSF1159 (17th) and C-130H 1602 Rome-Jeddah as RSF888 (20th).

5th   Sabena's passenger flight SN617/8, was operated by B.707 OO-SJH today, due to the cancellation of yesterday's flight.

8th   Overseas National operated two DC-8 flights for Laker Airways; N868F was today and N867F on the 11th.

8th   Transavia B707 PH-TVA (GK3107 Gatwick-Gander) was also a sub-charter for Laker. The recent sub-charters were due to the airlines DC-10s being used on Hajj pilgrimage flights to Mecca.

12th   German Air Force Transall 50+91, arriving at 1206 as DCN9542 operating Cologne-Luton, were their first training flight through Manchester since July.

14th   Another diversion day provided eleven from Heathrow, six of which were first visits: TWA B.707 N8733 at 0706 (TW754 from Boston), Pan American B.747 N738PA at 0753 (PA002 from New York), Malaysian Airlines B.707 9M-MCS at 0708 (MH894 from Kuwait), Singapore Airlines B.707 9V-BDC at 0802 (SQ743A from Frankfurt), Iran Air Boeing 707 EP-IRN at 0855 (IR776 from New York) and Qantas B.747 VH-EBD at 0922 (QF001 from Frankfurt). Malaysian and Singapore Airlines had operated as a combined airline until 1972 and today was their first visit to Manchester in their separate identities. Disappointingly, the diversions had dried up by mid-morning, probably due to British Airways ongoing handling issues. Gatwick handled a large number of Heathrow diversions and by late afternoon, they were full to capacity. Over 1,500 passengers from the diverted aircraft were dealt at Manchester, before being railed to London - eventually! Several more started to arrive from the Midlands early evening, just as fog was descending on Manchester, but due to low pressure sweeping across the country, it didn't last for long.

15th   Skyline Sweden Viscount SE-CNK positioned in from Kristiansand, on a dull, wet Saturday afternoon, to operate an outbound charter to Gothenburg. Registered in Sweden in 1967, it was first operated by Falconair, before going to Skyline Sweden in 1971 and seeing five more year's service before its withdrawal in August 1976.

16th   Lufthansa operated the following Boeing 727s this month – two first visits, D-ABKF today & D-ABLI on the 17th/30th and D-ABHI on the 23rd.

16th   On a dull, wet and windy Sunday, British Airways Trident G-AWZH and L.1011 Tristar G-BBAE, which was the first Tristar to operate a passenger flight from Manchester, both operated charters to Malaga. The return flights were operated by Trident G-AWZZ and first visit L.1011 Tristar G-BBAJ on the 19th.

17th   Austrian Airlines DC-9 OE-LDE (OS3857/8) brought in the Austrian football team for a Euro 76 qualifier with Wales, taking place at the Racecourse Ground, Wrexham. Wales won 1-0 and qualified for Euro 76. The Austrians returned home on the 20th, again on DC-9 OE-LDE.

21st   Belgian Air Force DC-3 K-10/OT-CWE arrived at 1049, routing Brussels-RAF Northolt.

29th   Light snow and black ice early on gave way to a cold and sunny day, but Heathrow and Gatwick were badly affected by fog throughout the day. I saw four 'Speedbird' arrivals during the morning, including B.747 G-AWNA at 1104 (BA660 from Miami), which was observed overhead during my sister's wedding at Stockport Registry Office. I was looking forward to the prospect of more diversions, but by lunchtime the only diverted aircraft were the four Speedbird flights. British Airways were still having industrial problems, as far as handling diversions was concerned and flight BA598 Air New Zealand DC-10 ZK-NZP (LAX-LHR) was one of many turned away. It ended up making its way to Prestwick, joining several other trails heading northwards. By early evening the airport was fairly quiet, but it soon got busy when the southern airports fell below most aircrafts landing limits. Of the thirty-one arrivals Manchester received between 2021 and 2359, twenty-three were diversions and the non-British aircraft were KLM DC-9 PH-DNL at 2038 (KL141 from Amsterdam), TWA B.707 N18706 at 2052 (TW702 from New York), Alitalia DC-9 I-DIKT at 2054 (AZ292 from Milan) and SAS DC-9 LN-RLA at 2120 (SK505 from Stockholm).

29th   Loganair continued operating a Birmingham-Glasgow flight through Manchester on Saturday evenings and today's Islander, G-AYXK, was a first time visitor.

30th November 1975 – British West Indian Airlines (BWIA), made its second visit to Manchester with first visit Boeing 707 9Y-TEE, which served the airline up until 1982. They made several diversionary visits to Manchester with Boeing 707s up until 1982, when the type was replaced with Tristar 500s on their London services. First visit Singapore Airlines Boeing 707 9V-BFW, which served the airline up until 1981, is seen here on a frosty apron, having recently arrived from Zurich as SQ765A. The B.707 was soon to be replaced by the airlines Boeing 747s. (Geoff Ball)

30th November 1975 – The only airline seen at Manchester operating the Ilyushin IL-62 was Tarom, but the arrival of LOT IL-62 SP-LAC broke that sequence! It's seen here still in old colours, having just arrived from Warsaw on diversion from Heathrow. Exactly an hour later, JAL Boeing 747 JA-8122 touched down as JL421 from Tokyo/Copenhagen, also making its first visit to Manchester. (Geoff Ball)

30th November 1975 – A fantastic shot of three diverted Alitalia Douglas DC-9s. From front to back, I-DIKT, which had appeared the previous evening (AZ292 from Milan) and today's arrivals I-DIBO (AZ282 from Rome) & I-DIKE (AZ8216 from Milan). (Geoff Ball)

30th   A large variety of diversions continued arriving throughout the day and although I missed some of the early ones, I did see LOT IL-62 SP-LAC arriving at 1019 (LO341 from Warsaw), closely followed by B.747 G-AWNL at 1040 (BA570 from Chicago) and Swissair DC-9 HB-ISM at 1053 (SR810 from Geneva) - a stretched DC-9 Series -51 and the first one to visit Manchester. I saw further diversions: British Airways Trident 3 G-AWZP at 1100 (BE753 from Stockholm) and Air Malta B.720 AP-AMJ at 1114 (KM744 from Malta), before hearing a noise that got louder and louder, which I soon realised was an aircraft not following its standard approach. It was about to appear directly over the flats where I lived and make a visual approach to Runway 24, which it did in a spectacular and noisy fashion! It was awesome enough it was a Boeing 747, but even more thrilling it was a Japan Airlines B.747 (JA-8122 JL411 from Copenhagen). Its visual approach and angle had made it difficult to identify, as it was the first time I'd seen a Japan Airlines aircraft. Tunis Air made their first visit to Manchester with B.727 TS-JHO at 1121 (TU790 from Tunis) and there was another appearance by British West Indian Airlines with B.707 9Y-TEE at 1134 (BW900 from Bridgetown), making its first visit. Also arriving were two Alitalia DC-9s: I-DIBO at 1142 (AZ282 from Rome) & I-DIKE at 1306 (AZ8216 from Milan); first visit Singapore Airlines B.707 9V-BFW at 1324 (SQ763A from Zurich), RAF VC-10 XV101 at 1243 (RR2495 from Akrotiri) and Irish Cessna 182 EI-AOD at 1409, which was also a Heathrow diversion! There was a temporary improvement in the London weather by late afternoon, but it fell below limits again around teatime, when two further Heathrow diversions arrived including another first time visitor: Kuwait Airways B.707 9K-ACU at 1842 (KU181 from Rome) and Nigeria Airways B.707 5N-ABJ at 2014 (WT914 from Rome). Aircraft turned away from Manchester today because of handling problems or ground congestion included Qantas B.747 VH-EBG (QF001), EL AL B.707 (LY315) and MEA B.720 (ME201).

December 1975

British Airways reported an 800% increase in bookings for next summer, compared to the same time last year! Passengers carried on their Manchester-London route in 1975 were the highest for ten years, up 10% on last year.

There were fifty-one weather diversions during the month, with the main sessions on the 12th and 15th. Saturday 20th also had potential, when London's main airports were affected by fog for long periods, but Manchester could only take a few due to the industrial action.

There were numerous Tradewinds CL-44 visits during the month, in connection with exporting bridge sections to Baghdad.

Japan Airlines B.747 JA-8122, which diverted in on 30th November, was involved in a serious incident during the month, after skidding off the runway at Anchorage and sustaining $21m worth of damage!

ILS traffic observed and identified were Brazilian Air Force HS.748 C91-2511 (4th), BFS HS.748 D-AFSI (6th) & RAF Victor XL188 (10th).

2nd   Royal Saudi Air Force operated just two flights during the month. C-130H 465 from/to Jeddah via Milan as RSF812 today and C-130E 1602 from/to Jeddah as RSF889 on the 19th.

2nd   BAF Carvair G-ASDC, arriving at 1110 to operate a cattle charter to Ostend, was in a bare metal colour scheme.

12th   Dove G-AJGT was one of the oldest British registered aircraft to visit this year, arriving at 1614 from Heathrow as FC550, having already been in twice this year. Registered in 1947, it spent the first twenty-seven years operating for Bristol Siddeley Engines, who later became Rolls-Royce. In late-1974, it was purchased by Fairflight Charter, to add to their growing inventory of Dove's and Heron's, although not all of these were airworthy. From 1976-1979 it was operated by Alderney Air Ferries, before being withdrawn and broken up in 1979.

12th   Today saw the arrival of six Heathrow diversions, all 'Speedbird' flights. There were three Boeing 747s, two Boeing 707s and one SVC-10. The passengers were kept onboard, pending an improvement in the weather.

14th   Lufthansa operated Boeing 727 D-ABKJ on today's Frankfurt LH076/7 and again on the 21st. Others were D-ABLI (28th) and D-ABKE (30th).

15th   This diversion day started off with low cloud and 200m visibility and although the fog soon cleared, it remained a dull day. Heathrow however remained below limits for most landing aircraft until the following morning, but even so the only diversions arriving at Manchester by midday were two British Airways 747s: G-AWNI at 1100 (BA881 from Tehran) & G-BBPU at 1046 (BA600 from Montreal) and one of our Heathrow-bound services that had returned back to Manchester (BE4405). At lunchtime I witnessed the arrival of Aer Lingus B.707 EI-ANV (EI9164 from Dublin). In the meantime, Air New Zealand DC-10 ZK-NZN 'Speedbird 598' was holding at Pole Hill beacon and had decided to divert to Gatwick, but by the time he was southbound approaching

Honiley beacon he was told Gatwick was full after accepting diversions all morning, so he did a 180° turn and proceeded to divert to Prestwick. However, on his way north he heard B.747 G-AWNL (BA941) en route Prestwick-Heathrow hoping in vain for a clearance in the London weather, but soon after he requested a diversion to Manchester, the pilot of the Air New Zealand DC-10 did the same and became the first visit of the airline to Manchester. I caught its arrival just before returning to school and by mid-afternoon I was lucky enough to see first time visitor Qantas B.747 VH-EBC at 1357 (QF007 from Frankfurt) and the first visit of a Singapore Airlines B.747 when 9V-SIB arrived at 1402 (SQ773A from Frankfurt). I also saw the first Gulf-Air VC-10 into Manchester when A4O-VK arrived at 1412 (GF005 from Abu Dhabi) and the very final visit of an Alitalia DC-8 with I-DIWG at 1518 (AZ280 from Rome), which was the same aircraft that arrived on Friday 24th October. I didn't see any more diversions after the arrival of SVC-10 G-ASGR at 1526 (BA801 from Kuwait), by which time there were six wide-bodied aircraft on the ground at Manchester, a record that lasted over twelve hours. The evening saw further diversions: Nigeria Airways Boeing 707 5N-ABJ at 1748 (WT902 from Kano), LOT Ilyushin IL-18 SP-LSE at 1832 (LO3909 from Krakow), Alitalia DC-9 I-DIKW at 1904 (AZ298 from Milan), first visit TWA B.707 N18704 at 2028 (TW702 from New York) and Alitalia DC-9 I-DIBD at 2115 (AZ316 from Pisa).

16th December 1975 – By this morning, there were five TWA aircraft on the ground. Joining B.707 N18704 (nearest) which arrived the previous night, were B.707's N28727 (TWA6754 from Boston) and N18707 (TW1756 from Philadelphia). The other two TWA aircraft not in shot, but making up the numbers were B.747 N93104 (TW700 from New York) & N93108 (TW760 from Los Angeles). (Geoff Ball)

16th December 1975 – Air New Zealand DC-10 ZK-NZN arrived yesterday afternoon with twenty-one other diversions. The airline operated long-haul routes on behalf of British Airways from 1975-1980. (Geoff Ball)

16th   Even though the morning's visibility was around 150m in fog, four TWA diversions arrived, two of which were first visits: B.707 N18707 at 0913 (TW1756 from Philadelphia) and B.747 N93108 at 0612 (TW760 from Los Angeles). By midmorning, when the fog started to clear, there were seven B.747s and a DC10 on the ground at the same time. When Wardair B.747 C-FDJC arrived at 1238 from Gatwick to operate a charter to Toronto, it meant that for three minutes, there were eight 747s and a DC10 on the ground at the same time. The previous record was set on 29th August 1973 with four B.747s and a DC-10. Later in the evening Wardair's other B.747, C-FFUN, arrived at 2250 to operate a charter direct to Vancouver, which meant there'd been ten different wide-bodied aircraft at Manchester within a 24-hour period.

18th   Unless the 7 inch crack, observed running the entire width of the landing strip near a point where the original runway joins the extension on the main 06/24 runway, gets any worse it will remain operational. The centre section of the runway, constructed after the war had no proper foundations and the original extension completed in 1951, added 600 yards at the eastern end of Runway 06/24. As the threshold of the original Runway 24 was at the highest point of the airport, extending from this point had created the infamous hump. Engineers feared there maybe problems, after several further extensions were carried out, hence the need for a second runway. Although there's no current danger to aircraft, the situations being closely monitored and night closures for several weeks are expected from March next year, so that repairs can be carried out.

20th   As fog affected Heathrow all day, Manchester should have received another influx of diversions, but instead it was handicapped by British Airway's continuing handling issues and a cabin crew strike from today to the 22nd. However, a small number of diversions did arrive, including a couple of first visits: MEA Boeing 720 OD-AFP at 1858 (ME201 from Beirut) and Kuwait Airways B.707 9K-ACJ at 1845 (KU197 from Frankfurt). Over the next few days the cabin crew strike was responsible for British Airways flights being sub-chartered by other airlines such as BIA, BMA, Britannia, Dan-Air, Spantax & Martinair.

22nd   Air Canada DC-8F C-FTJL arrived at 1534 (AC092 from Toronto), to operate an outbound cattle charter to Toronto.

23rd   Rousseau Aviation HS.748 F-BSRU arrived from Tours on a TAT flight, routing via Manchester to pick up spares.

25th   Yippee - I got my first pair of binoculars, a pair of Zenith 10x50's! From now on, weather permitting, I could read off most registrations, although there was little activity as it was Christmas Day. By this time, I was recording everything I saw, no matter how mundane and my ever growing logs were boosted by choosing window seats whenever in class, so I could see all the aircraft! With so many interesting and memorable diversion days towards the end of the year, my interest in the hobby increased, especially now I had my own binoculars.

26th   Alidair Viscount G-ARGR operated the final outbound newspaper flight, QA433, at 2330 to Lossiemouth, as they've been transferred to Liverpool.

First/Last Arrivals & Departures 1975

First arrival:	B.707 G-APFN/BA648 from Prestwick at 0948
First departure:	BAC 1-11 G-AVMO/BE842 to Dublin at 0841
Last arrival:	PA-27 G-BBTL from Dusseldorf at 2137
Last departure:	B.737 EI-ASC/EI9213 to Dublin at 2255

(+/- % on Previous Year)		
Scheduled Passengers	1,409,000	+ 3.5%
I.T/Charter Passengers	1,179,000	+23.0%
Transit Passengers	101,000	+2.0%
Total	2.689,000	+11.2%
Freight & Mail (Tonnes)	37,400	-19.3%
Movements	68,400	+5.0%

Airport Diary 1976

January 1976

The New Year brought a major development to Manchester Airport, when Dan-Air opened a maintenance facility in one of the old hangars for their 1-11s and HS.748s. Other Dan-Air types, such as Comets and B.727s, were also seen during the first month. From an enthusiast's perspective, most aircraft passing through the hangar for maintenance, overhaul or re-spray were fairly mundane, interspersed with the occasional interesting visitor. Fairey Aviation next door wasn't creating much interest either, except for two sporadic occasions when there was an influx of Islanders during the summer and Trislanders towards the end of the year.

Due to disappointing passenger numbers, British Airways will drop their Manchester-Munich service by the end of March. The load-factor on the route, set up to entice local businessmen to use Manchester instead of Heathrow, had dropped to around 20%. A new flight to Nice will commence at the end of March with new services to Frankfurt and Zurich planned for next year. Advance booking charters to Canada & USA, to be reintroduced this summer with return fares from £117, will supplement existing scheduled services and operate via Prestwick. A weekly summer flight will commence to Toronto on 31st May and to New York on 2nd June.

Crew training flights at Manchester were recommenced by British Airways, who operated SVC-10 G-ASGG (28th), L.1011s G-BBAE (12th/14th) & G-BBAI (9th/26th) along with Gulf Air example L.1011 G-BDCW (28th/30th).

ILS traffic observed included BFS D-AFSJ (23rd/27th/29th), RAF Victor XL512 (20th), RAF Canberra XH137 (23rd) and Dove G-ARHW (13th).

2nd The tail end of a hurricane passed through Manchester last evening and for most of today. Cessna 172 G-AVBZ diverted in yesterday from Crossland Moor, with wing-tip damage caused by the very high winds. £6,000 of damage was caused, when a crossbar of lights was ripped off a pole in the Bollin Valley and thanks to the valiant efforts of light aircraft owners, a wind-tunnel effect was avoided when they managed to close the doors of the South Side hangars.

5th Gulfstream 2 N677S arrived on a demonstration tour, routing Birmingham- Leeds.

5th RAF operated VC-10 trooping flights: XV105 RR2175 Brize Norton-Gutersloh & RR2176 from/to Gutersloh today and XV107 RR2180 Brize Norton- Gutersloh on the 7th.

6th Two Royal Saudi Air Force flights arriving today, C-130H 465 from/to Jeddah via Milan as RSF800 and C-130E 1606 from/to Jeddah as RSF1214, departed on the 8th.

9th Lufthansa operated Boeing 727 D-ABKG on today's Frankfurt LH072/3. Others were D-ABKJ (11th), D-ABKF (13th) and first visits D-ABKH (18th) & D-ABKG (25th).

13th French Air Force Paris No.93 stopped for fuel, en route Villacoublay-Aberdeen. It returned south on the 15th, again via Manchester.

19th French Air Force Falcon 20 No. 260 was also a fuel stop, from Shannon to Villacoublay.

21st Dan-Air Comet G-APME was slightly damaged after being struck by a pair of steps, whilst being moved in gale force winds.

22nd The Belgian Air Force were scheduled to operate a flight through Woodford today, with a customs clearance stop at Manchester, but due to high winds it was put off until the following day.

23rd C-130 CH-06 made its first visit, arriving at 1503 from Brussels, operating yesterdays delayed flight. C-130H CH-03 was the aircraft being used, but due to engine failure downwind at Woodford, it returned to Brussels without landing.

23rd RAF Canberra XH137 was carrying out a photo survey in the Trafford Park area, when it departed the Manchester Control Zone by performing an ILS, before leaving via Congleton.

28th Making its first appearance for the start of an extensive training programme, was Gulf Air L.1011 G-BDCW today. Delivered new only six days earlier, this and their second aircraft, G-BDCX, are currently based at Prestwick and will enter service on 1st April.

February 1976

Despite industrial action during the first quarter of 1975, the airport still managed an 11% passenger increase overall for the year, compared to 1974. Last month's passenger numbers of 155,000 showed an 8% increase compared to January 1975, although aircraft movements for the same period showed a reduction on the previous year.

The Airport Authority has been assured that although increased traffic would be inevitable, aircraft noise from a second runway would not spread, as it would only be used for landing traffic. The airports Director, Gordon Sweetapple, said it would be used for heavy or long range flights needing the additional length, or occasionally when the 06/24 was closed for maintenance.

Car park charges are to rise again from 1st March, with an hour's stay going up from 20p to 25p and daily parking from £1.10 to £1.30.

British Airways and Gulf Air undertook extensive crew training this month with B.707s G-APFJ (16th/18th), G-APFM (26th) & G-ARRC (15th); VC-10 G-ARVM (8th), SVC-10 G-ASGF (5th), L.1011s G-BBAE (4th/9th/23rd), G-BBAF (2nd/4th), G-BBAG (16th) and Gulf Air L.1011's G-BDCW (1st/6th/8th/13th/18th/20th & G-BDCX (22nd/25th/27th).

HS.748 ILS traffic included Ecuadorian Air Force FAE-739 (12th/18th). RAF traffic noted and identified were Victor XL512 (20th), Canberra XH137 (23rd) and Dove G-ARHW (2nd/13th).

1st February 1976 – British Airways used Manchester and Prestwick for extensive crew training on their new L.1011 Tristars since November 1974. By January 1976, they were joined by Gulf Air with their first L.1011, G-BDCW, seen here sporting the airlines new livery. It eventually became A4O-TW. (Geoff Ball)

2nd   Today finally saw the arrival of the first Belgian Air Force Pembroke to Manchester, when RM-9/OT-ZAI arrived at 0942 from/to Brussels.

3rd   The current European Cessna 500 Citation demonstrator, N287CC, stayed overnight at Manchester on a flight from Saarbrucken.

3rd   Two Royal Saudi Air Force C-130s made their first visits this month. The first, C-130H 1604 was today as RSF802 from/to Jeddah via Milan, before departing on the 5th. The second, C-130H 464 as RSF803 from/to Jeddah, was on the 24th.

3rd   Sabena Boeing 737 OO-SDJ, operating the inbound SN617 from Brussels, landed safely having declared a full emergency with no flaps!

3rd   Dan-Air's latest Comet, G-BDIF, made its first appearance today positioning in from Edinburgh at 1649. Bought by Dan-Air in 1975, it was formerly ST-AAX with Sudan Airways.

5th   Condor B.727 D-ABNI made its first visit this evening, operating Lufthansa LH072/3, unobserved by most as it arrived in total cloud cover at 200ft.

7th   Last night's failure of the areas main electricity substation hit Ringway, Styal and Heald Green. More than 10,000 homes were without power, but the airport was unaffected thanks to its emergency back-up system.

8th   Lufthansa operated Boeing 727 D-ABKA on today's Frankfurt LH076/7, which was also a first visit. Others used were D-ABKH (15th) and D-ABFI (22nd).

8th   The Royal Marines operated Gazelle XX376 through Manchester from Blackburn to Chester. The return flight in the opposite direction, passed through the following day.

9th   It's my thirteenth birthday and I was given the aircraft radio I'd been promised. The Kingsonic, approximately 12" x 7", was encased in black vinyl crocodile type skin, except for the facia. It had the standard bands, AM/FM/LW/MW, short wave/airband/PB (police band) and WB (weather band), although I never heard any police or weather transmissions on it. It took months to master and understand the jargon, radio frequencies and which traffic could be heard on which band was hard to say the least! Because the airway frequencies were so confusing, I decided to concentrate purely on the local ones and by the summer I was familiar with them and their traffic.

After lots of practice, I was confident enough to tackle other frequencies and adopted a simple logging system, one I would use for another ten years, which I referred to as my tracking-books. Going up and down the frequencies on the tuning dial and noting everything I heard was the name of the game, although the scatter-gun approach had more purpose if there were any diversions!

9th Skyways Cargo Douglas DC-3 G-AGYZ arrived at 2006, on a freight flight from Dusseldorf. It had seen service for over thirty years and was a piece of history! Operating for BEA for many years, based at Berlin-Templehof, it had been involved in the Berlin Airlift of 1948-49. Skyways sold the aircraft in Ethiopia in 1977.

12th Gulfstream 2 N711SC made its first visit, arriving at 1535 from Aberdeen.

17th British Airways Viscount G-AMON made its final visit, before being withdrawn on 31st March. It was ferrying passengers from/to Prestwick, when Montreal/Toronto flight BA648/9 was terminated at Prestwick, after B.707 G-APFN became unserviceable.

18th British Caledonian B.707F G-BDLM (BR6196) was inbound with cattle from Australia.

18th Belgian Air Force DC-6 KY-2/OT-CDB arrived at 1145 on a return flight from Brussels.

19th In a repeat performance of the 17th, British Airways Viscount G-AMOG arrived ferrying passengers from/to Prestwick, due to unserviceable B.707 G-ARRC. It was also its final visit, as it too was withdrawn on 31st March. Both G-AMOG & G-AMON had been used primarily on a feeder service between Prestwick, Edinburgh & Aberdeen.

21st A short diversion session brought the first visit of Bangladesh Biman B.707 S2-ABN at 1023 (BG001 from Dacca/Dubai). Today also saw the first visit of a Braathens B.737 since 17th October 1973, when B.737 LN-SUP diverted in from Stansted at 0052 (BU731 from Gothenburg). The only other diversion of note was East African Airways VC-10 at 0836 (EC654 from Athens).

22nd Gulf Air L.1011 G-BDCX made the first of many crew training flights during the month, supplemented by their other L.1011, G-BDCW.

22nd HS.125 AN-BPR, arriving briefly to clear customs whilst on its delivery flight, was the first ever visit of a Nicaraguan registered aircraft.

23rd British Air Ferries Herald G-BDFE, with its VIP interior, arrived as part of a nationwide demonstration tour from Birmingham to Aberdeen.

24th PA-31 G-OLLY visited during the day. It had one of the early out-of-sequence registrations and although it wasn't the first, it spawned a phenomenon! No prizes for guessing it was owned by Robertson's Foods, even using the call-sign 'Gollywog'!

24th The North West Flying School based at Manchester was formed on this date.

29th Mooney N6934V arrived at 1917 clear customs, en route from Le Touquet to Blackpool.

29th PA-22 Colt G-ARUC was blown over by a freak gust! It was eventually dismantled in the South Side hangars after being declared a write-off!

March 1976

The Airport Authority's monthly figures for February showed an overall growth in aircraft movements of 10%, compared to the same month last year.

British Airways will reintroduce the Aberdeen service from next month, with retimed flights to give passengers longer at Aberdeen. From April, they will also reintroduce their early morning Manchester-Heathrow flight, (BE4403), after being suspended for the winter.

More crew training flights took place during month including British Airways L.1011s G-BBAJ (28th) & G-BEAK (11th) and Gulf Air L.1011 G-BDCX (7th/10th/19th/21st/24th).

HS.748 ILS traffic observed were Ecuadorian Air Force FAE-739 (2nd) and private 5H-WDL (23rd), which first flew from Woodford on the 19th and will be delivered eventually to Williamsons Diamond Mines of Tanzania. RAF traffic noted and identified were Nimrod XZ283 (5th/16th), C-130 XV178 (15th) and Victor XL158 (23rd).

1st Today's arrival of Belgian Air Force Pembroke RM-7 was the second to visit and the first of several Belgian Air Force flights this month. Although most flights were scheduled to be operated by Pembroke's, the type and/or the timings nearly always changed!

2nd German Air Force operated their first training flight through Manchester this year, when Transall 50+05 arrived at 1047 as DCN2184, from Alhorn to Northolt.

7th A crated Rothmans Pitts Special, identity unknown, was observed today outside the Fairey hangar. It arrived on 15th February onboard Tradewinds CL-44 G-AWGS (IK2078 from Baghdad) and then spent time outside the freight import warehouse, before being removed by road. The Pitts Special had originated from Bahrain, after performing at air shows.

11th Martinair DC-9F PH-MAO departed with day-old chicks, ultimately bound for Libya. A further flight with more chicks was operated on the 16th by PH-MAR.

11th The arrival of Belgian Air Force C-130H CH-08 at 1108 from Brussels, originally started out as a DC-3 flight, but before departure it was then changed to a DC-6. However, after the DC-6 burst its tyres on landing at Northolt, C-130 CH-08 was sent to continue the mission and flew direct from Northolt to Manchester, instead of via Woodford as originally scheduled.

15th Lufthansa operated Boeing 727 D-ABKJ on Frankfurt LH072/3 today and 26th/31st.

16th Saturn C-130 N10ST arrived at 2315 (TV10 from Stuttgart) as a Stansted diversion and N12ST routing Frankfurt-Gander, called in on the 18th with a fresh crew to take N10ST out.

16th Sabena B.737 OO-SDA arrived at 1345 from Brussels, bringing in Anderlecht FC to play Wrexham the following evening.

16th Korean B.707F N370WA was the first visit of a Korean Airlines aircraft, albeit a leased one from World Airways. It was taking out large sections of steel for a power station, but loading the cargo was so chaotic, it departed sixteen hours late! Due to the fiasco, it was the only flight of this nature.

17th Trans European A.300 OO-TEF and B.720 OO-TEB brought in Anderlecht FC supporters for their European Cup-Winners Cup tie with Wrexham. The 1-1 draw meant the Belgian's progressed and Wrexham were out of the competition.

17th PA-30 G-AWKF made a wheels-up landing on Runway 24. After extensive repairs it finally departed on the 30th July.

18th Aer Turas Britannia EI-BBH arrived at 0344 on its first visit, operating from/to Venice on a cattle charter. Purchased from the RAF in August 1975, it served with the airline until October 1981.

19th Bergen Air Transport DC-4F LN-MOB, arriving on a return freight flight to Stavanger, was only to last with the airline for another year before being sold in Zaire as 9Q-CPB. Its ex-United States Coast Guard and it first flew in 1945.

19th The first of Dan-Air's five recently purchased ex-RAF Comets to visit was G-BDIV at 1647, operating a City-link flight from Newcastle to Teeside. First visit dates of the others were G-BDIT (4th June), G-BDIU (12th August), G-BDIV (19th March), G-BDIW (8th July) and G-BDIX (21st May).

21st March 1976 – Belgian Air Force made four visits with Douglas DC-3 aircraft between September 1975 - March 1976. This shot shows of KY-8/OT-CND in basic Sabena colours, having just arrived from East Midlands on a wet, quiet Sunday afternoon. (Geoff Ball)

24th Royal Saudi Air Force C-130H 1603 made its first visit today, arriving at 1123 as RSAF85 from/to Jeddah via Milan, before departing on the 26th.

26th   The third Belgian Air Force Pembroke to visit was RM-11/OT-ZAK, arriving at 1651 from Brussels. It also visited on the 28th from Northolt to Brussels.

29th March 1976 – Air Botswana HS.748 A2-ABB arrived for maintenance after being on a two-year lease from Dan-Air. It departed on 16th April as G-AZSU and served with Dan-Air until March 1982 before being leased to British Airways. (Geoff Ball)

April 1976

British Airways new evening scheduled service from/to Aberdeen with a HS.748, was cancelled due to a staff dispute and didn't commence until 31st May.

     Dan-Air's city-link service introduced in 1970 may cease, if the airports concerned remove the special concessions they've been operating under and decide to increase landing and handling fees. Despite improvements over the past twelve months, services between Teeside, Newcastle, Manchester, Birmingham, Bristol, Cardiff & Bournemouth, are still not breaking even.

     Another batch of British Airways Viscounts withdrawn in March/April will be scrapped and their last visit details are as follows:

G-AOHJ   29/03   Last flight 06/04/76, stored at Newcastle
G-AOHK   09/03   Last flight during 04/76, stored at Leeds
G-AOHO   18/03   Last flight during 03/76, stored at Jersey
G-AOJB   22/03   Last flight 01/04/76, stored at Liverpool
G-AOJD   19/03   Last flight during 03/76, stored at Jersey

     The following airlines made changes from this month. Air France became a weekday operation with Boeing 727s. British Airways will operate B.707s on New York service (BA538/9) and SVC-10s on Montreal/Toronto (BA648/9), cargo flights will operate twice-weekly to Montreal/New York (BA467) and inbound direct from New York on Fridays (BA468), a new service to Nice will be introduced, but flights to Munich ceased last month. Morning KLM flight KL153/4 operates daily, but the lunchtime KL155/6 has been dropped. Lufthansa will continue five-weekly freight flights to Frankfurt with Boeing 727s. Sabena's passenger flight SN617/8 has been re-timed to evenings daily, except Saturdays and the cargo flight will remain five-weekly.

     HS.748 ILS traffic observed was confined to Ecuadorian Air Force FAE-739 (5th/6th). RAF traffic noted and identified were Canberra XH137 (1st), Dominie XS732 (23rd), British Airways VC-10 G-ARVM (3rd/4th/7th), Dove G-ARHW (7th/27th) and RAE Comet XS235 (29th).

1st   Today's arrival of Sabena B.737 OO-SDM was the first of the airlines six B.737s making their first visits this month. The others were OO-SDD (6th), OO-SDE (14th), OO-SDL (11th), OO-SDN (4th) and OO-SDO (26th).

5th   RAF VC-10 XV106 (RR2412 Brize Norton-Belfast) and C-130 XV223 (RR4984 Lyneham-Belfast), were taking part in an emergency airlift to Northern Ireland today. Other trooping flights were VC-10 XR806 (RR2339 to/from Hanover-8th) and VC-10 XV101 (RR2344 to Gutersloh-20th).

5th   This month's Belgian Air Force flights were C-130H CH-07 at 1244 Northolt-Brussels today, Douglas DC-6s KY-2/OT-CDB at 1538 from/to Brussels (6th), KY-1/OT-CDA at 1420 from/to Brussels (9th) and Merlin CF-01 at 1154 from/to Brussels (13th).

8th   Lufthansa operated Boeing 727 D-ABIZ on today's Frankfurt LH072/3. Others during the month were D-ABIJ (9th) and D-ABIY (23rd).

9th   Skyways DC-3 G-AGJV operated a return cargo flight from Aberdeen.

9th   Beech 95 G-APUB, currently owned by famous World War II pilot Douglas Bader, arrived at Fairey's for a check-up, before departing to White Waltham on the 30th.

13th   British Airways BAC 1-11 G-BBMG operating BE188, diverted in en route Birmingham-Dublin with a suspected bomb onboard, but following a thorough search it was found to be clean.

14th   Swissair used a stretched Douglas DC-9-51 for the first time, when HB-ISM operated this evening's SR840 from Zurich.

24th   US Army CH-47 20954 hovered over the Freight Apron for three minutes this morning, en route Burtonwood-Northolt.

27th   Portuguese national carrier TAP operated a charter to Funchal with first time visitor Boeing 727 CS-TBS, which also operated the return leg on the 30th.

28th   Norwegian carrier Nor-Fly, made its first visit to Manchester today with the arrival of CV-440 LN-KLK at 1857 from Torp. Formerly SE-BSR with SAS, this aircraft was purchased by Nor-Fly in December 1975 and made numerous appearances until its last on 25th April 1980.

May 1976

British Airways Cargo increased Montreal/New York flight (BA467) to three-weekly and passenger services to New York (BA538/9) and Montreal/Toronto (BA648/9) will be operated by SVC-10s.

The following airlines have summer IT programmes from Manchester: Aviaco, Aviogenex, Balkan, Inex-Adria, JAT, LOT, Spantax, Tarom & Trans-Europa; as does a variety of UK operators: Britannia Airways, British Airtours, British Airways, British Caledonian, Dan-Air & Laker Airways. Airlines operating regular flights to the USA/Canada this summer are British Caledonian (B.707), CP Air (DC-8), Dan-Air (B.707), Laker Airways (B.707/DC-10) and Wardair (B.707/B.747). Other USA/Canada flights were operated by Pan American B.707s N403PA (29th) & N493PA (8th) and TWA B.707s N8729 (28th), N18709 (1st) & N28728 (22nd).

ILS traffic included Belgian Air Force HS.748 CS-01 (28th/31st) and Dove's G-ARHW (6th/7th/25th/26th) & G-ASMG (27th). British Airways crew training flights were B.707 G-APFM (2nd), B.747s G-AWNM (25th/26th) & G-AWNN (4th/5th/7th) and VC-10 G-ARVM (27th).

3rd   USAF Douglas C-9 71-0876, the military version of the DC-9, made its first visit today on a flight from Saragossa to Mildenhall.

5th   Long-term resident Beagle 206 G-AWRO left for Leeds at 1202, after being stored since 27th April 1975.

6th   The Belgian Air Force operated a couple more flights during the month. C-130H CH-06 Northolt-Bristol was at 1240 today and the last visit of one of their Pembroke's was RM-11/OT-ZAK, operating from Northolt to Brussels on the 28th.

9th May 1976 – Iranian Air Force Boeing 707 5-244, noted with a refuelling boom, was the first of sixteen freight charters from/to Tehran operating between today and the 19th September 1977. Note the 'AF' on the forward fuselage with the proceeding letters 'II' (Imperial Iranian) scrubbed out. Also note that the Jackson brickworks chimney in the background is no longer operating. (Geoff Ball)

12th   PA-23 F-BVUC arrived at 0939 on a fuel stop, en route Nancy-Glasgow.

12th   Martinair operated a charter from/to Amsterdam as MP3768, with DC-8 PH-MAU.

12th   Manchester received a couple of visitors in connection with the European Cup Final in Glasgow, between Bayern Munich and St. Etienne. Falcon 20 D-COLL and Lear Jet D-CONI arrived to park, as there was no room at Glasgow or Prestwick!, A massive airlift of French and German fans to Glasgow was undertaken, as the French contingent alone was estimated at 25,000. The teams contested an excellent final, which was won by Bayern Munich 1-0.

13th Only the second aircraft of its type to visit was Falcon 10 F-BXAG, arriving at 1013 from Glasgow, before its departure for Gatwick.

17th After undertaking numerous test flights over several weeks, long time resident Beagle 206 G-AVCI finally departed at 1032. Routing Liverpool-Leeds-Prestwick-Stornaway, it was on delivery to its new owners in the USA.

19th A pair of CV-440s, N14278 & N25278, owned by the Armstrong Cork Company, arrived closely together this morning from Newcastle. They were making their first visits since 1970, before departing for Dusseldorf.

22nd VC-10 XR806 RR2405 Brize Norton-Brussels and C-130 XV191 RR4937 Lyneham-Hanover were on trooping flights.

27th Shorts demonstrator, SD-330 G-BDMA, made its first visit to Manchester today. The twin-engine transport aircraft is designed to carry up to thirty passengers and it first flew in August 1974.

28th Swissair used a stretched Douglas DC-9-51 again this month, when HB-ISS operated this evening's SR840 from Zurich.

29th May 1976 – HS.748 C-GMAA, arriving at 1741 on a Saturday afternoon, was in a very 'seventies' scheme. It was on delivery for Austin Airways routing Bastia-Stornaway, before its departure for Stornaway on the 31st. Delivered new to British airline BKS in 1965, it only saw a year's service, before being sold in Mexico. (Geoff Ball)

30th Monarch Airlines BAC 1-11 G-AWWZ arrived at 0111 to operate Laker Airways flight, GK628, to Palma.

31st Trans European A.300 OO-TEF positioned in from Brussels to operate a pilgrimage flight to Lourdes. The return flight was operated by three Britannia Airways B.737s!

June 1976

British Airways started a weekly Wednesday New York charter flight (BA431/0) from the 2nd until October, with the return operating Mondays and a weekly Monday Toronto flight (BA411/0) from the 7th, returning on Wednesdays. Lufthansa used two Boeing 727s on its Frankfurt passenger service, D-ABKG (19th) and D-ABSI (23rd). Swissair changed types twice during the month, when the Douglas DC-9-51 operated SR840/1with two first visits, HB-ISP (6th) and HB-ISL (30th).

Non-scheduled transatlantic flights were operated by Pan American B.707s N406PA (24th), N424PA (18th), N491PA (26th), N885PA (27th) and TWA B.707s N8729 (12th), N8731 (26th), N18709 (19th), N28727 (12th/19th) & N28728 (5th).

The only ILS traffic observed and identified were Belgian Air Force HS.748 CS-01 (25th) and Mosquito RR299 (25th).

2nd Norwegian operator Bergen Air Transport, made its final visit to Manchester today when Douglas DC-4F LN-MOJ operated from Southend to Belgrade, on behalf of British Air Ferries.

3rd Laker Airways BAC 1-11 G-AVBW (GK243 to Palma), reported a bird strike on takeoff.

4th My sisters fiancé, Steve Sayles, took me to the Blackpool Air Show today, in his white 1967 Hillman Minx. Apart from my annual bus trip to Woodford Air Show, it was my first official spotting trip outside of Manchester. Amongst the exhibits was the future of the RAF, the Panavia Tornado XX946, performing stunning aerobatic displays.

5th VC-10 XV105 RR2451 Brussels-Brize Norton and C-130 XV214 RR5389 Brussels-Lyneham were both trooping flights.

6th Alaska International C-130 N107AK arrived from Manston at 1209, to transport a very large piece of machinery. The aircraft, white with a thin blue cheatline, had an interesting '1776-1976' bi-centenary motif. Their last C-130 to visit Manchester, N9263R in 1970, was in a very different scheme of all-silver with 'Alaska' written in large red letters on the forward fuselage.

8th Tunis Air Cessna 414 TS-DMH arrived at 1402, operating a training flight from Brussels. It had flight planned touch-and-goes at Gatwick and Birmingham, before stopping at Manchester prior to returning to Brussels via Liverpool, Bournemouth & Jersey.

8th Another Merchantman leaving the British Airways fleet during the month was G-APEM, making its last visit today operating BE3023/18. It was sold to Europe Air Service as F-BYCE.

9th Belgian Air Force operated C-130H CH-07 at 1037 from/to Brussels today and C-130H CH-04 at 1204 from Lyneham-Brussels on the 21st.

9th Witnessed by the writer from a classroom, was the only visit of Argosy G-APRM. Owned by Rolls-Royce since 1970, it's used for various duties, including transporting the company's aero engines. Routing from Bristol-Filton to Munich, it regularly flies to Toulouse in connection with the Olympus engine development for Concorde.

13th Mooney HB-DWH was on delivery when it arrived at 1839 to night-stop, en route Reykjavik-Zurich.

15th Today was the second visit of an Imperial Iranian Air Force Boeing 707, when 5-242 arrived at 1817 (ELF137 Heathrow-Tehran), before departing on the 17th.

16th Transavia SE.210 Caravelle PH-TRY, arriving at 1558 operating a return flight to Amsterdam as HV7849/50, was heard by the writer - but not seen due to annoyingly low cloud!

18th RAF HS.125 XX508, operating from RAF Northolt to Cardiff, was carrying the Prime Minister, James Callaghan.

18th The writer was treated to another daytrip by Steve Sayles, this time to Heathrow - or so he thought! After being on the road for twenty minutes, it was obvious his car wouldn't make it, so we headed for Castle Donnington instead, which took a further three hours! It was my first visit and although it was quiet for a summer Saturday, it was good to be somewhere different. The only activity was British Midland B.707 G-AYVG, with Syrian Arab titles, carrying out endless approaches and overshoots. British Midland Herald G-ATIG also came and went, along with several light aircraft, but that was pretty much it. On the airfield were several Viscounts in various states of dereliction and an all-white ex-Pan American B.707, N701PA, present since 1972 and missing its tail. The weather, which had been warm and sunny, had clouded over by the time we left, but before going home we headed off to Salford Docks to see the ex-RAF Comet XR659 we'd heard was being used as a restaurant. It had been flown to Ringway in 1975, dismantled then transported to its present location and reassembled. Named "Westward Ho", it was located next to the owners other toy, a floating nightclub also called "Westward Ho". I was glad the Comet hadn't been consigned to the scrapyard, but I couldn't help feeling sad that instead living out its final days transporting military top brass or troops around Europe, it now had the indignity of satisfying the seventies veracious appetite for chicken-in-a-basket and scampi-and-chips! As we watched endless pairs of platform shoes traipsing on and off the graceful machine, it started to rain and the fading light only added to the depressing scene! On the way back I thought that in spite of its current circumstances and lack of former prestige, I was still pleased I'd seen it!

22nd Jetstream G-AWVK called in to carry out trials on the ILS, using the call-sign 'Decca Navigator'.

24th HS.125 F-BOHU arrived at 0834 from Lille for pre-customs clearance, bound for Hawarden. It returned on the 26th, again to clear customs prior to its return to France.

25th An unidentified RAF Buccaneer performing a practice ILS, came within 30ft of landing. In conjunction with the Woodford Air Show, it was followed minutes later by Mosquito RR299.

26th US Army Beech U-21 18010, operating from Leeds to Berlin, was the first US Army aircraft to visit Manchester since 10th October 1973.

26th   The RAF were busy with trooping flights this weekend, transporting 400 plus Territorial Army soldiers out for a two-week camp in Germany. Four C-130 aircraft were involved today, operating from Lyneham to Bruggen: XV183 (RR5088), XV186 (RR5086), XV200 (RR5090) and XV296 (RR5084). The following flights operated from/to Bruggen on the 27th: XV183 (RR5089), XV196 (RR5087) & XV296 (RR5085).

26th   Heron G-AOZN had only operated for Fairflight Charter since early 1975 and today it made the last of its three visits, routing Biggin Hill-Gatwick before being sold in New Zealand in September. It was a regular visitor during the 1960's, when it was operated by Mercury Airlines.

27th   Two Pan American Boeing 727s made their first visits during the month, both from/to Berlin-Tegel. N357PA as PA366G was today and N323PA as PA367G on the 28th.

28th   Swedish Air Force C-47 79002, arriving from Karup in a natural and metal day-glo scheme, was carrying the King's Head Badge of F8 (Transport Wing) and the F13 Squadron code.

28th   Greek registered aircraft are extremely rare at Manchester and the only arrivals over the years have been from Olympic Airways, mainly on diversion from Heathrow. However, Mitsubishi MU-2 SX-AGQ arrived at 1053 today from Leavesden.

30th   Sterling will operate a series of weekly charters to/from Copenhagen via Dublin using SE.210 Caravelle's on alternate Wednesdays or Thursdays, dependant on the route (Wednesday NB548 Dublin-Copenhagen & Thursday NB547 Copenhagen-Dublin). The first flight operated today with SE.210 OY-SAK, arriving at 1430 (NB548 Dublin-Copenhagen) and the last was on the 2nd September with SE.210 OY-SBW at 1229 (NB547 Copenhagen-Dublin).

July 1976

Local based air-taxi operator Manchester Air Taxis was acquired during the month by NEA.

British Airways further reduced their cargo flights. The Montreal/New York flight (BA467) finished at the end of the month, which just left the Friday morning New York flight (BA468).

Lufthansa used the following Boeing 727s on its Frankfurt passenger service: D-ABGI (27th), D-ABKI (2nd), D-ABQI (23rd/24th) & D-ABRI (5th). Swissair operated the Douglas DC-9-51 on SR840/1 twice and both were first visits, HB-ISK (15th) and HB-ISR (7th).

Non-scheduled transatlantic flights were operated by Pan American B.707s N404PA (24th), N428PA (25th) & N885PA (17th) and TWA B.707s N8729 (3rd/11th), N8731 (31st), N18709 (31st), N18712 (31st) & N28728 (24th).

The only ILS traffic observed and identified were Belgian Air Force HS.748 CS-02 (14th) and RAF Dominie XS735 (22nd). British Airways crew training flights were B.707 G-ARRA (1st) and VC-10 G-ARVM (8th).

1st   Three German light aircraft; Cessna 310 D-ILGT, Beech 55 D-IHAT and Cessna 210 D-EAMK, were all seen at Manchester today, which is not a common occurrence!

2nd   Based Airview Cessna 172 G-AYGO departed during the morning, but never returned as it crashed shortly afterwards in Ireland.

4th   Loganair Trislander G-AZZM called in at 1725, en route Leeds-Glasgow.

5th   IAS DC-8F G-BDDE, arriving at 1110 (FF9242 from Rome) on a hot Monday morning, was to transport an outbound load of computer equipment for Melbourne.

5th   Two Ilyushin IL-18 flights, arriving this afternoon were on the ground together for six minutes! LOT IL-18 SP-LSH at 1615 (LO3271/2 Krakow-Warsaw) and Balkan IL-18 LZ-BEV at 1817 (LZ6047/8), brought in a band from Sofia, taking part in a concert in Manchester.

8th   Lufthansa B.707F D-ABUA arrived at 1129 as LH6072/3 with a consignment of cheesecloth shirts from India – and who wasn't wearing one in 1976?

10th   Another busy weekend for the RAF, returning the Territorial Army soldiers from Germany, who'd gone out last month. Two C-130s, XV188 (RR5249/5250) and XV217 (RR5248/5249) operated two return flights from Wildenrath today.

11th   BAC 1-11 N504T arriving at 1448 from Nice, was the first non Dan-Air aircraft to receive attention at their hangar. It left for Le Bourget on the 15th, after an engine change.

11th   Air Malta leased World Airways B.727 N692WA for the summer season, which made the first of three visits today, operating KM106/7.

12th The latest Iranian Air Force B.707 to visit was 5-249 (ELF138 from/to Tehran). It differs from the previous two, as it has attachments for refuelling drogues on its wingtips, a double width window on either side near the rear of the fuselage and like the previous aircraft it had a flying-boom refuelling probe.

14th The first HS.748 for the Belgian Air Force, CS-01, was delivered ex-Woodford on 28th June. Although it carried out numerous training flights, it hadn't actually landed at Manchester until today, when it arrived at 1225 from/to Brussels to night-stop.

15th Canadian Air Force Boeing 707 13701 made a brief stop at 1330, en route Prestwick-Mildenhall, operating the first training flight through Manchester since 26th June 1974.

18th Gulf Air L.1011 A40-TY, arriving at 1902 as GF100 en route from the Montreal Olympics, had the Sultan of Oman and his travelling entourage onboard. An entire floor of the Excelsior Hotel was booked for their exclusive use, prior to departure back to Doha.

19th Lufthansa B.747F D-ABYE (LH7072/3), made its second visit to Manchester, arriving at 0223. Its cargo, from the USA via Frankfurt, included a piece of freight weighing 31 tonnes.

21st French Air Force Falcon 20 No. 167 operated a touch-and-go at 1333, en route from Shannon to Villacoublay.

23rd Overseas National made two first visits this month. Douglas DC-8 N821F arriving at 1201 today inbound from Gander, was carrying an organ society and DC-8 N819F operated from Prestwick to Gatwick on the 16th.

24th Besides Balkan and LOT, another airline operating Ilyushin IL-18 flights this month was Hungarian state-airline Malev, with two first visits. HA-MOE arrived at 1300 (MA0560/1 from/to Budapest) today and HA-MOG operated the return flight (MA0562/3) on the 14th August.

27th Cargolux CL-44 TF-LLI operated an outbound charter today, taking bridge sections to Benghazi on behalf of Tradewinds, even using a Tradewinds flight-number.

28th German Air Force Transall 50+79 was the first this year and unusually it used its serial as its call sign (DCN5079).

28th July 1976 – .One of the best movements of the year was the one and only visit of a Royal Saudi Air Force Jetstar 101. Arriving a day later than planned, it attempted to leave on the 31st, only to return ninety minutes later with fuel pump trouble, before eventually departing on the 5th August. (Geoff Ball)

31st Today's arrival of Tupolev TU-154 CCCP-85139 at 1315 (SU3637/8 from/to Leningrad), was the first Aeroflot charter to Manchester since August 1974. The return flight operated on 15th August with TU-154 CCCP-85054 (SU2243/4) and both were first visits.

August 1976

Environment Secretary, Peter Shore, has given approval for the airports £6m cargo terminal. It's to be sited on the north western side of the airport, with initial capacity for 200,000 tonnes per year and provision for future expansion. The commencement date for the work however, won't be given until the airport authorities see an improvement in the freight figures.

British Airways are planning to operate the six long-range L.1011 Tristars they have on order, on services out of Manchester by 1979. They will replace SVC-10s on the Manchester-New

York service and greatly reduce noise levels. The 235-seater aircraft are capable of flying up to 6,000 miles without refuelling.

A work-to-rule and go-slow by Barcelona ATC at the end of the month seriously disrupted charter and scheduled flights to Spain. It's a non-union strike, as Spanish law forbids the forming of a trade association, which is one of the reasons for the strike! They also want to see drastic improvements in ATC facilities, before a major incident occurs.

Lufthansa used two Boeing 727s on their Frankfurt passenger service: D-ABIW (1st) and D-ABKQ (31st). Non-scheduled transatlantic flights were Pacific Western B.707 C-FPWV (26th), Pan American B.707s N435PA (16th), N496PA (28th), N885PA (14th), N887PA (7th) and TWA B.707s N763TW (first visit-21st), N764TW (21st), N8729 (14th/28th), N18712 (21st) & N28728 (7th/22nd).

The only ILS traffic observed and identified was Citation 500 PH-CTF (24th).

6th   Spantax CV-990 EC-BQQ, arriving at 2205 (BX2503/2 from/to Palma), was actually delayed Dan-Air flight DA2502/3.

7th   Pan American B.707 N457PA, delivered new to the airline in 1967 as a pure-cargo aircraft, made its first visit today. It was operating a freight charter from Heathrow, before eventually departing for Shannon.

7th   Dan-Air B.707 G-AYSL landed as a full emergency at 1012 inbound from Gatwick, operating a transatlantic charter on behalf of British Caledonian. It was half way between Gatwick and Manchester, when the pilot suspected the landing mechanism had jammed. As the instrument panel showed a suspected hydraulic failure, the situation was serious enough to alert RAF Scampton of a possible foam-landing. He made several holds and a low sweep over the Tower, so a visual check could be made by ATC, who confirmed the undercarriage was down and it landed safely. The aircraft and its passengers continued their onward journey 24-hours later.

9th   Iranian Air Force B.707 5-244 arrived at 1903 as ELF157 (from/to Tehran), before departing on the 11th.

10th   Ex-RAF Andover XS607, civil registered as G-BEBY, is being used by Hawker Siddeley on a sales tour. Its military markings were covered and it carried Hawker-Siddeley titling.

12th   Intra Airways DC-3 G-AMPO arrived at 1627 from Jersey to transport oil rig equipment to Sumburgh.

14th   Cessna 411 C-GTUR arrived at 1633, returning home from Le Touquet after a European holiday tour. It was carrying badges from several countries on the nose-wheel door and the passengers were observed as mostly teenagers.

14th   The Red Arrows performed a loop prior to their arrival at 1900 from Waddington. They left for their performance at the Manchester Air Show at Barton the following afternoon, returning thirty minutes later, before departing via Buxton to Waddington.

19th   African Safari Britannia 5Y-AZP arrived at 1923, operating a flight on behalf of 'reborn' Invicta International, which is now a pure-cargo airline. The aircraft was eventually purchased by Invicta and restored to its original registration of G-ANCF in January 1977.

21st   British Airways Malta-Manchester flight BE935 operated by Boeing 707 G-APFG, landed twelve hours late due to a rabies scare at Malta. The delay was caused by the aircraft having to be fumigated at Malta, after the crew suspected a rat had got onboard!

23rd   Dutch Government F.28 PH-PBX was in civilian marks and flown by a Martinair crew. Used by Government Ministers and VIP's, today's arrival at 0901 from Amsterdam brought in the Dutch Minister of Housing, undertaking a tour of urban renewal in Manchester.

24th   Royal Saudi Air Force C-130E 460 made its first visit today, arriving at 1035 as RSF815 from/to Jeddah via Milan, before departing on the 26th.

24th   Dan-Air Comet G-BBUV operating DA4482 to Palma with 115 passengers onboard, returned to Manchester for an emergency landing, with a fire-warning light on. It circled for forty-five minutes to dump fuel before landing safely. Met by several fire engines, there was no sign of any fire! After an inspection, the problem was found to be a faulty instrument.

29th   In the midst of a long hot summer, dense fog in the South East provided Manchester with twenty-one diversions from London. Those of note were the first visit of a National Airlines DC-10, when N82NA arrived at 0806 (NA002 from Miami); the first diversion arrival of a British Airways L.1011 with G-BBAE at 0835 (BE309 from Malta) and the first visit of Pan American B.747 N657PA at 0824 (PA002 from New York). In all there were eleven wide-bodied jets during the day and as ten were on the ground at the same time, a new record was set. Diversions in such quantities are rare for August and the last time this happened was in 1973, which coincidentally was also on the 29th August! I decided to go to the airport rather late in the day, to see if anything was still there. The day had been warm but unusually cloudy, but by the time we got to the terraces the sun was breaking out and there were plenty of diverted aircraft still on the ground, mostly long-haul probably due the crews going 'out of hours' and being unable to fly them back to London.

29th August 1976 – Included in this shot of parked diverted aircraft are three British Airways Boeing 747s: G-AWNO 'Speedbird 660', G-AWND 'Speedbird 500' still in full BOAC colours but BA titles, G-BBPU 'Speedbird 010' and departing B.707 G-AYLT operating BA539 Prestwick/New York. (Geoff Ball)

29th August 1976 – National Airlines had recently replaced DC-8s and were now using Douglas DC-10s on their NA002/1 Miami-Heathrow-Miami service. N82NA, which had arrived during the morning on its first visit to Manchester, is seen taxiing for departure back to Heathrow. (Geoff Ball)

September 1976

Pelican Air Transport, currently being set-up by two pilots, will be the first all-cargo airline based at Manchester. They plan to acquire two Douglas DC-8s, which can carry up to 35 tonnes of cargo non-stop to the Middle East and beyond, serving points in East and West Africa. Operations will start next April and seventy-five staff will be employed initially. They hope to plug an obvious gap, currently being served by the motorway network, as air freight continues to be roaded to London.

British Caledonian will operate BAC 1-11s on the Manchester-Gatwick route from January 1977. The BIA Heralds currently being used will be transferred to the airlines Rotterdam services. A new midday Manchester-Gatwick service will also be added, operated by Heralds.

British Island Airway's application to operate a Manchester-Isle of Man route has been rejected. Had they have been successful; they would be competing with British Airways.

British Airways will introduce the Boeing 747 on their Manchester flights to Canada & USA from next May. Flights to New York will operate three days a week, with the SVC-10 being used for the rest of the week. Toronto will be served by the B.747 four days a week and again, the SVC-10 will operate the rest. They announced that in a bad year generally for airlines, passenger figures across the Atlantic from the North showed a 40% growth!

European football returned to the North West after several years. Manchester City had not played European football since 1971, but having won the League Cup Final in March, they had qualified for the UEFA Cup, which would be played over two legs. It was not a happy return however, as although they won the first leg at home against Juventus 1-0, they lost the away leg 2-0 and were out of the competition. Manchester Utd were also playing European football again. They won the European Cup in 1968, but were knocked out the following year and the side went into decline. In 1974 they were dealt the ultimate embarrassment of being relegated from Division One, after being defeated on the final day of the season by one of their former greats, Dennis Law, back-heeling a goal for City and condemning them to Division Two football the following season. United fans tried their best to get the game abandoned, by spilling onto the pitch and although it was stopped temporarily with several minutes left to play, the referee decided the result would stand without returning the players to the field. Manchester United were relegated, but returned to the First Division at their first attempt, even reaching the FA Cup Final in May 1976 as red-hot favourites, only to be humbled by Southampton; but despite losing they entered the UEFA Cup the following season. In September 1976 they overcame Ajax of Amsterdam over two legs. Ironically, in the second round they met the conquerors of Manchester City, Juventus. Like City, they won the first leg 1-0 at home, but lost at Juventus again, going down 3-0 in Rome. All this provided some much missed football traffic into Manchester Airport, albeit short-lived.

Lufthansa used two Boeing 727s again on their Frankfurt passenger service, D-ABHI (5th) and D-ABKD (14th). Non-scheduled transatlantic flights were Pacific Western B.707 C-FPWV (26th), Pan American B.707s N428PA (3rd), N433PA (26th), N884PA (2nd), N887PA (4th) and TWA B.707s N18709 (4th/17th), N18712 (25th) & N28727 (9th/11th).

ILS traffic observed and identified was just French Air Force Falcon 20 F-RAFL (15th).

2nd   RAF HS.125 XX507, operating from/to Northolt (RR1533), was dropping off the Prime Minister, James Callaghan for various local engagements.

5th   RAF VC-10 XV104 (RR2633 from Gutersloh), operated the months sole trooping flight.

6th   Two British Airtours B.707s made their final visits to Manchester today. G-APFB arrived at 0847 (KT891 from Malta) and G-APFI arrived at 2203 (KT995 from Athens). Both aircraft departed Gatwick bound for Kingman, Arizona in November, for eventual scrapping.

8th   Belgian Air Force operated the following aircraft during the month: C-130 CH-07 arrived today at 1023 from Brussels to Bristol, C-130 CH-02 at 1019 from/to Brussels on the 14th and first visit HS.748 CS-02 at 0953 from/to Brussels on the 29th.

8th   Iranian Air Force B.707 5-250 was a first visit, arriving at 1433 operating from/to Tehran as ELF158, before departing on the 10th. Another flight on the 30th, B.707 5-8310 arriving at 0915 as ELF159 from/to Tehran, wasn't technically a first visit, as it had visited earlier in the month in its previous incarnation as 5-250.

9th   PA-28 Cherokee PH-NSF arrived from Luton at 1737, to be British registered at NEA. It eventually became G-BEFF and departed for Woodvale on the 20th January 1977.

10th   British Airways Trident 3 G-AWZT and Inex Adria DC-9-51 YU-AJR were completely destroyed in a mid-air collision over Yugoslavia, with a combined loss of 176 lives.

11th   Lufthansa B.707F D-ABUO made its first visit today, operating cargo flight LH4072/3.

11th   Air Algeria operated a freight flight with leased Boeing 707 ET-ACD today. AH7548 arrived at 0904 from Algiers and departed at 1740 for the central Sahara town of Hassi Messaud.

13th   Gulfstream 2 N677S, operated by Sentry Insurance, arrived on a round-trip from Luton in a very smart white, brown and gold colour scheme.

14th   Royal Saudi Air Force C-130H 462 made its first visit, arriving at 1130 as RSF630 from/to Jeddah via Milan, before departing on the 16th.

14th   Alitalia DC-9 I-DIBJ arrived with Juventus FC for their UEFA Cup tie against Manchester City, which City won 1-0 and the team returned on DC-9 I-DIKE on the 16th. Their return two weeks later brought bad news for the plane-spotting fraternity, when the Blues lost 2-0 in Rome and were out of the UEFA Cup and Europe for the season.

15th KLM operated Douglas DC-8-63 PH-DEA on KL153/4, due to an increased inbound load bringing Manchester United fans back from Amsterdam, after their game with Ajax FC.

19th British Caledonian BAC 1-11 G-AXJL made its last visit, (BR694/3 from/to Alicante). It was sold in January 1977 to Philippine Airlines as RP-C1188.

24th HS.125 EC-CMU, arriving at 1708 from Stansted, was making a first visit. After night-stopping it proceeded onwards to Hawarden for a major overhaul.

27th Martinair F.28 PH-MOL arrived with Ajax FC to play Manchester Utd in the return leg of their UEFA Cup Tie, having won their home tie 1-0. The team returned on the 29th on Fokker F.28 PH-MAT, after losing 2-0 and consequently being knocked out of the European Cup. Manchester Utd progressed to the second round and will meet the conquerors of Manchester City, Juventus!

27th This morning's arrival of Jetstar N731A was the second visit of the type this year. It was also only the third different aircraft since N3E in 1971.

27th For the sixth successive weekend, major delays were recorded at Manchester Airport due to an ongoing work-to-rule by Spanish ATC. The longest delay was DA2372 (Manchester-Malaga), operated by Comet G-APYD, which was fourteen hours late. Several other flights were also delayed by two to five hours and British Airtours flight KT891 (Malta-Manchester) operated by Boeing 707 G-APFF, was fifteen hours late due to technical trouble.

29th The second British Caledonian aircraft making its last visit this month was B.707 G-AZJM, (BR2840 from New York). It was sold to British Midland, to add to their growing collection of B.707s for leasing out.

October 1976

The second runway planning application has been called in by the Secretary of State for the Environment, Peter Shore, which means a public enquiry will be held at a date to be announced.

Remedial concreting work is being carried out, due to holes appearing all over the apron. When the taxiway opposite the end of Pier 'B' was repaired earlier, it resulted in three stands being withdrawn for a month and now Pier 'A' is receiving similar attention. Eventually the red-island between the two piers and the complex taxiway junction near the end of Pier 'A' will be strengthened. The work will be carried out over two nights in November, when the runway will be closed for five to seven hours.

Due to high demand, British Airways will continue to operate the Nice service through the winter. Five more Boeing 707s were disposed of during the year and their last visits were as follows:

G-APFM	18/10	Withdrawn 01/11/76, flown to the USA for scrapping
G-APFN	27/02	Withdrawn 03/76, flown to the USA for scrapping
G-ARRA	11/08	Transferred to British Airtours during 10/76
G-ARRB	08/01	Withdrawn 01/76, flown to the USA for scrapping
G-ARRC	06/10	Transferred to British Airtours during 03/77

This just leaves G-APFJ from the original batch, which is being used for crew training purposes only.

My friend and fellow spotter Michael Sutcliffe had been a member of an aviation society called PB Enterprises for a while and each month he received their publication covering Manchester movements, trip reports, features and various aviation related articles. It was a good source of tying up aircraft I'd seen but needed the registrations for, so this month I decided to join, along with several of my school friends. Soon afterwards Pete Wilson, Ian Barrie and I booked places on a day's excursion to Heathrow, which included Biggin Hill and even though the trip wasn't until Saturday 29th January 1977, our anticipation was 'off the register'!

It was another lean month for ILS traffic. Observed and identified were French Air Force SE.210 Caravelle 141/F-RAFG (20th) & RAF Whirlwind XP338 (22nd). British Airways crew training flights were B.707 APFJ (14th) & VC-10 G-ARVM (21st).

2nd Tarom TU-154 YR-TPB, operating the last IT flight of their summer programme (RO769/770), was replacing an unserviceable B.707 which in turn was replacing an unserviceable IL-62!

4th   Pacific Western B.707 C-FPWJ, arriving at 0910, was operating a flight on behalf of CP Air (PW773 Prestwick-Gatwick).

4th   No less than four Gulfstream 2s made their first visits this month. N663P arrived at 0614 from Gander today, N4290X at 1536 from Birmingham (14th), C-FFNM at 1609 from Dusseldorf (20th) and Luton diversion N530SW at 2357 from Gander (26th).

5th   HS.125 G-BDOA arrived with Fulham FC titling, in connection with their League Cup replay with Bolton Wanderers. It's believed Rodney Marsh, George Best and Bobby Moore were onboard. It left bound for Tel Aviv via Rome and Heraklion after the game, which was nothing short of farcical, when Bolton equalized in the sixth minute of extra time, added on for time-wasting! When the Fulham players protested, the referee sent Bobby Moore off for the first time since 1961 and only the second time in his career! To cool the situation, the manager Alec Stock took the team off the field, but the referee in the company of two policemen, issued an ultimatum that unless Fulham were back on the pitch within two minutes, he would abandon the tie in favour of the home team Bolton. Ten-man Fulham returned to the match and the League Cup replay ended in a draw.

13th   Argosy 9Q-COA arrived at 2002 for attention with Dan-Air. Formerly ex-RAF XR136, it had been stored at Shackletons Aviation in Bournemouth. It was in basic RAF colours, with the cheatline and registration on the tail boom sprayed out with blue aerosol paint, except for the last three numbers of the serial on the tail which were untouched, as was the squadron badge. The 'Borough of Wallingford's' crest was also still visible on the cockpit window, as was the Royal Air Force titling on the nose. The new registration was taped onto the booms with red tape and the military serial was still visible under the wings. Upon arrival at Manchester, it spent a couple of days in the South Bay before being towed to the hangar, where it was stripped to bare metal and had the nose radome removed. It's to be refurbished and re-sprayed for Otrag Range Air Services, who plan to use two aircraft as support for the assembly of a missile launch facility in Zaire, which is in competition with NASA and the European rocket, Arianne.

17th   Dan-Air Comet G-ARJK made its last visit to Manchester, arriving at 1912 (DA1341 from Athens), before positioning out to Birmingham the next day at 1438. It's very final flight was Birmingham-Lasham on 1st November, for withdrawal from service.

18th   Dan-Air Comet G-AYVS was also making its last visit, arriving at 0123 (DA4493 from Alicante), before positioning out to Glasgow at 1608. It's very final flight was Gatwick-Lasham on 6th January 1977, for withdrawal.

19th   Alitalia DC-9 I-DIKQ arrived with Juventus FC for their UEFA Cup Tie against Manchester Utd, which they lost 1-0. The team returned on DC-9 I-DIBQ on the 21st and as Utd lost the return leg 3-0, the aggregate score meant they wouldn't be playing anymore European football this season.

19th   The sole Douglas C-54F operated by Aer Turas, EI-ARS, made its last visit when it diverted in at 1913, due to fog at Leeds. Purchased from Balair in 1969, it was sold in 1977 as N88887.

20th October 1976 - Alisarda DC-9 I-SARV (IG962/3), arriving with Juventus fans in connection with their UEFA Cup tie with Manchester Utd, was the airlines only visit to Manchester. This particular DC-9 operated with the airline until 1980, when it was sold to a private company as N5NE. (Geoff Ball)

21st   TWA B.707 N18709 was operating TW8131, an outbound charter for the Yorkshire Evening Post to San Francisco and Las Vegas.

22nd   The day started off ordinarily enough. It was half-term week and I'd gone to the airport for the day with a few friends, but early on we were evicted from the terraces for kicking a sugar cube around!! We relocated to the landing lights at the corner of Shadow Moss Road and Ringway Road where we stayed until 4pm, by which time the weather had deteriorated considerably. It got to around 800m visibility in drizzle and it was getting quite windy, when out the gloom came RAF Whirlwind XP338 performing an ILS approach, which was a great and unexpected treat!

23rd   Air Anglia F.27 G-BDDH arrived at 1212 as AQ1024, transporting Norwich FC for a First Division match with Manchester Utd, which ended in a 2-2 draw.

24th October 1976 – McCulloch International Boeing 720 N7201U arrived on a gloomy Sunday. The aircraft had a VIP interior, with a maximum capacity of forty passengers. The starboard side of fuselage carried the inscription "Gary Wright" and the port side read "Frampton Comes Alive", referring to his multi-million selling live album and "Bandana does it again" was written in small letters over the port forward door. It was the personal transport of Peter Frampton, one of the biggest superstars at the time, while undertaking a world tour and he'd arrived at Manchester for a concert that evening. The aircraft, which had the notoriety of being the first Boeing 720 ever produced, was repossessed in November 1977 and eventually scrapped at Luton in 1982. (Geoff Ball)

November 1976

British Air Ferries have been granted a licence to operate to Antwerp and Rotterdam from Manchester. They will use Heralds, but as yet, no start date has been announced.

Having already confirmed their Nice service will continue through the winter, British Airways will also operate five-times weekly to Milan, as opposed last winter's four flights a week.

Jetsave, the country's largest advanced booking charter company, will increase flights between Manchester, Canada & USA by 40% next year. Montreal has also been added to their existing destinations of Toronto, Vancouver, New York, Los Angeles & Chicago.

FOG! It was responsible for an awful lot this month, from blotting the place out to playing host to many interesting diversions from other airfields. However, most of the foggy periods in the South East were short lived, as either Gatwick or Heathrow tended to be open at any one time, but this month we did teach them a lesson in how to produce persistent fogs! One airfield that rivalled Manchester for poor visibility this month was Leeds-Bradford, which was fog-bound on many days. Manchester received an incredible thirty-eight diversions, with Air Anglia being particularly common.

Airline changes this month were: Air France reverted to a six-weekly service with SE.210 Caravelle's. British Airways operated a Trident 3 on Friday evening (BE4436/4407) departing on Saturday morning, but in-between operated to/from Malta as BE934/5. New York (BA538/9) was reduced to five-weekly and Montreal/Toronto (BA648/9) to six-weekly, although both went back to a daily service December-mid-January. KLM flight KL153/4 operated Monday-Saturday, lunchtime flight KL155/6 on Sundays and cargo flights remained at three-weekly. Winter IT flights are operated by Britannia Airways, British Airways, British Caledonian, Dan-Air, Monarch Airlines and Laker Airways, who are also operating weekly ABC flights to Los Angeles, New York & Toronto.

Lufthansa used the following Boeing 727s on their Frankfurt passenger service: D-ABDI (26th), D-ABHI (16th), D-ABIE (28th), D-ABII (17th) & D-ABKB (22nd).

ILS traffic observed and identified were RAF Whirlwind XP338 (1st), HS.125 5N-AKT (2nd) & Dove G-AREA (18th). British Airways crew training flights were B.707s APFJ (5th) & G-AYLT (30th).

1st   Canadian Air Force B.707 13701, arriving at 1421 operating a further training flight from Prestwick to Mildenhall, was noted with UN badges on the tail.

3rd   A cold and clear winters morning produced eight fog diversions from Heathrow, six of which were British Airways. The other two arrivals were first visitor Qantas B.747 VH-EBL at 0645 (QF007 from Bombay) and Olympic Airways B.720 SX-DBK at 1150 (OA2594 from Athens), bringing in fans from AEK Athens for their UEFA Cup game with Derby County that evening.

4th   British Airtours B.707 G-APFK, operating inbound charter from Turin as KT071, was making its last visit as it crashed on a crew training detail at Prestwick in March 1977.

4th   Another two Gulfstream 2s made their first visits this month. Fluor Corporation N400M arrived today at 1604 from Amsterdam and made numerous visits up until 1983 and N200A arrived at 2106 from Gander, as a Heathrow diversion on the 14th.

5th   Heron G-AOTI arrived from East Midlands to operate a return flight to Glasgow. Registered new in 1956, it's been operated by Rolls-Royce ever since and continued to serve them until it was sold in 1982.

7th   Long-time resident Beagle 206 G-BCJA suddenly sprang to life today, after sitting inside the South Side hangars since August last year. It departed at 1147 to be overhauled at Biggin Hill, before flying to the USA.

9th   The airport had virtually ceased functioning due to dense and persistent fog, but one of the few flights that made it on a very foggy evening was the first visit of an Aeroflot AN-12. CCCP-11526 arrived at 1845 (SU2241/2 from/to Riga) in 400m visibility, to fly out a consignment of rabbits and luckily the cloud broke long enough for the writer to see it!

9th   A group chartering Peter Aviation Herons G-ANSZ & G-ANXA to fly them from Manchester to Norwich, left by coach instead due to persistent fog delaying their departure. Both aircraft finally positioned back to Norwich on the 11th.

9th   Argosy 9Q-COA was fully painted this month, in a mainly day-glo red scheme. Due to be named 'Jason', it spent most of the month inside the hangar.

9th   Fairey received no less than eight Trislanders and two Islanders for storage this month and with the exception of one Islander, they were all new, effectively straight from the production line. With the hangar being so crowded they were frequently parked outside for long periods, which made viewing much easier for the spotters!

9th   Two RAF Pumas, XW222 & XW224, made fuel stops en route Wittering-Crosby.

10th   Today saw a mere eight arrivals, due to dense fog.

11th   Once Manchester's fog had cleared, the other airports suffered, particularly Leeds which was fog-bound all day. As a result, Manchester received seventeen diversions, including five Air Anglia flights with four different aircraft: G-BAKL, G-BAUR, G-BDDH & G-BDVS. Heathrow and Gatwick were also affected for a short time in the morning, but the only diversion from Gatwick was World Airways DC-8 N806WA, arriving at 0029 (WO806 from Athens). Heathrow was affected for longer and produced first time visitors TWA B.707 N8730 at 0627 (TW754 from Boston) and National Airlines DC-10 N81NA at 0657 (NA002 from Miami). Other diversions were British Airways B.747 G-AWNK at 0644 (BA010 from Nairobi), British Airways B.707 G-AYLT at 0843 (BA560 from Boston) and TWA B.707F N15713 at 0925 (TW622 from New York).

12th   There were no arrivals from 1514 today until 0134 on the 14th. SK537 operated by Douglas DC-9 LN-RLN left Manchester for Dublin, only to return due to their weather and then find itself fogged in at Manchester, unable to leave for another 24 hours.

13th   The airport was at a virtual standstill due to fog. There were no arrivals and only twelve departures. Flights were diverted to Liverpool, East Midlands & Birmingham and buses were organised to transport the passengers to their diverted planes.

14th   Normal operations resumed today after visibility increased just enough to make it possible. Although Manchester still had some fog in the afternoon, it had dispersed by the evening but all the southern airports were affected by early evening. The first diversion into Manchester was Heathrow regular Gulf 2 N200A at 2106, followed by seven diversions in a twenty-two minute period, including British Airways L.1011 G-BBAI at 2112 (BE745 from Copenhagen), SAS DC-9 OY-KGH at 2120 (SK505 from Stockholm), Alitalia DC-9 I-DIKU at 2124 (AZ316 from Pisa) and two first visits: TWA B.707 N773TW at 2127 (TW702 from New York) & TAP B.727 CS-TBR at 2248 (TP9817 from Oporto).

14th November 1976 – After an extremely foggy last few days, Dove G-APSO and Heron G-ANNO are seen here having recently arrived to operate outbound charters to Lyon. Operated by Biggin Hill-based Fairflight Charter, they served with the company until 1977 and 1980 respectively. (Geoff Ball)

14th The highlight of the evening was the arrival of the first Concorde to Manchester. I was puzzled when I heard 'Speedbird 578' for the first time on approach 119.4, although I was a regular listener of the airways, I'd never picked up this flight before and as it got closer and closer, I still wasn't sure what type of aircraft it was. It wasn't until it transferred to Tower 118.7 as 'Speedbird Concorde 578' that I realised what it was. It was still around 7-miles from touchdown and as I wouldn't be able to see it until it was 5-miles out, I turned the lights off in the lounge so I could see it better and even at 7-miles out it was an awesome sound! She did not disappoint once she'd sailed over, such a fantastic sight, even in the dark! Her flying time was three hours thirty-nine minutes from Washington and she'd spent no time holding at Heathrow prior to diversion to Manchester. The passengers were held onboard until the pilots checked the weather forecast and as no improvement was imminent they were offloaded. Some chose to spend the night at the Excelsior Hotel and others completed their journeys to London on a specially chartered train.

15th November 1976 – Gulf Air VC-10 A40-VK was an early morning diversion. None of the airlines VC-10s were ever painted in the new colour scheme, but it still looks impressive. British Airways Boeing 747s G-AWNE & G-BDPV can be seen in the background. (Geoff Ball)

15th I was hoping the day would start where the previous one left off, so I faked a cold and took the day off school in anticipation of what might arrive! The day showed early promise when Gulf Air VC-10 A4O-VK arrived at 0624 (GF121 from Bahrain). Further flights followed with British Airways B.707 G-AXGX at 0741 (BA560 from Boston) and B.747s G-BDPV at 0732 (BA600 from Toronto) & G-AWNE at 0941 (BA510 from New York), but by midmorning they'd petered out. This may have been due to handling issues, as by lunchtime aircraft were still diverting from Heathrow to other airports. Yesterday's Concorde had been parked at the end of Pier B, which was soon closed off due to the sheer number of spectators. The afternoon was fairly quiet and just as operations seemed back to normal, fog descended on the south again. By teatime Manchester was handling a varied selection of diversions and the first to arrive was IAS CL-44 G-BCWJ at 1702 (IK2704 from Istanbul), followed by British Airways L.1011 G-BBAF at 1706 (BE009 from Paris) and Alitalia DC-9 I-DIZE at 1710 (AZ280 from Rome). There was a slight gap before the next batch, starting with British Airways SVC-10 G-ASGI at 1737 (BA317 from Jeddah), the first visit of a Lufthansa A.300 with D-AIAB at 1758 (LH034 from Frankfurt) and British Caledonian B.707 G-BDSJ at 1809 (BR3111 from San Francisco). The final diversion was Tradewinds CL-44 G-AWGS at 2252 (IK2722 from Lagos).

22nd   First time visitor Iranian Air Force B.707 5-8311 arrived at 1331 as ELF201 (from/to Tehran), before departing on the 24th.

22nd   Oman Air Force Viscount 502 arrived for maintenance/overhaul with Dan-Air Engineering, work which had previously been carried out by Airwork at Bournemouth. It was present until the 23rd January 1977, when it departed to Bournemouth for further work.

30th   Norwegian Air Force Falcon 20 No 53 diverted in from RAF Binbrook at 1256, after failing to divert to Leeds-Bradford.

December 1976

The month started where the last one left off, with fog disrupting operations. For six of the first fourteen days, including the 3rd, there was just one arrival all day and six on the 4th. Leeds-Bradford fared just as badly and the South East was affected by fog and snow.

A drop in last month's passenger figures, caused by fog, meant the airports annual target of 3 million wouldn't be reached. However, it was still a record as a figure 2,726,659 was reached by the end of November, compared to 2,538,129 for the same period last year.

9th   HS.748s PK-IHK & PK-IHM arrived from Reykjavik, en route for Nice, whilst on delivery for Bouraq of Indonesia. Although not strictly hangar movements, they were looked after by Dan-Air.

13th   Sterling SE.210 OY-SAM, arriving at 1134 on a shopping charter from Billund, actually arrived via Birmingham, having diverted there earlier in the day due to fog at Manchester.

13th   On a very murky morning, Malaysian Airlines B.707 9M-MCR made its first visit to Manchester, arriving at 1019 (MH894 from Kuwait). Another Heathrow diversion of interest was Simbair Boeing 707 5X-UWM, operating East African Airways flight (EC556 from Cairo).

14th   Lufthansa operated just one B.727 on LH072/3 with today's visit of B.727 D-ABFI.

15th   Twenty Leeds diversions arriving at Manchester over the last two days were mainly Air Anglia and British Airways flights, with nothing of interest amongst them.

16th   Canadian Air Force B.707 13703, arriving at 1349, was another training flight routing Prestwick to Brize Norton. Like the previous visitor 13701, it had UN badges on the tail.

16th   Another Bouraq HS.748, PK-IHG, passed through Manchester on delivery today, before its departure for Nice on the 22nd.

17th   Private VC-10 A40-AB arrived at 1459, on diversion from Gatwick with burns patients for treatment in the UK.

17th   Overseas National DC-8 N866F arrived from Frankfurt to operate a Laker Airways outbound flight to Toronto, before returning the following day.

18th   HS.125 N51993 (formerly G-AZAF), was on delivery to the USA via Keflavik, when it arrived to clear customs.

20th   First time visitor Iranian Air Force B.707 5-8312, arrived at 1347 as ELF178 (from/to Tehran), before departing on the 22nd.

20th   There was a severe lack of sunshine at Manchester this month and today was no exception. However, the airport soon brightened up with the arrival of thirty-one diversions from airports such as Heathrow, Gatwick, Luton, Birmingham, East Midlands, Leeds, Humberside, Finningley, Gamston & Brough; but the only one of note was Gulf Air VC-10 A4O-VC at 0901 (GF121 form Dubai), making its first visit.

21st   The second Nor-Fly aircraft to visit Manchester was CV-440 LN-MAP. Arriving today at 2046 from East Midlands to Glasgow, it returned on the 29th at 1701 from Stavanger.

21ˢᵗ December 1976 - Otrag Argosy 9Q-COA is seen leaving for Bournemouth, several weeks late after its refurbishment. Due to the number of problems incurred, the second aircraft 9Q-COE 'Sharon' was converted at East Midlands. (Geoff Ball)

23rd British Airways Concorde arrived at a very cold Manchester for the second time today, when G-BOAA landed at 1158 as BA301 from Bahrain, again diverting in due to fog at Heathrow.

24ᵗʰ December 1976 - HS.748 G-BEJD, arriving for Dan-Air on delivery, was formally LV-HHE. It was previously owned by Aerolineas Argentinas and later by YPF (Yacimientos Petroliferos Fiscales), an Argentinean Oil Company. It was present until the 7ᵗʰ March 1977. (Geoff Ball)

29ᵗʰ On a cold crisp morning, seven diversions arrived from Heathrow. Amongst three British Airways arrivals were B.747 N93107 at 0655 (TW760 from Los Angeles), Qantas B.747 VH-EBE at 0714 (QF007 from Bombay) plus first visits South African Airways B.747 ZS-SAN at 0701 (SA226 form Sal Island) & BWIA B.707 9Y-TEK at 0755 (BW900 from Port of Spain).

First/Last Arrivals & Departures 1976

First arrival:	B.737 G-AVRO/BY356Y from Malta at 0040
First departure:	B.737 G-BADR/BY320W to Malta at 0811
Last arrival:	B.737 G-BAZI/BY330G from Alicante at 2246
Last departure:	Trident 3 G-AWZD/BE934 to Malta at 2227

(+/- % on Previous Year)		
Scheduled Passengers	1,499,000	+6.3%
I.T/Charter Passengers	1,264,000	+7.2%
Transit Passengers	112,000	+10.8%
Total	2,875,000	+6.9%
Freight & Mail (Tonnes)	36,400	-2.7%
Movements	73,900	+8.0%

Airport Diary 1977

January 1977

Fog and snow continued to affect operations at Manchester and other UK airports, particularly midmonth, during a severe wintry spell.

British Airways Super 1-11 Division, set up five years ago as Manchester's airline, is to be axed as part of a reorganisation plan. The airline has made it clear that the changes will not affect Manchester services, although it does reverse the thinking behind the original plan of giving the division the flexibility to organise its own capacity and schedules. Manchester services and their eighteen strong Super BAC 1-11 fleet will become part of the new UK & Ireland Division on 1st April.

British Airways have lodged an appeal against BAF's proposed Manchester-Antwerp/Rotterdam service. British Air Ferries are intending to make Manchester their Midlands and North base and introduce more services. The Antwerp/Rotterdam service, originally due to commence in April, is likely to be put back due to the appeal.

Air Malta will lease a Boeing 707 (G-AZTG) from Dan-Air for the summer season, to supplement the airlines B.720s.

Of particular note this month was the arrival of three HS.748s: PK-IHI (4th), PK-IHH (9th) and PK-IHJ (12th), passing through on their delivery flights to Bouraq-Indonesia.

KLM utilised Douglas DC-8 PH-DCU on KL155/6 (2nd) and Lufthansa used the following Boeing 727s on their Frankfurt passenger service: D-ABKB (11th), D-ABKD (14th) and D-ABKF (16th). Sabena operated Boeing 707s OO-SJG (16th) and OO-SJO (13th) on passenger flight SN617/8.

ILS traffic observed and identified was French Air Force Falcon 20 167/F-RAFL (19th). British Airways crew training flights were VC-10 G-ARVM (22nd), SVC-10s G-ASGE (8th) & G-ASGH (17th) and B.707 G-APFJ (12th/14th/15th/16th/18th/24th/26th).

1st   British Caledonian began operating BAC 1-11s on two of its three Manchester-Gatwick services today. BAC 1-11s will operate the morning rotation (BR981/4) and teatime (BR985/992); but Heralds will still operate the last Gatwick-Manchester flight of the day (BR991) and the first outbound Manchester-Gatwick (BR982).

4th   Two military flights operated today. Belgian Air Force HS.748 CS-02 arrived at 1229 from/to Brussels and the latest Iranian Air Force flight, B.707 5-8313, arrived at 1902 as ELF179 (from/to Tehran) before departing on the 6th.

6th   Fog affected operations today when fourteen flights were diverted away mostly to Liverpool, including BY400G B.737 (Palma-MAN), BE4414 & BE4418 BAC 1-11s (Heathrow-MAN), BE917 BAC 1-11 (Brussels-MAN), EI206 BAC 1-11 (Dublin-MAN) and Viscount G-AOJE (Jersey-MAN). Others were LH4072 (Frankfurt-MAN) diverting to Amsterdam, SK059B (Copenhagen-MAN) diverting to Glasgow and SN131 (Brussels-MAN) diverting back to Brussels.

10th   British Midland B.707 G-AZWA operated an inbound Jetsave charter (BR2792 from New York), on behalf of British Caledonian. Formerly a Donaldson International aircraft, it was sold later in the year in October as N70798, having operated for British Midland since March 1975.

11th   French Air Force Nord 262 No. 86 was a Warton diversion, but when it was due to depart the following day, it developed an unserviceable starboard engine. French Air Force Paris No.53 was dispatched from Villacoublay with the necessary spare parts, but by the time the Nord 262 was ready to leave on the 13th, Manchester had closed due to snow, but it managed to depart just before midnight.

13th   Manchester saw the third arrival of a British Airways Concorde, when G-BOAD made its first visit as 'Speedbird Concorde 301' from Bahrain, with twenty-nine passengers onboard. Although Heathrow was suffering from snow showers during the day, it diverted in for fuel due to lengthy holding delays caused by Heathrow running single runway operations. However, from 1600 onwards it was Manchester's turn to be affected, when numerous flights were diverted away.

13th   Hawker-Siddeley demonstrator HS.748 G-BDVH arrived at 1601 as a Woodford diversion due to snow.

13th   Sabena B.707 OO-SJO (SN617), held for over two hours at Brookmans Park beacon, awaiting snow clearance. When it finally landed on Runway 06 at 2245, it was making its first visit.

16th SN617/8 was operated by a B.707 again, this time OO-SJG which encountered none of the problems experienced by OO-SJO three days earlier!

16th Oman Air Force BAC 1-11 551 made its first visit today, arriving at 1119 (OU551 from Bournemouth) for maintenance with Dan-Air Engineering, before departing on the 21st.

16th January 1977 – Oman Air Force BAC 1-11 551 was present with Dan-Air until the 21st. On the 23rd, Viscount 502, which had been present since November undergoing major refurbishment, is seen here departing to Bournemouth for further work. (Geoff Ball)

17th Amidst some early Heathrow diversions were TWA B.707 N793TW at 0845 (TW754 from Boston), making it first visit and another appearance by Malaysian Airlines, with Boeing 707 9M-MCS at 0833 (MH894 from Kuwait).

19th Geminair Britannia 9G-ACE arrived at 1931 on a freight charter, departing for Tripoli with equipment for the Libyan Armed Forces.

25th Dan-Air HS.748 G-BEBA diverted into Manchester with hydraulic problems, operating DA060 routing Leeds-Glasgow. Emergency services were standing by as the aircraft landed and then shot off the runway onto the grass. Although it was quickly towed off to the Dan-Air hangar, the incident stopped all movements between 0808 and 0909, during which time Air France AF960 and British Caledonian BR981 diverted to Liverpool and DA052 was diverted to Leeds.

26th British Airways B.707 G-APFJ, the last of the original batch ordered by BOAC, made its final visit to Manchester on a crew training flight, before being transferred to British Airtours in April.

29th Dan-Air HS.748 G-AZSU was severely damaged while landing in bad weather at Sumburgh on the 10th. After temporary repairs, it was flown into Manchester today, unpressurised with its gear down for further work with Dan-Air Engineering, before finally leaving for Glasgow on the 29th March.

29th Saturday 29th January, the day of my first spotting trip to London had almost arrived! The meeting point was Mersey Square, Stockport at 23.30 (28th), to catch the PB Enterprises coach to Heathrow and Biggin Hill. After several local pick-up stops, the coach eventually sped to Heathrow, arriving around 5am. I was told the established spotting place was the Queens Building, but as it was closed until 9am, the place to go was to one of three car parks, although Terminal 3 was the favoured one. It was absolutely freezing on the top car park and the biting wind was very cold and very strong! I had no gloves with me and the only respite was to shelter inside one of the stairwells every few minutes, before going outside again to read off the next arrival. Despite the cold, I was at one of the world's busiest airports and it was very exciting. Once the Queens Building had opened, we had four hours to collect numbers and thaw out. It had fantastic views of the two runways, the terminals and various hangars on the far side. There were shops selling snacks, confectionery, aviation books and magazines as well as a sheltered seating area and toilets. It also had a PA system that gave a running commentary on aircraft arriving and departing, although it wasn't working on this particular day, but it was definitely in operation throughout the 1960's and into the 1970's. I still hadn't thawed out fully when we boarded the coach at Terminal 1 at 1pm, to be whisked off to Biggin Hill, via a tour of the Heathrow perimeter. This allowed us to see aircraft parked on the various maintenance areas and aprons, good for spotting the odd exotic executive visitor. Amongst the aircraft seen was Simbair B.707 5X-UWM, which had been operating for East African Airways. It had visited Manchester on one occasion and although I didn't know it at the time, it was impounded by the authorities, as the airline had ceased trading the day before. Its regular practice when an airline goes bust for the airport authorities and leasing companies to impound aircraft to recover any fees or debts. We arrived at Biggin Hill at 2.30pm and saw two aircraft dominating the scene - the withdrawn ex-IAS Britannia G-AOVP and antique Percival Prince N206UP, formerly G-ALWH, which was ready for its ferry flight to its new Stateside owners. The airfield itself, the hangars, its aprons and even the surrounding woods, provided all sorts of small and medium light aircraft, in various states of airworthiness. The hangars had been opened for us and we saw many Doves and Herons, some of which were quite literally 'out to grass'. The place was an aviation version of an antiques shop and being given a full tour of the airfield and all its curios was very enjoyable, but even though we were given a thoroughly warm welcome by all concerned, we were still frozen to the bone!

February 1977

Last year's hot summer and the severe winter frosts that followed, have taken their toll on large parts of the apron, which are in urgent need of repair. The deterioration of the concrete surface has reached such an extent that any available funds will be used to carry out thin layer repairs to the worst areas. Funding is also available for repairs to one of the main taxiways, which is a danger to movements, after suffering extensive frost damage.

Equipment changes on European scheduled services were Air France (AF960): B.707 F-BHSF (4th) and Lufthansa (LH072/076): B.727s D-ABDI (15th), D-ABII (27th), D-ABIU (6th), D-ABKA (11th) & D-ABKI (1st).

ILS traffic observed and identified were RAF Whirlwind XJ727 (4th), Strikemaster G-27-299 (7th), French Air Force Falcon 20 167/F-RAFL (19th) and the first HS.748 from Woodford since July 1976, Guyana Airways 8R-GEU (25th). British Airways operated the only crew training flight, VC-10 G-ARVM (15th).

4th   Air France B.707 F-BHSF was utilised on AF960/1, due to an increased load for the England v French Rugby Union International.

6th February 1977 – Making its fourth visit, operating in what is effectively a RAF livery, is Interconair Britannia EI-BBY, seen parked on the Freight Apron. It made numerous visits during the year operating cattle charters, but unfortunately it was written-off in a landing accident at Shannon in September. (Geoff Ball)

6th   Iranian Air Force operated two flights this month from/to Tehran. B.707 5-8304 arrived at 1406 as ELF537 today and 5-8311 at 1525 as ELF538 on the 27th.

7th   Gulfstream 2 N401M, Fluor Corporation's replacement for C-FFNM arrived at 0838 from Frobisher Bay at the start of its European/Asian tour.

10th   The arrival of Nor-Fly CV-440 LN-KLK wasn't particularly remarkable; but due to there being more passengers than it could carry, PA-31s LN-NPY & LN-NPZ followed with the rest. Both flights, operating from/to Torp via Aberdeen, were transporting seamen.

15th   The major excitement of the month was an influx of predominantly Heathrow diversions. The timing was perfect as it was the school holidays, but I wasn't up early enough to catch British AW SVC-10 G-ASGP at 0733 operating as MK042 for Air Mauritius, TIA DC-8 N4868T at 0758 and British Midland B.707 G-AYVE at 0828 (KQ114 from Nairobi). But I was up in time for British Airways B.747 G-AWNJ 'Speedbird 889' calling up on Tower 118.7. Not that I could see anything as the visibility wasn't great and the cloud cover was below 1000ft. In amongst the arrivals was National Airlines DC-10 N82NA at 0847 (NA002 from Miami), followed by two more BA 747s: G-AWNI at 0906 (BA520 from Washington) & G-AWNA at 0910 (BA660 from Miami), both within 5-miles of each other on the final approach. It was the first visit of Ghana VC-10 9G-ABO since September 1975 and the first visit of Sudan Airways B.707 ST-AFB at 1008 (SD112 from Rome), whose radio had to be heard to be believed! It had a very loud whine in the background, making any conversation from the pilot almost inaudible, which wouldn't be allowed by ATC nowadays! Swissair flight SR800 diverted to Manchester when its alternate, Birmingham, fell below limits, whilst another, 'Swissair 810', opted to divert to Castle Donnington. Tridents are rare diversions now they are CAT.III equipped, capable of landing in the thickest of 'pea-soups', yet one arrived diverting in as 'Shuttle 713'. Lufthansa also diverted two flights into Manchester: B.737s D-ABEM at 1021 (LH040 from Hamburg) and D-ABGE at 1030 (LH056 from Cologne). The star movement was Thai DC-8 HS-TGZ 'Thai International 900' diverting inbound from Bangkok via Athens. It was the first lander I'd seen all morning, as it broke through the clouds at just the right moment. It sounded very impressive on the radio and it would be another twelve years before Thai visited again. Finally, there was an Alitalia B.727 flight planned direct into Manchester, but this eventually arrived at Heathrow instead.

15th　　Brymon Twin Otter G-BDHC, arriving at 1017 amid a flurry of diversions, prompted the idea that this too was a diversion, as it rarely deviates from its regular Plymouth-Heathrow-Plymouth rotation. However, it was bringing a party of French businessmen into Manchester.

17th　　Dan-Air took delivery of another new HS.748, G-BEJE. It was formerly LV-IDV and as with G-BEJD, it too was owned by YPF and arrived in their full colours, having departed Buenos Aires on the 10th. Its full routing was Buenos Aires-Sao Paulo–Brasilia–Belem–Paramaribo-Port of Spain-San Juan–Miami–Wilmington-Boston-Goose Bay-Sudbury–Sondre Stromfjord–Kulusuk–Stornaway-Manchester. After a lengthy overhaul, it departed to Aberdeen on the 2nd May.

19th　　RAF C-130s XV176 (RR5040) & XV304 (RR5041) were taking troops to Gibraltar.

23rd　　USAF Beech U-21A 18019, arriving at 1330 as a Leeds diversion operating a flight on behalf of the US European Command, was in standard US VIP colours with large stars and stripes on the tail. It was based with the 1st Aviation Detachment at Stuttgart.

23rd　　Dan-Air City-Link flight DA057 was operated by Alidair Viscount G-ARBY.

24th　　IAS CL-44 G-BCWJ arrived from Gatwick, operating on behalf of Tradewinds for the continuation of flights to Iraq with prefabricated bridges.

26th　　202 Squadron RAF Whirlwind XP354 called in for fuel during a search and rescue sortie, looking for a missing bank clerk in the Prestbury area, before eventually departing for Leconfield.

26th　　KLM operated DC-8F PH-DCT on freighter flight KL909/10 today. Other KLM DC-8F freight substitutions during the year were DC-8F PH-DCZ on the 4th June and 26th August.

27th　　Air Anglia flight AQ823 (Amsterdam-Leeds) was diverting into Manchester with technical trouble and was on its descent, when his company advised him to divert to East Midlands instead.

March 1977

The airport will receive its first scheduled air services from Finland in April, when Finnair commence a once-weekly cargo flight. It will be operated by Kar-Air DC-6F OH-KDA, which is capable of carrying up to 12 tonnes. Finnair also plan to increase frequency to twice-weekly from the autumn and start passenger services next year.

Equipment changes on the European scheduled services were Air France (AF960): B.707 F-BHSN (5th) and Lufthansa (LH072/076): B.727 D-ABKG (6th).

ILS traffic observed and identified were Guyana Airways HS.748 8R-GEU (1st) & HS.125 G-MFEU (25th). British Airways crew training flight L.1011 G-BEAL was also a first visit (21st).

4th　　Bell 206 Jet Ranger G-BEKH, frequently seen on television advertisements for Barratt Homes, declared a full emergency and landed with engine trouble.

4th　　PA-34 Seneca VQ-SAM, arriving from Lyon at 2029 for NEA, will eventually take up residency on the South Side as G-BEVG.

4th   Dan-Air HS.748 G-ARAY caused a ground incident today, after a fire warning light came on while the starboard engine was starting up on Stand 43. After being surrounded by fire engines, the problem was found to be an instrument fault.

5th   The RAF operated the following C-130 trooping flights: XV214 (RR5345) & XV296 (RR5346) Lyneham-Gibraltar today and XV191 (RR5591) & XV296 (RR5590) Gibraltar-Lyneham on the 7th.

5th   Another heavy load on Air France Paris flight AF960/1 produced a further B.707, F-BHSN this time.

7th   A short lived colonial diversion session produced an interesting selection, including the only appearance of Air Jamaica this decade when DC-8 6Y-JII arrived at 0735 (JM002 from Kingston). Qantas B.747 VH-EBG at 0752 (QF007 from Bombay) and National DC-10 N83NA at 0805 (NA002 from Miami) were both first visits and other arrivals were Gulf Air VC-10 A4O-VK at 0729 (GF121 from Dubai), South African Airways B.747 ZS-SAL at 0802 (SA258 from Sal Island) and British Airways B.747 G-BDPV at 0811 (BA600 from Toronto). Approximately 1,000 diverted passengers were affected.

7th   French Air Force Falcon 20 49/F-RAFJ performed a touch-and-go at 1624, en route Shannon to Villacoublay.

7th   Due to the lack of HS.748s, Dan-Air's been using British Midland and Alidair Viscounts since last month. As far as the Manchester flights were concerned, British Midland Viscount G-AZNA was used on today's City-link flight DA050.

8th   HS.125 N20S was on delivery to the USA, using the call-sign 'De Havilland 20 Sugar', routing Hawarden-Reykjavik.

8th   The third Argentinean HS.748 on delivery to Dan-Air was G-BEKC. Arriving today in basic Aerolineas Argentinas colours with no titles, it went inside the hangar on the 25th.

9th   TWA B.707 N18712, arriving at 1546 as TW8366, was operating a charter for JCB employees outbound for New York.

9th   Iranian Air Force B.707 5-8311, arriving at 1330 as ELF539 (from/to Tehran), departed on the 11th.

12th March 1977 – This colourful aircraft, Ted Smith Aerostar N300AM, aborted its attempt on a round-the-world speed record after developing technical trouble. It was a first visit of type, arriving en route Gander-Frankfurt after being forced to divert in with low pressure. It left after receiving two hours attention on the South Side. (Geoff Ball)

14th   Granada TV filmed an episode of the drama series, The XYY Man, at the airport from the 14th to the 17th. It involved Northern Executive Aviation PA-31 G-AYLJ, titled 'Southern Executive Aviation' in exciting scenes, including fights on the apron, fire engines dashing around, security vans being chased and screaming vehicles crashing through the West Gate near Dan-Air's hangar. The climax was the blowing up of a PA-31 Navajo replica on the fire dump, but due to continuity problems, it was eventually carried out at Stretton Airfield instead.

15th   Swedish Air Force sent a C-130 into Manchester for the first time today, when 84001/71 arrived at 1007 from Malmo and stayed until the 17th. Another C-130 visitor today was Belgian Air Force CH-12, arriving at 1457 from RAF Leeming.

16th   The day produced a French invasion for the European Cup game between Liverpool and St. Etienne. Amongst the arrivals were seven SE.210 Caravelle's from various operators, a couple of Vanguards and a selection of French light/biz-aircraft, but unfortunately they all operated into

Liverpool. Due to the amount of fans making the trip, two flights operated into Ringway: Europe Air Service Vanguard F-BXAS (EY4262/3) and Air Charter SE.210 F-BJTO (SF184).

18th A rare executive type, the Jet Commander, paid a visit when N77NR operated from/to Geneva, where the aircraft is based.

19th Air Bridge Carriers Argosy G-APRL arrived at 1532 to clear customs, en route from Marseilles to Liverpool (AK312).

21st British Airways L.1011 G-BEAL made its first visit, operating the first L.1011 Tristar crew training flight of the year through Manchester.

23rd HS.125 9Q-CHD arrived at 1714 to clear customs after maintenance at Hawarden and returning back to Zaire.

23rd CL-44 LV-JTN flew into Gatwick from Buenos Aires, via Las Palmas. Its relevance to Manchester is that it was bringing HS.748 spares into the UK, in conjunction with the recent sale of a number second-hand Argentinean HS.748s to Dan-Air.

27th The world's worst aviation disaster happened today. Pan American Boeing 747 N736PA (Clipper 1736) left Los Angeles yesterday, Saturday 26th March, with 364 passengers and 16 crew bound for the Canary Islands. It stopped off at New York first to collect a further 14 passengers and 2 crew, taking the total number onboard up to 396. The flight continued bound for Las Palmas, where the passengers were to join their ship for a cruise around the Mediterranean. KLM Boeing 747 PH-BUF (KL4805) was also Las Palmas bound, operating a charter from Amsterdam with 248 passengers and crew onboard. In the meantime, because of a bomb explosion at Las Palmas Airport, all flights were being diverted to Santa Cruz in Tenerife, including the Pan American and the KLM; but once the ban was lifted, the Captains of both flights were anxious to take their aircraft over to Las Palmas. The actual causes of what happened next are a matter of controversy and conjecture, but the established facts are that the KLM B.747 was at the end of the Tenerife runway waiting clearance to depart for Las Palmas, during which time the Pan American B.747 was taxiing at the opposite end of the runway, from a remote parking spot towards the terminal. He was having to taxi along the runway facing the KLM aircraft, when the Pan American had difficulty finding the exit off the runway, due to thick fog. For whatever reason, the KLM aircraft attempted to depart whilst the Pan American aircraft was still on the runway and upon collision, the top of the Pan American was instantly sliced off. The impact killed everyone onboard the KLM flight and all but 61 on the Pan American aircraft.

28th Dan-Air BAC 1-11 G-BDAE (DA1790 Gatwick-Geneva) made a full emergency landing with undercarriage problems.

30th One that didn't make it was a Canadian Air Force C-130, due in on a training flight which was cancelled.

31st The end of an era occurred today when the British Airways Super 1-11 Division, branded as Manchester's own airline, was disbanded. The honour of the last flight under this guise went to BE4438 from Heathrow, arriving at 2142 operated by G-AVMR.

April 1977

A heated Airport Authority meeting took place on the 29th, when they decided to press ahead with the second runway scheme, in preference to rebuilding the existing one. The planning application has been called in and is subject to a public enquiry on a date still to be announced, nine months after the plans were originally submitted.

Rumours that Woodford would be used for Manchester's night-cargo flights have been refuted by the airport's Director, Gordon Sweetapple. In reply to a question in the Houses of Parliament from Macclesfield M.P. Nicholas Winterton, Mr Sweetapple explained that Woodford didn't have the proper night lighting or navigational aids, its runway length was restricted and aircraft parking space was limited. He added there would be major problems moving and loading equipment, but in any event, it wasn't even licensed by the CAA to operate such operations.

Besides Laker DC-10 G-BBSZ on the 10th (details below), other aircraft experiencing problems were Comet G-APZM with an engine fire warning (3rd), Britannia Airways B.737 G-AXNB with a suspected nose wheel fault (15th), unidentified Dan-Air BAC 1-11 with undercarriage problems (15th) and British Airways BAC 1-11 G-AVMS aborting takeoff on BE904 Manchester-Paris (19th).

Although Dan-Air hangar engineers were on strike from the 2nd - 7th, the airline took delivery of two more HS.748s: G-BEKF (14th) and G-BEKE (22nd). However, due to the amount of work being undertaken, both aircraft repositioned to Lasham to have the job done there instead.

The following airlines made changes from this month. Aer Lingus no longer operates to Amsterdam (last flight was 31st March). Air France will operate daily with SE.210 Caravelle's. British Airways are back to daily flights to New York (BA538/9) and Montreal/Toronto (BA648/9) both with SVC-10s and new routes to Frankfurt and Zurich have been introduced. Finnair introduced a once-weekly cargo flight to Helsinki, via Heathrow.

Equipment changes on the European scheduled services were Lufthansa (LH074/076): B.727s D-ABFI (24th/26th), D-ABKD (12th), D-ABKG (22nd), D-ABLI (20th) & D-ABQI (13th) and Swissair (SR842): DC-9-51 (SR842) HB-ISL (5th).

ILS traffic observed and identified were HS.125 G-MFEU (5th) and RAF Devon VP977 (14th). The only British Airways training flight was B.747 G-AWNN (22nd).

3rd RAF operated two inbound trooping flights when C-130s XV210 (RR54589) & XV223 (RR5488) arrived from Gibraltar.

3rd Making the first of many visits throughout the summer was Dan-Air B.707 G-AZTG, operating on behalf of Air Malta. Its final visit for the airline was 23rd October as KM106/7.

4th Capitol DC-8 N8763, operating to New York on behalf of Laker Airways, was the airlines only visit to Manchester this year. It was delivered new to Eastern Airlines in 1968, before being purchased by Capitol in May 1976, who operated the aircraft until December 1982. The last Capitol DC-8 to visit was N900CL on 6th September 1975.

4th Iranian Air Force B.707 5-8311 arrived at 1330 as ELF553 (from/to Tehran), before departing on the 6th.

4th All flights between Manchester and Heathrow were cancelled today, due to industrial action by 4,000 maintenance engineers at Heathrow. The unofficial action in restricting shift working was not supported by Manchester's engineers. Several flights from Manchester to Belfast and the Isle of Man were also affected, but all other British Airways flights out of Ringway operated normally.

5th British Air Ferries Herald G-BAVX, operating Glasgow-Heathrow in a VIP configuration, was carrying Fleetwood Mac on their nationwide tour promoting their latest album, Rumours.

5th Swissair DC-9-51 HB-ISL was used on SR842/3, due to an increased load transporting Liverpool supporters for their European Cup Semi-Final first leg with Zurich FC.

5th Another Canadian C-130 training flight due in on the 1st was cancelled again, but one finally showed up today when 130315 arrived at 1428, routing Bardafoss-Lyneham.

5th Corvette F-BUQP was only the second of its type to visit Manchester, arriving at 1120 from Le Touquet, before its departure for Epinal at 1216.

6th Spantax CV-990 EC-BTE operated BX669/670 (from/to Palma); on behalf of tour operator Intasun and EC-BJC operated the flight the following week.

7th Lufthansa cargo flight LH4072/3 was operated by B.707F D-ABUY.

9th Hughes 500 G-BDOY landed at Ferranti's Wythenshawe plant, close to the airport today.

10th Laker Airways DC-10 G-BBSZ aborted takeoff after bursting a tyre on departure for Niagara at 0337. Before the aircraft was removed, it had to be emptied of fuel and a full load of passengers, which caused the runway to be blocked until 0715.

12th BIA Herald G-APWE, (UK8284/3 from/to Rotterdam), was the first aircraft noted in the airlines new colours.

12th Following a walk-out by British Airways maintenance men in support of their Heathrow colleagues, all BA flights out of Manchester were cancelled until the 18th, when Manchester engineers abandoned support for their Heathrow counterparts and voted to end the strike. Although flights had started again, full operations weren't restored until the 1st May.

12th Dan-Air City-Link flight DA056 was operated by Peters Aviation Heron G-ANXB.

15th   Iranian AF B.707 5-8302 (ELF554) arriving at 1349, has been doctored since its last visit (as 5-242) and now has large rear windows.

16th   Aviaco SE.210 EC-CAE operated a flight from/to Palma (AO1900/1) today on behalf of British Airtours, due to the ongoing strike action.

17th   Martinair DC-9 PH-MAR, arriving at 0710 to operate an outbound freight charter to Bergen, was also due to the British Airways strike.

17th   The strike by maintenance men continues. Apart from several BAC 1-11 positioning flights and a British Airtours B.707 flight carrying 180 passengers returning from a pilgrimage to Lourdes, all British Airways flights have remained cancelled.

23rd   Transmeridian CL-44 G-AZIN arrived to transport more bridge sections and Dove G-ANVU brought in another crew to take the CL-44 out to Kuwait.

24th   HS.125 G-BEFZ called in to pick up the Junior Minister for the Department of Industry, Gerald Kaufman, en route to Heathrow.

26th April 1977 – After last year's visit of a Swedish Air Force DC-3, another turned up today. Douglas DC-3 79007/77 appeared in bare metal and day-glo and closer examination revealed the titling 'Scandinavian Airlines System' over the windows. It's seen here parked on the South Bay, after arriving from Gothenburg, before its departure for Vasterias on the afternoon of the 29th. (Geoff Ball)

May 1977

British Airways ceased their weekly New York freight service (BA468) on the 20th; leaving the twice-weekly service as the only British Airways dedicated freight flight, operating from Manchester. On the positive side, the following changes will operate until mid-October: New York passenger flight (BA538/9) to operate a mix of SVC-10/B.747 aircraft, Canadian flights will be split into two with Toronto four-weekly with B.747s (BA648/9) and Montreal five-weekly with SVC-10s (BA658/9).

The following airlines have summer IT programmes from Manchester: Air Malta, Aviaco, Aviogenex, Balkan, Inex-Adria, JAT, LOT, Tarom & Trans-Europa; as do a variety of UK operators: Britannia Airways, British Airtours, British Airways, British Island Airways, Dan-Air & Laker Airways. Operating regular flights to the USA/Canada this summer are British Caledonian (B.707), CP Air (DC-8), Laker Airways (DC-10) & Wardair (B.707 & B.747).

Equipment changes on the European scheduled services during the month were Lufthansa (LH074/076): B.727s D-ABGI (9th), D-ABIU (1st), D-ABKA (6th) & D-ABKJ (13th).

ILS traffic observed and identified were Lufthansa Beech 90 D-ILHB (20th), Dove's G-AREA (23rd) & G-ASMG (23rd/24th) and RAE Comet XS235 (25th).

1st   British Airways finally operated a full schedule today after April's strike. The dispute cost the airport £150,000 in lost revenue, 800 movements and over 50,000 passengers.

4th   One of my greatest regrets was missing a fantastic school trip to RAF Leuchars in Scotland. It involved a British Airways BAC 1-11 flight to Edinburgh on the early morning departure (BE4472), then a coach direct to Leuchars for a thorough tour of the RAF base, before returning on the evening flight (BE4483). The idea of flying in 1977 didn't have great appeal for me, after the Tenerife air crash and all the strikes and delays, but hearing about it afterwards, I was determined to go next year.

7th British Caledonian B.707 G-BDCN made its last visit today (BR5084 to Prestwick). It was sold to TAAG Angola as D2-TAC in October.

11th Lufthansa's cargo flight (LH4072/3) was operated by B.707s on three occasions this month, with D-ABUE today and D-ABUY on the 18th/25th.

13th HS.125 HZ-DAC, arriving at 1242 from its Geneva base on its way to Hawarden for maintenance, returned on the 27th to clear customs again before its flight back to Geneva.

14th Today was the day of our coach trip to Heathrow and Biggin Hill Air Show and unlike last time, it was warm, sunny and not too windy. We made an initial stop at Luton, a major charter/IT airport with extensive maintenance facilities and a healthy collection of light aircraft. The next stop en route was Stansted, which had little activity, but it did have several disused airliners in various states of destruction and dereliction. They were mainly used by the fire services and in amongst them was a pair of ex-Martinair Douglas DC-7s, PH-DSL & PH-DSO, although they were barely recognisable. We reached Heathrow by midmorning, where copious amounts of foreign numbers were collected and after a couple of hours we left for Biggin Hill. This time round it seemed to have less to offer and because it was an air show day, there was no access to the hangars. The IAS Britannia G-AOVP we saw last time had gone, having been broken up for scrap, as had the geriatric Percival Prince N206UP. The magic of the place was missing this time, but nevertheless it was still a very enjoyable day. It was also Cup Final day, when Manchester United overcame the team of the moment and beat Liverpool 2-1.

15th Aer Arran Islanders, EI-BCE today and EI-BBR on the 16th, were used to take ICI employees on a plant visiting exercise to Ireland.

16th Iranian Air Force operated two flights this month from/to Tehran. B.707 5-8311 arrived at 1340 today as ELF556 and B.707 5-8304 at 1418 as ELF557 (31st).

19th Pan American B.707 N404PA arrived at 1253, to operate British Caledonian flight BR2113 to New York.

20th British Airways operated their final transatlantic cargo flight out of Manchester today, when B.707 G-ASZG arrived inbound from New York as BA468. At its peak in late-1971, their forerunner BOAC was operating thirteen transatlantic cargo flights a week and since starting cargo operations from Manchester in 1961, they have served New York, Chicago, Boston, Montreal, Detroit & Philadelphia.

22nd British Airways inaugurated B.747 flights from Manchester today, when G-AWNE positioned in from Heathrow to operate BA539 onwards to Prestwick/New York.

22nd Oman Air Force's second Viscount, 501, arrived at 1413 (OU501 from Bournemouth) for a major overhaul with Dan-Air Engineering, before departing for Bournemouth on 14th July.

25th Air Freight DC-3 G-APBC arrived from Lydd at 1907 to operate a cargo charter to Linz the next day.

25th Nord 262 F-BPNX arrived at 1437 on a crew training flight from/to Gatwick.

26th Monarch BAC 1-11 G-AXMG arrived as a Dan-Air sub-charter from Malaga (OM871).

28th Monarch BAC 1-11 G-BCXR was operating a British Airways outbound sub-charter to Alicante (OM888).

June 1977

British Airways lost their appeal against British Air Ferries proposed Manchester-Antwerp/Rotterdam service, but no start date has been announced, as there are now Dutch objections and the route still has to be approved by their Government.

Details are emerging of the aircraft Pelican Air Transport plan to use for their forthcoming operations. It's believed they are acquiring ex-British Caledonian B.707s G-AZJM & G-BDCN and the first of these will be delivered by the end of the month. Their colour scheme will be a navy-blue tail with a white stripe containing a red pelican and a red/white/blue cheat line with blue titles.

Equipment changes on the European scheduled services were Air France (AF960): B.707 F-BHSJ (4th) and Lufthansa (LH074/076): B.727s D-ABBI (24th), D-ABKG (17th) & D-ABSI (14th).

ILS traffic observed and identified were RAE Andover XS606 (2nd), RAF C-130 XV206 (10th), Dove G-ASMG (21st), RAE C-130 XV208 (23rd), RAE Comet XS235 (23rd/30th), AEW Comet XW626 (28th) and Army Air Corps Gazelle XZ313 (30th).

2nd TWA B.707 N8729 arrived at 1606 as TW8501 to operate an outbound flight to Montreal, on behalf of CP Air.

3rd Today's JAT flights, JU218/207 & JU206/219, were operated by the Yugoslav Government's B.727, YU-AKD.

4th Monarch Airlines B.720 G-BCBA positioned up from Luton to operate a return flight to Gerona (OM918/9), on behalf of Dan-Air.

4th Air France B.707 F-BHSJ, operating Paris flight AF960/1, was the third of four B.707 substitutions this year.

7th Viscount G-AVJB, operated by Intra Airways, arrived on a flight from Teeside to Cork as JY207/8. It was previously operated by British Midland twice and also by Kestrel Aviation.

9th British Caledonian used a recently delivered Douglas DC-10, G-BEBM, on a transatlantic service from Manchester for the first time (BR2113 to New York).

10th Pacific Western B.707 C-FPWJ arrived at 1151 from Helsinki to operate a CP Air flight to Toronto the following day (PW767/8). It was formerly a full cargo operation, but due to fierce competition, the airline withdrew from this market and converted the aircraft to carry passengers.

13th TAE SE.210 EC-CUM operated Dan-Air flight DA2433/2 from/to Gerona.

13th Iranian Air Force operated another two flights during the month, from/to Tehran. B.707 5-8313 arrived at 1603 as ELF558 today and B.707 5-8304 at 1430 as ELF559 on the 28th.

15th TWA B.707 N18712 arrived at 1627 as TW8501, operating an outbound flight to Toronto, on behalf of CP Air.

15th Laker Airways DC-10 G-BELO made its first visit to Manchester today and was distinguishable by the lack of titles on the roof.

17th Monarch operated two sub-charters on behalf of Dan-Air today. BAC 1-11 G-BCXR arrived at 0657 inbound from Faro as OM953 and G-AXMG at 2053 from Alicante as OM955.

17th June 1977 - Brightening up a cloudy but humid day was KLM DC-8 PH-DEM, operating a KLM charter (KL2667) bound for Munich. This aircraft had been leased to Surinam Airways since 1975 and is seen here in full colours with KLM stickers. (Geoff Ball)

17th Corvette F-BTTP arrived at 1422 from Blackpool, before departing later for Gatwick.

17th Partenavia P.68 D-GITE, arriving at 1745 on a flight originally destined for Liverpool, was forced to divert to Manchester due to lack of customs.

18th Dan-Air took delivery of their sixth HS.748 when G-BEKD arrived from Reykjavik. After a major overhaul, it departed for Aberdeen on 26th October.

21st Beech 99 SE-GRB, arriving at 1528 from Amsterdam, was operated by Baron Air. It departed the following morning on a round trip to Malmo.

23rd Lear Jet D-CONO arrived at 1928 on an ambulance flight from Tobruk.

23rd A very rare type to Manchester was the Beech 18, but N5959F arrived at 1141 today from Gatwick, before its departure for Heathrow later. It's based in New York State and the last one to visit Manchester was Loganair's G-ASUG on 29th July 1973.

24th June 1977 – Canadian Airline Quebecair made its first visit to Manchester, when B.707 C-GQBH arrived from Gatwick, operating on behalf of CP Air to Montreal (QB903). It saw service with the airline until February 1979, when it was written-off in a landing accident in St. Lucia. Note the vintage Foden coach in the background. (Geoff Ball)

26th My third and final excursion of the year was to Greenham Common Air Show, again courtesy of PB Enterprises. Due to the regulations surrounding coach drivers having to take regular breaks, their trips rarely went directly to the final destination, so extra airfields were visited along the way. Before reaching the show, early morning stops were made at Thruxton, Bournemouth & Southampton. Thruxton is well known for its motor-racing circuit, but it also has an airstrip and we were given a tour of the hangars, which contained lots of aircraft in dismantled states, including a Panamanian registered Bell 206 Jet Ranger. Bournemouth and Southampton produced nothing out of the ordinary and we arrived at Greenham Common at 1pm. It was a sprawling mass of an airbase and large amounts of military numbers went into my book. We saw various types and it was the first time I'd seen some of the Air Force's present and overall it was a most enjoyable experience.

27th Cessna 404 N37094 arrived at 0748 from Reykjavik on delivery to the Kenya Police Air Wing, before departing for Bastia the following day.

28th HS.125 9K-ACR, arriving at 1725 from Geneva, was probably the star executive visitor of the month. It was also the first visit of a privately registered Kuwaiti aircraft.

28th Comet XW626 performed an ILS at Manchester on its maiden test flight, originating from Woodford. It's been converted to an airborne early warning version of the Nimrod.

30th Making its first visit was Lear Jet HB-VCY, arriving at 1044 to operate an outbound ambulance flight to Verona.

July 1977

ILS traffic observed and identified were RAF Dominie XS732 (19th), Dove G-ASMG (21st), RAE C-130 XV208 (23rd), RAE Comet XS235 (23rd/30th), AEW Comet XW626 (28th) and Army Air Corps Gazelle XZ313 (30th).

3rd Another aircraft on delivery was Cessna 404 N23PG, arriving at 2327 for a night-stop, before departing for Humberside the following morning.

5th Two East European flights, arriving in connection with the Eisteddfod Festival today, were Balkan IL-18 LZ-BEP (LZ8371 from Varna) and Malev IL-18 HA-MOG (MA1787 from Budapest).

5th Philadelphia based PA-30 Twin Comanche N740AF arrived at 1435 from Jersey, on its current tour of Europe.

6th Islander G-AZGU, formerly EC-CFY, arrived on delivery to NEA after being based in the Canary Islands operating for Aerocasa. It remained with NEA for overhaul and modification before leaving for Khartoum on the 22nd, where it will operate on contract.

6th RAE 1-11 XX105 operated a training flight as 'Nugget 85' from/to Bedford.

11th Royal Navy Wessex XT764 was based at Manchester until the 13th, whilst in the region on a nationwide tour as part of the 'Navy Presentation Team'.

13th Pan American B.707 N894PA arrived from Heathrow at 0708 to operate BR2901 to Chicago, on behalf of British Caledonian.

9th July 1977- Finnair DC-8 OH-LFY arrived at 1023 on a sunny Saturday morning, operating on behalf of British Caledonian (AY6444 from Toronto). It would be a further eight years before another Finnair DC-8 was seen at Manchester. OH-LFY only served with Finnair until 1980, when it was sold to the French Air Force. (Geoff Ball)

14th   British Airways B.747 G-AWNL went tech on arrival, after positioning up from Heathrow to operate BA539 to Prestwick/New York. It finally departed the following afternoon.

14th   Although USAF confirmed one of their pilots made an error last month, confusing Manchester for Woodford, the CAA declined to comment. The aircraft, an F-111, was due to appear at the Woodford Air Show on the 25th June, but instead it made a low-level run at Manchester, even finding time to show its credentials as a swing-wing bomber!

17th   LOT TU-134 SP-LGC (LO3097/8 from/to Warsaw), was the first aircraft to visit in the new colour scheme.

17th   The Red Arrows arrived from Shawbury to take part in the Barton Air Show and for the second year running, they used Manchester as their temporary base.

17th   Vintage pair Meteor WF791 and Vampire XH304 arrived from Shobdon, in conjunction with the Barton Air Show.

18th   Iranian Air Force B.707 5-8304 arrived at 1639 as ELF714 (from/to Tehran), before departing on the 20th.

19th   Air Afrique DC-8 TU-TCH was the first of five flights, arriving between the 19th and 23rd. Each was scheduled to carry 53 tonnes of the chemical known as yellowcake, a form of uranium concentrate powder used in the preparation of uranium fuel for nuclear reactors. The cargo originated from Niamey, Nigeria and other aircraft used were DC-8 TU-TCG and UTA DC-8 F-BOLI. Both Air Afrique DC-8s had two-tone green tails and green cheatlines. UTA DC-8F was in basic UTA colours, but neither carried external titling. Originally, these flights were to be operated by Pelican Air Transport, but they are still in the process of setting up.

18th   There were two CP Air Boeing 747s on the ground at the same time today. The first, B.747 C-C-FCRD, arrived this evening from Amsterdam to operate the much delayed outbound CP819 to Toronto. The second, B.747 C-FCRE, operated yesterdays inbound CP818 from Toronto, but after going tech on arrival, it didn't depart until later in the evening (CP992 to Amsterdam).

19th   Dan-Air took delivery of their seventh and final ex-Argentinean HS.748, G-BEKG. After another lengthy major overhaul, it positioned to Aberdeen on the 29th December.

20th   It was a good morning for biz-jet first visits. Citation 500 HZ-NCI arrived at 0827 operating a return flight from Heathrow and Gulfstream 2 N130A arrived at 0909, operating a return flight from Brussels.

24th   Balkan started operating Tupolev TU-134s on LZ917/8 and subsequent fortnightly flights and today's was operated by first time visitor LZ-TUN.

26th   Uni-Air DC-3 F-BCYT operated a passenger charter from/to Caen, before departing on the 28th.

26th   Beech 60 Duke N4556S arrived at 1021, operating from/to its current base at Cardiff.

26th   Eagle Air Boeing 720 TF-VLB operated Aer Lingus EI620/1 to/from Copenhagen today and EI204/5 from/to Dublin on the 28th. Aer Lingus are currently affected by an industrial dispute involving maintenance staff.

28th   British Air Ferries Carvair G-ASDC, arriving at 1052 to operate an outbound cargo flight to Rotterdam, was sporting the new style BAF colours currently worn by Heralds.

29th   Aer Lingus evening freighter, EI9212/3, was operated by Boeing 707 EI-ANV.

31st   Alitalia DC-9F I-DIBK operated their final cargo flight (AZ1969) out of Manchester today. The original service that started in April 1970 was operated by SAM Cargo Douglas DC-6s initially. The airline also operated a passenger service serving Milan/Rome from 1968-1972.

August 1977

This month's big story was the commencement of a five-day strike on the 12th by UK ATC assistants, over a pay deal negotiated last year not being honoured. On this particular weekend, the situation was made worse when further traffic restrictions were imposed by French and Spanish ATC. To minimise the damage of the stoppage, airline services were rescheduled and co-ordinated in a joint effort to limit demands on the major airports and as a result, traffic levels were reduced and handled with minimal delay. Another strike by ATC assistants on the 26th however, was an indefinite one and the only winners were the air-taxi operators, who were booked up solidly for weeks in advance and the owners of piston-engined aircraft, who could operate outside of controlled airspace.

Pelican Air Transport expects to commence operations on the 1st November, even though they are still in the process of securing financial backing. Their first aircraft is being painted in Hong Kong but it's neither of the two ex-British Caledonian B.707s mentioned in June, as B.707 G-AZJM remained with British Midland and G-BDCN was sold to TAAG Angola in October.

A new customer for Dan-Air Engineering is Ford Motors, based at Stansted. They operate two BAC 1-11s and both passed through Manchester during the month for maintenance: G-BEJW (1st) and G-BEJM (27th).

British Airways has undertaken a major investment programme, including modernising some of their handling equipment. Although other airports have benefitted, Manchester will see a range of cargo improvements including expansion to the bonded areas, a new fleet of fork-lift trucks for the import/export warehouse and new accommodation for administration staff, due for completion by November. A new computer system will monitor cargo progress and help with information regarding cargo capacity.

Equipment changes on the European scheduled services were Aer Lingus (EI620/1): TEA B.720 OO-TEB (29th) and Lufthansa (LH074/076): B.727s D-ABCI (24th) & D-ABIE (16th).

The only ILS traffic observed and identified during the month were Israeli Air Force B.707 4X-BYD (10th) and British Airways VC-10 G-ARVM on a crew training flight (9th).

2nd   Iranian Air Force operated two more flights this month, from/to Tehran. B.707 5-8302 arrived at 1523 as ELF715 today and B.707 5-8304 at 1828 as ELF716 on the 15th.

3rd   British Caledonian's second DC-10, G-BEBL, arrived at 0952 from Gatwick to operate BR2183 onwards to Boston.

3rd   SATA SE.210 Caravelle HB-ICQ arrived from Venice at 1429, before departing later for Zurich as VS869.

4th   Ford Gulfstream I G-ASXT, arriving at 1027, was ferrying a crew up to take BAC 1-11 G-BEJW back to Stansted after maintenance with Dan-Air.

5th   PA-39 F-GALF, formerly G-AVJT and ex-resident of the Manchester School of Flying, arrived from Jersey for an overnight stay. It flew a return flight to/from Isle of Man the following day, before departing to Sumburgh on the 8th.

6th   Britannia Airways started a weekly newspaper flight to Belfast, but by the 20th it had been taken over by Air Bridge Carriers aircraft. This was due to the unavailability of their own B.737s, after being over-worked on IT flights because of the high level of ATC delays.

6th   Intra Airways immaculate looking DC-3 G-AKNB, arriving at 2227 to operate a return freight from Jersey, was carrying Express Air Freight titles.

10th   Israeli AF B.707 4X-BYD operated a round trip training detail from Frankfurt, overshooting at 1204 on a quiet Wednesday lunchtime.

12th   Royal Saudi Air Force C-130H 1605 was notable for routing from Jeddah to Dover AFB via Gander, as transatlantic flights normally operate through Shannon. It returned eastbound on the 19th via Gander, again routing via Manchester.

13th   Cessna 404 N24PG, arriving at 1218 from Reykjavik, was on delivery to Geosurvey of Nairobi. Displaying magnetometer booms front and back, it left for Luton the following day.

13th   Cessna 310 N8578G was also on delivery today. It was bound for Kenya, routing Reykjavik-Gatwick, when it was forced to divert to Manchester after developing a technical fault.

16th   Pacific Western B.707 C-FPWJ arrived 1648 (PW767 Gatwick-Calgary), operating on behalf of British Caledonian.

16th   Although it's not related to aviation, one of the big stories of the year was today's death of Elvis Presley. It was massive news for months, when TV programmes and documentaries on the star were shown and re-shown, along with old clips dug out from archives. Weeks before he died he'd released a rather good single, 'Way Down', which was floundering in the lower reaches of the charts, but following his death it was Number One by the end of the month.

21st   The transportation of Airbus wings from Manchester appears to have recommenced, with today's arrival of F-BPPA, the first Guppy flight since the 26th June.

21st   Emergency services were put on standby today, when inbound PA-34 Seneca G-BCID reported it had no greens indication showing, when it should have had three to confirm the undercarriage was down. It made a low pass so ATC could check the undercarriage and after being observed as normal, the aircraft landed safely.

24th   Army bomb squad officers were called in to attend to an unclaimed case, about to be loaded on the mornings British Airways Belfast flight (BE4452). It was removed to a blast-proof bunker in a remote corner of the airport, after X-rays revealed it contained a mystery cylinder. After being blown up, the contents were found to be nothing more than harmless electronic equipment.

25th   Swissair DC-9F HB-IFW, operating SR847 to Zurich, returned after takeoff due to a suspected bird strike.

25th   The emergency services were on full alert today, when British Airtours B.707 G-APFL (KT996 to Corfu), carrying 156 passenger, reported its No. 3 engine had failed just after takeoff. The pilot initially requested a fly-past, so ATC could observe it at close quarters, but he then asked permission to dump the aircrafts 12 tonnes of fuel. ATC agreed and he was sent to Congleton NDB to carry out the procedure. Seven minutes later he requested a diversion to Gatwick, where he landed safely. The passengers finally left onboard B.707 G-ARRC two hours later.

26th   Today was the start of an indefinite strike by ATC assistants, which coincided with a ten-day go-slow by French ATC over pay and working conditions. All traffic overflying France was affected, as were the three main Paris airports. Flights were mostly on time, but passengers were advised to prepare for delays and bring blankets in case evening flights were affected. British Airways cancelled eight Manchester-Heathrow flights when ATC assistants set up a picket line near the Tower.

26th   An ATC watch log entry reported the driver of a British Airways works vehicle almost collided with an aircraft, taxiing without lights. PA-30 G-BAWN had just left Stand 21, en route to the South Side, when the incident happened. Under airport rules, it's the driver's responsibility to look out for and give way to any aircraft, but as the plane was without lights, the driver was told he was within his rights to make an official complaint in writing!

27th   Another flight on behalf of British Caledonian, Dan-Air B.707 G-AYSL (BR2184 from Boston), arrived over twenty-one hours late after being delayed by the ATC strike.

29th   Aer Lingus EI620/1 to/from Copenhagen was operated by Trans European B.720 OO-TEB today, as Aer Lingus are still being affected by the strike by maintenance staff.

29th   SAS DC-8 SE-DBG operated an outbound charter on behalf of SAAB (SK7590 to Munich). DC-8 LN-MOW operated the return flight (SK7591) the following day and both aircraft were first visits to Manchester.

September 1977

A mass meeting of thousands of airport staff took place on the 2nd, when workers demanded their views be heard before any decisions made to drop plans for the second runway. It's the first time in the airport's history that trade unions have combined on any issue. The decision to hold the meeting was made by union officials, on the same day the Greater Manchester Policy Committee voted unanimously to shelve the second runway, in favour of a £20m improvement scheme to extend the present runway by 10,000ft; work which would close the airport for two months. However, it was announced on the 23rd that any decision would be deferred until next month, after the Government produced its white paper on the future strategy for Britain's airports. The white paper, three years in the making, follows a Government decision to scrap plans for a new London airport at Maplin. Last month the Policy Committee of the conservative dominated GMC backed the extension, but the labour controlled City Council were reluctant to drop the scheme.

British Airways temporarily dropped their schedules to Frankfurt and Zurich at the end of the month, due a lack of aircraft. A number of Super 1-11s have been transferred to Heathrow to cover capacity shortages caused by the grounding of Trident 3s for checks, after wing cracks were discovered. The defects were found during a routine check of G-AWZL in August. They also cancelled a number of Manchester-London services due to the ATC assistant's dispute.

As the ATC assistants strike continued into this month, British Airways reported losing £1m a day. The grounding of their Trident 3 fleet only added to the problem and many domestic services were cancelled, as precious slots were better utilised for international routes. The impact on holiday traffic was considerable and the regular strikes by the French and Spanish contributed to frequent and major delays. Many sub-charters took place to get airline schedules back on track.

The continuing strikes by English, French & Spanish ATC assistants resulted in lengthy delays, especially at weekends, when other airlines were drafted in to help clear the backlog. Despite the strikes, the poor summer had created extra demand for late holidays, hence the appearance of a late-summer programme by Trans Europa. As last minute requirements were so high, even more pressure was put on the airport and airlines reported domestic flights being cancelled and international flights being regularly delayed, although this did recede towards the end of month. By the time the peak travel times had passed, it was proven that the aviation industry had adapted positively to the challenging circumstances.

Equipment changes on the European scheduled services were Lufthansa (LH074/076): B.727s D-ABBI (20th/21st/27th), D-ABIE (28th), D-ABIO (16th/23rd), D-ABIX (30th), D-ABKB (13th) and D-ABKH (14th).

ILS traffic observed and identified were Dove G-ARHW (9th) & RAF Victor XM717 (29th).

1st   Dan-Air used Alidair Viscount G-ARGR on today's City-Link DA059 (Cardiff-Newcastle).

2nd   The ATC watch log recorded that an aircraft had reported seeing a hole in Runway 24, near the western taxiway. Following an inspection and the discovery of a 2ft square hole, the runway was closed at 1825 for thirty minutes, while temporary repairs were carried out.

2nd   Alidair Viscount G-AZNH, arriving at 0918 (BR2114 from Gatwick), was bringing transatlantic passengers back to Manchester from a flight terminated at Gatwick.

2nd   Dan-Air City-Link flight DA050 Teeside-Cardiff was operated by British Air Ferries Herald G-BDZV.

2nd   HS.125 HZ-DAC arriving at 1303 was one of several HS.125s passing through Manchester to clear customs, en route to/from Hawarden for maintenance. Others during the month were HB-VBZ (3rd), 9Q-CFW (9th) and HZ-DAC again (16th).

3rd   Martinair DC-8 PH-MAU positioned in from Luton to operate the much delayed Dan-Air DA2418 to Alicante. It returned later in the day as DA2419, before positioning out to Amsterdam.

3rd   Dove G-ARYM, a long time regular over many years, arrived at 1545 on a flight from Biggin Hill. It's now owned and operated by Volkswagen.

4th September 1977 – British Caledonian B.707 G-BDSJ is seen here being prepared for its departure to Toronto as BR2251 on a sunny, Sunday afternoon. Delivered new to Qantas as VH-EAJ in 1968, it was sold to British Caledonian in March 1976 and served them until 1981, by which time it had been converted to cargo operations. (Geoff Ball)

4th   Skyline Sweden operated two flights this month. Viscount SE-FOX arrived on a charter from Gothenburg at 1715 as OX201 today and their other Viscount, SE-FOY, arrived at 1917 as OX203 from Stockholm on the 14th. The airline would make one final appearance in 1978, the same year it ceased operating.

4th   The ATC watch log recorded that passengers had been observed walking across the apron towards Pier B, from recently arrived Balkan TU-134 LZ-TUL (LZ917). It was parked on the South Bay with coaches arranged to collect them, so it was unclear why they were wandering across the taxiways!

6th   Iranian Air Force operated two further freight flights this month, from/to Tehran. B.707 5-8302 arrived at 1329 as ELF716 today and B.707 5-8312 at 1358 as ELF718A on the 19th, which was the final flight to operate into Manchester.

9th   TIA DC.10 N102TV, arriving from Gatwick at 1641, was operating another sub-charter on British Caledonian's behalf.

10th   CP Air B.747 C-FCRB, made its first visit to Manchester, arriving as CP817 from Gatwick. It's been based at Vancouver, operating the airlines Pacific flights.

10th   The arrival of four RAF C-130s: XV187 (RR5578), XV207 (RR5577), XV212 (RR5579) and XV222 (RR5580), which all departed to Leipheim, was in connection with a NATO exercise in Germany.

12th   Continuing industrial action by English, French & Spanish ATC assistants was responsible for major delays over the weekend.

12th   PA-23 Aztec G-BBOJ declared a full emergency, due to a suspected undercarriage fault. It overshot initially, but landed safely on its second approach.

12th   USAF T-39 Sabre 61-0653 arrived at 2013 from Cologne, before departing later to Upper Heyford.

13th   Monarch Airlines BAC 1-11 G-AXMG, operating (DA2431 from Milan-Malpensa) on behalf of Dan-Air, reported an unusual noise on takeoff. A burst tyre was suspected, but following an inspection of the runway, nothing was found.

13th   Manchester United started a new European campaign away to St. Etienne, flying out on Aer Lingus 1-11 EI-ANG (EI7950). The game played the following day resulted in a 1-1 draw.

14th   A KLM Boeing 747, due to take Manchester Utd fans out to Lyon for their game with St. Etienne, was cancelled the week before due to the lack of passengers.

14th   Condor B.727 D-ABWI arrived at 2058, operating from/to Frankfurt. It was heard but not seen by the writer, due to a very low cloud base.

14th   British Caledonian B.707 G-AWWD (BR2904 from Chicago) made its last visit to Manchester today, as it was sold the following month to TAAG Angola as D2-TAD.

14th   The first of three Dan-Air Comets to be withdrawn this year was G-AROV. It made its last visit to Manchester today, arriving at 0157 (DA2461 from Catania), before positioning out to Gatwick at 0840. It flew its final flight, Birmingham-Lasham on 31st October, where it was withdrawn.

16th   Pan American operated two flights on behalf of British Caledonian this month. B.707 N496PA departed today at 1809 for New York and B.707 N894PA arrived at 1114 from New York on the 23rd.

19th   Spantax DC-8 EC-CZE operated delayed Dan-Air flight DA2667/6 from/to Ibiza.

20th   One aircraft that didn't make it was Beech 55 D-IFTH. It was on its way en route from Frankfurt, when it crashed in Germany killing all six onboard.

20th   RAE BAC 1-11 XX105 arrived at 1358, operating a training flight from Prestwick-Thurleigh.

21st   Passengers turning up to catch their morning flight to Heathrow were in for a treat! The flight was operated by B.707 G-AWHU, which had arrived the previous day (BA596 from New York) and rather than it positioning out empty, it was used on flight BE4405.

21st   Queens Flight HS.748 XS789 arrived at 1057 from Benson, with a member of the Saudi Royal Family onboard.

24th   RAF C-130s XV193 (RR5582) and XV199 (RR5584), arriving from Menningen, were returning troops from a recent NATO exercise. A further C-130 flight from Menningen operated on the 26th with XV207 as RR4295.

25th   Aviaco SE.210 EC-BIF, operating AO1046/1523 & AO1522/1047, was making its last visit to Manchester today. It was sold to Aero-Lloyd as D-ABAK in March 1980.

26th   History was made today, when the first Skytrain service left Gatwick for New York. The CAA caved in to Laker Airways at the eleventh hour, by finally allowing them to use Gatwick instead of Stansted. The capacity restriction of 189 seats was also lifted and fares started from just £59 one-way.

27th   Nord 262 F-BPNU arrived at 1504, operating a crew training flight from/to Gatwick.

27th   The second Dan-Air Comet to be withdrawn this year was G-APMG. Arriving at 1523 (DA2437 from Palma), it positioned out to Aberdeen the following day at 1617. Its final revenue flight was 16th November and positioned to Lasham on the 21st November.

29th   Quebecair's second visit this year took place today when B.707 C-GQBH arrived at 0700 (QB816 from Toronto).

30th   Martinair DC-9 PH-MAR arrived at 2118 as MP2361, operating a freight charter on behalf of Interflug.

October 1977

The ATC assistant's strike moved into its third month, causing more delays and cancellations. ATC officers were managing to move around 80% of all movements, as they had the benefit of accessing the main ATC computer at West Drayton, which they hadn't been able to do during the previous work-to-rule. The strikers felt the union had misjudged their situation by calling an indefinite strike, as many wanted to return to work. By midmonth the dispute had taken several twists and turns, following their rejection of the CAA's improved pay and conditions, due to unacceptable clauses. A picket line was crossed at West Drayton ATC centre by drivers delivering fuel to the RAF offices and by the end of October the ATC officers bearing the brunt of the extra work weren't prepared to put up with it much longer, at which point the CAA put forward a revised pay deal, which brought the strike to an end in November.

A Trident shortage and lack of BAC 1-11s at Manchester was the reason for the cancellation of a number of British Airways London services. Also, due to a dispute by airport security staff, they had to operate their Manchester-Belfast flights from Liverpool towards the end of the month.

The inauguration of Pelican Air Transports first service has been postponed indefinitely, as the two founding members have sold the airline to freight agents Hill & Delamain.

Interconair, who were due to start their regular cattle flights again, lost their only Britannia, EI-BBY, last month in a training accident at Shannon. This meant the following aircraft had to be sub-chartered: Martinair DC-9 PH-MAR (5th), African Safari Britannia 5Y-AYR (7th) and Air Bridge Carriers Merchantman G-APES (26th).

Equipment changes on the European scheduled services were Air France (AF960): B.707 F-BHSO (2nd) & B.727 F-BPJP (3rd); Lufthansa (LH074/076): B.727s D-ABBI (7th/11th), D-ABIA (4th), D-ABII (5th) & D-ABSI (19th) and Swissair (SR842): DC-9-51 HB-ISL (8th) & HB-ISS (9th).

The only ILS traffic observed and identified were RAF Nimrod XV236 (12th) and RAF Victor XM717 (21st).

1st   Spantax CV-990 EC-BQA operated Dan-Air flight DA4455/4 from/to Barcelona.

1st   Dan-Air B.707 G-BEAF arrived at 1951 (DA7531 from Toronto) on a freight charter.

1st   KLM DC-8F PH-DCZ, arriving at 1141 (KL9597 from/to Amsterdam), was another freight charter, but this one was on behalf of Interflug.

2nd   Martinair DC-9F PH-MAO, arriving at 0123 (MP2362 from/to Amsterdam), was another Interflug freight flight. These flights are transporting television tubes that are too large to fit through the doors of their own planes! Another Martinair DC-9F, PH-MAR, also operated a freight flight (MP2374 to Venice) on the 15th.

3rd   The second Spantax CV-990 in three days, EC-CNG, operated a much delayed British Airtours flight (KT497/6 from/to Mahon). It was also the first visit of one of their ex-Swissair acquisitions (formerly HB-ICA).

3rd   Oman Air Force BAC 1-11 551 made its second appearance (OU551 from Bournemouth) for further maintenance with Dan-Air, before departing on the 9th.

5th   The second-leg of the Cup Winners Cup tie between Manchester Utd and St. Etienne took place today. No French fans appear to have flown in and it's unclear how the team arrived. However, the match was won by United, 2-0, which meant they were through to the next round and would face Portuguese team, FC Porto.

5th   Pan American B.707 N894PA arrived at 1210 today (BR2904 from Chicago), on behalf of British Caledonian. Another B.707, N892PA, operated Istanbul-New York on the 12th.

6th   Tradewinds CL-44 G-AWOV, arriving as Gatwick diversion (IK822 from Larnaca), was in a revised colour scheme. The titling had been removed from the roof and placed on the cheatline below the cockpit windows.

6th   The ATC watch log recorded that from 1000-2359 Manchester was the number two diversion airfield for Scampton and would accept up to thirteen aircraft.

6th   Air Anglia F.27 G-BDDH, diverting in due to high winds at Leeds-Bradford (AQ823 from Amsterdam), marked the return of Air Anglia to Manchester and judging by the amount of flights this month, Ringway is clearly back in favour!

7th   Okanagan Bell 212 C-GOKT arrived into Amsterdam by ship yesterday. After being off-loaded, it flew Grantham-Manchester-Cork today and joined the other Okanagan helicopters temporarily based at Grantham for off-shore work.

8th October 1977 – African Safari Britannia 5Y-AYR arrived last night as a Luton diversion. Remarkably it still wore the blue cheatline from its days with British United, almost nine years after last operating with them as G-ANCD. It remained in service with several operators until August 1982, when it was withdrawn. (Geoff Ball)

9th   Aviaco SE.210 EC-BIE, operating AO1046/1523 & AO1522/1047, was the second SE.210 making its last visit this year. It was sold to Aero-Lloyd as D-AAST in February 1980.

9th   The last of the three Dan-Air Comets withdrawn from service this year was G-ARJN. It made its final visit today at 2016 (DA4489 from Barcelona), before positioning out to Gatwick at 2059. Its final flight was from Gatwick to Lasham on the 24th December.

10th   Ford HS.125 G-AYFM operated a crew ferry flight to return BAC 1-11 G-BEJM to Stansted, after maintenance with Dan-Air.

10th   HS.125 HB-VFA called in at 1650 from Hawarden as 'Newpin 29', to clear customs on a pre-delivery flight.

13th   Sobelair SE.210 OO-SRB, arriving at 1215 from/to Brussels, was a businessmen's charter.

14th   British Caledonian BAC 1-11 G-ASJC (BR985 from Gatwick) landed with a major hydraulic leak.

14th   Tradewinds CL-44 G-AWGT landed on its second attempt, after the RVR fell below its limits on the first approach, while diverting in from Gatwick (IK122 from Lagos).

15th   British Caledonian DC-10 G-BEBM was diverting to Manchester (BR368 from Accra), when the RVR fell below its minimum requirements on approach, so it eventually overshot and went to Prestwick instead. After the fog started to clear, fourteen diversions arrived during the morning including Qantas B.747 VH-EBD at 0727 (QF007 from Bombay).

16th   The ATC watch log recorded at 0330, that the barriers would be removed from disused Runway 02/20 for any diverted aircraft. A total of thirty-nine arrived, thirteen of which appeared before 0700 when Heathrow and Gatwick were both out. The figure could have been higher, had Manchester not been affected by fog, as even though it never fell below limits, it was bad enough to restrict diversions from 0700-0900 when only two arrived. Leased Gulf Air L.1011 N81027 'Gulf 1027' arriving at 0910 (GF1027 from Dubai) started the next wave, when seventeen arrived within ninety minutes, including the first visit of Air India B.747 VT-EDU at 0914 (AI112 from New York). Others included CP Air DC-8 C-FCPL at 0934 (CP816 from Toronto), Swissair DC-9-51 HB-ISM at 1011 (SR800 from Zurich), KLM DC-9 PH-DNO at 1047 (KL115 from Amsterdam) and the last of this batch, British Airways SVC-10 G-ASGE at 1139 (BA383 from Tehran). By early evening another session was threatening, when the Midlands and later the South East, were affected by fog. By the time Jetstar N40XY arrived at 2100 as a Luton diversion, Manchester was also affected and to such an extent that its own flights were diverted away.

16th   Today's arrival of Air India B.747 VT-EDU was the first by the airline since 1971 and also the first time they used Manchester as a weather diversion alternate. As if this wasn't enough, they also diverted in two more during the month, VT-EBE (17th) and VT-EBD (25th).

16th   Gulf Air VC-10 A4O-VG arriving at 1432 (BA1242 from Heathrow) stayed for ninety minutes for reasons unknown, before continuing its flight to Prestwick. The airline is currently phasing out the type and operated under a British Airways call-sign.

16th October 1977 – Spanish charter-airline Trans Europa operated regular IT flights from Manchester between 1976-1981, although they had been in existence since 1965. Seen here is SE.210 EC-CIZ, which arrived the previous evening as an East Midlands diversion. (Geoff Ball)

17th   The ATC watch log recorded that from 0830-1500, Manchester was the primary diversion alternate for Finningley and would accept up to ten Dominies. The airport was also given number two diversion status for Waddington from 1100-1300.

17th   Another day when the diversion tally could have been much higher, as both Heathrow and Gatwick were below limits all morning, but so was Manchester! By midday, Ringway's weather had improved enough to accept diversions, amongst these were first visits Qantas B.747 VH-EBA at 1217 (QF007 from Frankfurt) and Air India B.747 VT-EBE at 1258 (AI116 from New York). Aer Lingus B.707 EI-ASO overshot at 1344 (IN6015 from Chicago) on diversion into Manchester, operating a Dan-Air flight with a Shamrock call-sign. It got to 2-miles final when its company instructed him not to land at Manchester, but to overshoot and proceed to Gatwick instead. When the fog returned late evening and affected Birmingham, Luton & Gatwick, Manchester handled further diversions.

18th   Poor weather affected UK airports for the fourth consecutive day. Leeds was fog-bound all day and Heathrow was below limits briefly. British Airways L.1011 G-BEAM (BA483 from Dhahran), was noted heading towards Prestwick early in the morning.

18th   Evergreen International DC-8 N800EV arrived at 1406 (EV800 from Gatwick), to operate a Laker Airways flight to Los Angeles, via Niagara. It was the airlines first visit to Manchester.

18th   Manchester Utd flew out to Porto on Aer Lingus 1-11 EI-ANE as EI7966, for their second round first-leg match with FC Porto the following day, when Utd were comprehensively beaten 4-0.

19th   Monarch Airlines BAC 1-11 G-BCXR left this morning with Manchester Utd fans (OM912 to Oporto) for their second round European Cup-Winners Cup game with FC Porto.

19th   RAE Devon XM223 arriving at Manchester today, was in connection with the trial installation of the British Doppler MLS (Microwave Landing System), with further visits by XM223 and Devon XG496 on the 27th. When the system was installed for the trial, the CAA and the manufacturers, Plessey, gave it maximum publicity by inviting 'Tomorrow's World' and other television crews to film the proceedings.

20th   The ATC watch log recorded that from 0240-1000, Manchester was given number two diversion status for Scampton and would accept up to seven Vulcan aircraft.

22nd   Aer Lingus B.747 EI-ASI made its first visit today at 1255 (EI7206 from Dublin) to operate outbound ESSO charter KM787, on behalf of Air Malta.

23rd   Monarch BAC 1-11 G-AXMG arrived at 0908 (OM521 from Palma), operating on behalf of Dan-Air.

23rd   East German-airline Interflug, made their first appearance at Manchester today, sending in two aircraft carrying an orchestra and their equipment. TU-134 DM-SCX arrived at 1500 (IF2014/5) and IL-18 DM-STK at 1849 (IF2016/7).

24th   The dwindling number of Comets continues! Dan-Air Comet G-AYWX made its final visit today, arriving at 1752 (DA4465 from Malaga), before departing the following day at 0937 (DA1466 to Split). In 1978 it made its very last flight, Palma-Bristol on 29th April and on the 2nd May, it was flown to Lasham for withdrawal.

25th   The ATC watch log recorded that when Islander G-AVKC was on a test flight after its overhaul with NEA, it had landed without clearance.

25th   Four Heathrow diversions arrived this morning. British Airways B.747s G-AWNO at 0819 (BA560 from Boston) & G-AWNP at 0726 (BA500 from New York) and two first visits from New-York: TWA B.707 N18703 at 0930 (TW708) & Air India B.747 VT-EBD at 1015 (AI102).

25th   British Airways L.1011 G-BBAI was operating the return leg of the ESSO charter to Malta.

27th   Europe Air Service Herald F-BLOY called in at 1024 (EY4506 to Inverness) to clear customs.

28th   Air France SE.210 F-BHRF reported it may have hit an object on landing, but it turned out that three blades in one of the engines had broken. The problem was so serious the aircraft needed a new engine and it was grounded until the 30th.

28th   Government B.727 YU-AKD operated JAT's last summer flight, JU206/7.

29th   French Air Force Noratlas 121/IL, arriving from Villacoublay at 1226, brought in a new engine for Air France SE.210 F-BHRF.

31st   TAP B.707 CS-TBI, arriving at 0847 (GK3088 from Toronto), was a first visit operating a Laker Airways flight.

31st   Another TAP aircraft making its first visit was B.727 CS-TBL, bringing in FC Porto today for their European Cup-Winners Cup second leg game with Manchester Utd.

November 1977

After last month's bad weather and diversions, there were only strong winds this month and virtually no diversions, but Manchester did benefit from extra flights due to the fireman's strike at Liverpool.

CAA HS.748 G-AVXI, RAE Andover XS646 & RAE HS.748 XW750 were all involved in further intensive trials on the British Doppler MLS. In direct competition with an American version, whichever wins will replace systems at airports all over the world. Although the ILS (Instrument Landing System) is accurate, it has limitations. It guides aircraft in on a narrow radio beam 8° wide, but it cannot be installed at all airports, as the beam can be affected by interference from surrounding terrain and buildings. However, the new MLS is even more accurate, with a beam ten times wider than the ILS and tests have already proved it can cope with difficult airports. One of the reasons tests are being carried out at Manchester, with a hundred landings so far, including ten 'blind', is because the CAA wants to see the effects of the runways hump. Tests have also been carried out at Brussels, Gatwick, Stansted & Kristiansand and more are planned at other airports. A final decision will be announced at next April's meeting of the International Civil Aviation Organisation, which represents 135 countries.

British Airways have based a 'short' BAC 1-11 at Manchester, replacing another Super 1-11 currently covering services out of Heathrow. They will have more holiday flights next summer, increased frequencies to Amsterdam, Berlin & Geneva and a new service to Faro.

The UK Government has prevented SAS from operating the Dublin sector of their SK537/8, in retaliation over a Danish ban on British Midlands newly proposed Birmingham-Copenhagen service.

Britannia Airways increased frequency on their newspaper service to Belfast to a daily operation. Most of these flights are still operated by Air Bridge Carriers, although British Midland DC-9 OH-LYB was used on the 17th and Alidair Viscount G-ARIR on the 18th. Air Bridge Carriers and Aer Turas are continuing their cattle flights to Milan and Venice.

The following airlines made changes this month: Air France reverted back to a six-weekly service with SE.210 Caravelle's (AF962/1). British Airways Montreal/Toronto (BA648/9) operates as a Boeing 707 flight and a Trident 3 operates Friday evenings BE4436/4413, departing on Saturday mornings. Finnair increased their Helsinki cargo flights to twice-weekly. KLM morning-flight KL153/4 continues daily through the winter and the lunchtime KL155/6 continues on weekdays. Winter IT flights will be operated by Aviaco, Britannia Airways, British Airways, Dan-Air & Laker Airways and there are no ABC flights to the USA.

Equipment changes on the European scheduled services during the month were Finnair (AY032): DC-9 OH-LYI (4th), Lufthansa (LH074/076): B.727s D-ABCI (29th), D-ABGI (24th), D-ABII (11th), D-ABIW (20th), D-ABKA (21st), D-ABKC (25th), D-ABKG (22nd), D-ABQI (23rd) and Swissair (SR842): DC-9-51s HB-ISK (28th) & HB-ISL (6th).

ILS traffic observed and identified were RAE Andover XS646 (1st/2nd/3rd/4th) and RAE HS.748 XW750 (1st/2nd). British Airways crew training flights were G-AXGW (8th/9th/10th) and VC-10 G-ARVM (23rd).

1st   Merlin N49MZ, arriving at 1755 en route Gothenburg-Cork, was a technical diversion with undercarriage problems. After attention with Dan-Air, it departed the following day.

3rd   Alidair Viscount G-BDRC, operated an outbound flight to Deauville today (QA755). Previously owned by Intra Airways, it still wears their basic colours, but has no titles.

3rd   Another TAP B.727 first visit was CS-TBQ, arriving to take FC Porto home after knocking Manchester Utd out of the Cup Winners Cup, even though Utd won tonight's game 5-2.

7th   British Caledonian B.707 G-CDHW, made its first visit today (BR2792 from New York). Still a relatively new aircraft, having been built in 1975, it only operated with British Caledonian until January 1979, when it was sold as A6-HRM.

11th   Even though Manchester was affected by winds of up to 50kts during the day, the airport still received a number of evening diversions due to strong cross-winds.

11th   Royal Saudi Air Force C-130Hs 463 (RSF230) and 465 (RSF287) operated USA-bound flights through Manchester, transporting F-5 parts back to Northrop.

12th   Flights between Manchester and Belfast were operating normally today after six weeks, when airport security staff finally resumed normal working.

14th   Strong winds were still affecting the airport when BE985 from Frankfurt overshot due to a 42kt gust, but it still managed to land after a second attempt! Other flights weren't as lucky - BE917 (from Brussels) diverted to Heathrow, EI620 (from Dublin) diverted to Shannon, BE953 (from Geneva) diverted to Birmingham, GK307 positioning from Gatwick diverted to East Midlands, DA1213 diverted to East Midlands and KL155 (from Amsterdam) diverted to Heathrow.

14th   HS.125 5N-ANG arrived at 1903 to clear customs, en route for maintenance at Hawarden.

14th   RAF VC-10 XV109, arriving at 2324 (RR2600 from Hanover), was operating an inbound trooping flight on behalf of Britannia Airways!

15th   Ford Air commenced a Tuesday flight from/to Cologne today with the first flight being operated by Gulf 1 G-ASXT (FD251/2). Due to the lack of fire-cover at Liverpool, they used Manchester until the 20th December.

16th   Falcon 20 F-BVPN was on departure for Clermont-Ferrand, but it had to return due to a cracked windscreen.

17th   Severe ice and poor braking action during the morning caused the following flights to divert to other airports: BY085B to Birmingham, Dan-Air HS.748 G-ARMW to Leeds, EI9216 returned to Dublin, SK057 went onwards to Copenhagen and SR846 returned to Zurich.

18th   Falcon 20 I-EKET diverted in at 1547 en route to Blackpool, due to the unavailability of customs at Blackpool.

19th   PA-32 F-BOJV, owned by Aeromaritime the operators of the Guppy flights, operated from/to Paris le Bourget today.

21st   British Airways flights returned to normal following five hours of talks to resolve a dispute involving sixty semi-skilled men. Their walk-out over grading, led to the grounding of all BA flights since the 17th. They returned to work yesterday morning, after being promised talks at a national level to discuss their grievances.

22nd   After many months of legal and political wrangling, the first British Airways Concorde flights between London-New York were finally underway, complimenting the existing Washington and Bahrain services.

24th   Air Freight Douglas DC-3 G-AMWW, arriving at 1913, was operating a cargo flight from Aberdeen, before departing later for Gatwick.

26th   Another Air France SE.210 Caravelle leaving the fleet was F-BHRB, making its final visit to Manchester today, before its withdrawal from service the following month.

27th   Biz-jet arrivals at the weekend weren't too common in 1977, particularly in winter, but two arrived today and both were first visits. Diamond-Shamrock Gulfstream 2 N24DS arrived at 1500 from Munich, before departing to Le Bourget the following day and Lear Jet N54YR from Keflavik arrived at 1943, before leaving for Torp on the 29th.

28th   Two British Air Ferries Carvair's visited Manchester in the new BAF colour scheme. G-ASHZ landed with the port outer engine feathered, after it was shut down due to overheating. Its cargo of nine yearling racehorses continued their journey to Ireland the next day on Carvair G-ASDC, which had positioned from Dublin. Meanwhile, G-ASHZ returned to Southend on three engines.

28th   HS.125s D-CJET today and 9Q-CCF on the 29th, called in to clear customs, en route for maintenance at Hawarden.

30th   Early freezing fog caused the diversion away of the following flights: BY990V to Birmingham, DA1549 to East Midlands, LH4072 to Amsterdam and SK057 to Copenhagen.

30th   PA-31 916, landing in a visibility of 700m in freezing fog and outside temperature of -7c, was the first arrival of a French Navy PA-31 since April 1973.

30th   PA-31 SE-FNE and Cessna 404 SE-GZG arrived in the afternoon, when the visibility went from bad to worse, but even though it was right down to 400m - they still made it!

December 1977

Car parking charges will go up from April next year. The main increases are in terminal parking at the multi-storey, when rates will rise from 40p to 45p for 2-hours, 50p to 60p for 3-hours, 60p to 70p for 4-hours, £1.00 to £1.20 for 12-hours and £1.50 for 24-hours. Approval was also given for increased landing charges, passenger load supplements and aircraft parking. It's estimated the increases will net the airport £1.3m a year.

Cargo flights by Air Bridge Carriers and Aer Turas continued during the month, transporting cattle to Milan and Venice.

Numerous charters carrying car parts for Ford operated through Manchester, due to continuing industrial action at Liverpool.

Equipment changes on the European scheduled services during the month were Air France (AF962): Air Charter SE.210 F-BJTG (6th), Lufthansa (LH074/076): B.727 D-ABKJ (5th) and Swissair (SR842): DC-9-51s HB-ISL (17th) & HB-ISS (12th).

ILS traffic observed and identified were Hawker-Siddeley HS.748 G-11-8 (7th), RAF Dominie XS732 (14th), CAA HS.125 G-AVDX (14th) & RAF C-130 XV178 (19th). HS.748 G-11-8 was on its very first flight, in full Trinidad & Tobago Air Services colours, prior to being delivered as 9Y-TFS on the 23rd. It was also the first HS.748 seen on the ILS since March.

1st   Dan-Air B.727 G-BFGN, arriving at 2257 was in basic Delta colours, but with no titles. It was on delivery, en route Goose Bay-Gatwick, when it diverted in due to strong headwinds.

3rd   Jet Commander N7KR arrived on a fuel stop at 1823, en route Reykjavik-Milan.

4th   Due to the continuing strike by firemen at Liverpool; Hamburg FC flew into Manchester for their match with Liverpool FC on Hapag-Lloyd B.727 D-AHLS.

4th   TWA operated a charter using B.707 N18712 (TW8778 from New York). Next summer will operate a weekly ABC charter from/to New York, on behalf of Jetsave.

5th   Falcon 20 N121EU owned by IBM, arrived from Le Bourget transporting the President of IBM to and from various points over the next few days.

7th   Intra Airways DC-3 G-AMPO, arriving at 2045 from Saarbrucken, was transporting car parts from Germany on behalf of Ford.

7th   PA-28 SE-GVA was on delivery from Gander-Aarhus, when it diverted in due to strong headwinds.

7th   Another inbound diversion today was Cessna 310 D-ICAL, after declaring a full emergency with an oil leak.

8th   The ATC watch log recorded that from 0640 Manchester was the primary diversion for Finningley and would accept up to ten Dominies.

8th   PA-23 N101VH, arriving for British registry with NEA, was G-BNPD by the 10th. It performed various test flights during the month, but was still present at the end of the year.

11th   PA-23 G-AYBO inbound from Ipswich, reported it had no nose-wheel down indication and would feather the engines on landing. A full emergency was declared and when it touched down, it immediately swung onto Runway 28. Luckily, no damage was done to either the aircraft or the occupants!

12th   A full four years after the rest of the airline succumbed to ATC flight numbers, Dan-Air's City Link flights finally stopped using their registration and adopted ATC flight numbers.

12th   Royal Saudi Air Force C-130H 469 made its first visit today. It arrived at 1604 as RSF711 Jeddah-Milan and departed on the 15th.

13th   British Airways Viscount G-AOHV, (BZ541 from Ronaldsway) made a safe landing after declaring a full emergency with a nose-wheel unlocked indication.

14th   British Air Ferries Carvair G-ASDC arrived at 0116 from Saarbrucken, on a Fords car parts charter.

15th   Air Atlantique DC-3 G-AMCA at 0351 and BAF Carvair G-ASHZ at 0830, arriving from Cologne, were also bringing in car parts on behalf of Fords.

15th   Beech 80 G-BDKG suffered an undercarriage collapse on landing. It had just departed to Cork, when the fault developed and it held over Stretton for an hour before returning and landing on Runway 28. It departed to Liverpool on the 5th January, after receiving attention.

16th   IFA Douglas DC-6 OO-IFA (ex-Air Djibouti) arrived at 0012 from Frankfurt, transporting car parts on behalf of Ford. The new airline formed this year, made its first revenue flight on 16th June, carrying eighty-six passengers from Brussels to Jersey. It's also capable of carrying freight, after having a cargo door fitted during a major overhaul in 1975. Arriving in a stylish orange and blue livery, this was its only visit to Manchester, as the airline ceased trading in May 1978 and it was sold as N799TA.

16th   In a month plagued by aircraft incidents, SVC-10 G-ASGK (BA538 from New York direct), declared a full emergency today, with a hydraulic fault.

19th   Today's major diversion session produced some interesting aircraft. There was some local fog around early on, but it was clearing when the first divert, South African Airways B.747 ZS-SAM arrived at 0702 (SA858 from Sal Island). It was missed by the writer, as it was the first day of the school holidays and there was no rush to be up early, although I was up by 9am and oblivious to the weather situation in the south. My current tracking book was coming to an end and as I walked back from Stockport after buying a new one, I saw Trident 3 G-AWYZ (Shuttle 863 from Glasgow) and Laker Airways B.707 G-AVZZ (GK8614 from Detroit) arrive in quick succession. I wasn't convinced they were diversions, but the next two arrivals dispelled all such doubts! British Airways B.747 G-AWNM at 0947 (BA889 from Bahrain) was quickly followed by British Caledonian DC-

10 G-BEBL at 0950 (BR366 from Kano) and a further flight, British Airways SVC-10 G-ASGI at 1000 (BA610 from Montreal) went overhead as I was putting the key in the door. For the next hour there was a steady flow of diversions, mainly mundane apart from Saudia B.747 OD-AGI at 1025 (SV071 from Rome). Saudia was a new airline to Manchester, but this particular aircraft, leased from MEA, was in full SV colours. Also in this session was the first visit of a Kenya Airways new Boeing 707, 5Y-BBI (KQ714 from Rome) and when SVC-10 G-ASGD landed at 1114 (BA317 from Jeddah), it was the end of the session. No other diversions arrived in the next two hours, despite the weather remaining the same, so it was probably due to lack of space or handling facilities. B.747 9V-SQD 'Singapore 077' was turned away during this time and I heard it was diverting to Prestwick. Aircraft started diverting into Manchester again from 1300, but as the runway had changed to Runway 06, I wasn't going see anything now! I considered going to the airport, but decided to stay at home with my radio in full use. A slight easterly breeze had picked up, which was obviously the reason for the runway change and although there was patchy cloud in the morning, it had developed into a cold but sunny day. The next session began with the three first visits; the first visit of a British Airways Rolls-Royce powered Boeing 747 when G-BDXA arrived at 1322 (BA510 from New York), EL AL B.707 4X-ATS at 1354 (LY315 from Tel Aviv) was the first visit by the airline since November 1971 and Malaysian Airlines DC-10 9M-MAS arrived at 1359 (MH002 from Frankfurt). Laker DC-10 G-AZZD arrived at 1407 operating a Skytrain service (GK020 from New York). Others of note were first visit Swissair DC-9-51 HB-IST at 1429 (SR816 from Geneva), KLM DC-8 PH-DEM at 1433 (KL119 from Amsterdam) and KLM DC-9 PH-DNB at 1439 (KL101 from Rotterdam). Again, this batch of diversions lasted for about an hour and more aircraft were turned away, including British Airways Concorde G-BOAD (BA301 Bahrain-Heathrow), British Airways B.747 G-BDXB (BA660 Miami-Heathrow), MEA B.707 OD-AFD (ME201 Beirut-Heathrow which diverted to Paris-Orly), Alia B.707 JY-ADP (RJ111 Amman-Heathrow) and British Airways L.1011 G-BBAH (BE003 Paris-Heathrow, diverted to Glasgow). Swissair DC-9-51 HB-ISM (SR804 Zurich-Heathrow) was actually inbound to Manchester when it followed company instructions and diverted to Gatwick instead. British Airways Trident 2 G-AVFB (BE355 Rome-Heathrow) was also inbound to Manchester, but it eventually ended up diverting to Bournemouth. Two further Heathrow diversions arrived around teatime: BAC 1-11 G-AVMR at 1655 (BZ705 from Aberdeen) and another Saudia visitor, this time one of their own aircraft when L.1011 HZ-AHD arrived at 1739 (SV173 from Paris). Unfortunately, another Saudia L.1011, HZ-AHH, on delivery direct from the Lockheed factory routing Palmdale-Heathrow and a possible diversion contender, ended up diverting to Paris. There were no more diversions after 'Saudi 173', apart from a final SVC-10 nearly four hours later, when G-ASGF arrived at 2123 (BA717 from Doha), even though Heathrow was still effectively closed due to fog.

19th   Royal Saudi AF C-130H 470 made its first visit to Manchester today. It was operating westbound as RSF228, transporting more F-5 parts back to Northrop, before returning eastbound on the 28th.

20th December 1977 – Having not visited Manchester before, Saudia diverted two aircraft in due to fog at Heathrow: L.1011 Tristar HZ-AHD & B.747 OD-AGI. Both had joined the mass exodus of aircraft departing for Heathrow by lunchtime. (Geoff Ball)

20th   Hawker-Siddeley HS.748 demonstrator, G-BCDZ, was a Woodford diversion, arriving from Nice at 1357 after returning from a sales tour of the Far East.

21st   Balair DC-6F HB-IBS operated a freight charter on behalf of Swissair as SR1844/5, from/to Basle.

21st   LOT TU-134 SP-LGD (LO4035/6), operating one of three Christmas charters this month, was a last minute substitute as it was originally planned for IL-62 SP-LAE.

22nd   LOT IL-18 SP-LSE arrived at 2116, operating Teeside-Warsaw as LO4013/4.

23rd   LOT IL-18 SP-LSI, making its first visit operating LO4017/8, was formerly operated by the Polish Air Force.

30th   This was the second consecutive day of strong winds, when three early morning arrivals were diverted away: AF962 (from Paris) to Birmingham, AY032 (from Helsinki) to Heathrow and BA538 (from New York/Prestwick) also went to Heathrow, after making an aborted approach when cross-wind strength became too severe.

30th December 1977 – CV-240 N12WA arrived with engine trouble on the 28th, en route Reykjavik-Cairo for its new owners. It was parked outside the Dan-Air hangars until its departure for Heathrow on 1st January 1978. Built in 1948, it was registered as SU-AZW, but was withdrawn in 1982. (Geoff Ball)

First/Last Arrivals & Departures 1977

First arrival:	PA-23 G-AWDI from Edinburgh at 0158
First departure:	PA-23 G-AXOW to Heathrow to 0710
Last arrival:	BAC 1-11 G-AVYZ/GK324 from Palma at 2317
Last departure:	BAC 1-11/G-AVYZ to Gatwick at 2359

(+/- % on Previous Year)		
Scheduled Passengers	1,483,000	-1.1%
I.T/Charter Passengers	1,310,000	+3.6%
Transit Passengers	111,000	-0.9%
Total	2,904,000	+1.0%
Freight & Mail (Tonnes)	37,500	+3.0%
Movements	75,800	+2.5%

Airport Diary 1978

January 1978

The Airport Authority voiced its concern over plans by British Airways to introduce a 'no-bookings' shuttle service between London and Manchester. They fear it will take traffic away from Manchester's direct services; but the airline made assurances they were developing services from Ringway. The airport blamed last summer's ATC strikes and cancelled flights, particularly by British Airways, for failing to reach last year's 3 million passenger target.

British Airways announced further expansion of their Manchester services this year, with increased frequencies to Paris, Copenhagen & Heathrow. New 'advanced purchase excursion' fares are also being introduced, bookable two months in advance, which will bring down the price of a return ticket to £139 for Manchester-Toronto and £140 for Manchester-New York. Also being considered are a number of new scheduled services including Jeddah, Bahrain, Johannesburg & Los Angeles. Routes to Rawalpindi and the Persian Gulf are also being given serious consideration. Other changes will see the Aberdeen service upgraded to a Viscount and the reintroduction of the Zurich service, suspended last year. Finally, from May there will be a twice-weekly direct service to Montreal with Boeing 747s, which will also be reintroduced on their New York and Toronto flights.

Dan-Air won contracts to carry out maintenance on behalf of four overseas operators: Cyprus Airways, Fred Olsen, Royal Swazi National Airways & Oman Air Force. When their new Manchester maintenance facility first opened in January 1976, they employed 100 staff which has now has risen to 350.

Due to the high demand, Britain's second largest tour operator, Arrowsmith, have added an extra 5,000 holiday seats from Manchester. They have sold half of their 100,000 holiday quota for this year already and extra flights will be added to Corfu, Barcelona, Palma & Malaga.

Northern Executive Aviation saw a 28% increase in passengers last year, when more than 13,000 were carried.

Equipment changes on the European scheduled services were Lufthansa (LH074/076): B.727s D-ABIU (22nd), D-ABIZ (12th), D-ABKH (10th); Swissair (SR842): DC-9-51s HB-ISK (23rd), HB-ISP (16th) and B.747 HB-IGB (18th).

ILS traffic observed and identified were RAF Dominie XS733 (10th), French Air Force Falcon 20 238/F-RAFM (11th) and HS.125 G-AXDM (17th).

1st New resident, Chipmunk G-BFAW, has remained with the North West Flying School since its arrival at Manchester last month. It's predominantly dark blue, with a red and white check rudder, a multi-coloured growl on the engine cowling and white bands on the wings.

2nd Ford Motors BAC 1-11 G-BEJM arrived at 1100 from Stansted for work with Dan-Air, before departing on the 6th. Their other two BAC 1-11s also visited Dan-Air during the year and G-BFMC made its first visit on 7th July.

3rd Corvette PH-JSC was en route from Amsterdam to Leeds today, when it was forced to divert into a very windy Manchester at 1059 due to flap trouble.

4th Laker Airways BAC 1-11 G-AVBW, (GK2843 Manchester-Munster) had to abort takeoff due loss of power in its starboard engine.

5th HS.125 5N-ANG arrived at 1307 from Hawarden for customs clearance after maintenance.

7th Two Air France SE.210 Caravelle's making their last appearances at Manchester this month were F-BHRO today and F-BHRN on the 11th. Both aircraft had been withdrawn by April.

8th Manchester was on standby to accept weather diversions from the south and had space to accommodate up to fourteen aircraft, including six wide-bodied, until it had problems of its own with fog. British Airways B.747 G-AWNC, operating 'Speedbird 010', was on its way in but it overshot at 0840 when visibility fell below its landing limits and it eventually diverted to Prestwick. Qantas B.747 VH-EBJ arriving at 0810 (QF001 from Bahrain), was making a first visit.

8th World Airways DC-8 N801WA arrived at 1450, operating a charter from New York. They will be operating a summer programme on behalf of Jetsave Holidays this year.

10th The arrival of British Caledonian B.707 G-AYEX at 0857 (BR2212 from Toronto), marked the airlines final ABC flight from Manchester. They were pulling out of the transatlantic charter market to concentrate on building up their scheduled route network, as part an effort to increase their worldwide presence as a major scheduled airline. Caledonian, as it was known prior to its merger with BUA in 1971, had been the dominant affinity-group carrier across the Atlantic, with a market share of 22.5%.

11th The airport was warned to expect high cross-winds, which increased in intensity by the afternoon and by the evening, they were quite ferocious! They came from a northerly direction, reaching speeds of up to 50kts, with temperatures barely above freezing. From around 1800 aircraft inbound to the major southern airports were holding, mainly at the Honiley beacon and Manchester was in a position to receive up to twenty diversions, including five wide-bodied. The first diversion was British Airways Trident 3 G-AWZF at 1904 (BE625 from Cologne). This aircraft and subsequent arrivals, found Manchester's high winds weren't much of an improvement than those in the south! Because of this, only five diverted aircraft made it into Manchester, all arriving within thirty minutes of each other. Birmingham on the other hand was deluged with arrivals, including seven McAlpine Aviation HS.125s, diverting in from Luton. Manchester lost a flight late evening when Comet G-BDIV (DA1519 from Malaga) overshot, due to the strong winds and diverted to Birmingham.

12th PA-23 Aztec G-BAVZ slid off Runway 28, having declared an emergency with an undercarriage fault. It was towed off to the South Side hangars for attention, before leaving later in the day.

17th Due to weather conditions on the east coast, Manchester was put on standby for Scampton, Waddington & Finningley, after being declared the primary alternate for any aircraft inbound to these RAF bases.

18th January 1978 – As Swissair operations into Heathrow were severely affected by today's fog, they used Boeing 747 HB-IGB on Manchester's SR842 Zurich flight; with additional passengers for Heathrow, who were subsequently transported to London by surface transport. (Geoff Ball)

18th Following a deterioration in Heathrow's weather in the early hours, Manchester Apron Control advised that should the need arise, eighteen narrow-bodied and four wide-bodied aircraft could be accepted. Although Heathrow had fallen below the limits for most landing aircraft and remained so for the rest of the day, Gatwick was unaffected and operated as normal until 1500, but after the congestion of so many diverted aircraft and having difficulties coping with their own flights, they became PPO (Prior Permission Only). Apart from the very first diversion into Manchester of B.747 VH-EBD at 0641 (QF001 from Bahrain), in a very low cloud base, little else of excitement appeared until the arrival of Alitalia DC-9 I-DIBC at 1122 (AZ282 from Rome), which heralded the start of a little more variety, as soon to follow was Austrian Airlines DC-9-51 OE-LDN at 1145 (OS451 from Vienna), Kenya Airways B.707 5Y-BBK at 1149 (KQ214 from Frankfurt) and Finnair DC-9-51 OH-LYR at 1156 (AY831 from Helsinki). After B.747 G-AWNC arrived at 1204 (BA510 from New York), there were no more diversions for three hours, so I assumed the Heathrow weather had improved, but when I got home from school I heard a large aircraft overhead and saw British Airways L.1011 G-BBAF (BE079 from Nice), disappearing into the backdrop of the setting sun on its final descent into Manchester. I later discovered the weather had not cleared during those 'three hours' and I'd missed two B747s. The first, TWA B.747 N93107 at 1501, (TW1754 from Shannon) had diverted there originally and then made an attempt to return to Heathrow, before landing at Manchester. The second, Alia JY-AFA at 1547 (RJ111 from Amman) was one of the highlights and a first visit, but I was perplexed as to how I'd missed it during my walk home, as the flight path was always in direct view, it must have arrived when I called in at the sweetshop! Soon to follow was Trident 3 G-AWZU at 1635 (BE195 from Barcelona) and EL AL B.707 4X-ATB at 1638 (LY315A from Paris) which was also a first visit. There were further sporadic arrivals throughout the evening, culminating in another visit of a British Airways Concorde, G-BOAE this time, which arrived at 2047 (BA170 from New York). The Concorde flights to New York had been subjected to legal wrangling for many months, prior to their commencement on 22nd November 1977, initially operating twice a week. The final highlight of the day was Swissair Boeing 747 HB-IGB, which was not a diversion, but operating our own Zurich flight SR842/3. Due to fog at Heathrow, none of their Zurich flights had operated and the majority of London-bound passengers had made their way by surface transport, onwards to Heathrow. Although Manchester was still preparing to accept further diversions, with space being made for nine aircraft, including three wide-bodied, no more arrived after the final diversion of the evening, Alitalia DC-9 I-DIZE at 2200 (AZ292 from Milan). The forecast predicted a vigorous low pressure, bringing wind and rain which would sweep across the country, so a weather standby was issued to expect strong winds. Aircraft that didn't make it into Manchester for various reasons were MEA Boeing 720 OD-AFS (ME201), Kuwait Airways B.707 9K-ACJ (KU183), National Airlines DC-10 N83NA (NA002) and British Airways B.747 G-AWNP (BA250).

18th January 1978 – An evening shot of three aircraft that diverted in from Heathrow during the afternoon/early-evening. Seen here is El Al Boeing 707 4X-ATB (LY315A), Ghana Airways (GH700) & British Airways L.1011 Tristar G-BBAF (BE079). (Geoff Ball)

20th Partenavia P.68 G-BCPO made an emergency landing and parked outside the South Side hangars awaiting engine spares. It finally left on 2nd February after repairs.
20th The ATC watch log recorded that upon leaving Stand 46, the pilot of G-AVMK (BE4407) complained that a Shell tanker drove across his path. The Shell supervisor was contacted and instructed to reprimand the driver!
22nd Oman Air Force BAC 1-11 551 arrived at 1110 (OU551 from Bournemouth) for attention with Dan-Air, before departing on the 27th.

24th British Airways Trident 1E G-ASWU made its first visit (BE4424/35 from/to Heathrow). Formerly Cyprus Airways 5B-DAD, it was rescued from the aftermath of the Turkish invasion of Cyprus in 1974!

24th The RAF retired its final Argosy today, when XR143 made its last operational flight from Brize Norton. Originally fifty-six were delivered to the RAF, from November 1961. The Argosy had never been a regular visitor to Manchester and the last military appearance was RAE example XN817, making an ILS approach on 12th November 1975. The last RAF Argosy to actually land was 29th August 1971, when XR136 took part in a Heaton Park fun weekend.

25th Two French Air Force Falcon 20s, on training flights from Shannon to Villacoublay, made touch-and-goes today: 93/F-RAFN at 1256 and 167/F-RAFL at 1633.

25th NEA took delivery of another Islander when SE-FTA arrived at 2001 from Groningen. It will eventually become G-BNEA and although it should have gone to Leavesden for painting, in the end it was done in the South Side hangars.

26th The ATC watch log recorded that an inbound Air Bridge Argosy flight (AK720P from East Midlands) overshot at 0026 due to technical trouble. It had only been showing two greens, when there should have been three, to indicate its full landing gear was down, so it subsequently diverted to back to East Midlands.

28th US Army Beech U-21 18019 arrived at 1432 to clear customs, en route Liverpool to Coleman Barracks.

31st Dan-Air HS.748 G-ARAY, en route Cardiff-Leeds, diverted in with a fire warning light on. It departed an hour later, but returned immediately, this time declaring a full emergency with a fire in the port engine. It made a safe landing, after closing down the offending engine.

31st The airport was closed from 0915-1200, due to snow.

February 1978

The Government finally published its white paper on the UK's airports and announced that Manchester has been nominated as one of only two Category A Gateway International Airports outside of London, with the other being Prestwick. Qantas and Saudia are already interested in serving Manchester, but any new services are still subject to Government approval. British Airways and PIA are looking to serve Rawalpindi, due to demand by the large Pakistani community in the North. Although regional airport policy was clarified in the white paper, the Government has no intention of stimulating growth by artificial means and insists traffic growth will still have to stand on its own two feet. Despite Manchester's nomination as the only new international gateway in England, traffic is not expected to rise above 6 million passengers per year for the foreseeable future. Second-tier regional airports are likely to be identified as Birmingham, East Midlands, Newcastle, Cardiff and possibly Leeds. It's hoped a clear policy on regional airports will settle some of the conflicts between the catchment areas, e.g. the designation of Manchester as an international gateway and Liverpool's reduction to a third-level local status. Ringway suffered badly from last year's strikes, industrial action by British ATC assistants, British Airways engineers and the fire services, all of which contributed to the slump in traffic.

The other major announcement of the month was that a decision was made on the 24th regarding the future of Manchester's proposed second runway. After a 10-10 split, the outcome was finalised on the casting vote of the Airport Authority Chairman. After taking advice from engineers and considering the lack of central government funding and insufficient traffic, he voted to defer the project and carry out improvements on the existing runway instead. The work would involve strengthening the runway's weak centre section by adding up to 25 inches of asphalt to the depth and extending it by 800ft to a total length of 10,000ft. The work will be carried out during the summers of 1979 and 1980 at night, to avoid closing the airport completely for two months. The airport authorities have stressed that the second runway has not been abandoned, but merely delayed. The unions pledged to fight the decision and warned of serious industrial relations in the future.

The problem of night-time flight noise is not appreciably decreasing, despite controls and incentives. Most infringements were caused by the various ATC disputes, delaying aircraft into the night. The nosiest culprits are BAC 1-11s and Boeing 727s. It was recorded that the 1-11 flew 10%

of the night flights between 1973-August 1977 and contributed 24% of the noise infringements, while the Boeing 727 flew 13% of the night flights and contributed 25% of the infringements.

Having introduced a second weekly service between Manchester and Malta during the summer last year, Air Malta will reintroduce the second flight again this summer, but this time it will be scheduled rather than a charter. The new Thursday flight will operate between June and September and complement the existing Sunday service.

Equipment changes on the European scheduled services were Lufthansa (LH074/076): B.727s D-ABFI (17th), D-ABIY (14th), D-ABKA (10th), D-ABKC (24th) & Swissair (SR842): DC-9-51s HB-ISK (27th), HB-ISR (6th) plus first visit HB-ISU (20th).

ILS traffic observed and identified were French Air Force SE.210 141/F-RAFG (7th), RAF Vulcan XJ782 (28th) and RAF C-130 XV178 (28th).

1st During a very wet and windy evening, Air Alsace VFW-614 F-GATG made a first visit of type, appearing at 1951 from Glasgow. It arrived at Manchester as part of a sales tour of the UK, before departing for Bristol the following evening.

1st Invicta Britannia G-ANCF diverted in due to high winds, en route from Nicosia to Manston as IM849, operating a 3-engined ferry.

4th Swissair cargo flight SR846/7 was operated by Balair DC-8 HB-IDU.

5th Fred Olsen HS.748 LN-FOM arrived for a minor check with Dan-Air. It's used as a calibration aircraft and rarely ventures outside of Scandinavia. Its colour scheme consisted of a white upper fuselage, orange stripe and tail with a white flag. It performed a test flight on the 23rd before departing back to Oslo.

5th AA-5 G-BCCJ was taxiing from the South Side to the Freight Apron, when it got stuck in the grass after one of its wheels left the taxiway, so the pilot and his passenger had to push it back onto the taxiway!

7th French Navy PA-31 918 arrived at 0931 as F-YEFU, on a return flight to Le Bourget.

7th Air Wales made its first appearance at Manchester when PA-31 G-BWAL, operating Cardiff-Hawarden, diverted in due to fog.

7th The star military visitor of the month was Venezuelan Air Force C-130 4224 diverting in from Salmesbury, as its regular alternate Warton, was also affected by fog. These aircraft are regular visitors to Salmesbury, bringing in BAC Canberra fuselages for refurbishment.

10th Cessna 414 G-AZZK, inbound from Edinburgh, landed with a misted-up windscreen after the pilot reported 'he had great difficulty seeing the runway'!

10th Dan-Air HS.748 G-ARAY positioned out to Bristol, only to return with a faulty engine de-icer. The problem was not severe and left again for Bristol later in the day.

11th Oman Air Force Viscount 501 arrived for attention with Dan-Air today, followed by Viscount 502 on the 14th. They are due to become 3D-ACM & 3D-ACN respectively, with the Royal Swazi National Airways. As they couldn't be accommodated inside the hangar, they were parked on Fairey's Apron during the month.

16th The ATC watch log recorded that from 0030-0300, Manchester was given primary diversion status for Waddington, but will only accept one Vulcan aircraft and from 0700-1800 it was given primary diversion status for Finningley and could accept up to five aircraft.

16th Geminair Britannia 9G-ACE arriving at 2028 (IM170 from Venice), was making the first of its two visits to Manchester this year, operating a cattle charter on behalf of Invicta International.

19th British Airways B.707 G-AWHU was observed with smoke coming from the port undercarriage, when landing on a positioning flight (BA649 from Heathrow). After nothing major was found, it departed as normal to Prestwick.

20th The second Oman Air Force BAC 1-11 to arrive for attention with Dan-Air was 553 (OU553 from Bournemouth), before its departure on the 25th. It was a day later than planned, due to snow affecting its ferry flight up from Bournemouth.

20th Dan-Air Comet G-APYC, (DA1558 to Birmingham), reported 'it may have struck something on departure'. After landing safely at Birmingham, it was discovered to have burst a tyre on takeoff.

21st Another bleak overcast day, followed a week of cold temperatures and occasional snow in the region. Other parts of the country fared a lot worse, with severe blizzards over the previous weekend. The morning produced a couple of early diversions in the shape of Ford Motor's Gulf 1 G-AWYF, diverting from Liverpool and Warton regular Hansa Jet D-COSA. The weather elsewhere was cold and misty, but as the morning progressed it turned into fog in some parts. At 1120 Heathrow's visibility of 450m was deteriorating and by lunchtime Manchester had space to accept fourteen narrow-bodied and six wide-bodied diversions and moves were made to open up disused Runway 20 for parking. It wasn't too long before Manchester was receiving a steady stream of diversions from Heathrow and a couple from Gatwick. The first of interest was new Caribbean Airways B.707 G-BFBZ arriving at 1156 (IQ060 from Frankfurt), which later departed direct to Bridgetown. British Airways B.707 G-AYLT was next at 1205 (BA453 from Athens), followed by first visit Alitalia B.727 I-DIRU at 1242 (AZ290 from Milan). British Caledonian B.707 G-AYSI arrived at 1306 on behalf of Flamingo Cargo (SE112 from Athens). British Airways sent in two L.1011 Tristars: G-BBAJ at 1314 (BA329 from Amman) and G-BEAM at 1338 (BA491 from Dhahran). Finally, VC-10 A4O-VL, arriving at 1325 (AE781 from Rome), was operating an Air Ceylon flight in full Gulf Air colours, with a British Airways crew. Unfortunately there was no requirement for parking on Runway 20, so the barriers were replaced again.

22nd Another military type being retired and phased out was the Army Air Corps six remaining Sioux helicopters, used by the Blue Eagles display team. The type had seen fourteen years of active service and the last to visit Manchester was XT124 on 29th March 1976, which incidentally was sold in 1977 as G-BFFV.

23rd Hundreds of airport staff stopped work for two hours today, timed for the quietist period from 1400-1600, in support of the second runway. Only four flights were delayed for up to an hour and as there was sufficient fire cover, the airport remained operational.

24th Queens Flight HS.748 XS789 had Her Majesty the Queen onboard, en route from Heathrow to Kinloss. It had stopped off at Manchester to pick up the Duke of Edinburgh, after carrying out a local engagement.

25th The ATC watch log recorded that at 1628 a Dan-Air vehicle narrowly missed a British Airways 1-11 being towed from the South Bay to Stand 25, via Taxiway 3. Dan-Air were contacted and asked to explain why the driver didn't give way and wasn't listening out on the ground UHF channel. Half an hour later, when there was still no telephone call of explanation from the offending driver, the police were called in to investigate the incident. By 1715 the police reported that as Dan-Air were unable to identify the driver, no further action was possible!

26th Sunday morning saw two Shannon diversions: Aer Lingus B.707 EI-ASO at 0820 (IN104 from New York) and first visit TWA B.707 freighter N792TW at 0933 (TW8904 from Boston).

26th Air Bridge Carriers Argosy G-APRL operated the final Manchester-Belfast newspaper flight, AK721/0. The flights, which started last September on behalf of Britannia Airways, have been transferred to Liverpool, but will continue to be operated by Air Bridge Carriers.

28th RAF Vulcan XJ782 made two ILS approaches late this morning, en route from RAF Scampton to Lajes, in the Azores.

March 1978

The airport has taken the preferred option of carrying out the runway strengthening work at night over a period of two years, rather than closing down fully for two months. Although it's the more expensive option, it will save the problem of passengers checking in as normal and then being taken by bus to one of several possible departure airports.

From 1st May another 1,300 parking spaces will be available, as more long-term car parks are opened near the Excelsior Hotel. Charges will be 85p a day, compared to the 2,500 multi-storey spaces at £1.50 per day and the 341 surface spaces at £1 per day. Meanwhile a sobering thought; parking one's light plane at Manchester would cost £1.10 a day, which is 30% cheaper than parking a car in the multi-storey!

Aer Lingus was affected by industrial action from the 14th and had to cancel all Manchester-Cork flights for the rest of the month, as well as a number of Dublin passenger flights and both freighters, EI9212/3 & EI9216/7. They were forced into sub-chartering numerous aircraft and using management crews to operate their own aircraft.

Equipment changes on the European scheduled services were KLM (KL153): Martinair DC-9 PH-MAR (15th), Lufthansa (LH074/076): B.727s D-ABIZ (18th) & D-ABLI (27th), SAS (SK537): DC-9-21s OY-KGF (22nd), SE-DBS (3rd) and Swissair (SR842): DC-9-51s HB-ISM (25th) & HB-ISR (22nd).

ILS traffic observed and identified were HS.125s G-BART (7th), G-BFMO (21st) & F-GASL (14th). RAF C-130's were XV176 (15th) & XV215 (28th). The only crew training flight was British Airways with G-AXGW (2nd).

4th   Cessna 182 EI-ATF arrived at 1144 from Dublin for maintenance with Northern Executive, before departing on the 19th.

4th   Sabena B.737 OO-SDH was operating the early morning freighter, SN129, when it overshot due to a sudden fog bank drastically reducing visibility. The situation was hampered further when the RVR machine was unserviceable and as it was unable to give an accurate reading, the aircraft returned back to Brussels.

5th   The airport was having bird problems around lunchtime, when seagulls were encouraged to hang around the fast turn off/Link A area of Runway 24, by spectators feeding them from the end of the Domestic pier. BAC 1-11 G-AVMN (BE4423 to Heathrow) reported hitting a gull on takeoff, which was confirmed later, but it carried on as normal.

5th   First visit HS.125 5N-AQY arrived from Palma at 1908 to night-stop, prior to its departure to Hawarden for maintenance.

11th   The airport was on standby to receive weather diversions and space was confirmed for eighteen narrow-bodied and seven wide-bodied aircraft. In the end seven diversions arrived, mostly from British Airways. There was a rare diversion from Stansted when Sterling SE.210 OY-SAM arrived at 0935 (NB425 from Stockholm), one of many flights from Scandinavia into London each weekend. Another two diversions were first visits: B.747 VH-EBI at 0739 (QF007 from Bombay) and Zambia Airways B.707 9J-AEL at 0735 (QZ704 from Lusaka), which had recently been converted to passenger operations. Also notable was the diversion to Shannon of PIA B.747 AP-AYW, which was possibly the one and only time during the decade that this airline diverted anywhere north of Watford!

12th   Ralleye F-BSTJ which had arrived on the 10th, made an attempt to depart only to be blown onto its side by Guppy F-BPPA. Remarkably no injuries or significant damage was sustained and it finally departed for Cardiff the next day.

13th   The ATC watch log recorded that a telephone call had been received at lunchtime from a resident in Mobberley, complaining that a departing aircraft passing over at approximately 1220, had sprayed oil all over his car and washing. The offending aircraft was possibly one of four, but the actual culprit remained unidentified!

14th   The final flight took place today of Aer Lingus' sole remaining fifth-freedom service to Europe, when B.737 EI-ASD operated EI620/1 (DUB-MAN-CPH-MAN-DUB). Their withdrawal was the result of an inter-Governmental agreement, terminating their fifth freedom rights to pick passengers up from Manchester to the Continent. At its peak, Aer Lingus operated from Manchester to Amsterdam, Brussels, Copenhagen, Dusseldorf, Frankfurt & Zurich, but from April they will only operate to Dublin and Cork.

14th   Philippine Air Transport C-130 RP-C101 arrived at 0222 to transport a number of generators to Lagos, via Algiers.

16th   Aer Lingus evening Dublin flight EI214/5 has been operated by various outside aircraft this month, starting with Dan-Air Comet G-BDIX today. Others included British Midland Viscount's G-BAPG (20th), G-BAPE (23rd), G-AZLR (24th) & G-BAPD (28th) and British Airways BAC 1-11 G-AVMP (22nd). The most interesting sub-charter was B.707 9G-ACJ, operating the much delayed flight. Owned by Templewood Aviation, it arrived in a Bahamas World colour scheme with Ariana titles, operated by a Trans Asian Airways crew.

17th   The ATC watch log recorded that from 1300-1800 Manchester was given number two diversion status for Scampton and would accept up to six Vulcan aircraft.

17ᵗʰ   The airport was put on standby for PA-23 Aztec G-BBXE. It was on a test flight out of Manchester, when it was forced to return after the pilot shut down the port engine. Fortunately it made a safe landing and was able to taxi to the South Side.

18ᵗʰ   British Airways introduced a £64 one-way standby fare on the Manchester-New York route, compared to the current standard return fare of over £300!

21ˢᵗ   Dan-Air took delivery of yet another HS.748 today. G-BFLL, formerly HK-1409, arrived in full Avianca orange colours but no titles. It entered the hangar during the afternoon and departed for Aberdeen on 22ⁿᵈ April.

26ᵗʰ   Dan-Air/IAS B.707 G-BEVN arrived at 1907 (FF586A from Palma) to operate an outbound freight flight to Lusaka, via Athens.

28ᵗʰ   Another new airline for Dan-Air engineering was Cyprus Airways, who brought BAC 1-11 5B-DAG in for minor work today (CY007 from Larnaca/Naples), before departing the following day. It made further appearances for maintenance throughout the year.

28ᵗʰ   NEA took delivery of new PA-23 Aztec N40270, which will eventually become G-TAXI. Leaving the NEA fleet is veteran PA-23 Aztec G-AXOW, which has been sold as EI-BDN.

29ᵗʰ   Skyline Sweden Viscount SE-FOY arrived at 2015 (OX201 from Esbjerg). It was the airlines last visit to Manchester, as they ceased operating during the year.

30ᵗʰ   Merchantman G-APEP operated the final Manchester-Amsterdam cargo flight (BE3023/18). BEA/British Airways have operated Merchantman flights to Heathrow, Belfast, Brussels, Amsterdam, Paris, Frankfurt & Dusseldorf over the years and the cargo variant of the Vanguard will be withdrawn over the next few years. The further loss of cargo services follows British Airways withdrawal of the Boeing 707 transatlantic freighter services from Ringway last year, which means they no longer operate any direct cargo services from Manchester.

31ˢᵗ   World Airways commenced their first scheduled programme out of Manchester today, when DC-10 N103WA arrived at 1146, making its first visit operating Gatwick-New York.

April 1978

Wrangling amongst elected members of the Airport Authority is threatening its long term future. Currently, the representation of the authority is split equally between Councillors from Manchester Corporation and the Greater Manchester Council. The city faction believes a second runway should be built to ensure Manchester can meet the challenges of the future, while GMC representatives, with the backing of the Government's white paper, are convinced the scheme to strengthen and extend the existing runway will suffice. The cheaper and quicker alternative was finally approved on the casting vote of the Chairman, a GMC man; although it's likely when the City Council's turn comes to elect the next Chairman in June, they will be in a position to reverse the decision.

Last November, several RAE aircraft were involved in extensive trials on the potential replacement for the ILS, the Doppler MLS system. The International Civil Aviation Organisation (ICAO) will meet this month to decide the fate of the British system, in competition with their American rivals. The Americans have developed their own system, the Time Reference Scanning Beam or TRSB, but the ICAO wants to adopt the MLS as the successor to the ILS system. The ILS, installed at airports throughout the world, operates at long radio wavelengths and is sensitive to obstruction and reflection from terrain, whereas the MLS benefits by providing shorter wavelengths, less sensitive to interference, providing guidance over a wider area than the ILS.

British Airways dropped the Albion (BZ) prefix from the 1st. The Manchester flights to Aberdeen, Jersey & Isle of Man have been renumbered and are using 'Speedbird' call-signs. For example, inbound flight from Ronaldsway BZ541, is now BA5699. Also of note are the transatlantic flights which have operated as BA538/9 (New York) & BA648/9 (Montreal/Toronto) for many years, are now operating as BA184/5 & BA080/1 respectively. The Aberdeen flight is being operated by Viscounts and Copenhagen has been increased to six-weekly. Other changes for the summer are that Air France will operate daily with SE.210 Caravelle's. KLM morning flight KL153/4 remains daily, but the Saturday flight operates with DC-8s. The weekend Lufthansa flight via Dublin operates as LH078/9 and freight flight LH4072/3 operates with B.737s. SAS passenger flights will now operate six-weekly direct from/to Copenhagen.

Due to the continuing Aer Lingus pilot strike, the following were cancelled: Cork passenger flights, morning Dublin flight EI204/5 and freight flights EI9212/3 & EI9216/7. However, they did manage to operate a number of Dublin flights with their own B.737s, but their BAC 1-11s were grounded throughout the month. The following aircraft were used on the Dublin flight EI214/5: Alidair Viscount G-ARGR (1st), Britannia Airways B.737s G-AXNC (14th) & G-AZNZ (21st); Dan-Air Comets G-APME (19th), G-APZM (3rd/17th/18th) & BAC 1-11 G-BCWA (20th/27th); Montana Austria B.707 OE-INA (4th/16th/26th) and Transavia B.737 PH-TVH (7th).

Equipment changes on the European scheduled services were Lufthansa (LH074/078): B.727s D-ABIY (10th) & D-ABLI (27th); SAS (SK539): DC-9-21s OY-KGE (28th), OY-KGF (9th), SE-DBR (4th) and Swissair (SR842): DC-9-51s HB-ISL (4th/10th) & HB-ISR (22nd).

ILS traffic observed and identified were HS.125s G-BART (6th), G-BFMO (21st) & F-GASL (14th); RAF C-130s XV176 (26th) & XV201 (6th); RAF Dominie XS709 (11th) and two RAF Vulcan's performing practice diversions: XH560 at 1215 (20th) & XJ782 at 1127 (20th).

3rd British Airways was affected by a 24-hour unofficial strike, despite talks at the weekend to try and avoid industrial action. It involved 2,200 stewards and stewardesses, wanting better promotional prospects and easier access to career opportunities within the airline's long-haul fleet.

3rd Trans Asian Boeing 707 9G-ACJ arrived at 1259 as EI6542 (Dublin-Tarbes), to drop off some passengers bound for Manchester.

3rd Sotramat HS.125 OO-SKJ made its first visit today, arriving at 1214 from/to Antwerp. It was the only HS.125 that made it onto the Belgian register.

4th Sabena B.737 OO-SDH was written-off today, on a training accident at Brussels.

7th World Airways operated further flights during the month. DC-8 N804WA today and N801WA on the 14th were outbound to New York and DC-8 N803WA operated inbound flights on the 22nd & 29th. They also operated a flight to Los Angeles via New York on Friday 28th with B.747 N748WA.

7th TAP B.707 CS-TBA, arriving at 1202 operating an outbound charter to Lisbon as TP8620 on behalf of Massey-Ferguson, also operated the return flight TP8621 on the 10th.

13th British Caledonian's new once-weekly cargo service between Manchester and Houston, Texas, was inaugurated by B.707F G-BDEA. The airline is hoping its introduction will eliminate the need for North West industry to take US-bound exports to London by road. It's the first pure-freight air link between Manchester-USA, since British Airways withdrew their New York service in May 1977.

16th The third and final Oman Air Force BAC 1-11 to visit Dan-Air for attention was 552, arriving at 1040 (OU552 from Bournemouth), before departing on the 22nd.

17th Corvette PH-JSB, arriving at 0942, was operating MP4707/8 from/to Amsterdam on behalf of Martinair.

29th April 1978 – Following on from a number of flights last year, another series transporting yellowcake for the BNFL plant at Salwick nr Preston started today. Air Afrique Douglas DC-8F TU-TCG was the first of six and Douglas DC-8-55F F-BUOR is seen here in the afternoon, about to position itself onto the Freight Apron. The plant at Salwick was the first commercial power station in the world to produce nuclear fuel. Each aircraft carried 60 tonnes of the yellowcake powder, which has been extracted and packed at the remote Arlette mine in Niger, before being taken to Niamey for the flight to Manchester, via Marseilles. (Geoff Ball)

18th Rockwell 690 N81547, currently based at Norwich, arrived to operate a day return to Plymouth.

25th The Fairchild-Swearingen Metroliner is a new 19-seat turboprop aircraft that went into production in 1974. Today's arrival of European Air Transport Metroliner OO-JPI at 0921, operating in full Sabena colours, was a first visit of type to Manchester.

26th Today saw the first French Air Force Noratlas training flight since April 1974, when Noratlas 89/62-WL arrived at 1512, on a flight from Amsterdam to Bournemouth.

30th The dwindling number of Dan-Air Comets was further reduced today when G-APME arrived at 1919 on its final revenue flight (DA1327 from Malaga). It positioned out from Manchester to Lasham on 2nd May, where it was retired from service.

May 1978

The heavily discussed plan to strengthen and improve the airports main 06/24 runway was approved during the month by city planners and work will start next year.

Following a meeting in Montreal last month, the International Civil Aviation Organisation (ICAO), has given their endorsement to the American version of the MLS system. The Time Reference Scanning Beam (TRSB) is now the planned replacement for the world-wide ILS system.

The much delayed launch of Manchester's very own freight airline, Pelican Cargo, is now likely to be early July.

The North West Flying School became official agents for Grumman. Cougar N730GA, arriving on the 22nd, was in connection with this and they planning to replace their existing PA-28 Cherokees with Grumman types.

The habit of using out of sequence registrations has become an obsession with UK civil aircraft owners. Seen during the month were Beech 200 G-BKTI (31st), Cessna 340 G-VAUN (17th), Cessna 421 G-BTDK (31st), PA-23s G-BTHS (16th) & G-SHIP (28th), PA-28 G-JOHN (19th) and PA-31s G-BTLE (11th) & G-MDRB (16th).

The recent industrial action affecting Aer Lingus came to an end on the 8th. Both Dublin passenger flights resumed on the 10th and Cork the following day, but the only freight flight that returned was EI9216/7.

From the 22nd, British Airways will operate a mix of SVC-10/B.747s on the New York passenger flight (BA184/5). The Canadian flights are split into two until the 19th October: Toronto three-weekly with B.747s (BA080/1) and Montreal direct twice-weekly with B.747s (BA082/3).

The following airlines have summer IT programmes from Manchester: Air Malta, Aviaco, Aviogenex, Balkan, Inex-Adria, JAT, LOT, Spantax, Tarom, Trans-Europa & Trans European. As well as a variety of UK operators: Britannia Airways, British Airtours, British Airways, British Caledonian, British Island Airways, Dan-Air & Laker Airways. Airlines operating regular flights to the USA/Canada this summer are CP Air (DC-8), Laker Airways (B.707 & DC-10), TWA (B.707), Wardair (B.707 & B.747) and World Airways (DC-8 & DC-10).

Equipment changes on the European scheduled services were Lufthansa (LH074/078): B.727s D-ABGI (27th) & D-ABKD (31st); SAS (SK539): DC-9-21s LN-RLL (31st), SE-DBR (8th) and Swissair (SR842): DC-9-51s HB-ISL (6th), HB-ISM (7th) & HB-ISS (3rd).

ILS traffic observed and identified were RAF Dominies XS709 & XS726 (11th) and RAF C-130s XV189 (19th) & XV203 (12th).

1st Today was the first May Bank Holiday, after it was added to the calendar. It was also the day when two Dublin flights arrived at Manchester to fill the gap of the cancelled EI214/5. Boeing 737 EI-ASB routed Dublin-Manchester-Brussels (EI646), while Maersk B.737 OY-APH routed Copenhagen-Manchester-Dublin (EI625).

2nd Air Atlantique DC-3 G-AMCA and Air Freight DC-3 G-AMSV operated outbound to Glasgow, on oil related freight flights.

2nd HS.125 N100GB arrived at 1219 en route to Hawarden for maintenance, sporting a stars and stripes colour scheme.

3rd Over 2,000 passengers arrived on various flights, diverting into Manchester due to fog at Heathrow and Gatwick. Space was made available for up to twenty aircraft, including five wide-bodied, but in the end nine wide-bodied were accepted. Amongst four British Airways B.747 flights was Delta L.1011 Tristar N81028 at 0754 (DL010 from Atlanta), diverting from Gatwick on only its third day of operation. Another new Qantas arrived, this time B.747 VH-EBN at 0749 (QF001 from Bombay), National Airlines DC-10 N81NA at 0802 (NA002 from Miami) and Air India B.747 VT-EDU at 0950 (AI104 from New York). Also notable was the Hong Kong registered Transmeridian CL-44 VR-HHC, arriving at 0443 (KK2733 from Lagos).

3rd   Today was the day of our school trip to RAF Leuchars and the sight of inbound diversions at Manchester Airport only added to the excitement! My first ever flight was onboard BAC 1-11 G-AVMX, BE4472 bound for Edinburgh. The departure time of 0750 was on schedule and the whole flight was a fantastic experience. Upon landing at Edinburgh, we boarded a coach for RAF Leuchars, but stopped off first at the famous St Andrews Golf Club for a round of - yes you guessed it - Pitch & Putt! The origins of Leuchars airbase can be traced as far back as 1911 and it's the most northerly air defence station in the UK. Equipped with F-4 Phantoms, we were allowed to inspect one at close quarters, as well being taken on a tour of the base and its facilities. Once completed, we took the coach back to Edinburgh for our flight to Manchester. BE4483 operated by G-AVMI arrived roughly on time and to a very warm evening, which rounded off a very enjoyable day.

5th   Invicta International Britannia G-ANCF operated the regular livestock charter to Italy today, on behalf of Air Bridge Carriers and again on the 11th/12th.

5th   Having been parked outside since its arrival in February, Ex-Oman Air Force Viscount 502 finally entered the hangar today, but Viscount 501 remained outside.

5th   Puma's XW226 & XW228 were routing in formation from Odiham to Belfast, when XW228 reported rotor blade trouble and was forced to land at Manchester. Puma XW226 landed with it and stayed for over an hour before continuing its journey, while Puma XW228 departed the following afternoon. Another RAF Puma arrived on the 21st, when XW216 called in on a flight from Halfpenny Green to Lossiemouth.

6th   Resident Cessna 172 G-BAEO had an accident at Barton after overrunning the runway on landing. Luckily none of the four onboard were injured, but the aircraft suffered considerable damage and had to be transported by road to NEA for repair on the 10th.

10th   Belgian Air Force Merlin CF-04, arriving at 0946 from/to Brussels, also operated to Lee on Solent-Brussels on the 12th.

11th   TIA C-130 N12ST arrived at 0341 on a fuel stop, en route from Frobisher Bay to Emmen, Germany.

13th May 1978 – On a glorious Saturday morning, KLM Douglas DC-8-55 PH-DCU is seen here in the company of two Laker Airways BAC 1-11's. KLM operated the Douglas DC-8 on their Saturday morning service during the summer of 1978 using just two aircraft, PH-DCU & DCW. (Ian Barrie)

13th   British Midland Viscount G-AZLS and first visit DC-9 N48075 operated outbound flights to Tarbes. N48075 was on a short-term lease from Southern Airways, before returning in June.

16th   Pacific Western B.707 C-FPWV (PW604) arrived at 1823 to operate a delayed flight to Vancouver, on behalf of CP Air.

17th   Dan-Air B.727 G-BAFZ was noted in the airlines new revised colour scheme. The basic difference is a broader red cheatline along the fuselage.

18th   Bristow's Puma G-BFSV arrived at 0659 on a tech stop, en route Redhill-Aberdeen.

19th   Star visitor of the month was 'blue' Braniff DC-8 N813BN; operating a trooping flight taking US soldiers back to Texas after a NATO exchange with UK troops from Weeton Barracks, near Preston. The US troops had arrived by RAF VC-10 XV102 on the 22nd April. This was also the first visit to Ringway of Braniff International, who confirmed Manchester as their designated primary alternate for their European flights.

21st   HS.125 HZ-DAC, arriving to clear customs before its onward flight to Hawarden for maintenance, was officially detained following instructions from customs. It eventually left for Hawarden the following morning.

22nd   British Airways resumed Boeing 747 operations from Manchester today, when G-AWNC positioned up from Heathrow to operate BA083. It's the first of a twice-weekly service to Montreal and they will also operate to New York and Toronto.

22nd   Another new type, the Grumman Cougar, appeared when N730GA arrived from Elstree on a demonstration tour of the UK.

22nd   NEA received yet another PA-23, this time N40475. It was re-registered as G-CDBI and left on the 26th for further work.

22nd   German Air Force Dornier Do.28 59+01, arriving at 1351 (DCN5901 from/to Cologne), was a first visit of type. The aircraft was in full VIP colours, consisting of a cream fuselage and a dark blue cheatline, with day-glo on the wings and tail tips.

24th   Gulfstream 2 N1806P arrived from Liverpool and parked up for three days in connection with the PGA British Open at Birkdale, Southport.

25th   Cessna 150 G-AWPU, en route Coventry-Blackpool, was transiting the low level corridor through the zone when the pilot stated he was lost. His Automatic Direction Finder (ADF) was not registering, but it was established he was near Congleton and as a consequence a number of departures from Manchester were delayed. He was eventually guided towards Barton, in order to land there, but ATC had noted that throughout the incident 'the pilot had acted in a confused manner'. Once on the ground at Barton, he was contacted by Manchester ATC and told his performance, namely confused radio transmissions and haphazard obedience to ATC instructions, was unsatisfactory, particularly in the vicinity of an international airport. He was warned that while no further action would be taken, other than logging the incident, any repeat performance would definitely lead to action. It transpired he was on a final cross-country flight for his PPL (Private Pilots Licence) and admitted to being totally confused!

25th   British Airways B.747 G-AWNP was taxiing out for departure to Prestwick/New York (BA185), when the pilot asked ATC if he could pull over in a convenient position, as they had a sparrow zooming up and down in the cabin and the crew wouldn't leave until it was evicted!

25th   Wessex XT764 arrived at 1733 as part of the Royal Navy presentation team. It made several local visits and also flew to/from Congleton Festival before going tech and finally departing to Wittering on 2nd June.

25th   Quebecair B.707 C-GQBH, arriving at 1349 (QB999), was operating a flight to Montreal via Shannon on behalf of CP Air.

26th   Resident Chipmunk G-BFAW returned from Coventry after having radio equipment fitted. It departed to Bassingbourn on the 28th for an air event and returned in June.

27th   JAT flight JR2206/7 is a weekly IT operation from/to Dubrovnik and today it was operated by Tarom TU-154 YR-TPG, making its first visit.

28th   Italian registered biz-jets are quite rare at Manchester, as too are Sabreliner business jets, yet I-FBCA arrived on a very hot afternoon, operating from/to Milan.

29th Air France SE.210 F-BHRG made its final visit to Manchester, operating AF962/1 before being withdrawn from service in August.

31st Out of sequence Cessna 421 G-BTDK, owned by British Air Ferries, was bringing airline officials to Manchester prior to the commencement of their new service to Rotterdam.

31st May 1978 – A fine aerial shot of Hangar 522, the home of Manchester's light-aircraft residents, taken from Nor-Fly Convair CV-440 LN-MAP. It was operating two pleasure flights on behalf of the Manchester branch of Air Britain, before its departure back to Stavanger on 2nd June. (Geoff Ball)

June 1978

Tour operator, Intasun are planning an in-house airline, with bases at Gatwick and eventually Manchester. Three Boeing 737s have been ordered for operations commencing next year and the first in February, will undertake route-proving and crew-training exercises, before the first IT flights in May.

Dan-Air B.707 G-AZTG, a regular visitor to Manchester since its first visit in July 1972, will be withdrawn by the end of the year, when it's likely to be scrapped. The airline's already in the process of offloading their remaining B.707s to other operators.

Equipment changes on the European scheduled services were SAS (SK539): DC-9-21s LN-RLO (30th), SE-DBP (1st/23rd) and Swissair (SR842): DC-9-51s HB-ISL (6th/25th), HB-ISM (7th/19th/23rd), HB-ISN (21st/24th), HB-ISP (13th), HB-ISS (3rd/28th) & HB-ISU (20th).

ILS traffic observed and identified were RAF Jetstreams XX492 (5th) & XS726 (11th). RAF traffic observed were C-130s XV200 (29th), XV293 (7th) & XV298 (15th); RAF Nimrod XV256 (12th) and RAF Vulcan XM602 (29th). This month's selection included the first appearance of a RAF Jetstream and the first Nimrod since October 1977.

1st British Air Ferries finally inaugurated their twice-daily service to Rotterdam, when Herald G-BCZG operated VF919/20 & VF995/6. It's configured to carry 25 passengers and 2 tonnes of freight.

1st Dove G-ANUW paid its final visit to Manchester, arriving at 1157, operating from/to Stansted. Delivered new in 1955, it remained a Government aircraft throughout its flying life and it was being operated by the CAA, before being permanently withdrawn in 1980.

1st Invicta International Britannia G-ANCF operated today's once-weekly livestock charter to Milan (IM820), in place of Air Bridge Carriers.

1st Court Helicopters Sikorsky S.61 ZS-HDK diverted into Manchester at 1944 due to bad weather, en route from Aberdeen to Gatwick, before continuing its journey the following morning. It became G-BFPF, after being sold to British Airways Helicopters.

3rd The Red Arrows arrived late afternoon from RAF Cosford, to use Manchester as a temporary base before their performance at the annual Barton Air Show, the following afternoon.

Flight support was provided by C-130 XV218, arriving at 1803 (RR4658 from RAF Kemble). After completing their display, they departed at 1550 for Linton-On-Ouse, just before the rains came.

4th Vintage pair Vampire XH304 and Meteor WF791 also arrived for the show, as did the star of the day, B-17 'Flying Fortress' G-BEDF nicknamed 'Sally B', which landed at 1413 prior to its performance at Barton.

4th Aerostar N90693 landed at 0213 on its delivery flight routing Reykjavik-Luton, when it was forced to make a fuel stop.

7th Transavia B.737 PH-TVN, positioned in to operate BY166A/B to/from Malaga on behalf of Britannia Airways. It made the return flight, landing in a very heavy thunderstorm!

7th Busy Bee F.27 LN-SUL, arriving at 1019 operating an inbound charter from Stavanger, also operated the return flight on the 10th from Bodo, via Bergen. It was wearing a sticker reading 'On charter to the Norwegian Armed Forces'.

12th RAF Nimrod XV256 performed a practice ILS at 1000, prior to landing at Woodford.

13th PA-31T VH-MWT, arriving at 1315 on delivery routing from Gothenburg-Heathrow, was clearly taking the long route home!

14th British Airways Trident 3 G-AWZS (BE4863 Glasgow-Heathrow) diverted into Manchester at 0856, due to a bomb threat.

17th Air Anglia Bell 47 G-ATFV arrived at Manchester today by road. It was made airworthy before taking part in pleasure flights over the coming weekend. It was thought to be the first time a helicopter had travelled by road to its destination, been assembled and then taken-off from the trailer transporting it!

18th First visit Lear Jet D-CHER, arriving from Nuremberg at 1742 as HD735 (Holsteinflug), was unusual as biz-jets don't normally use a flight number.

18th Yet another aircraft on delivery was Beech 36 N256RE, routing Reykjavik-Rome. Arriving at 1646 today, it stayed until the 20th.

18th Dan-Air took delivery of Mount Cook HS.748 ZK-MCF for the summer, which departed for Aberdeen on the 22nd as G-AYYG. Once owned by Howard Hughes, it had been stored at Woodford just in case he ever visited Britain! The only time it ever flew was for demonstration or airworthiness purposes, before being sold to the New Zealand airline in 1976.

18th Aviaco SE.210 EC-CAE operated an extra flight, AO1522A/1523A from/to Alicante, which was also the last visit of an Aviaco SE.210 to Manchester. It was sold to Aero-Lloyd as D-ACVK in February 1980.

19th Wardair B.747 C-GXRA paid its first visit to Manchester today and was recognisable by the airlines new titles on the tail.

20th British Airways B.747 G-AWNG was an early arrival (BA082 from Montreal) onto Runway 06. The pilot commented 'that the sun would be directly in his eyes, but he would still continue'. However, at his own request he ended up breaking off the approach before repositioning visually and landing on Runway 24.

20th Another aircraft on delivery was CAP-10 TF-UFO, Deauville-Glasgow. It was a first visit of type, arriving at 1532 on a fuel stop, staying for just over an hour. The aircraft is a two-seat training aerobatic type, first flown in 1968.

22nd The arrival of first visit LOT Ilyushin IL-62 SP-LAG (LO3605/6) at 1822, was the start of a series of flights from/to Warsaw, on behalf of Laing Construction.

24th The annual Woodford Air Show took place today, the same day an iconic piece of the airports skyline passed into history. The Jacksons Brickworks built in 1948 at Oversley Ford at the southern end of the airport, had fallen victim to the 1970's building recession. When the company was forced to shut down a number of factories and combine others, sadly the Oversley Ford plant was one of the closures. The buildings were quickly demolished, but the famous chimney remained intact until 1.55pm, when it too was raised to the ground!

26th Spantax DC-9 EC-CGY operated the late running GK229/230 from/to Palma.

26th Three LOT aircraft appeared mid-evening to take personnel from Laing Construction to Warsaw. The arrival of TU-134 SP-LHC at 1801 (LO3619/20) and IL-62s SP-LAA at 1748 (LO3611/2) & SP-LAF at 1855 (LO3617/8), made an impressive sight on the ground together.

27th Intra Airways DC-3 G-AMHJ arrived at 1244 to operate a freight charter to Lisbon, via Jersey.

27th Queens Flight Wessex XV733 had Princess Anne onboard, en route from Gatcombe Park to a local event in Bolton.

29th RAF Vulcan XM602 performed an ILS at 1325 on another practice diversion.

30th Aer Lingus Cork flight EI763/0 was operated by British Midland Viscount G-BAPD.

July 1978

Increases of 18% in passenger numbers and 32% in IT movements have been recorded for the first six months of 1978, compared to the same period last year. Airports forming the British Airports Authority, such as Heathrow and Gatwick showed increases of 5% and 13% respectively.

EL AL Charter announced their intention to commence a once-weekly flight between Manchester and Tel Aviv from next April.

Increasing amounts of traffic restrictions into French airspace caused long weekend delays from mid-month, right through to September. The French ATC controllers are in dispute with their management over inadequate equipment, pay and an increasing workload.

Cessna 182 G-BAEO, which has been with NEA for repair since its accident at Barton, has been declared an insurance write-off and is now dumped outside the South Side hangars.

Equipment changes on the European schedules were Air France (AF962): Air Charter SE.210 F-BJTO (7th), Lufthansa (LH074/078): B.727 D-ABKB (14th), SAS (SK539): DC-9-21s OY-KGD (4th), SE-DBP (6th), SE-DBS (26th) and Swissair (SR842): DC-9-51s HB-ISN (29th) & HB-ISP (22nd).

ILS traffic observed and identified were all RAF examples: XV211 (4th), Dominie XS736 (17th) and Jetstreams XX495 (21st) & XX497 (21st). Crew training flights were operated by British Airways B.707 G-ASZG (11th/14th) and Air Anglia F.28 PH-MOL (28th/29th).

1st 'New' NEA PA-23 G-CDBI, arriving back from Stapleford, was in full service by the 21st.

1st Corvette F-BTTL was making its first visit today on a crew training flight on behalf of Air France, who also used Nord 262s F-BLHX, F-BPNT & F-BPNX, during the year.

2nd British Airways Trident G-ARPZ (BE4623 Belfast-Heathrow) diverted into Manchester this afternoon declaring a full emergency, when the pilot reported smoke in the cockpit.

2nd Aer Lingus Dublin flight EI214/5 was operated by British Midland Viscount G-AZNA.

3rd Uni-Air F.27 G-BYAO, arriving at 1638, was operating from/to Jersey covering for a delayed British Island Airways flight.

6th After several days of extensive crew training at Shannon, Pelican Cargo - the first all-cargo airline based at Manchester, finally started operations with Boeing 707 G-BPAT. They took delivery of the aircraft on the 28th June, when it arrived at Gatwick for completion of its customs documentation. It stayed there until the 1st when it left for crew training at Shannon, prior to its arrival at Manchester. It departed at 1555 today (DP2001) bound for N'dola, Zambia via Athens, before returning on the 10th with 33 tonnes of grapes from Cyprus. Currently employing fifty-two staff, the airline plans to add a second Boeing 707 in September. They are confident they can attract customers currently sending thousands of tonnes of cargo to Heathrow by road, for onward transportation by air. Once their second aircraft arrives, they plan to operate four flights a week, to various points in Africa.

6th First time visitor Lear Jet HB-VFB arrived at 1130, to operate an outbound ambulance flight to Malaga.

7th TIA DC-10 N103TV arrived at 0839, operating a charter from Los Angeles on behalf of World Airways.

8th German-based Mitsubishi MU-2 N99KC made the first of two visits this month, arriving at 1802 operating from/to Frankfurt.

10th Cyprus Airways BAC 1-11 5B-DAH made its first visit to Manchester (CY018 from Larnaca/Naples), arriving for work with Dan-Air Engineering, before its departure on the 12th.

11th Laker Airways B.707 G-BFBS and Air Canada DC-8 C-FTIO were both covering Laker's DC-10 flight GK091/2. The DC-8 covered the inbound flight (AC070 from Toronto) and the B.707 operated the outbound sector (GK092).

11th   My final week of the school term produced some highlights. The first was today, when 'Air Canada 070' DC-8 C-FTIO caught me by surprise as I was leaving for school, although I had seen it before. This was the first visit by the airline since 1975. I was up early enough on the 13th to see Pan American B.707 N882PA arrive at 0627 (PA021 from Bahrain). Considering the amount of Pan American B.707s appearing over the years, it was amazing that this one was a first visit, fifteen years after their first. Finally, Friday 14th saw the first visit of a RAF Bulldog, when XX615 arrived before I left for school.

12th   Dan-Air B.727 G-BEGZ paid its first visit today, positioning up from Gatwick to operate a return flight to Naples (DA7956/7). Rarely seen in the UK, as it's based at Berlin-Tegel, it made another visit on the 18th.

13th   BAC 1-11 G-AVMT (BE4468 to Belfast) declared a full emergency due to hydraulic trouble shortly after departure. It returned to Manchester, where engineers were standing by with locking pins. After landing safely, it was towed off Runway 06/Link A to Stand 46.

13th   Eagle Air B.707 TF-VLC paid its first visit to Manchester today, operating KM776/7 from/to Malta. Leased to Air Malta for the summer season, it's in their full colours.

14th   RAF VC-10 XV102 (RR2753 from Hanover) arrived at 2309 with 126 school children onboard. The ATC arrival controller confused everybody by continually referring to the flight as 'Ascot 2573'!

15th   Aer Turas Britannia EI-BBH positioned in from Milan at 1716, to transport live minks to Dublin. When the cargo was being loaded on the 17th, it was noticed that most of the animals had died due to lack of water. At this point the RSPCA was called in and the uproar that followed caused the flight to be further delayed. The surviving minks were taken to Dublin on the 18th by Invicta International Britannia G-ANCF.

16th   A member of the public contacted Manchester ATC to say he'd been watching Guppy F-BPPA taxiing out on a flat tyre and once airborne, 'something had come off the wheel'. An immediate inspection was carried out on the runway, where part of a wheel rim was found. The aircraft had carried onto Bremen, where it made a safe landing.

17th   Cessna 206 N756JM, the company's current demonstrator, called in for fuel at 1447 en route Brussels-Dublin.

17th   Royal Saudi Air Force C-130H 1619 made its first visit today, arriving at 1727 as RSF817 from/to Jeddah via Milan, before its departure on the 20th.

21st July 1978 – Air Malta used two classic aircraft, owned and operated by Airtrust Singapore, during the summer. Today's arrival of N48062 (KM780 from Malta) had been anticipated for many weeks and was the first visit of a Convair CV-880. It's seen here having just arrived on a warm Friday evening, still in basic Cathay Pacific colours. It was memorable for the smoke when it arrived and the smoke and noise when it left! Remarkably two weeks later, their second CV-880, N48059, made an appearance on the 4th August (KM780 from Malta). Sadly, these were the only visits of the Convair CV-880 to Manchester and although they'd been around since 1959, they weren't considered a success. The only major airlines operating them were Cathay Pacific, JAL, Delta & TWA and none of these made it into Manchester. This aircraft was withdrawn at Singapore in 1979 and broken up in 1984. (Geoff Ball)

21st   Capitol DC-8 N906CL, a short -33 series, operated a one-off charter from/to Philadelphia, arriving at 1442. The outbound flight, departing at 1636, routed via Prestwick.

21st   CAA HS.748 G-ATMJ acquired by Dan-Air, arrived at 1702 for an overhaul and re-spray, which was achieved during the nine days prior to its departure to Aberdeen on the 31st.

22nd   The writer had another away day to Heathrow, courtesy of PB Enterprises and spent a solid twelve hours number crunching endless modern airliners - heaven or hell?

22nd   For the second time this summer, JAT flight JR2206/7 was operated by a Tarom TU-154, YR-TPH this time, which was also making its first visit.

23rd   Ex-Oman Air Force Viscount 502, which had arrived on 14th February, emerged from Dan-Air's hangar earlier in the month as 3D-ACN. It departed for Rome today on delivery to the Royal Swazi National Airways.

25th   Arab Wings Lear Jet JY-AFD arrived at 1402 from Vienna on an ambulance flight, before its departure to Amman on the 27th.

26th   This morning's Aer Lingus Dublin flight EI204/5 was operated by Montana's second B.707, OE-IRA, which was also a first visit.

26th   French Navy PA-31 No.232, arriving at 1320 on a refuelling stop, was en route Dublin-Paris-Le Bourget.

28th   RAE Andover XS607 arrived from West Freugh at 1619 (Nugget 48 from West Freugh) for a re-spray with Dan-Air and departed 9th August for Farnborough in a most colourful red, white and blue scheme. Devon XM223 arrived on 9th August at 1302 as a crew ferry, also in the new RAE scheme.

28th   Fokker F.28 PH-MOL, formerly operated by Martinair, appeared on a crew training flight today and again on the 29th. It's on short-term lease to Air Anglia, who have two aircraft on order for delivery next year, to operate services from Leeds and Norwich.

29th   Arriving at 1415 on a very hot Saturday afternoon was Mitsubishi Mu-2 VH-MIT, on delivery. It left on the 3rd August for Nice, although its eventual destination was Melbourne.

31st   Saudia DC-8F N8636, arriving at 0441 (SV8585 from Cairo), was transporting an outbound cargo of laboratory equipment.

August 1978

After several trouble free months, Manchester was affected by two sets of industrial action. Firemen were the first to go on strike on the 9th from 0930-1300, which left the airport unlicensed and unable to accept commercial movements. The second involved British Airways engineers, striking for 24-hours on the 23rd from 0630. Threats of blacking by other staff prevented British Airways movements and seventy flights were cancelled.

Major news of the month concerned heightened security at Manchester Airport. Due to emergency anti-terrorist rules brought in by the Government, only passengers were allowed into the terminal. The new measures, introduced during the weekend, coincided with a French ATC dispute, which caused delays of up to fourteen hours. Further casualties were the spectator terraces, which were closed and the top floor of the multi-storey car park, which was sealed off. The police stopped anyone attempting to enter the terminal building and only those with tickets were admitted. These precautions were in response to an attack on an El Al bus in London on the 19th August.

British Airways will introduce a shuttle on the Manchester-London service from next April, using BAC 1-11s and Trident 3s. They say the new service, which is already successfully operating between Heathrow & Belfast/Glasgow/Edinburgh, will open up a whole new concept in travel between the two cities. Operating every two hours, passengers arriving up to ten minutes before departure will be guaranteed a seat and if the plane is full, another will be provided within fifteen minutes! The airline has said the new service will not result in the running down of other services from Manchester and its being launched in direct competition with British Rail's vigorous pricing policy at selective times. They hope the new service will increase passenger numbers by 15% to 460,000 and a new departure lounge is being planned to cater for the extra loads. It was also announced that from October, new standby fares will start from £13 one way and a reduction of 40% for pensioners travelling midweek to Aberdeen, Edinburgh, Glasgow, Belfast, London, Guernsey, Jersey and the Isle of Man, will also come into operation. New major intercontinental routes are still being considered with Johannesburg, Tehran & Sydney being strong contenders.

Intra Airways have applied to the Civil Aviation Authority to operate a scheduled service between Jersey and Manchester, in direct competition with British Airways.

British Caledonian will introduce a £15 single weekend fare between London-Gatwick and Manchester this winter.

In addition to the once-weekly charter previously announced to begin next April, El Al is also expected to operate a twice-weekly cargo service between Manchester and Tel Aviv. Although its main cargo will be flowers and fresh fruit, extra security would be required before the start of any flights. Britannia Airways are also due to commence the first direct passenger flights from Manchester to Tel Aviv in October, on behalf of Horizon and Thomson Holidays.

The continuing go-slow by French ATC this month left Manchester coping with 3,000 delayed passengers. To help pass the time, feature films were shown in the Brabazon Suite. A plan to use schools as holding centres during the holidays for delayed passengers is being seriously considered and the education authorities have already been contacted. Transporting people offsite would take huge pressure off the airport's facilities and keep everyone together in case the delays were suddenly reduced and the passengers were needed back at the airport quickly.

Traffic problems caused by aircraft spotters around the airport's perimeter road in the Styal area will be discussed at this month's Airport Authority meeting. To help elevate the problem, they are considering turning the site of the former Jackson brickworks, at the South West side of the airport, into a dedicated site for enthusiasts, with car parking, viewing areas and catering facilities.

Pelican Cargo B.707F G-BPAT has been deployed elsewhere during August, spending considerable time on charter to IAS and Tradewinds out of Gatwick and Maastricht.

Equipment changes on the European scheduled services were Lufthansa (LH074/078): B.727s D-ABDI (17th), D-ABGI (20th), D-ABKF (13th) & D-ABKM (14th); SAS (SK539): DC-9-21s OY-KGD (28th), OY-KGF (11th) and Swissair (SR842): DC-9-51s HB-ISO (12th/14th) & HB-ISS (6th).

ILS traffic observed and identified was Dove G-ARHW (14th/15th). RAF traffic observed were C-130 XV304 (17th) & RAF Jetstream XX495 (30th). The only crew training flight was British Airways VC-10 G-ARVM (27th).

1st   Rockwell 112 G-BEFS, arriving from Stansted, made a wheels-up landing due to an undercarriage fault. It received attention with NEA and finally left in February 1979.

1st   Aer Turas Britannia EI-BAA operated Aer Lingus freighter service EI9216/7 and again the following evening.

2nd   Today was the first visit of an EMB-110 Bandeirante, when G-BWTV arrived routing Aberdeen-Leeds. Originally destined for Westward Airways, it's currently operating for Air Ecosse.

4th   Jet Ranger G-OJCB, owned by JCB Excavators, undertook a shuttle service between Manchester and Haydock Park in connection with an industrial plant exhibition at the racecourse.

5th   Aeroflot operated the first passenger charter from Manchester since August 1976, when Tupolev TU-154 CCCP-85218 arrived at 1147 (SU1637/8 from/to Leningrad). The return flight on the 19th utilised TU-154 CCCP-85220 as SU1637/8 and both were first visits.

7th   CAA HS.125 G-AVDX arrived at 1227 from Birmingham, carrying the Chairman of the CAA (Civil Aviation Authority).

8th   Private B.707 N5038 arrived at 1005 from Aberdeen, before departing later at 1458 to Stavanger. The aircraft (ex-N7525A of American Airlines), with a VIP configuration to carry forty passengers, is owned by Dresser Industries who have a factory in nearby Wythenshawe. They also own Jetstar N7782, which visited on the 25th.

9th   Beech 55 EI-BEW, formerly D-IHAT, arrived at 1800 for a major overhaul with NEA, before eventually leaving on 30th January 1979.

9th   Dan-Air HS.748 G-ASPL, (DA054 Manchester-Cardiff), had been airborne for only six minutes, when a loud explosion was heard onboard. An emergency return to Manchester was requested, where the aircraft made a safe landing, before positioning out to Leeds the following day after attention with Dan-Air Engineering.

9th   The major recipient of the 4½ hour strike by Manchester's firemen was Liverpool. They received six British Airways flights, the morning British Air Ferries Rotterdam flight and Wardair B.707 C-FZYP, operating direct to Vancouver with 185 passengers.

11th   Early morning fog at Gatwick caused American-airline, Delta, to make a second visit to Manchester when L.1011 N81028 arrived at 0816 (DL010 from Atlanta). The ground controller initially advised the pilot to park on the South Bay and the reply back from a very bemused Delta Captain, made it quite clear 'he didn't know where that was, as this was his first time'! Thirty minutes later, the Delta was followed by a second Gatwick diversion, when B.707 G-BFBS arrived at 0841 (GK070 from Montreal).

13th   Citation 500 EP-PBC was the first Iranian biz-jet to visit Manchester. It was bringing an injured oil worker back from Iran, when it arrived at 2322 from Tehran, via Luton.

14th   RAF VC-10 XR810, arriving at 1608 (RR2624 Brize Norton-Hanover), was operating an outbound trooping flight.

18th   Jordanian World/Alia B.707F JY-AED arrived at 0001, operating a cargo flight on behalf of Saudia (SV8628), routing from/to Amman.

19th   LOT TU-134 SP-LHF, arriving at 1947 (LO4279/80 from/to Krakow), was a first visit. Formerly with the Polish Air Force, it was still painted in their old colour scheme.

25th   Due to the constant threat of terrorist organisations, an order was issued by the Government to the UK's airports, to close all public viewing areas until further notice. This order came into effect at 1130, when the spectator terraces and the top levels of the multi-storey car park were all closed. Apparently, the majority of airlines using the airport have been requesting closure of the terraces for years and it's only through the determination of the Airport Authority that they remained open. Manchester's terraces are regarded as the best in the country and thankfully the airport valued the need to keep them!

26th   LOT IL-62 SP-LAE, arriving at 2045 (LO4291/2 from/to Warsaw), was the fifth and final IL-62 first visit this year.

26th   NLM F.27s PH KFG at 1050 (HN4317/8) and PH-KFH at 1315 (HN4307/8), brought in a party of Dutch shoppers for a weekend in Manchester.

28th   Aer Lingus Dublin flight EI214/5 was operated by British Midland Viscount G-BAPE.

29th   Maersk B.720 OY-APY, arriving at 0652 operating Britannia Airways flight BY142 from Gerona, was twenty-eight hours late due to the French ATC action.

31st   Britannia Airways had to sub-charter again, this time with SATA DC-8 HB-IDM, positioning in at 2145 from Geneva to operate BY458A flight to Malta.

September 1978

Companies have been invited to tender for work on Manchester's main runway improvement scheme, due to start next March. The airport will close at night for eight months and a further six months in 1980, when it should be completed. A plan for the 200,000 tonnes of materials needed for the job to be transported by road at night and dumped directly onto the required areas has already caused controversy with adjoining councils and local residents.

A feasibility study will examine whether a link to the Manchester-Wilmslow main railway line is possible. Apart from the obvious long-term benefits, the Airport Authority sees it as an ideal solution for coping with diverted passengers. If the study favours the scheme, a planning application will be forwarded to the Government.

The second B.707 for Pelican Cargo, due early October, is former the Dan-Air/IAS example G-BEVN.

Equipment changes on the European scheduled services were Lufthansa (LH074/078): B.727 D-ABPI (2nd) and SAS (SK539): DC-9-21s OY-KGE (24th), SE-DBO (18th) & SE-DBS (14th).

ILS traffic observed and identified were RAF C-130s XV206 (4th), XV210 (8th) & XV213 (25th); RAF Jetstream XX496 (20th) and RAF Vulcan XH560 (20th). The only crew training flight was British Airways VC-10 G-ARVM (8th).

1st   SATA DC-8 HB-IDM arrived at 0742, operating delayed BY455 from Malta. More French ATC industrial action provided further sub-charters by Britannia Airways, including Tunis Air

B.727 TS-JHQ (1st), British Midland B.707 G-AYVG (3rd), Kar-Air DC-8 OH-KDM (6th/7th) and British Midland B.707 G-AZJM in full Air Algerie colours (25th).

3rd   Citation G-BCRM arrived at 0623 on an air ambulance flight from Nice.

4th   Pacific Western made their last visit to Manchester, when B.707 C-FPWV arrived at 1127 (PW607 Keflavik-Gatwick). They withdrew from transatlantic operations in 1979 and B.707 C-FPWV was sold as N138TA in October 1978. Their other B.707, C-FPWJ, was sold in May 1979 to Abelag Aviation as OO-ABA.

5th   It appears Aer Lingus are still suffering from aircraft shortages, as Pan American 727 N329PA arrived at 1003 (EI204/5 from/to Dublin). They were also using Pan American B.707s on numerous Dublin-Heathrow services around this time.

6th   Dan-Air was also severely affected by the French ATC industrial action. Geminair B.707 9G-ACK positioned in at 1834 from Brussels to operate a return flight to Malta (DA4448/9), before positioning to Manston. The airline also utilised Aviaco DC-8 EC-AUM to operate DA2161/0 from/to Las Palmas, which was nearly fifty hours late!

7th   Lear Jet D-CBRK, arriving at 1537, operated an outbound ambulance flight to Munich.

7th   Dan-Air Comet G-APYC, was making its final visit to Manchester today (DA4489 from Corfu), before departing at 1724 on the 9th (DA2318 to Palma). It was sold to the Ministry of Defence in December.

8th   This was a Friday that produced four first visits and an interesting variety of movements. Capitol DC-8 N912CL at 0134 (CL912 Philadelphia-Shannon), World Airways DC-10 N105WA at 0617 (WO105 Los Angeles-Gatwick), French Navy Nord 262 45/F-YDAW at 0928 (Lorient-Macrihanish) clearing customs at Manchester and SAS DC-8 SE-DBK at 1445 (SK8504/7504 Copenhagen-Stockholm) operating an outbound charter on behalf of Volvo, with the same aircraft returning on the 11th (SK7506).

8th   British Airways sole remaining VC-10 paid its last visit today, when G-ARVM arrived at 1748 from Prestwick. Used as a training aircraft before being withdrawn during the summer of 1979, it ended up as an exhibit at the RAF Cosford Air Museum.

9th   Saudia operated a number of freight flights this month with DC-8F N8636. SV8630 Jeddah-Riyadh was today, SV8639 Jeddah-Riyadh (18th) and SV8634 Paris-Riyadh (23rd).

9th   There were two interesting light aircraft movements today. The first, PA-31T Cheyenne N51BJ arriving at 1213 from/to Elstree, was being used short term by Yorkshire-based Trident Television. The second was Cessna 305 OE-CCG, arriving at 1512 from Liverpool to Gatwick. This Cessna type first flew in 1949 and saw extensive military service with many Air Forces around the world as a single engine, high-wing liaison and observation aircraft.

10th   Eastern Airways DC-3 G-AMRA made a fuel-stop, en route from Luton-Belfast.

10th   RAF C-130s XV214 (RR3508) & XV307 (RR3507) were taking troops out to Germany to participate in NATO's annual series of 'Autumn Forge Exercises', which started in 1975 and have been conducted every year since. Designed to link-up a number of training exercises under a common scenario, they test the readiness of combat forces and the capability of NATO forces to work together.

11th   Ex-Oman Air Force Viscount 501 which arrived on 11th February, emerged from the Dan-Air hangar today as 3D-ACM, destined for Royal Swazi National Airways. It was ferried to East Midlands the next day in preparation for its delivery flight, but it never saw service with the airline. After a period in storage, it was eventually sold to British Midland in March 1979 as G-BFZL.

12th   Aer Lingus BAC 1-11 EI-ANH took Manchester City out to Enschede (EI7952) for their UEFA Cup first-round, first-leg with FC Twenthe.

12th   When resident Meta-Sokol G-APVU arrived from Taunton and landed on Runway 28, its tail wheel collapsed and it had to be manually recovered to the South Side for repair.

14th   GAF Nomad VH-BLY arrived on demonstration to NEA. It flew to Caernarfon and returned to Manchester via Barton, where it demonstrated its credentials as a short landing and takeoff aircraft. Another Nomad, VH-AUI that had visited in June 1975 was also on demonstration to NEA.

14th   HS.125 G-BGKN arrived at 1828 to collect the Leader of the Opposition, Margaret Thatcher, who'd been visiting the region.

15th   American airline Overseas National ceased operations today, after struggling to compete with low scheduled fares from its competitors. For the record, their last visit to Manchester was 17th October 1977 when DC-8 N866F diverted in from Gatwick.

16th   RAF VC-10 XV104 arrived at 1427 (RR3230 Brize Norton-Hohn) to airlift more troops out to Germany for the 'Autumn Forge Exercise'.

16th   Both HS.748 demonstrators were on the ground at the same time over the weekend. G-BCDZ arrived late last night after Woodford had closed and G-BDVH arrived this evening. They both left for Woodford on the morning of the 18th, within a minute of each other.

17th   Pelican B.707 G-BPAT made only one visit this month, which was also its first appearance since 30th July. It's been operating for Sabena recently, due to aircraft shortages and arrived today on a Tradewinds flight number from Lagos (IK139A), before departing for Muscat (DP119) the following day.

17th   Clyden Airways commenced a new six-times weekly mail flight to Dublin today for the Post Office, when DC-3 EI-BDT (CE100/1) arrived at 2145, before departing at 2245. Kerry Airways had secured the contract originally, but they went into receivership before the flights began.

18th   Royal Saudi Air Force C-130H 468 made its first visit today, arriving at 1525 as RSF625 from/to Jeddah via Milan, before its departure on the 21st.

19th   Pan American B.707 N495PA positioned in from Hanover at 1756 to operate the delayed GK092 to Toronto, on behalf of Laker Airways.

20th   RAF Rescue Sea King XZ593, arriving at 0001 from Gatwick, was a first visit of type.

20th   Braathens Boeing 737 LN-SUS, arriving at 1321 (BU539 from Gothenburg), was their first visit since B.737 LN-SUP diverted into Manchester on 21st February 1976.

21st   British Airways Trident G-AVFC, arriving at 1235, was returning the England football team from Copenhagen, after winning a European Championship qualifier with Denmark 4-3. Local players were dropped off first and then the aircraft departed for Luton.

23rd   British Airways B.747 G-AWNA, operating inbound BA080 from Toronto/Prestwick, managed a safe landing on three engines. The fault was significant enough to delay its departure back to Prestwick/Toronto by five hours as BA081.

25th   Pan American B.707 N885PA arriving at 0754 from Prestwick, was operating outbound Laker Airways GK093 flight to Toronto. The inbound GK094, operated by Laker Airways DC-10 G-BELO, normally operates the outbound GK093 as well, but it positioned out to Gatwick instead.

27th   RAF Rescue Whirlwind XP395 arrived at 1543 to pick up a stretcher case off BY166B from Malaga, operated by British Midland B.707 G-AZJM. It then flew to Middlesbrough, where the patient was despatched to hospital.

27th   European football returned to Manchester. Although City was drawn to play FC Twenthe of Holland and lost the first-leg 2-0, they won this evening's home tie 4-0 and progressed to the next round. Unfortunately, no FC Twenthe fans came over on extra flights and the team arrived courtesy of a KLM scheduled flight.

28th   Transmeridian DC-8F G-BTAC, arriving at 1839, was making its first visit to Manchester on a cargo flight ultimately destined for Brisbane.

October 1978

The increased security measures introduced in August, have been relaxed and the frequent sightings of spotters standing on the junction of Ringway Road and Shadow Moss Road, with their large protest banners reading 'Give us back our Terraces' are now a thing of the past! The spectator terraces and the top tier of the multi-storey car park were both reopened on the 1st. Their closure is estimated to have lost the airport £40,000 and as a result, they are looking to the Government for reimbursement, who have also rejected the airport's proposal for direct rail access, after deciding it wasn't economically viable. The decision came as a blow, as the plan had been actively encouraged in the Government's white paper only last February.

Due to the night-time closures coming into force next year, most airlines have retimed their operations, although Liverpool will be used for some IT and freight flights. Delayed aircraft will also have to use Liverpool, but they will be allowed to fly back to Manchester in the morning when the airport reopens and have their landing fees waived!

Dan-Air's recent application to extend their City-Link service to Sumburgh has been rejected.

Equipment changes on the European scheduled services were Finnair (AY032): DC-9 OH-LYI (18th/20th/25th/27th), Lufthansa (LH4072): B.727 D-ABIX (6th/7th) and SAS (SK539): DC-9-21s LN-RLL (26th) & LN-RLO (17th).

ILS traffic observed and identified were RAF Jetstream XX497 (4th), RAF C-130 XV199 (19th), RAF Whirlwind XJ435 (30th), HS.125 HZ-DAC (30th) and Dove G-ARBE (31st).

1st   Saudia cargo flights to Dhahran/Riyadh continued throughout the month, but they weren't weekly as promised and were finished altogether by the 28th. DC-8 N8632 operated inbound on a Seaboard World flight number, SB1304, today and outbound to Riyadh as SV8637. Others were DC-8 N8636 (SV8642 Dhahran-Athens-21st) and DC-8 N8639 arriving amongst the diversions at 1010 (SV8655 Jeddah-Riyadh-28th).

2nd   Laker Airways GK094 inbound from Toronto, was normally operated by a DC-10, but this morning's was operated by Laker B.707 G-BFBS (GK094) and Quebecair B.707 C-GQBH (QB984). The Quebecair B.707 was the airlines final visit, as they ceased operating charter flights in 1979 and their Boeing 707s were all sold.

3rd   French Air Force Noratlas 146/64-KQ arrived at 1551, on a training flight from Lyneham to Bournemouth.

4th   USAF VC-137 (B.707) 58-6970 arriving at 0825 from Cologne, was carrying President Carter's security advisor for talks with the Prime Minister, James Callaghan, who was attending the Labour Party Conference in Blackpool.

5th   LOT IL-18 SP-LSI arrived at 1316 (LO3143/4), as part of an ongoing series of flights for Laing Construction. Another flight with IL-18 SP-LSD (LO4145) was on the 9th.

5th   Transmeridian CL-44-0 Skymonster N447T arrived at 0044 as KK6999, transporting a 15 tonne transformer from Norway.

5th   New Pelican Cargo B.707 G-BEVN, arriving at 1718 from Lasham, left three hours later for Maastricht where it operated for the rest of the month to various points in the Far East. Their other aircraft, G-BPAT, was present on the 1st, 16th & 20th.

6th   Wardair B.707 C-FFAN, arriving at 0928 (WD416 from Vancouver), was making its final visit to Manchester. Both B.707s will be sold and replaced by Douglas DC-10s.

7th   When Europe Air Service Vanguard F-BVRZ diverted in at 0956 from East Midlands (SF497A from Le Bourget), it was also the last visit of a passenger configured Vanguard.

7th   'New' British Airways 1-11 G-BFWN arrived at 1900 on lease from Cyprus Airways (ex 5B-DAJ). It went into the BA hangar and departed for Heathrow on the 11th.

8th   Dan-Air HS.748 G-AYYG arrived at 1054 from Aberdeen, for pre-lease return maintenance, before departing back to Mount Cook on the 13th as ZK-MCF.

10th   Laker Airway's sub-chartered the following two aircraft today: Balair DC-8 HB-IDM at 1526 as (GK3838 from New York) and Pan American B.707 N495PA at 0956 (PA1495 from New York).

10th   Peters Aviation Heron G-ANSZ arrived at 1127, operating a return flight from Norwich as NP950/1. A regular visitor to Manchester over many years since it was first registered in 1954 it saw regular operations with Mercury Airlines between 1966-1969, before it was sold to Peters Aviation in 1972 and left for pastures new in St. Lucia in 1980.

12th   Aeroflot TU-154 CCCP-85130 arrived at 1724 (SU1637/8) to return the Leningrad Philharmonic Orchestra back home.

12th   Noted by the writer was the first visit of a Greek Air Force aircraft to Manchester, when C-130 No.750 arrived at 1250, operating from/to Chateauroux with an outbound cargo of fifty one-gallon tanks of fluid.

12th   PA-27 EI-BDM arrived at 1357 for maintenance with NEA, before its eventual departure on 30th March 1979. PA-27 EI-BDN, arriving at 1430, acted as the crew ferry.

13th

13th   The country had been enjoying an Indian summer all week, with temperatures in the early 70's, but all that came to an abrupt end by the arrival of dense fog last night. I'd taken my aircraft radio to bed with me, so I could check the weather as soon as I woke, but it was difficult to sleep after seeing television's weather chart covered in the letters F-O-G, predicted for the following day. The morning finally came, but when I switched the radio on there was no mention of bad weather, but that quickly changed when I heard Gulfstream II N1806P talking to ground control about where he was parking, 'as he was not familiar with Manchester'. This sounded promising, but not yet proof there was fog around the country. I then heard 'Midland 210F' (Intra Airways DC-3 G-AMPO), a regular DC-3 freight flight into East Midlands, calling up on Manchester Tower frequency. OK, so the Gulfstream was a possible Luton diversion. I knew the DC-3 was an East Midlands diversion, but deep joy as following right behind was 'Speedbird 3670', a regular early morning New York-Heathrow freight flight (B.707F G-ATWV). However, there was a major problem as the landing runway was 06 and all I could usually see from our flat were the lights in the distance. Anyway, I quickly repositioned my radio back to the kitchen, where it was normally set up. It wasn't long before 'Delta 010' was heard on the Manchester control frequency 125.1 diverting inbound to Manchester, confirming the landing runway would be Runway 6 (his words!), but by the time he'd been transferred to Manchester approach, it was changed to Runway 24! This was Delta's third diversion into Manchester (L.1011 N81028), so they were clearly happy with us. By the time Kenya Airways B.707 5Y-BBI arrived at 0805 (KQ414 from Rome), unbeknown to me, there had already been twenty-one diversions up to this point, including JAT DC-9 YU-AHM at 0130 (JR2210 from Belgrade), Alaska International C-130 N107AK at 0219 (AK107 from Khartoum) and two British Airways Tristars: G-BEAL at 0229 (BE327 from Paris) and G-BEAM at 0538 (BA120 from Bombay). The next was Air India B.747 VT-EBN, which was already diverting into Manchester due to fog at Heathrow, when he declared an emergency with smoke in the cabin. It landed at 0828, just as the fog at Manchester was closing in and parked close to the fire station, where a full evacuation via the escape chutes took place. It was the airports first emergency evacuation of a Boeing 747. The Captain noticed a fire warning light in one of the cargo holds over the Atlantic, but only declared an emergency about 40-miles from touchdown. Forty-five firemen were involved with the incident, found to have been caused by an electronic organ in one of the cargo holds catching fire. By the time the Air India landed, no traffic was being accepted for Heathrow or Gatwick, unless they were Cat.III equipped. The weather situation at the London airports eased slightly around 1030, but even then landing was by prior permission only, which remained in force for most of the day. Manchester was affected by dense fog during the morning and received just one diversion when Tradewinds CL-44 G-AWGS arrived at 1006 (IK4148B from Montreal), after which there were no more arrivals until 1333, although normal operations were returning by 1530. Today's winner for diversions was definitely Prestwick. Amongst the endless trails heading northbound was an Iraqi Airways B.747, YI-AGO (IA237) and the 'big orange' B.747 N601BN as 'Braniff 602'. By the afternoon, the fog at Manchester was still patchy enough to prevent further diversions, so preparations were made for what might come later with space being made available for up to twelve narrow-bodied aircraft plus six wide-bodied. The first of these were two diverted Trident flights: G-AWZJ at 1643 (BE691 from Warsaw) and G-AVFI at 1656 (BE601 from Vienna). Ironically at the same time they arrived, L.1011 G-BEAL left Manchester as 'Beeline 327X', attempting a return to Heathrow. The next three hours were fairly uneventful, but the anticipation of more diversions to Manchester was high, as the forecast for the southern airports was predicting a rapid deterioration. By 2000 there were diversions on their way from Heathrow and Gatwick and although they were mostly mundane, there were a couple of interest, such as the first visit of Royal Air Maroc with the arrival of B.727 CN-CCG at 2114 (AT5262 from Casablanca) and IAS DC-8F G-BDDE at 2122 (FF513A from Lagos). By 2030, Heathrow was below limits for most aircraft and Manchester ATIS was advising that due to visibility restrictions no traffic was being accepted for Gatwick. Today had not been a good one for Air India and its diverted flight 'Air India 108' - and it was about to get worse! By 2050 it was ready to depart back to Heathrow, but during its takeoff run it burst a tyre and remained on the runway. During this time, several inbounds had to overshoot and go into the hold over Manchester but fortunately it managed to exit the runway before too long. I stayed on watch up until Dan-Air

Comet G-APMB arrived at 2152 (DA2305 from Gerona), before retiring around 2200. I took my radio and listened in, but when there weren't any more diversions, I called it a night at 2300. After that and unbeknown to me, another eight British Airways diversions arrived. There were six Tridents: G-AVFB at 0020 (BE617 from Zurich), G-AWZF at 0023 (BE507 from Rome), G-AWZA at 0033 (BE4683 from Belfast), G-AWZP at 0037 (BE455 from Madrid), G-AWZJ at 0042 (BE737 from Hamburg) & G-AWZB at 0128 (BE619 from Zurich) and Tristars: G-BBAI at 2339 (BE387 from Brussels) & G-BBAE at 0118 (BE639 from Copenhagen) and first visit Alitalia B.727 I-DIRI at 2348 (AZ316 from Pisa). By the early hours, after the last diversions had arrived, not only was disused Runway 20 being used for parking, but Runway 10/28 was also in use.

14th As the morning weather steadily improved, large numbers of diverted aircraft making their way back to Heathrow were causing problems for ATC. Gatwick however was another story as even though their weather had been marginal during the morning, aircraft carried on landing. Meanwhile, back in Manchester the writer was in the kitchen having his lunch when he heard something about to fly over and it was no 1-11! It was the 'big orange' Braniff B.747 N601BN, diverting in at 1242 (BN602 from Dallas). Ironically before stopping to eat, I'd been listening to the pilot of this aircraft talking on his company frequency, confirming Gatwick's weather was improving and at this point he was unsure whether he would be allowed a slot-time for an approach at Gatwick, so when I saw it pass overhead - I was surprised to say the least! Two Dan-Air BAC 1-11s followed in quick succession, G-AWWX at 1247 (DA4027 from Hanover) and G-ATPL at 1255 (DA5568 from Berlin) and one more Gatwick diversion, LOT TU-134 SP-LHF arrived at 1612 (LO4265 from Krakow). As a final comment, it's interesting to note that although Braniff had made Manchester their primary diversion airport for Gatwick and subsequent European flights, they only made one more visit, in November 1979. Between now and then, they had many opportunities to divert to Ringway, but as they didn't, it put the credibility of their intent regarding Manchester into question!

14th Dan-Air Comet G-APZM made its final visit to Manchester today, arriving at 0205 (DA2313 from Gerona), before its departure at 0925 (DA2336 to Alicante). It's very last flight was 14th November (Dubrovnik-Gatwick), then onto Lasham the very same day for scrapping.

14th Air Canada DC-8 C-FTIS, arriving at 1604, was operating a delayed CP Air flight. Another, DC-8 C-FTIP, operated Montreal-Toronto as AC070/1 on the 25th.

15th October 1978 – Gulf 2s N24DS & N1807Z, owned by Diamond Shamrock Industries, are seen having just arrived from Shannon on their first visits. They were bringing in the Board of Directors on a tour of their European facilities.
(Geoff Ball)

16th Laker Airways Toronto flight GK094 was operated by a mix of aircraft again, their own B.707 G-BFBS and Wardair B.707 C-FFAN. The reason for the sub-charters and equipment changes to B.707s was due to a temporary shortage of aircraft, after the commencement of their daily Gatwick-Los Angeles Skytrain operation.

17th Manchester City's second round UEFA Cup tie against Standard Liege, brought in a number of extra flights with fans for the game. The team arrived at 1246 on Sobelair SE.210 OO-SRI and the first set of fans arrived at 1725 on first visit Sobelair B.737 OO-SBQ. The 18th saw the arrival of another Sobelair aircraft, B.707 OO-SJA and Martinair F.28 PH-MAT. City won 4-0 and the return was two weeks later and even though City lost that game 2-0, they were still through to the next round, when they would meet the mighty AC Milan!

17th   Pan American B.707 N887PA arriving at 1324 from Paris, was operating outbound to Atlanta.

18th   HS.125 aircraft passing through Manchester to/from Hawarden for maintenance are becoming less common, but HS.125 N605W arrived at 1338 today for customs clearance, en route to Hawarden and again on its return on the 23rd.

19th   It's not every day a Gabon registered aircraft can be seen at Manchester, but Beech 36 TR-LUX, currently based in the UK, arrived at 1511 from Leavesden and stayed around thirty minutes.

19th   Dan-Air Comet G-BBUV also made its final visit to Manchester, arriving at 0008 (DA4463 from Gerona), before its departure at 0916 (DA4488 to Corfu). It's very last flight was on the 22nd routing Palma-Gatwick, before flying to Lasham the following day for scrapping.

21st   An inquiry was held today to discover why Britannia Airways B.737 G-AVRL, bound for Monastir, had left on the 19th with a hole in the fuselage and why it had only come to light when a pressurisation leak warning light sounded on final descent. It's believed that the aircraft was struck by a ground vehicle at Manchester, possibly the tractor that removed the steps. Engineers were flown to Monastir to carry out temporary repairs so it could depart to Luton for full maintenance.

23rd   Sterling SE.210 OY-SAH arrived at 1417 (NB3311 from Billund), with a party bound for the Motor Show at Birmingham.

23rd   Beech 95 G-ASYJ lost its starboard engine on landing from Blackpool. As it was blocking Runway 24 and unable to taxi, it was pushed onto Link A and then the Freight Apron.

25th   British Airways Trident G-AVFB arrived at 1935 from Dublin, to drop off local England players, returning after a European Championship qualifier with the Republic of Ireland, ending 1-1.

25th   Private BAC 1-11 N1543, arriving at 2234 from Heathrow to undergo maintenance with Dan-Air, is reportedly up for sale. It remained parked outside Fairey's until 28th November, when it operated a return flight to Gatwick. It then went inside the Dan-Air hangar until the 30th, when it departed for Athens.

27th   It had been an unsettled week, with rain and windy spells, but it was foggy today until teatime. It wasn't dense enough to affect landing traffic, so the airport received a variety of aircraft. American Aerostar N99RW at 0928, Skyvan G-ASZJ at 1601, PA-31 N7XB at 1652, PA-31T OY-BRL at 1740 and Italian Cessna 421 I-DLGG at 2030. Visibility steadily improved in the evening, but Heathrow and Gatwick's slowly deteriorated and it was forecast that visibility would be down to 100m by midnight.

27th   British Airways Merchantman G-APEP, arriving at 1651 (BE9105C from Dusseldorf), was making its last visit to Manchester as a British Airways aircraft, as it was sold to Air Bridge Carriers in November 1979.

28th October 1978 – Sudan Airways B.707 ST-AFB arrived just after midnight as 'Sudan 128' from Frankfurt. Other diverted aircraft in this shot include British Caledonian Boeing 707 G-CDHW & Laker Airways Douglas DC-10 G-AZZD. (Geoff Ball)

28th   The writer had little sleep in anticipation of what might happen with regards to the weather, so he was ready when the first two diversions arrived. British Caledonian B.707 G-CDHW arrived at 0641 (BR352 from Dakar), DC-10 G-BEBM at 0653 (BR368 from Accra), followed closely by British Airways L.1011 G-BBAJ at 0655 with a great sounding radio and SVC-10 G-ASGH at 0722 (BA058 from Cairo). The next was Air India B.747 VT-EDU at 0912 (AI110 from New York) and two first visits: South African Airways B.747 ZS-SAP at 1054 (SA228 from Sal Island) and Finnair DC-9-51 OH-LYO at 1121 (AY831 from Helsinki), which was the first time

Finnair had used Manchester for a weather diversion. Although Heathrow and Gatwick were affected by fog right up until lunchtime, there were remarkably few diversions into Manchester. British Airways had sent their B.747s into other airports again, as none arrived at Ringway. The final two diversions, BCAL B.707s G-AXRS at 1220 (BR246 from Houston) and G-BDLM at 1224 (BR676 from Caracas), were heard talking to each other on their company frequency an hour before arrival. 'Caledonian 246' was holding over South Wales and 'Caledonian 676' from Caracas was holding in the Southampton area. Both were concerned they were low on fuel and 'if they didn't make Gatwick at the first attempt, they were going to have problems'. In the end they decided it was too much of a risk and subsequently made the trip northwards!

28ᵗʰ October 1978 –
Making their first visit of
the year was South
African Airways. It was
also the airlines fifth
B.747 to visit
Manchester. ZS-SAP
served the airline its entire
operating life, from
1972-2003
(Geoff Ball)

29ᵗʰ   An early morning diversion witnessed by the writer was B.747 N93109, arriving at 0556 (TW760 from Los Angeles). Heathrow was affected by fog until midmorning and at 0720 their visibility was 0m with an RVR of 150m. As Ringway received just the one arrival, it appeared the weather diversions had gone elsewhere, even though Manchester could accept up to ten narrow-bodied and four wide-bodied aircraft. Today was also the date British Airways totally dropped their call-sign 'Beeline', in favour of the universal 'Speedbird'.

29ᵗʰ   British Airways leased another BAC 1-11, G-AZMF, from British Caledonian, which arrived today. It's now based at Manchester, operating Zurich, Frankfurt & Heathrow flights.

November 1978

The airport reported a 23% increase in passenger traffic during October, over the same month last year. The number of passengers using Manchester for the first ten months totalled 3,038,371, but during the same period, freight was down by 8%.

British Airways reduced fares between Manchester and West German destinations by up to 30%, with the biggest reductions on weekend return flights. They also increased winter frequencies between Manchester and the Isle of Man to twice-daily.

Owing to next year's night-time runway closures, the following airlines outlined their provisional plans. Swissair will re-route freight flights through Liverpool, SAS will re-time to operate in the day, Lufthansa will re-time night operations and Sabena will drop night freight flights and operate a Boeing 737 Combi on the daytime passenger service instead.

The year saw an increasing number of light aircraft operators using call-signs/flight prefixes, rather than their registration. McAlpine Aviation (RM) started the trend last year and Thurston (HZ) and Air London (JF) also started using call-signs this year. As far as the Manchester based ones go, Apache Air Taxi's are using (IN) 'Indian' with PA-31 G-BFFI, Otter Controls (OC) are using 'Otter' with Cessna 340 G-AZRB and Air Kilroe are using 'Kilroe'.

The following airlines have made changes from this month: Air France will remain a daily operation throughout the winter for the first time. British Airways Montreal/Toronto (BA080/1) will operate four-weekly and New York (BA184/5) daily, both with SVC-10's and Malta has been dropped for the winter. The morning KLM (KL153/4) reverts to a daily DC-9 and the cargo flights five-weekly direct, with one arriving via Glasgow. Winter IT flights are operated by Air Malta, Britannia Airways, British Airways, Dan-Air and Laker Airways - who will not be operating ABC flights to USA/Canada for the second winter season running.

Equipment changes on the European scheduled services were Finnair (AY032): DC-9s OH-LYH (10ᵗʰ) & OH-LYI (1ˢᵗ/8ᵗʰ/10ᵗʰ/17ᵗʰ/24ᵗʰ), Lufthansa (LH074/078): B.727s D-ABKF (15ᵗʰ), D-ABKN (20ᵗʰ) & D-ABSI (19ᵗʰ/24ᵗʰ) and SAS (SK539): DC-9-21 SE-DBS (11ᵗʰ).

ILS traffic observed and identified were CAA HS.748 G-AVXI (8ᵗʰ), RAF Nimrod XV227 (15ᵗʰ), HS.748s G-BCDZ (21ˢᵗ/23ʳᵈ) & LIAT VP-LAZ (24ᵗʰ); RAE BAC 1-11 XX919 (21ˢᵗ), RAF C-130 XV221 (28ᵗʰ) and RAF Jetstream XX481 (30ᵗʰ).

1ˢᵗ   British Airways have completely standardised their flight numbers/call-signs. All flights, irrespective of whether they are Domestic, European or Long-haul, are now operating under the call-sign 'Speedbird' and the only flight code used is 'BA'.

1ˢᵗ   The very final visit to Manchester of a Wardair B.707 took place today, when B.707 C-FZYP positioned up from Gatwick, to operate outbound WD416 to Vancouver.

1ˢᵗ   Spantax operated their final flights of their summer programme today and both were operated by CV-990s: EC-CNG (BX723/4 & BX725/6) and EC-BTE (BX023/4 & BX025/6).

1ˢᵗ   HS.125 5N-ANG arrived at 0142 from Madrid, eventually bound for maintenance at Hawarden, before returning on the 30ᵗʰ in the opposite direction. The following day, HS.125 N605W arrived at 1303 from Copenhagen for customs clearance, en route to Hawarden.

6ᵗʰ   TMA began a series of Monday freight flights through Manchester. The first was first visit Boeing 707F OD-AGP today and further flights were N7096 (20ᵗʰ) & OD-AFX (27ᵗʰ).

6ᵗʰ   Dan-Air has won a maintenance contract with Bavaria-Germanair, for the overhaul of their BAC 1-11s. The first aircraft, D-ALFA, arrived today at 0709 from Frankfurt and the second, D-AMAS, on the 21ˢᵗ.

6ᵗʰ   When Dan-Air Comet G-BDIT touched down at 2241, (DA4441 from Ibiza), it was the final flight from Manchester of a based Comet. From tomorrow, the airline will only have Boeing 727s and BAC 1-11s based at Manchester. There were numerous visits by Dan-Air Comets from this date, but they were one-offs or operated by Gatwick based aircraft.

7ᵗʰ   The first visit of an Air France Boeing 747 took place today, when B.747F F-BPVV made a technical stop at 0503 as AF1315, en route from Houston to Paris-CDG.

7ᵗʰ   Dan-Air commenced a weekly IT flight from/to Malta, which was notable for being operated by a Berlin based B.727 on a 'w' pattern.

8ᵗʰ   The second Italian Sabreliner to visit this year was I-MORA, arriving at 1055 operating from/to Milan-Malpensa.

9ᵗʰ   LOT TU-134 SP-LHC, operating outbound flight LO4094, suffered an engine failure on takeoff. It remained at the airport and was moved between the South Bay and the Fairey Apron at regular intervals, until it finally departed for Warsaw on the 20ᵗʰ.

9ᵗʰ   Tomorrows weather forecast for the South East was looking promising, as widespread fog was predicted, although fog was notoriously hit-and-miss to forecast in terms of how extensive or dense. When the BBC weather forecast had the letters F-O-G on the chart, the bigger the letters the more dense it was going to be and the more spread out the letters, the more extensive it would be! In reality though, the opposite usually applied, when the smaller the letters the more chaos seemed to arise and the bigger the letters, nothing much seemed to happen! Not long after the writer had retired in anticipation of the next day, diversions started to arrive after 2200. Of the four from Gatwick and one from Heathrow, the only one of interest was the first visit of Italian charter-airline Itavia, who sent in DC-9 I-TIGI at 2300 (IH1538 from Genoa). The ATC watch log recorded that at this point, the airport would accept ten narrow-bodied and four wide-bodied diversions.

10ᵗʰ   The day saw another major diversion session. I switched my aircraft radio on as soon as I woke at 0600, just in time to see Saudia B.747 OD-AGH at 0623 (SV077 from Riyadh), but I'd already missed four early morning British Airways diverts: L.1011 G-BEAL at 0230 (BA120X from Dhahran), SVC-10 G-ASGA at 0539 (BA130 from Jeddah), L.1011 G-BBAJ at 0551 (BA120 from Jeddah) and L.1011 G-BEAM at 0602 (BA100 from Bahrain). The local weather didn't forecast fog for the region and for once they were right as it was a dull, nondescript day. I couldn't contain my excitement and anticipation of what was to come, as I settled down to listen in before leaving for school at 0820, when another three arrived: B.747 G-BDXA at 0700 (BA012 from Bombay), British Caledonian B.707 G-AYEX at 0741 (BR214 from Lusaka) and Kenya Airways B.707 5Y-BBJ at 0810 (KQ416 from Rome). According to the ATC watch log, the number of diversions the airport was willing to accept had been revised just before G-BDXA arrived, to two narrow-bodied only. The next two diversions, G-AYEX and 5Y-BBJ, were in keeping with the revised quota, but B.747 G-BDXA seemed to dispel this! By 0820 the quota was revised again, this time to accept six narrow-bodied and no wide-bodied diversions. By now, fifteen diversions had arrived since last night, including five wide-bodied. Before leaving for school I was listening to flight 'Delta 10' talking to his company. He was advised his alternate had been changed to Manchester, so what it was originally is a mystery! Reluctantly I left home and walked to school with my friend Ian Barrie and we were both excited about the day ahead. We got as far as Heaton Chapel, with another ten minutes to go before we arrived at school, when we heard a distinct aircraft noise. We turned around as the flight path was directly behind us and saw it was a VC-10, with what looked like a dark tail. It was difficult to make out the airline, as it was such a grey day, so we gathered it could only be British Airways or the RAF, as they were the only operators of VC-10s by now, or so we thought! When we got to school our friend told us it was actually Air Malawi (7Q-YKH), as he'd heard it inbound on his radio. Ironically, I had my portable radio with me, but hadn't thought to switch it on. Delta L.1011 N81028 was next to follow and we just about saw this from the classroom. There was nothing in the next hour but after 1000 two British Airways Manchester flights (BA5001 & BA5003) arrived back after abortive attempts to get into Heathrow. They were closely followed by Laker DC-10 G-AZZD at 1020 (GK020 from New York) and it was another hour before the next two arrived. Fortunately it was Maths, one of the best classrooms to view from, as it was perfectly located for the approach. I had my aircraft radio on in class, hidden under the desk, but it became a little too loud when 'Finnair 831' (DC-9-51 OH-LYR) called up on Manchester Tower and Mr Swales confiscated it until the end of the lesson! Ten minutes after the diverted Finnair, Air France SE.210 F-BJTF was seen on the descent. I was unsure if it was a diversion or our own flight that had been delayed, but it turned out it was 'Air France 1826' from Marseilles, again diverting from Heathrow. Although the official line was that the airport could not accept anymore diversions due to lack of space, it was prepared to accept Qantas B.747 VH-EBO (QF001), but it ultimately ended up at Prestwick, along with another twelve wide-bodied aircraft. Apart from seeing the Army Air Corps Beaver XP789 at 1209 (Army 366 from Belfast) which was not a diversion, no more arrived even though the lunchtime forecast had predicted foggy weather for the rest of the day. As Ian and I were walking back to school after lunch, in an almost repeat performance of the morning, we got to the same spot and heard a noise, but this time it was an aircraft we could identify, British Caledonian DC-10 G-BEBL (BR366 from Kano), closely followed by IAS DC-8 G-BDDE (FF306 from Manston). The afternoon lesson was in a classroom where no aircraft could be seen, but fortunately nothing was missed due to a short-lived clearance in the London weather, when several aircraft made it back to Heathrow. Gatwick however was still suffering from dense fog that precluded any arrivals all day. Once out of class and into the fading light, it couldn't have been better timed, as at that moment another British Caledonian appeared when B.707 G-ATZC arrived at 1605 (BR376 from Lagos). Once home, I took my aircraft radio into the lounge to do some monitoring of the frequencies, while watching Crackerjack which had barely started, when diversions started arriving again and in greater numbers! The first of this batch were two Speedbird flights: Merchantman G-APEK at 1712 (BA3773 from Frankfurt) and Trident 3 G-AWZV at 1714 (BA691 from Warsaw), followed by Sabena B.737 OO-SDA at 1749 (SN611 from Brussels) and another Speedbird, this time B.747 G-AWNP 'Speedbird 270', which had been making its way down from Prestwick to Heathrow when the RVR fell below its limits. Birmingham had stopped accepting diversions by this time, although it too was affected by fog later in the evening and East Midlands stopped accepting diversions by 2030. Another eighteen diversions arrived at Manchester throughout the evening, bringing the total to forty-two. Amongst these was the same Air France SE.210 that had been in earlier in the day, F-BJTF (AF1822 from Toulouse); Transavia B.737 PH-TVD in full British Airways colours (BA571 from Istanbul), a third Air France flight Fokker F.28 F-GBBR (AF1862 from Nantes) and CTA SE.210 HB-ICN again operating a British Airways flight (BA615 from Zurich), but the main highlights came later in the evening. Around 2015 I heard on the radio what was clearly a B.747, identifying itself as '141', but I couldn't make out which airline, as he didn't clarify and when he did

I kept missing what he said. I monitored it the whole time it was on the approach frequency and was still none the wiser. When it transferred to the Tower I thought I would pick up the airline then, but as I hadn't tuned in correctly I missed it again and had to wait until it went over in the hope I could identify it. Sure enough it appeared and its bright tail light made it easily identifiable as Kuwait Airways (B.747 9K-ADB). It was a fantastic sight and quite a surprise, as I didn't know they even had any Boeing 747s! The final highlight of the evening was the arrival of US Navy C-9 160049, diverting in from Upper Heyford, named 'City of Jacksonville'. Its full routing was Jacksonville-Andrews AFB-St. Johns and it was carrying a number of Admirals. It nearly didn't make it into Manchester, as by 2050 the airport had decided not to accept anymore diversions, except for Concorde if requested, but it made it into Heathrow. Twenty minutes later the airport agreed to accept C-9 160049 when 'Swing 78' arrived at 2141 and unlike the Kuwait B.747, I could easily identify the call-sign! After listening in to see if any more were coming, I decided that was probably it for the night as the frequencies had gone very quiet. I turned in around 2230, after ringing my friends to tell them I was going to the airport in the morning to see how many diversions were there. The conclusion to a very hectic and chaotic day was that British Airways and Servisair turned many more aircraft away, mainly because of handling problems caused by staff shortages, a situation that continued into the following day. Manchester wasn't the only airport suffering problems, as East Midlands took twenty-five diversions during the day and also turned many more away due to lack of space. Manchester called a management meeting later in the month, in an effort to improve organisation for any future large-scale diversion days.

10th   Mention was made earlier in the year of the phasing out of Dan-Air B.707 G-AZTG. It made its last revenue flight on a Britannia Airways flight (BY405B from Tenerife), diverting in from Gatwick today and left for Lasham on the 14th for storage. Their other B.707, G-AYSL, appeared on the 21st to operate a B.727 flight, which had gone tech. G-AYSL is now operating in a hybrid colour scheme of a British Airways fuselage and full Dan-Air tail-colours.

11th November 1978 – Towards the end of 1978, Manchester saw some lengthy diversion sessions and yesterday was such a day, when Heathrow, Gatwick and various other southern airports where affected by dense fog. This was the only visit of Air Malawi VC-10 7Q-YKH (QM142 from Nairobi). It remained in service until 1979, when it was withdrawn and eventually scrapped in the early-1990s. (Ian Barrie)

11th   The writer caught the 0700 bus to the airport and arrived forty-five minutes later to see if anything extra had sneaked in overnight. Before I left, it seemed that Heathrow was still suffering from fog and was below limits to most aircraft, but due to the lack of parking space and handling equipment, Manchester would only accept four narrow-bodied and one wide-bodied diversion. Not long after arriving at the airport and getting up onto the terraces, another British Airways B.747, G-AWNB, arrived as 'Speedbird 012', adding to the already congested apron, bays, disused runway and even a normally active taxiway. Although last night's star visitors, Kuwait Airways B.747 9K-ADB and US Navy C-9 160049 were still in, today's star visitor was Western B.720 N93145, diverting in from Stansted as 'Western 9040'. Arriving in basic Western colours, it was destined to become HZ-NAA. JAL B.747 'Japanair 423' was holding over Pole Hill for a while and could be seen circling in the distance, but it eventually ended up diverting to Copenhagen. Although RAF VC-10 XR806 (RR2298 from Nairobi) arrived on diversion just before midday, aircraft were starting to disperse from the aprons, departing to where they were meant to be. Heathrow at 1240 had visibility of 1200m and Gatwick 2000m. A few bits and pieces arrived during the afternoon, by which time we'd left the spectator terraces and were camped out at the landing lights, by the crossroads between Ringway Road and Shadow Moss Road. Between 1500 and 1600, the weather was deteriorating sharply and while we waited for the bus home, British Midland Viscount G-AZLT (BD932 from Ronaldsway) arrived at 1611 as a Liverpool diversion, in what was now very cold and swirling fog. By the time I got home, I wasn't expecting any more diversions, as the forecast predicted early evening fog, so I decided watch TV, oblivious I'd missed two Gatwick diversions, both first visits: Wardair DC-10 C-GXRB as 'Wardair 410' and Balair DC-9 HB-IDT (BB182 from Zurich).

11th November 1978 – Another shot of the morning shows US Navy C-9A 160049 parked on the Domestic pier, having diverted in the previous evening as 'Swing 78'. There are plenty of aircraft in the background and note the C-9A still has its thrust reversers open. (Ian Barrie)

11th November 1978 – In the days before British Airways had their own Boeing 737s, they regularly operated various Transavia examples, sometimes in full colours. B.737 PH-TVD had arrived at Manchester the previous evening as 'Speedbird 571' from Istanbul. (Geoff Ball).

12th TAP operated a short series of Sunday flights during the month. B.727 CS-TBP operated as TP9616/7 Gatwick-Faro today, B.727 CS-TBL TP9618/9 from/to Faro (19th) and first visit B.727 CS-TBM TP9620 Faro/Gatwick (26th).

13th The Royal Saudi Air Force appears to be using Manchester rather than Shannon for their transatlantic stopovers this month. The first was C-130H 467 making its first visit today, en route from Milan to Gander, before departing on the 15th.

14th Dan-Air BAC 1-11 G-AWWX arrived for a re-spray into their new colours. It was the first time a company BAC 1-11 had been re-sprayed at Manchester.

18th Royal Saudi Air Force C-130H 1601, arriving at 1450 as RSF831, declared an emergency after shutting down one of its four engines.

19th New British cargo airline, Scimitar, made its first visit when B.707F G-BFZF arrived at 2317 operating under a Tradewinds flight number. It positioned in from Amsterdam to transport a cargo of bridge sections out to Cairo, on behalf of Fairey (IK4340/801).

21st British Airways Trident G-AVFB arrived at 1153 from Heathrow to take Manchester City out to Milan, for their third round UEFA Cup match with AC Milan.

22nd Venezuelan Air Force C-130 3556 arrived from Lajes, in the Azores and offloaded the tail planes of five ex-Air Force Canberra's for transportation by road to Salmesbury.

23rd A new variant of the Cessna Citation, the 550, made its first visit today when G-DJBI arrived at 0842 from Teeside, to operate an outbound flight to Milan. They are easy to distinguish from a regular Citation, as they are longer and have more cabin windows.

24th British Airways Trident G-AVFJ arrived at 0035, returning Manchester City from their match with AC Milan. The game should have been played on the evening of the 22nd, but after it was cancelled due to fog, it was played on the afternoon of the 23rd. It ended as a 2-2 draw and City won the return leg 3-0 on 6th December. It's unknown which aircraft the AC Milan team arrived on, but it was either a scheduled flight into Manchester, or via Heathrow.

24th French Navy DC-3 No. 84 called in for fuel at 0923, en route from Dublin to Berlin.

25th Laker Airways DC-10 G-BBSZ (GK030 Manchester-Gatwick), with fifty passengers onboard, made a safe landing shortly after departure after being struck by lightning.

25th British Airways Trident G-AWZU, inbound from Dusseldorf at 2015, reported 'he had hit a hole or something on landing'. It wasn't established what was hit if anything, but when it reached the stand the two port main tyres were found to have burst.

30th Invicta International acquired a second Britannia, G-AOVF. In basic IAS colours, it positioned in to operate Air Bridge Carriers weekly cattle charter to Milan the following day.

30th French Air Force Noratlas 177/64-IV arrived at 1340, on a training flight from Prestwick to Evereux.

30th Cessna Citation N445CC arrived at 1627 from Heathrow to carry out a series of demonstration flights for NEA, performing several ILS approaches and touch-and-goes.

December 1978

Planning applications for the airports 800ft extension to Runway 06/24 will be considered in the New Year. Around 130 acres of open land will be used, but no buildings will be affected. The extension means long-haul aircraft will be more economic and safety margins for landing aircraft will be increased. It will also help reduce noise from departing traffic over Heald Green and Gatley, as aircraft would be at a higher altitude. The proposals involve diverting part of the River Bollin, a longer taxiway, new drainage and extending lighting systems. Two public footpaths would also have to be diverted and a mounded embankment would be built between the runway and the river. The scheme would take around eighteen months and if approved would involve the compulsory purchase of land and a public enquiry to approve the diverting of public footpaths. If the application is successful, it would commence next April to coincide with work on the runway's hump.

Manchester Airport's first television advertising campaign started this month with Granada TV, at a cost of £83,000. The forty-five second commercials over seven weeks, promoting the convenience to passengers and cargo operators of using Manchester as opposed to London, will include a big sell on direct services.

Danish company Tjaereborg have just opened a Manchester office and are offering 25,000 cut price holidays from Manchester next year. By cutting out the travel agents, they can sell direct to the public at 10% cheaper than their competitors. Prices start from £64 for a week in the Costa Brava and guarantee no surcharges or restrictions on child reduction places. They own their own airline, Sterling, but flights will be operated by Britannia Airways and Dan-Air.

Air Kilroe's recently completed hangar next to the main South Side hangars, will house their aircraft; Beagle 206 G-AWRO, PA-23 G-AZSZ and PA-31 G-BFON.

Equipment changes on the European scheduled services were Finnair (AY032): DC-9s OH-LYH (13th/20th) & OH-LYI (1st/8th/15th); KLM (KL153): DC-8 PH-DCU (1st/21st), Lufthansa (LH074/078): B.727 D-ABKE (5th) and Swissair (SR842) DC-9-51 HB-ISP (15th).

Civil ILS traffic included British Island Airways Herald G-ASBG (2nd), Jetstream G-BBYM (6th), Dove G-ARHW (8th) and HS.125 G-BFPI (12th). RAF traffic identified were C-130 XV199 (1st), Nimrod XV254 (4th) and Jetstreams XX496 (12th) & XX497 (12th). The only crew training flight was operated by British Airways L.1011 G-BBAJ (11th).

2nd   Air France SE.210 F-BHRE, operating AF962/1, was noted using its rarely deployed parachute brake due to the very wet conditions!

3rd   Allegedly, the owner of Manchester based private BAC 1-11 N1543 tried to sell it last month. It reappeared today, departed on the 11th, returned on the 18th and since then it's been stored inside the Dan-Air hangar, as it has a maintenance contract with them. Apparently it's been taken off the market, as the owner only advertised it to see how much he could get for it!

3rd   Manchester was cold and overcast with a biting easterly wind, but the south, Luton and Stansted in particular, were affected by fog during the morning. The weekends tend to see large numbers of Scandinavian charter flights into these airports and on this occasion most were diverted to Gatwick, when fourteen descended on it! When Gatwick itself was affected by fog very early on, British Caledonian B.707 G-ATZC arrived at Manchester at 0546 (BR322 from Banjul). British Airways SVC-10 G-ASGI also called in during the evening, operating Heathrow-New York flight BA179, for some unknown reason!

3rd   Dan-Air Comet G-BDIX made its final visit to Manchester, arriving at 2219 (DA1501 from Alicante), before positioning out to Gatwick the following day at 1302. It's very last service should have been 1st November 1979 (DA1833 Lanzarote-Gatwick), before being flown to Lasham on the 14th; but it returned to service in April 1980 and operated another 'last service' on 17th October 1980 (Hamburg-Gatwick), before positioning to Lasham on 29th October 1980 for final withdrawal.

4th   RAF Nimrod XV254 performed an ILS at 0941, prior to its arrival at Woodford.

4th   The day produced a number of Heathrow diversions and the ATC watch log recorded the apron was available for ten narrow-bodied diversions and four wide-bodied aircraft. Amongst the diversions was first visit British Airways B.747 G-BDXB arriving at 0923 (BA270 from Boston) and an infrequent visit by TWA when B.747 N93119 arrived at 1002 (TW770 from Detroit). Manchester's weather deteriorated around 1030, about the same time fog in the South East was starting to thin. By early evening, Blackpool and Warton were affected and a couple of British Island Airways Heralds from Ronaldsway arrived as Blackpool diversions: G-ASBG at 1844 (UK512) and G-APWF at 1847 (UK708). The ultra-rare HS.125, G-AVRF, usually only ever seen at Warton, also arrived at 1822. After this, I spent the rest of the evening waiting for the inevitable, for the south to be affected by the fog, as the weather forecast had promised. Sure enough it soon was and the British Airways SVC-10, G-ASGI, that had called in the previous evening on the outbound flight, arrived on diversion from London at 2152 (BA178 from New York). This was followed later by British Airtours B.707 G-APFL at 2333 (BA583 from Larnaca). It went quiet again after that, so I took my radio to bed with me and a short time later I heard a very loud and a prolonged roar. Unaware of the time, I jumped out of bed and as I looked through my bedroom window I saw a familiar shape on approach. It was Concorde! I rushed to the kitchen window and watched as it passed over. It was always a thrill seeing her and I was memorised as she descended into the distance. I went back to my bedroom and switched the radio on in time to hear 'Speedbird Concorde 172 clear right on the greens'. I didn't know what time it was, but it was actually not long before 0200!

5th   The early morning arrival of Concorde G-BOAD, as 'Speedbird Concorde 172' didn't appear to be any different from the others in the fleet, even though it was dark I could still make out it was in British Airway's scheme, at least on the starboard side, as unbeknown to me the port side was in full Singapore Airlines colours! British Airways commenced operations to Singapore in December 1976, but had only operated for a few weeks because of Malaysian objections to Concorde overflying their country and the route had been in dispute ever since. However, the service recommenced this month and in connection with this, G-BOAD was painted in full Singapore Airlines colours on the left-hand side!

5th   The fog was still affecting Heathrow by early morning and although L.1011 G-BEAL 'Speedbird 100' arrived before I was up, I heard it talking to its company at Manchester. Qantas B.747 VH-EBK 'Qantas 001', making a first visit arriving at 0651, sounded really good over the radio. Two more diversions arrived from Heathrow before I left for school: B.747 G-AWNF at 0838 (BA062 from Nairobi) and Merchantman G-APEK at 0842 (BE3773 from Frankfurt). The ATC watch log recorded that at 0805 the airport was in a position to receive ten narrow-bodied diversions and only two wide-bodied aircraft. Manchester received intermittent Heathrow diversions up until early afternoon when the RVR was sufficient enough for aircraft to start landing again, although they were subject to ATC flow control. A little burst around late-morning/early-afternoon produced Icelandair B.727 TF-FIE at 1119 (FI450 from Keflavik), the first visit of Air New Zealand since December 1975 when DC-10 ZK-NZS arrived at 1220 (BA282 from Los Angeles) as Prestwick had been firmly established as its primary alternate since then; British Airways flights B.707 G-ATZD at 1230 (BA264 from Kingston) and first visitor B.747 G-BDXF at 1231 (BA176 from New York), Air India B.747 VT-EBO at 1250 (AI102 from New York) and Kenya Airways B.707 5Y-BBJ at 1319 (KQ114 from Zurich). The number of Heathrow diversions would have been much higher if Gatwick had been affected and hadn't received so many diversions. It was also the first visit of the year of a Douglas DC-6 other than OH-KDA, when Balair's sole example, HB-IBS, diverted in at 1330 from Birmingham (BB774 from Zurich). Also worthy of mention was that Qantas B.747 VH-EBK returned to Manchester around lunchtime, nearly three hours after it departed and attempted to land at Heathrow. Overall the day will be remembered for the airport receiving a total of sixty-six diversions, from twelve airports, which was the highest number ever handled by Manchester in a single day! From late afternoon to early evening Ringway was deluged with diversions, particularly commuter aircraft. Weather-wise, the low pressure that had already arrived at Manchester would sweep eastwards and bring with it the usual wind and rain.

6th   French Air Force Noratlas 148/64-BK arrived at 1152, on a training flight routing from Prestwick to RAF Lyneham.

7th   HS.125 N605W arrived at 1126 for customs clearance, prior to its onward flight to Hawarden for maintenance. However, soon after departure it was forced to return to Manchester due to the Hawarden weather.

7th   Merchantman G-APEG made its last visit as a British Airways aircraft, operating BA3772 to Frankfurt. It was sold to Air Bridge Carriers in December 1979.

8th   British Caledonian BAC 1-11 G-ASJC, inbound from Gatwick as BR985, landed safely after declaring a full emergency and losing power in one of its engines.

8th   Transvalair CL-44 HB-IEN positioned in from Amsterdam at 1706. It left the following day for Dar-Es-Salaam via Cairo, transporting bridge sections on behalf of Fairey.

9th   Chipmunk G-BFAW still appears to be a Manchester resident. The aircraft returned from Barton today and its owner is rumoured to be purchasing a Harvard!

11th   The ATC watch log recorded that from 0525, Manchester was given primary diversion status for Scampton.

11th   Rockwell 690 N81877, inbound from Coventry at 1645, declared a full emergency 3-miles from touchdown with suspected controls failure. After making a safe landing, the pilot reported that the controls locked when he selected undercarriage down.

12th   Manchester City was in the quarter-final of the League Cup, which was a two-leg affair by now. The first leg had taken place at Maine Road where City's opponents, Southampton, drew 1-1. British Air Ferries Herald G-BEBB arrived at 1414 to take Manchester City to Southampton for the second-leg. Unfortunately Southampton won 2-1, which put them through to the semi-final. British Air Ferries Herald G-BDFE brought Manchester City home.

13th 'New' British Midland Viscount G-AYOX, formerly 4X-AVA with Israeli airline Arkia, arrived at 1247 from Liverpool to operate the morning Isle of Man service (BA5570/1).

13th Royal Saudi Air Force C-130H 1618 made its first visit today, arriving at 1450 as RSF923 from Rome, before departing on the 15th to Gander.

14th A new airline to Manchester, Southern International, appeared when Viscount G-CSZB arrived at 1542 from Sumburgh. It operated the next day's Aberdeen flight (BA5690/9), before finally positioning out to Glasgow.

16th Britannia 5Y-AYR, owned by Allcargo Airlines, arrived at 1612 to operate a delayed Air Bridge Carriers cattle flight.

18th Manchester and Liverpool were affected by morning fog and Aer Lingus operated their morning Manchester flight EI204/5 nearly four hours late, with Boeing 707 EI-ANV. The 707 was used because the flight was combined with their cancelled Liverpool flight, whose passengers were coached over to Manchester.

19th Trinidad & Tobago Air Services HS.748 9Y-TGD was on delivery when it arrived at Manchester at 1707 from Woodford, to clear customs. Earlier in the day when the airport was affected by fog, nothing landed between 1000 and 1630 and for long periods the visibility was officially recorded as zero, which was the first time I'd heard this!

20th Weather affected operations at various regional airports for the next three days. Birmingham in particular was hit by fog initially and then snow by the 21st. Manchester had cold easterly winds, little sunshine and some snow on the evening of the 21st, but not enough to affect operations. The diversion totals of fifteen on the 20th and eleven on the 21st were just a warm up for the 22nd!

20th Polish-airline LOT operated the first of four flights over the next three days. IL-18 SP-LSG LO4187/8 Moscow-Gatwick was today, TU-134 LO4195/6 from/to Warsaw & IL-18 SP-LSB LO4199/4200 Teeside-Warsaw (21st) and TU-134 SP-LHA LO4211/2 from/to Warsaw (22nd).

22nd Kar-Air DC-6F OH-KDA made its first visit since 13th October, having been on maintenance.

22nd As if the diversion session on the 5th wasn't enough for one month, today produced a further forty-eight diversions and unlike the arrivals on the 5th, virtually all were airliners. By 0920 Heathrow was only accepting Category III aircraft due to fog, but the fog affecting Gatwick earlier on had lifted sufficiently enough for it to accept arrivals, including some diversions from Heathrow. I finally realised what was going on when World Airways DC-10 N104WA diverted in at 1127 and from then on there was a steady flow, mainly from Heathrow. First visit Transavia B.737 PH-TVI at 1239 (EI154 from Dublin), KLM DC-9 PH-DNH at 1333 (KL125 from Amsterdam) and three British Airways Tridents: G-AVFF, G-AVYC & G-AVYE and another first visit Gulf Air L.1011, N41020 at 1421 (GF007 from Abu Dhabi). For a very short time after this, Heathrow was accepting traffic, although ATC restrictions were controlling the number of inbound flights. However, this was short-lived as by 1600 Heathrow was only accepting Cat.III traffic again and by 1720 Gatwick was closed for the rest of the day, due to the weather and congestion. The aircraft starting the late afternoon/early-evening rush was British Airways SVC-10 G-ASGL at 1554 (BA150 from Cairo) and the amount of diversions in the next three hours was staggering! Between 1715 and 1939 there were thirty-eight arrivals, twenty-six of which were diversions. Both arrival frequencies were in use throughout this time; 119.4 was manned by controller Gerry Stevens and 121.35 by Tony Brown, who both did a spectacular job! Amongst the highlights of this batch were Sobelair B.737 OO-SBQ at 1717, the first visit of another Alitalia B.727 with I-DIRJ at 1722 (AZ290 from Milan), Lufthansa B.727s D-ABKH at 1806 (LH052 from Dusseldorf) & D-ABHI at 1928 (LH070 from Munich) and B.737 D-ABHE at 1913 (LH052 from Hamburg); another Gulf Air L.1011 first visit with A4O-TW at 1811 (GF025 from Bahrain), first visit Itavia DC-9 I-TIGU at 1828 (IH1540 from Rome), the first visit of Olympic Airways since 1976 with Boeing 707 SX-DBE at 1837 (OA259 from Athens) which was another first visit. Swissair DC-9-51s HB-IST arrived at 1848 (SR806 from Zurich) & HB-ISK at 1920 (SR812 from Geneva); Dan-Air Comets G-APMB at 1852 (DA3269 from

Munich) & G-BDIT at 1904 (DA3215 from Hamburg); two British Airways Merchantman G-APEJ at 1925 (BA3765 form Geneva) & G-APET at 1931 (BA3795 from Alicante) and KLM DC-8 PH-DEL at 1933 (KL137 from Amsterdam). Finally Eastern Airways L.1011 N323EA, arriving at 1922 (BA453 from Madrid) and on lease to British Airways, had a heated argument with BA Ops at Manchester when they told him Ringway could no longer accept him, a situation he was none too happy with, to say the least! He said 'he really didn't have many other options' and stated in no uncertain terms 'he would be diverting into Manchester anyway!' BA Ops were in absolute chaos, with the frequency in constant use the whole time. The poor lady manning the frequency was recorded saying to 'Speedbird 623' (L.1011 G-BBAE BA623 from Geneva) 'we're up the wall here!' At one point around 1915 a union representative voiced his concerns over the number of diversions the airport was dealing with, as it was stretching the various handling agents to the limits, but he was told a number of diversions still up in the air had no alternative other than to divert into Manchester. By the time BAC 1-11 G-AWYV arrived at 1939 (BR404 from Geneva), the airport was refusing anymore until further notice, unless it was an emergency. All available space was taken by diverted aircraft, including the disused runway and Runway 28. Lufthansa B.727 D-ABHI parked on Domestic Stand 48, reported at 2203 that passengers waiting more than two hours to disembark were causing trouble and threatening to walk-off the aircraft. At 2215 people were observed leaving the aircraft and when it was towed to International Stand 3 ten minutes later, it was minus twelve passengers!

23rd   The morning after the night before! Even though Heathrow was affected by dense fog until midmorning, it comes as no surprise that Manchester didn't accept anymore arrivals!

22nd   After its arrival on 28th March and being a resident inside the South Side hangar with NEA ever since, PA-23 G-TAXI finally flew a couple of test flights today.

26th   Dan-Air BAC 1-11 G-BDAE (DA1536 Manchester-Malaga), reported a bird-strike on takeoff. The pilot thought he'd hit at least four gulls, but continued onto Malaga anyway. After an inspection of the runway, a large herring gull was found dead.

26th December 1978 - BAC 1-11 N1543, arriving on 25th October, spent the majority of the next six months in storage. It received maintenance from Dan-Air and flew on a few occasions, before finally departing for Heathrow on 19th April 1979. (Geoff Ball)

27th   Tradewinds CL-44 G-AWGT, arriving at 0028 operating from/to Larnaca under a Cyprus Airways call-sign (CY050/1), was bringing in Rolls-Royce Spey engines for overhaul.

27th   Although Leeds was badly affected by snow until the 30th; it only produced mundane aircraft when seventeen diverted into Manchester in a four day period, traditionally the quietest of the year. Gatwick was also affected by snow late on the 29th & 30th.

28th   Guernsey Airlines was a new airline to Manchester, when Viscount G-BFYZ arrived to operate a charter flight to Teeside. The evening return was operated by another Viscount, G-ARGR.

28th   Another Dan-Air Comet making its final visit was G-APMB, which arrived at 1439 (DA1229/8 from/to Palma). The flight had originated at Gatwick and upon its return, the aircraft was withdrawn.

30th Greater Manchester Council's application to sell lottery tickets within the airport concourse was rejected, as was a previous gambling application in March 1975, when the placing of slot machines within the terminal building was also turned down.

31st Today's diversions were due to heavy snow in the South East. Heathrow and Gatwick were both affected and the first arrivals came just after midnight, all on Runway 06. By 0700, Manchester had space for nine narrow-bodied and two wide-bodied diversions. This figure was amended frequently throughout the morning and early-afternoon. Liverpool Airport stated that although there was no refuelling available, they could accept up to forty-five diversions! Gatwick and Heathrow had reopened by 1500, but with ATC restrictions. Highlights of the day included first visits by Qantas B.747 VH-EBM at 0657 (QF001 from Bahrain), TMA B.707F OD-AGO at 0940 (TL171 from Beirut) and BWIA B.707 9Y-TEZ at 0953 (BW900 from Bridgetown). Delta diverted DL010 into Manchester again, operated by L.1011 N31029. Although Manchester saw some snow, it was not as much as elsewhere, but it was very cold, especially by sunset under a clearing sky.

31st British Airtours Boeing 707 G-ARWD made its final visit to Manchester, arriving at 0207 (KT635 from Palma) amidst many other South East snow diversions. It was leased to Air Mauritius from April 1979 to April 1981 and although it returned to British Airtours, it was sold immediately and flown to the USA in May 1981 to be broken up.

31st The final entry of the year is a spectacular one, although not directly to do with aircraft. My sister and her husband claimed to have seen a `UFO' about 1930. The sighting was a red-hot topic on the radio and numerous callers said they'd witnessed something in the sky around this time. The story carried extra weight when the Captain of a Safe Air Argosy freight flight in Christchurch, New Zealand, reported and filmed (courtesy of an Australian TV crew onboard at the time) a series of bright lights in front of him on the 30th. These lights have never been fully explained and unidentified blips on ATC radars in Wellington corroborate the sightings. The story came to the attention of the world's media and was frequently shown on the BBC news. The ATC watch log recorded the following at 1904: 'UFO observed by all staff in Tower. Report duly filed and we are inundated with phone calls reporting the UFO'. Another log report made at 1915 read 'Numerous telephone calls received concerning a bright light observed moving from west to east at high speed, with a persistent trail. Observations made from a diverse selection of locations, as far as apart as Leeds, Blackpool, Belfast & Liverpool'. The lights were also observed from the air and the most likely explanation offered, is that it was either space debris or a meteorite re-entering the earth's atmosphere. The airport also received sightings from various other parts of the country and a report was raised by Manchester Tower's Supervisor, on the evidence of 'personal observation'!

First/Last Arrivals & Departures 1978

First arrival:	Argosy G-APRN/AK721 from Belfast at 0017
First departure:	Argosy G-APRN/AK722 to Belfast at 0106
Last arrival:	BAC 1-11 G-AVYZ/GK314 from Palma at 2258
Last departure:	B.727 G-BDAN/DA1504 to Tenerife at 2334

(+/- % on Previous Year)		
Scheduled Passengers	1,786,000	+20.4%
I.T/Charter Passengers	1,636,000	+24.8%
Transit Passengers	72,000	-35.2%
Total	3,494,000	+20.3%
Freight & Mail (Tonnes)	33,700	-11.2%
Movements	77,600	+2.3%

Airport Diary 1979

January 1979

New Years day started brightly enough, but it soon clouded over and by early afternoon it was thick enough for snow. Sure enough it did, on and off until the following morning, which was another cold, grey day with more snow. By the 3rd it was back to school for the writer, but we were sent home the following day, for several weeks, as there was no heating oil and the water pipes had burst! The rest of the month was dominated by one strike or another and the winter of 1978/79 became known as the 'winter of discontent', as the period saw the biggest stoppage of labour since the general strike of 1926! Everyone seemed to be on strike, including ambulance drivers, lorry drivers, grave diggers, bin-men and car workers etc. The airport was affected when firemen took action during the last week of January. Customs Officers also went on strike on a number of occasions, but their action had less of an impact. The strikes and wintry weather all added to the country's problems, making January a thoroughly difficult and miserable month!

Blockades of the country's docks by lorry drivers and the bad weather gave Manchester a great variety of freight flights. Our own operators provided extra services or increased capacity and even our 'based' airline, Pelican Cargo, turned up. Lufthansa used B.707s on LH4072/3: D-ABUA (6th), D-ABUI (14th), D-ABUY (17th) plus B.727 D-ABIW (16th). KLM used DC-8F PH-DCZ (14th/15th), SAS used DC-8F SE-DBI (30th) and Fred Olsen used Electra LN-FOG (17th). Other freight flights included Tradewinds B.707 G-BFEO (14th), Eastern Airways DC-3 G-AMYJ (5th), Transavia B.737 PH-TVC (11th), Pelican B.707 G-BPAT (18th) and German Cargo B.707 D-ABUE (twice on 17th), but a third flight was cancelled after airport porters refused to handle it!

Dan-Air Engineering were kept busy throughout the year with the company's BAC 1-11s and HS.748s passing through. Other regular BAC 1-11s for maintenance were Cyprus Airways 5B-DAG/5B-DAH, Ford Motors G-BEJM/BEJW/BFMC and Oman Air Force 551/552/553.

The Runway 06 glidepath was back in service mid-month after being out of action since the middle of December, due to instrument failure and the 24 glidepath was out of service between 8th January and the end of February. The ATC watch log records on 13th January that a Laker Airways Captain voiced his concern over the length of time the Runway 06 glidepath had been out of service and commented 'He felt there had been a lack of urgency regarding the availability of all landing aids, especially during the current weather conditions'.

Air Europe were recruiting local cabin staff during the month. Operations will commence from Gatwick in May, with Manchester to follow, although no dates have been announced as yet.

British Caledonian has applied to the CAA for permission to operate services between Manchester and Stockholm.

British Island Airways will take over all scheduled routes by British Air Ferries, using the seven Heralds leased from them, but BAF will continue to operate their own cargo services. This will affect the Manchester-Rotterdam service, which will operate under BIA's 'UK' flight code from April, when it will route, Isle of Man-Blackpool-Manchester-Rotterdam-Manchester-Blackpool-Isle of Man.

Cyprus Airways will recommence services to Cyprus in April with a once-weekly flight to the southern resort of Larnaca. They previously flew to Nicosia in the North, but flights were halted in July 1974 when the Turkish invaded the island. The old airport has been annexed since the invasion and is a no-go area. The new flights are aimed at holidaymakers, businessmen and ethnic traffic, with fares starting at £173 return for an APEX ticket.

Trans International Airlines will operate a summer programme from Manchester for the first time this year, flying to New York and Los Angeles from May, with Douglas DC-10s. Fares will start at £95 return for an advance booking charter ticket.

Equipment changes on the European scheduled services were Air France (AF962): Air Charter SE.210 F-BJTG (11th), Lufthansa (LH074/078): B.727s D-ABKR first visit (12th), D-ABLI (13th) & D-ABQI (9th) and Swissair (SR842): DC-9-51 HB-ISP (15th).

The only civil ILS traffic noted was CAA HS.125 G-AVDX (31st) and the only RAF traffic identified was Nimrod XV249 (15th).

1st   The year was ushered in by freezing temperatures reaching -6°c under a clear and starry sky and although it was cold and sunny to begin with, cloud had spread by late morning/early afternoon. It was snowing by 3pm, which continued on and off all day, setting the precedence for the rest of the winter, as it snowed regularly well into March. The snow was accompanied by freezing temperatures and it became the worst winter since 1963!

2nd   Due to continuous snow since midnight, the airport was closed from 0200 to 0600, as ground staff struggled to clear the aprons and taxiways of snow and ice. It closed again from 1040 to 1730 for more clearance work, but even then the TGWU workers said they wouldn't handle aircraft on the stands until the apron was completely clear of snow. They also said if any aircraft came onto the apron before it was cleared, they would be blacked, which led to landing aircraft being handled on the taxiway!

3rd   Despite snow, ice and freezing temperatures, the airport started to function normally again, except for some routes and taxiways, which were still impassable. A minimum snow clearance width was created and regular de-icing runs took place on Runway 06, which was closed between 1430 and 1600 for major clearing work. PA-28 N4607F arrived from Luton at 1030 amidst the chaos and made its way precariously to Dan-Air's hangar, where it parked all day prior to its departure back to Luton. This aircraft is destined to become G-OODY, although when it appeared again on 3rd February it was still N4607F.

4th   The state of the airfield at 0700 was reported in the ATC watch log as follows: 'Runway's full length and width clear with slush in places up to 10mm, with some ice patches towards the edge, with braking action Runway 06 medium. Snow banks on runway edge and taxiways up to a depth of 1m. All major North Side taxiways are available, with the exception of 24 Link A. Southern taxiways not available to aircraft, only vehicles. Most aprons stands accessible'. The disruption continued and by 1045 apron staff once again refused to handle aircraft on un-cleared stands, because of the slippery surface conditions. However, by the afternoon the airport saw the arrival of a number of diversions, including a couple of Viscounts from Leeds: G-APEX at 1323 (BA873 from Dublin) and G-AOYJ at 1326 (BA'YJ from Heathrow). For the second day running, SVC-10 G-ASGK (BA184) arrived direct from New York, due to adverse weather at Prestwick.

4th   Several airports apart from Manchester benefitted from diversions, due to Heathrow being affected by snow and ice during the morning. The British Airport Authority came in for criticism for failing to clear Heathrow's apron areas. British Airways had to cancel 150 of their 180 scheduled flights, after several members of staff broke their bones after slipping on ice. Although the runways had been cleared earlier in the week, the apron areas outside the terminals were covered with compacted snow and ice and the airlines complained it was impossible for passengers and vehicles to move safely around parked aircraft.

4th   Today saw the first visit of an executive B.727, when Fluor Corporation's N4002M arrived at 1216 from Bangor. A space was cleared on the South Bay, courtesy of the ground handlers, as the porters refused to assist. It was also the first visit of an Irish Beech 200, when EI-BFT arrived at 0951. It was routing from Dublin to Brough when it called in to clear customs, before returning in the opposite direction the following day.

4th   Transvalair CL-44 HB-IEO arrived at 2336 (VX117 from Kano), before operating the following day to Cairo. Interestingly, it was parked and loaded on International Pier B, probably because of the precarious state of Freight Apron, where it would normally park.

5th   Wardair DC-10 C-GXRB diverted in at 1839, (WD801 Gatwick-Toronto) with an engine fire warning light on. It was the second Wardair DC-10 to visit and the first witnessed by the writer, arriving amidst a full emergency! After landing it was noted that a panel on the centre engine was missing.

5th   Eastern Airways DC-3 G-AMYJ arrived at 1739 to operate a freight flight to Cologne.

6th   Shorts SD-330 G-BSBH arrived at 1008 from Belfast Harbour to collect freight that had found its way to Manchester instead of Belfast!

8th   A new type appeared on the South Side, when PA-38 Tomahawk N4277E arrived at 1457. It was marked N4277E on the port side and incorrectly marked N42777 on the starboard. Ferried across by 71 year old ferry-pilot Mr H. Dubois, routing Fort Lauderdale-Bangor-Gander-Shannon-Manchester, it's thought to be the first time a PA-38 has been flown across the Atlantic.

Purchased by the Manchester Flying School, it's due to be registered as G-BMSF and it flew a local test flight as such on 14th February.

7th January 1979 – This shot shows a rapid thaw taking place after heavy snow during the first week of January. Polish Air Force Ilyushin Il-18 101 showed up on Sunday lunchtime, in full Polish military marks, operating LOT flight LO4223/4 from/to Warsaw, due to LOT suffering from aircraft problems caused by the poor weather in Poland. (Geoff Ball)

9th   Royal Saudi Air Force C-130H 466 made its first visit, arriving at 1431 as RSF900, en route Cairo-Gander, on their only transatlantic flight this month. The decline of these flights was probably due to the poor weather and industrial action.

10th   Bavaria-Germanair BAC 1-11 D-AMUC, arriving at 0744 from Munich for maintenance with Dan-Air, was present until the 25th.

10th   Although it hadn't snowed since the 2nd, a fresh batch arrived this afternoon. Heavy falls for the rest of the day caused frequent closures at the airport for snow clearance and de-icing.

11th   Continuing snow showers caused the airport to close for snow clearance and de-icing for an hour in the evening and again before midnight.

12th   Once the overnight snow had stopped, the airport had a new hazard to deal with - fog! The regions motorways were reduced to 50mph and there were only nine arrivals at Manchester all day, but not specifically due to the weather. It was due to an unofficial 24-hour strike by British Airways pilots over the use of a recently delivered 'long-haul' Tristar on the London-Paris route.

13th   The airport was hit by record low temperatures overnight when -12°c was recorded, making it the coldest January since 1945. Even the de-icing equipment was affected, when a number of vehicles were frozen solid. The airport struggled to operate normally until mid-afternoon, when it was subjected to patchy and occasionally dense freezing fog.

14th   Unusually for a Sunday, a number of cargo flights arrived due to the continuing lorry drivers strike. Swissair DC-9 HB-IFW (SR4846/7), KLM DC-8F PH-DCZ (KL909/9327), Lufthansa B.707F D-ABUI (LH4072/3) and first visit Tradewinds B.707F G-BFEO (IK4420/431).

14th   The major news of the day was the complete reversal of the weather, at least for the time being, when a major thaw took place. The majority of snow accumulated since New Year's Day had disappeared, except for some banks of un-melted snow around the airfield.

15th   The thaw continued, with temperatures reaching 5°c by the afternoon. Manchester handled twenty-eight diversions, after fog affected many airports at various times. Birmingham was fogbound all day, Luton from the afternoon onwards, East Midlands until tea-time and the North Eastern airports during the evening. Even though Heathrow was affected by the evening, Manchester didn't receive any of their diversions. However, Ringway had already received twenty-six diversions from other airports and at that point could still handle another four narrow-bodied and five wide-bodied aircraft. Three flights diverting to Liverpool late evening were two British Airways SVC-10s - G-ASGI (BA200), G-ASGK (BA064) and Nigeria Airways B.707 5N-ABK (WT802). For some unknown reason all these aircraft were handled by Manchester approach 119.4, then transferred to Manchester Director 121.35 and only transferred to Liverpool Tower when in sufficient enough range.

15th   SAS DC-9 OY-KGS made a first visit today, operating SK539 in an all-silver colour scheme. In contrast it was also the final visit of a TWA B.707, when N28726 arrived at 1006 as TW8761, operating a return Christmas charter from New York. The airline would not make any more charter visits and their Boeing 707s started to be phased out in 1980.

18ᵗʰ   British Air Ferries Herald G-BDZV, (VF995/6 from/to Rotterdam) is now wearing basic BAF colours, with British Island Airways titles on the port side only.

18ᵗʰ   Beagle 206 VH-FDH, arriving at 1749 from Biggin Hill, was on its way to the USA in Flying Doctor colours. It's been purchased by South Florida Aircraft Sales & Services of Fort Lauderdale and it departed on the 23ʳᵈ February to Stornaway.

19ᵗʰ   The airport was affected by strong winds, cold temperatures and snow showers throughout the day and due to the weather, restrictions were imposed for traffic landing at Heathrow and Gatwick during the morning. While both airports were closed between 1230 and 1400 for snow clearance, Manchester received four diversions in a thirty minute period: Air New Zealand DC-10 ZK-NZQ at 1236 (BA598 from Los Angeles), Aer Lingus B.737 EI-ASG at 1253 (EI158 from Dublin), Bangladesh Biman B.707 S2-ABN at 1300 (BG003 from Dubai), British Airways BAC 1-11 G-AVML at 1305 (BA743 from Cologne) and Transmeridian DC-8F G-BFHW at 1411 (KK7675 from Las Palmas) which was a first visit. The ATC watch log records that Manchester was preparing to accept up to twenty narrow-bodied and five wide-bodied aircraft, but in the end fifteen diversions were received, from various airports.

19ᵗʰ   After Air Malta flight KM704/5 was cancelled, Monarch Airlines Boeing 720 G-AZKM positioned up from Luton to operate the flight as OM756/7.

20ᵗʰ   The topsy-turvy weather continued, from snow the previous day, to fog today. The airport saw a varied selection of diversions from Liverpool, Birmingham, Luton & Leeds and the final visit of Balair DC-6 HB-IBS, diverting in at 0952 from Liverpool on a freight flight (BB891 from Stansted). Also on its final visit was BAF Carvair G-ASDC, which diverted from Liverpool at 1341. It was stored at Southend, after it's very final flight on the 3ʳᵈ April.

21ˢᵗ   Today started promising enough, when Zambia Airways B.707 9J-ADY arrived at 0641 (QZ038 from Lusaka). There had already been four diversions up to this point, including British Caledonian B.707 G-BDLM at 0532 (BR322 from Banjul) and DC-10 G-BEBM at 0556 (BR362 from Lagos). Heathrow was affected by patchy fog and as visibility was constantly fluctuating; most aircraft were landing normally. Other early morning arrivals into Manchester included Gatwick diversions Britannia Airways G-AVRM at 0749 (BY459B from Athens) & Transvalair CL-44 HB-IEN at 1011 (VX121 from Kano), Stansted diversion DC-8F G-BTAC at 0907 (KK7677 from Las Palmas) and East Midlands diversion Falcon 20 OY-AZT at 1011 from Billund. The Transvalair landed at a time when Manchester's weather was deteriorating rapidly and by 1030 the fog was so bad it precluded further movements until 1936! Simultaneously, Heathrow suffered the same fate, when it too fell below limits for most aircraft. A mad scramble soon took place for somewhere to land, when a number of holding aircraft were getting low on fuel. Gatwick, Stansted & Luton were also out for long periods and by 1100 the sight of six British Airways B.747s heading north to Prestwick, under a clear blue sky was frustrating, but also very impressive! They were interspersed with other aircraft heading north such as Air Canada B.747 C-FTOE, Braathens B.737 LN-SUM and two TWA flights: L.1011 N31031 (TW754) & B.747 N93106 (TW760). The situation became desperate when even Cardiff received a number of diversions and Aer Lingus Dublin-London flights were flight-planned straight into Cardiff for a time. Other rarely heard flights diverting as far north as Prestwick included Monarch Airlines B.720 G-BCBB (CY326 Larnaca-Heathrow) and B.707 4X-ATR (LY1315 Tel Aviv-Heathrow). Normality returned early evening, but as far as Manchester was concerned it went from the sublime to the ridiculous, when just as the fog was starting to clear; Ringway was hit by industrial action and was closed by 2300. Council workers on a 24-hour strike forced the cancellation of all scheduled flights from Manchester. Ten-thousand passengers were affected when porters, baggage handlers, car parking staff and firemen joined a nationwide stoppage. There were plans to coach some passengers to Liverpool to take their flights from there, but the union threatened to employ 'flying pickets' if this took place.

21ˢᵗ   One that didn't make it through the fog was Lufthansa B.727 D-ABKN, operating LH078/9. It bypassed Manchester completely and operated directly to/from Dublin on what would have been its first visit.

23ʳᵈ   All airports south of and including Manchester were closed, because of long periods of snow from early morning.

24th The airport was affected by industrial action again and was closed at 0800 because of a vacant chair in the fire-station watch room, left empty due to a work-to-rule. The fireman who'd been allocated the chair prior to the action had gone on holiday and following a meeting of shop stewards representing porters, marshallers, car park staff, baggage loaders and firemen, the union refused cover for him. The continuing action by six-hundred corporation employed airport staff left the management with no choice other than to close the airport, as constant watch room manning was a mandatory stipulation of the airports licence. The airport finally reopened at 1800, after an agreeable replacement filled the seat!

25th Having not long re-opened after the latest batch of industrial action, the airport suffered heavy snowfalls, which caused further delays and cancellations.

26th It was another day of passenger disruption and misery, when snow and industrial action closed the airport all day again.

27th The work-to-rule by six-hundred corporation airport workers, which had effectively closed the airport to traffic since the 21st, finally ended and the airport was reopened from 0800. A peace deal between unions and management gave the Airport Authority a four-week breathing space, time enough to finalise a local pay deal, giving workers wage parity with other UK airports. Manchester was fully operational again, although a restricted timetable was still in place, with some flights having to use Liverpool due to the weather and restrictions on ground handling facilities. Paris-flight AF962 (SE.210 F-BJTS) held for nearly two hours, waiting for the runway to be swept and de-iced, before finally landing at 0933. Not so lucky was SVC-10 G-ASGJ (BA184 from New York/Prestwick), which diverted back to Prestwick. Manchester was hit by flight restrictions from a different source later on, when more fog rolled in and nothing landed after 1548.

28th The airport battled to stay open after the arrival of more snow and strong winds. It was eventually closed between 1643 and 1852 for runway sweeping and de-icing. When SVC-10 G-ASGD operating positioning flight BA9440 back to Heathrow, got to the holding point of Runway 24 in the middle of driving snow, it was so bad he requested the runway be swept before takeoff! This was academic however, as the snow was so heavy the airport had to close and the SVC-10 eventually returned to stand.

29th The first French Air Force Transall to visit Manchester was F.17/61-ML, arriving at 1215 operating a crew training detail, en route Bristol-Amsterdam.

29th At 1322, Cessna 150 G-BFRP reported he was stuck in a hole near the South Side windsock, where work had been carried out laying a mains cable. Fire service assistance was requested and he was pulled clear ten minutes later.

29th Due to East Midlands being closed late evening for snow clearance, British Midland B.707 G-AYVG arrived at 2225 (BD720 from Shannon), in full PIA colours.

30th British Air Ferries Herald G-BDZV, (VF995 from Rotterdam), landed with partial hydraulic failure and had to be towed off Runway 24.

30th Having been in the NEA hangar since 9th August 1978, Beech 55 EI-BEW finally spread its wings, before returning later in the day. Larger style markings were applied and it left again on 9th February for Dublin.

30th Royal Swazi Viscount 3D-ACN arrived back at Manchester today. This aircraft was delivered last year, but never saw service with the airline. It's now been purchased by Dan-Air and departed on the 23rd April, on delivery as G-BGLC.

31st Sabena B.737 OO-SDP, operating the early morning freighter (SN131), diverted back to Brussels due to unavailability of the 06 glidepath.

February 1979

A private Airport Committee meeting chaired by the airport's Director, Mr Gordon Sweetapple, indicated a second runway could be operational by 1990. Another major development is that the building of the proposed new cargo centre could be brought forward by five years. Originally it was part of a development ear-marked for 1985-1990, but it may be introduced into a scheme starting next year. It's expected that the strengthening and rebuilding of the existing runway will start next month and work on the 800ft extension will be carried out next year.

During a meeting with the Airport Consultative Committee, tour operators expressed their concerns that Liverpool may not be able to cope when Manchester starts night-time closures next month. It was pointed out they had not fared well during last month's industrial action, when they struggled to deal with a number of Manchester flights over a four-day period, even though sufficient notice had been given. It was also mentioned that due to a shortage of staff, passengers were unable to obtain refreshments and massive queues had formed at the information desk when flight information boards weren't updated. In answer to their comments, Manchester's Deputy Director stated that Liverpool had assured him that arrangements to improve facilities were in hand and additional ground handling equipment had been acquired.

The airport is bracing itself for another boom year, despite being closed to night-flights from March to October. Increased holiday flights from airlines such as British Airways, will help the airport to achieve a 20% increase on last year.

After making just one flight from Manchester since November, Pelican Cargo announced relocation of their headquarters to London, as their operation now concentrates on Gatwick. This news and the fact that most night freighters will be using Liverpool from March, undoubtedly means a tough year for the airports cargo operations.

Equipment changes on the European scheduled services during the month were Lufthansa (LH074/078): B.727 D-ABLI (9th) and SAS (SK539): DC-9-21 LN-RLL (2nd).

The only civil ILS traffic noted was Dove G-ASMG (6th). RAF traffic identified included RAE Argosy XN817 (2nd), Hawk XX162 (9th), C-130s XV183 (14th), XV189 (26th), XV304 (23rd) and Jetstreams XX495 (19th/26th) & XX496 (19th). RAF Hawk XX162 was the first appearance of the type at Manchester (9th).

2nd   The last remaining UK military Argosy in service, RAE (Royal Aircraft Establishment) XN817, performed an ILS during the afternoon as 'Evergreen 14'.

2nd   Skyvan G-BFUM, arriving at 1425 for Dan-Air Engineering in primer and bare metal, was to be sprayed in Botswana Defence Force colours. The work was carried out in a spray area set up in the north east corner of Dan-Air's hangar, in a space large enough to take aircraft up to the size of a BAC 1-11. The Skyvan emerged on the 16th as OC-1 and departed within ten minutes on delivery. This was only time work of this kind was undertaken by Dan-Air engineering on an outside aircraft. There were plans for more Skyvan's to be re-sprayed at Manchester, but in the end Dan-Air decided they were too fiddly!

3rd   ATC delays through Spain and Portugal increased during the afternoon, when no ATC flight-plans were accepted for long periods.

4th   Long ATC delays continued throughout the day. Flights into and over Portugal were over seven hours late and from lunchtime, no more traffic was being accepted by the Canaries airports.

6th   Another visit of a French Air Force Transall, F.94/61-ZL this time, took place during a training detail from Lyneham to Amsterdam. It made an ILS approach, landed, then taxied straight round again before departing.

7th   The UK and its airports were suffering from snow and ice again. Even though Manchester had weather problems of their own, particularly with ice, it was still put on possible standby for snow diversions from Heathrow and was in a position to handle up to twenty narrow-bodied diversions, plus four wide-bodied aircraft. Nine diversions arrived between 0947 and 1238, including five from British Airways. Others were Kenya Airways B.707 5Y-BBJ at 0947 (KQ214 from Frankfurt), SAS DC-9 SE-DAL at 1118 (SK501 from Copenhagen), first visit Alitalia DC-9 I-DIZO at 1138 (AZ282 from Rome) and SAS DC-9 OY-KGK at 1238 (SK515 from Stavanger). More snow arrived at Manchester over the next few days and the trend of occasional snow, frosts, fog, ice and strong winds continued until end of the month.

7th   Korean Airlines made their first ever appearance at Manchester with their own aircraft, when B.707 HL-7427 arrived at 1411 (KE9007 from Brussels), before departing out to Seoul via Bahrain and Bangkok. They wanted to use a B.747F, but it couldn't be handled because of 'blacking' by the union of the use of a specialised piece of equipment for loading and unloading freight, the Super Hylo, which has remained unused in a hangar for more than a year!

7th   Following the visit of Beagle 206 VH-FDF last month, another ex-Flying Doctor example, VH-FDB, arriving at 1656 from Biggin Hill was also on its way to the USA. It was looked after by Air Kilroe and carried out a couple of return trips to Prestwick on the 8th/9th, before finally leaving on the 10th, bound for the USA via Prestwick.

7th   Making the first of three visits this year, was Lear Jet 25 I-KISS, arriving at 1653 from Turin.

11th February 1979 – Ex-Bouraq HS.748 C-GTLD arrived for engine and de-icing equipment work with Dan-Air. Incorrectly marked as CG-TLD, it was on its way to Bradley Air Services of Canada. (Geoff Ball).

12th   It was the second weekend of ATC delays, with some flights running up to fourteen hours late. The go-slow by Spanish ATC over better pay, conditions and equipment, remains unresolved and further chaos is expected as the summer approaches. Coupled with the knock-on effect of flights trying to reach Manchester before the 2300 curfew, it's more than likely that a greater number of flights will miss the deadline than previously anticipated!

12th   Due to snow in the south, Manchester was on weather standby and from 0500 could accept ten narrow-bodied plus six wide-bodied aircraft. Birmingham and East Midlands were closed for three hours in the morning due to snow, but nothing extraordinary appeared. The arrivals were three Britannia Airways B.737s, two British Airways Viscounts and two Dan-Air HS.748s.

13th   Twenty-five diversions arrived from Birmingham and Leeds (which were fog bound all day) and also from Coventry, Luton & Brize Norton. They mostly were mundane, with the exception of three RAF VC-10s: XV105 at 1059 (RR2159 from Washington), XV107 at 1458 (RR2534 from RAF Akrotiri) & XR807 at 1658 (RR2088 from RAF Akrotiri) and Andover XS605 at 1323 from Brize Norton, with a crew to take VC-10 XV105 out to Belfast.

13th   Allcargo Airlines Britannia 5Y-AYR, arriving at 0829 from Manston and departing later for Milan as IM391, was operating a cattle charter on behalf of Air Bridge Carriers. It operated again on the 16th from/to Milan as AK140.

14th   Alidair Viscount G-BDRC arrived at 1506 on a crew training flight from/to East Midlands.

15th   Snow closed Gatwick for a time during the afternoon, the same time Heathrow was on single runway operations. By the evening Manchester had received its first Heathrow diversion due to snow and holding delays, when Swissair DC-9-51 HB-ISR arrived at 1903 (SR812 from Geneva), just before it closed for snow clearance.

15th   Last year's use of several Nord 262s for training by Air France have begun again and the first this year was F-BPNU, arriving at 1555 from/to Gatwick. Other flights during the month were Nord 262 F-BPNX (28th), Corvettes F-BTTU (22nd/27th) & F-BVPK (22nd/23rd) and first time visitors MS.760 Paris F-BNRG (26th/27th) & F-BJLX (28th).

17th   Loganair Trislander G-AZZM arrived at 1618 on a fuel stop, en route Aberdeen-Exeter.

17th   A surprise diversion on a quiet Saturday evening was Cessna 441 5Y-NCA, routing from Keflavik-Luton on delivery. It had major engine trouble and was eventually moved to the Air Kilroe hangar for repair, before finally departing on 2nd March for Heraklion.

18th   The fourth and final Bavaria-Germanair BAC 1-11, D-AMAM, arrived at 1130 from Hamburg for maintenance with Dan-Air, before departing on 11th March.

18th   The first ever arrival of Flying Tigers took place today, when DC-8F N788FT appeared at 2359 (FT024 from Frankfurt). Much delayed due to technical problems, it was operating a livestock charter when it departed the following day to New York, via Shannon.

19th   British Airways BAC 1-11 G-AVMM (BA5642 Manchester-Glasgow) returned at 0809, having declared a full emergency with full engine failure.

19th   Another dull and overcast morning was also the writers first day back at school, after a week's break. We'd had so much time off since the New Year, due to lack of heating and holidays, I was beginning to miss the place! I was told about the Flying Tigers arrival by the other boys and a few of us skipped school at dinnertime to see if it was still in. Once we got to the airport, we were relieved to see it was sat on the Freight Apron, being loaded up. At that point we were oblivious the weather was causing problems at other airports, but we soon realised when two Trans-Europa SE.210s: (EC-BRJ TR262 Bristol diversion) and (EC-CIZ TR272 Cardiff diversion) arrived within twenty minutes of each other. It was an unexpected treat, as they didn't have a winter programme from Manchester. The airport had been advised to expect diversions from Leeds and Birmingham and could accept twenty narrow-bodied and four wide-bodied. By 1900 there had been nineteen diversions with a further eleven narrow-bodied plus four wide-bodied being prepared for. A total of twenty-six arrived overall and Runway 10/28 was also being used for parked aircraft, similar to the 13th, when Leeds and Birmingham remained fog-bound all day.

20th   For the second day running, fog was affecting mainly northern airfields and Leeds was out all day. Manchester was on standby for possible diversions from RAF Finningley and RAF Waddington.

24th February 1979 – The first Caribou to visit was former Kuwait Air Force example C-GVYZ, seen here on the South Bay. It arrived at 1955 on the 22nd having developed an engine fault whilst on delivery from Cherbourg to its new owner in Quebec. It finally left on the 4th March. (Geoff Ball)

28th   First time visitor Sabreliner N9NR, operated by McAlpine Aviation, arrived at 1712 from/to Luton.

March 1979

Following on from four days of industrial action in January, ground staff voted to accept a new pay offer, when a productivity deal was finalised after six weeks of discussions.

For the past few months, the apron outside the former Fairey hangar has been used for the storage of BAC 1-11 N1543 and the movement of aircraft in and out of Dan-Air's hangar. The space has been further reduced by a quantity of articulated lorry's using it for loading London-bound freight for consolidation from the Servisair warehouse, located in the old Fairey hangar, formerly used as Pelican's freight warehouse.

Clyden Airways mail flight CE100/1 has been suspended since the middle of February, due to a strike by the Irish Post Office.

Dan-Air has applied for a licence to fly Manchester-Cork from April 1980.

It's being rumoured that Iberia have been unable to obtain permission to operate scheduled flights to Barcelona/Madrid from Manchester this year.

From the 19th, British Caledonian will operate four-times a day between Manchester-Gatwick and three-times a day at weekends. KLM suspended their night-time freight flights on the 4th and Lufthansa, Sabena & Swissair suspended their night freight flights on the 3rd. SAS retimed cargo flights to operate during the day and extended Copenhagen passenger flights to operate onwards to Dublin twice-weekly.

Equipment changes on the European scheduled services were Finnair (AY032): DC-9 OH-LYI (7th), Lufthansa (LH074/078): B.727 D-ABRI (21st) and SAS (SK539): DC-9-21 LN-RLL (5th).

No civil ILS traffic was noted during the month. RAF traffic identified included C-130s XV219 (13th) & XV222 (14th) and Hawk XX223 (15th).

1st   Dan-Air Viscount G-BCZR arrived at 1252 for a brief stop, on an air test from East Midlands.

1st   LOT operated numerous charters during the month with Tupolev TU-134s from/to Warsaw. SP-LHA arrived at 1037 (LO3459/60) & SP-LHB at 1429 (LO3461/2) today and the others were SP-LHA LO3471/2 & SP-LHG LO3475/6 (5th), SP-LHB LO3479/80 (8th) and SP-LHC LO3485/6 (12th).

4th   The first night-flight to operate into Liverpool, Boeing 727 G-BAEF (DA1501), was running three hours late due to traffic delays at Alicante. When it was apparent the aircraft wouldn't make the 2300 curfew, a fleet of coaches set off from Manchester to collect the passengers from Liverpool and as the aircraft was due out again to Malta, those passengers were coached to Liverpool as well!

4th   Caribou C-GVYD finally departed after making two abortive attempts. The first was due to a radio problem and the second when the main rear door came open, so it was a case of third time lucky when it finally left at 1345, initially bound for Inverness!

5th   Today was the first of the six nights a week closures of Runway 06/24. Aer Lingus, KLM, Lufthansa & Swissair have transferred all their cargo operations to Liverpool for the duration of the work. Sabena used Liverpool initially, but then merged the daytime passenger flight with the night-time freighter into a daytime combi-flight.

6th   WDL F.27 D-BAKA brought Borussia Monchengladbach into Manchester for their UEFA Cup Quarter-Final first leg match with Manchester City, but due to the very early departure time of 0400, the fans arrived into Liverpool instead, onboard Condor B.727 D-ABKL.

8th   Aer Lingus B.707 EI-ANO, arriving at 1451 (EI9214 from Dublin), operated an extra cargo flight before departing for Shannon at 2052 as EI9215.

9th   Falcon 10 N77NR, arriving at 0912 from Frankfurt, had previously visited on 15th October 1978 as N183FJ.

9th   Air France SE.210 F-BHRL made its last visit to Manchester today operating AF962/1, as it was damaged beyond repair at Frankfurt three days later.

15th   Fokker F.28 PH-BBV was carrying out crew training flights. The aircraft, in basic NLM colours, is on lease to Air Anglia until the first of their own F.28s are delivered. Routing Norwich-Aberdeen, it appeared again on the 20th & 21st.

17th   Bad weather affecting the UK since New Year's Day continues to cause problems. Even though Manchester was affected by snow, the airport was still able to accept Teeside diversion British Air Ferries Herald G-BEYD, arriving at 1109 from Rotterdam.

17th   East Midlands was closed from 0830 to 1745, due to Lear Jet F-BSRL overrunning the runway on its departure for Paris.

19th   Owned and operated by the National Coal Board for a number of years, Dove G-ARUM arrived from Leavesden in connection with the Golborne pit disaster the previous day. Ten miners were killed in an underground explosion, thought to have been caused by a build up of methane.

20th   The third USA bound Beagle 206 passing through Manchester this year, was G-AWRM. Handled by Air Kilroe, it was on delivery to Fort Lauderdale to join the other two.

20th   Dan-Air HS.748 G-BEJE, arriving at 1808 from Aberdeen with the port engine shut down, was due for maintenance with Dan-Air Engineering.

23rd   Gulf Air B.737 A40-BG, currently leased to Britannia Airways, made its first visit on the 3rd and arrived again today from Toulouse. It was bringing in the French Rugby League team for the following afternoon's game with England at Warrington. An EAS Vanguard due to bring French rugby fans in was cancelled, due to lack of interest!

27th   The airport was put on standby for Beech 200 G-BFWH, diverting into Manchester en route from Heathrow to Aberdeen, with port engine failure.

27th   Private DC-9 N112AK arrived at 1708 from Athens, with the President of Sudan and his entourage onboard.

28th   Several arrivals were lost this evening due to strong crosswinds, including British Air Ferries Herald G-BEYF (VF995 from Rotterdam), Dan-Air B.727 G-BAEF (DA1037 from Lanzarote) which diverted to Liverpool and British Airways BAC 1-11 (BA5048 from Heathrow), which returned to Heathrow.

29th   Capitol DC-8 N906CL arrived at 1647 to operate a flight to New York, on behalf of Laker Airways.

29th   Arguably the best movement of the year so far was the arrival of Aero-Uruguay B.707 CX-BJV at 0728 on a wet Thursday morning, operating a freight flight on behalf of Air India. It was also the first visit of a Uruguayan aircraft to Manchester.

29th March 1979 – As if the Aero-Uruguay B.707 today wasn't enough, also arriving was private Electra N8LG, bringing John Denver in for a concert in Manchester as part of his UK tour. Its early evening arrival inbound from Dublin was later than intended, due to an engine fault. Immaculately presented inside and out with a full VIP interior, it operated as a VIP aircraft until July 1985. John Denver himself was a fully qualified pilot and the owner of a Lear Jet, which he bought new in 1974 and flew until the 1980's. He would regularly fly himself to his own concerts throughout America, often with his father, Henry John Deutschendorf Sr, as the co-pilot. He'd been an Air Force Lieutenant Colonel in the United States Air Force and set three speed records in the Convair B-58 Hustler bomber, which earned him a place in the Air Force Hall of Fame! (Geoff Ball)

30th   North West Flying School Grumman Cheetah G-BFTD crashed into the Welsh hillside today. After leaving Manchester at 1004 for Caernarfon, it was making the return flight when it found itself some miles off course. It wasn't found until 1st April, when NEA boss David Antrobus located the wreckage from one of the company's Islanders. Several local aircraft, as well as a RAF Rescue Whirlwind out of RAF Valley, had all taken part in the search.

April 1979

On instruction of the Airport Authority, the main South Side hangar No 522 and the apron outside, will be split into three sections and leased out. NEA will occupy the largest portion of the eastern end, Apache the small centre section and Barton Moss the rest, with each being responsible for their own customers. It's likely a number of existing residents will have to vacate, due to increased charges and the limit on the number of aircraft permitted inside the hangar for safety reasons.

Following a very cold spell, emergency repairs have been carried out on the roof section of the airport tunnel on the main A538 Altrincham to Wilmslow Road, running underneath the end of the main runway. Water seeping into the gaps of the construction joints, has frozen and formed large icicles, which are falling onto the traffic below and creating serious problems for motorists. The

Airport Authority has requested that the Department of Transport closes each bore of the tunnel consecutively from the 17th.

The following airlines have made changes from this month: Air France will operate Paris flight AF962/1 six-weekly. Air Malta will operate scheduled flight KM106/7 twice-weekly from June to October. British Airways transatlantic flights will operate daily to New York (BA184/5), Montreal/Toronto (BA080/1) six-weekly via Prestwick and once-weekly direct to Toronto (BA082/3). The B.747 will be reintroduced from 28th May to operate to Toronto via Prestwick five-weekly (BA080/1) and Montreal will be served four-weekly via Prestwick with a mix of SVC-10/B.747s (BA084/5). British Airways flights to Malta recommenced during the month with Trident 3s. British Island Airways now operate the twice-weekday Rotterdam service. Cyprus Airways introduced a once-weekly Larnaca flight from the 7th. Lufthansa now operate daily direct from/to Frankfurt (LH074/5), having dropped the weekend sector to/from Dublin.

Equipment changes on the European scheduled services were Air Malta (KM106): Transasian B.707s 9G-ACN (8th/22nd/29th) & 9G-ACO (1st/15th) and Swissair (SR842): DC-9-51s HB-IST (22nd) & HB-ISV (11th).

The only civil ILS traffic noted was Air Europe B.737 G-BMHG, operating various crew training flights on the 19th/20th/22nd/23rd/24th. Military traffic identified included Royal Navy Jetstream XX481 (5th), RAF Jetstreams XX492 (20th), XX493 (17th), XX496 (9th), XX497 (17th) & XX499 (26th); RAF Dominie XS710 (19th), RAE Comet XS235 (24th) and RAF C-130 XV212 (30th).

2nd   The first of two airlines making their first appearances during the month was Ontario Worldways with their single Boeing 707, C-GRYN, on their first transatlantic revenue flight. They commenced a return flight to Toronto on Mondays for Canadian originating traffic and will operate from Gatwick and Prestwick during the summer, but a planned service from Birmingham has been dropped.

2nd   PA-31 G-AXYA owned by Gill Aviation inbound from Newcastle, landed, then swung off the runway, before tilting onto its starboard wing. As it was causing an obstruction, the airport had to close for an hour in order to remove it. It was thought to have burst a tyre on landing, but an inspection of the runway confirmed it had hit an object. After extensive repairs by NEA, it departed back to Newcastle on the 11th July.

2nd   With the exception of the Chief Customs Officer and a senior colleague, all 130 Customs Officers joined a 24-hour civil servants strike. Honesty boxes were provided for passengers voluntarily declaring goods brought in from abroad! The strike also affected freight and the only consignments moving were by special arrangement. The absence of customs officials didn't affect flights, but the number of working ATC assistants was reduced which resulted in some minor delays, but it was the action by ATC assistants in the south that caused the cancellation of flights to Heathrow, Gatwick, Glasgow & Edinburgh.

2nd   The airport was closed from 1825, when the entire seventy-four man fire brigade was suspended without pay for three days, after refusing to lift a ban on overtime and flexible working in support of a pay claim. They said it would be Sunday the 8th before a full shift was available, because of days off and shift changes and even when they did return, they would resume their work-to-rule. The action affected up to 10,000 passengers a day and cost the airport £40,000 a day in lost revenue. Most flights operated out of Liverpool, although Birmingham was used more frequently by British Airways, as Liverpool found it increasingly difficult to cope. The trouble blew up when the firemen refused to participate in a self-financing productivity package for the airports ground and manual workers. Although the deal would have given them £13 a week more, their manning levels would be reduced from seventeen to fifteen firemen per shift to pay for it. A spokesman for the union said that while other airport departments had accepted manpower cuts, for the firemen it meant with fewer men the job would simply take longer, which was unacceptable due to the safety factor. The dispute was eventually settled and normal operations resumed from Saturday 7th at 0800.

7th   Dan-Air Comet G-BDIF (DA1631/10 from/to Milan) made its final visit to Manchester today. It operated its final service, Frankfurt-Gatwick on the 5th November, before positioning to Lasham on the 8th November for storage.

9th   Aer Lingus B.747 I-ASI arriving at 0938 (EI7938 from Bermuda), was returning a load of factory workers from Gloworm Radiators of Belper, Derbyshire. Due to the firemen's dispute, the outbound flight had operated from Liverpool. The trip was a staff reward for exceeding production targets.

11th   French Air Force Noratlas 185/64-KV arrived at 1019, operating a crew training flight from Evereux to Copenhagen.

13th   Belgian Air Force HS.748 CS-03 arrived at 1212 from/to Brussels.

14th   Dan-Air Comet G-APYD (DA1631/0 from/to Milan) also made its final visit to Manchester today and its final service (Heraklion-Gatwick) was on 23rd October. It's the last Comet 4B in service and will be preserved at Wroughton.

16th   Ontario Worldways B.707 C-GRYN operated OW705 from Toronto as normal, before positioning out to Dubrovnik, ultimately bound for South East Asia to assist with the Vietnamese refugee situation. Capitol DC-8 N8763 positioned in from Munich the following day at 1715 to operate the outbound OW706.

17th   The arrival of Capitol DC-8 N8763 was the second visit by the airline this year, but the major event as far as the writer's concerned was being told he and his family were moving to a fourteenth-floor flat on the other side of Stockport, but happily it was still on the flight path!

19th   Having been stored since last December, BAC 1-11 N1543 made a test flight routing Manchester-Biggin Hill-Stansted-Gatwick-Manchester and finally left for Heathrow on the 26th.

19th   The second airline making its first appearance this month was Air Europe, when B.737 G-BMHG operated a crew training flight and several more throughout the month. They will commence operations from Manchester in October.

21st   Another Dan-Air Comet, G-BDIU, made its final visit to Manchester (DA1335/4 from/to Ibiza). It's very last flight operated on 6th October 1980, before positioning out to Gatwick-Lasham two days later for storage.

22nd   Having fully relocated to Gatwick, Pelican Cargo B.707 G-BPAT arrived at 0939 from Athens (DP410), to operate an outbound freight flight to Malmo from Manchester, in preference to Gatwick. The same aircraft operated another flight on the 29th, when Gatwick was suffering handling and fuel supply problems.

23rd   Islander G-BESG arrived from Bembridge and went straight to Fairey's Apron, where several businessmen disembarked. As Fairey no longer has anything to do with Islanders, it was speculated they were visiting Dan-Air. With over thirty unpainted Islanders being held at Southampton and Dan-Air having spraying facilities, did 2 + 2 = 4? Ultimately, it didn't!

25th   Air Anglia F.27 G-BDDH, arriving at 1031 (AQ7902 from Norwich), was bringing in Norwich City to play Manchester Utd in a division one match, which was won by United 1-0.

25th April 1979 – Making its first visit to Manchester was HZ-RC1, arriving at 1745 from Corfu, ultimately bound for maintenance at Hawarden. It night-stopped, and resumed its objective in the morning, departing at 0929. (Geoff Ball)

26th   Charters on behalf of Laing Construction continue and LOT used IL-18 SP-LSB today, rather than a TU-134, operating from/to Warsaw as LO3783/4.

27th   Today was the third and final visit this year of US-airline Capitol, when Douglas DC-8 N8765 arrived at 1045, making its first visit on a flight from New York.

27th RAF C-130s XV181 (RR4382) & XV300 (RR4383) arriving from Lyneham, night-stopped before departing for Gibraltar the following morning.

29th Boeing 707 9G-ACN, operating KM107 to Malta, made two attempts to depart before officially going tech. Passengers said they'd seen flames coming from the engines and heard banging noises. After spending eight hours at the airport, the passengers were finally taken to the Palace Hotel, Buxton, for an overnight stay while they waited for news.

29th Mount Cook HS.748 ZK-MCF arrived at 1845 for its summer lease to Dan-Air as G-AYYG, before positioning out to Aberdeen on 3rd May.

30th Lufthansa B.727 D-ABKP arrived at 1142 with the West German National football team, for their European Championship qualifier match with Wales at Wrexham on 2nd May.

30th The hulk of Cessna 172 G-BAEO, which crashed at Barton in May last year, has finally been towed to Air Kilroe's hangar for final disposal, after a decision was made not to repair it.

30th Southern International's other Viscount, G-CSZA, made its first visit taking Manchester United down to Southampton for the evening's first division game, which ended 1-1.

30th The runway's strengthening work was progressing well after two months, but according to the ATC watch log, several aircraft reported the ramps or 'navvy boards' being used to protect a recently laid strip of asphalt were 'occasionally a little too steep for landing aircraft'.

May 1979

Amongst the winter destinations being offered by Thomson Holidays this year are Moscow, Reykjavik, & Banjul, Gambia along with Egypt, all available direct from Manchester. Cosmos Holidays will offer twin-centre breaks to Egypt and Israel this winter. Tourists will be flown to Israel for four days and then coached through the Gaza strip, onwards to Cairo.

Air Europe confirmed that from October, they will operate holiday flights from Manchester on behalf of Intasun, who expect to fly 40,000 passengers in the forthcoming winter season.

The following airlines have summer IT programmes from Manchester: Air Malta, Aviaco, Aviogenex, Balkan, Inex-Adria, JAT, LOT, Spantax, Tarom, TAE, TAP & Trans-Europa. As well as a variety of UK operators: Britannia Airways, British Airtours, British Airways, British Island Airways, Dan-Air, Monarch Airlines & Laker Airways. Airlines operating regular flights to the USA/Canada this summer are CP Air (DC-8 & B.747), Laker Airways (DC-10), Ontario World (B.707), TIA (DC-10) & Wardair (B.747 & DC-10).

Equipment changes on the European scheduled services were Air Malta (KM106): Transasian B.707 9G-ACN (6th/13th/20th/27th), Lufthansa (LH074): B.727s D-ABKD (1st), D-ABKI (17th), D-ABKN (18th) & D-ABRI (14th) and Swissair (SR842): DC-9-51 HB-ISU (26th).

RAF ILS traffic identified included Dominie XS711 (4th), C-130s XV184 (29th), XV210 (8th) & XV211 (24th); Hawks XX162 (22nd), XX163 (16th/21st), XX164 (10th), XX165 (22nd), XX172 (25th), XX174 (22nd), XX178 (18th), XX180 (16th), XX183 (16th), XX185 (10th), XX178 (10th), XX241 (10th), XX249 (28th) and Jaguar XZ115 (16th).

1st The airport closed between 1124 and 1422, after a strip of newly laid concrete was torn up by a departing aircraft, possibly BCAL BAC 1-11 G-ASJE (BR988 to Gatwick) and the last to land was HS.125 G-FOUR. The runways new surface, laid overnight as part of the strengthening work, was starting to break up and holes were appearing over large areas. During the closure, two exceptions were made for aircraft to land, for two different reasons. The first, BAC 1-11 G-AVMK (BA5018 from Heathrow), was carrying a passenger rushing to see a dying relative in hospital. The second resulted in BIA making a first visit with one of their newly acquired BAC 1-11s, G-AXOX (UK8216 from Gatwick). It was given special clearance due to Margaret Thatcher being onboard, for a pre-election tour of the region. Once it had landed, the runway was promptly closed again and unfortunately for Mrs Thatcher, the airport was still closed when she was due to return, so arrangements were made for her to fly from Liverpool instead.

1st Cessna 421 N6800C failed to make it this morning, due to heavy snow, when visibility was 400m with sky obscured. It was forced to overshoot and divert to Liverpool, before eventually arriving the following evening from Birmingham.

3rd   Lufthansa B.727 D-ABKF arrived at 1121 to take the West German football team back to Frankfurt, after comfortably beating Wales 2-0. This flight and the inbound on 30th April should have been operated by an Airbus A.300.

3rd   With the runway work in progress, departures particularly by Boeing 747s, were interesting to say the least! Due to their outbound engine pods being so close to the working areas at the edge of the runway, they are rising up great clouds of dust and debris and regularly sending the ramps used to protect them up into the air. Departing aircraft ripping up the newly laid asphalt have caused numerous runway closures for debris clearance and damage repair. A special team is now on standby for B.747 departures and one of those occasions was today's Wardair B.747 C-GXRD direct to Vancouver as WD421, which succeeded in blowing several ramps up and off the runway. In order for repairs to be carried out, the airport was closed from 1657-1801. The Wardair Captain was offered the chance to return after takeoff, but he opted to continue and requested an undercarriage check on arrival at Vancouver. Airline Captains are becoming increasingly cautious about the holes and the ramps coming loose, but even though the problems persisted all month, no delays were caused by it.

3rd   Sabena B.737 OO-SDP burst a tyre on departure, operating SN618 for Brussels. No debris was found on the runway and it carried onto Brussels.

6th   Eagle Air B.720 TF-VLC has been leased to Britannia Airways for the summer season. It arrived on its first visit at 1650 as BY027BF, on a positioning flight from Luton and since then it's spent most of its time at Manchester.

6th   The ATC watch log recorded that the Captain of Britannia Airways flight BY984A (B.737 G-BGNW) bound for Alicante, was at the holding point of Runway 24, when he saw children throwing stones at aircraft from inside the perimeter fence. The police sent to investigate the incident, found a large hole in the fence near the Airport Hotel.

11th   Air Kilroe's new hangar was officially opened today by Sir Matt Busby, even though they've been operating an air taxi service throughout the UK and Europe for several months already.

11th   Europe Air Service operated a series of flights from/to Tarbes with SE.210 Caravelle's. F-BXOO, formerly OO-SRF, was used on the first flight as EY1198/1201 today in basic Sabena colours and the others were F-BYCD EY1200/1 (16th), F-BXOO EY1198/9 and EY1200/1 (21st).

11th   The current company demonstrator, Citation 550 N55CC, arrived at 1206 from Malmo and then flew a return flight to Staverton on demonstration for Apache Air Taxis.

12th   RAF C-130s XV218 (RR4534) & XV210 (RR4535) were both outbound to Gibraltar, operating trooping flights.

14th   Air Kilroe Beagle 206 G-AWRO departed at 1014, initially for Prestwick, but its eventual destination is Fort Lauderdale. It's been sold in the USA and apart from a local test flight on the 26th March, it hadn't flown all year.

16th   French Air Force operated three training flights during the month. Noratlas 161/64-IM arrived at 1009 Evereux- Edinburgh today, Noratlas 199/64-KI at 1220 Lyneham-Edinburgh (29th) and Noratlas 119/64-BS at 1458 Edinburgh-Bournemouth (31st).

18th   Dan-Air BAC 1-11 G-BCWA, (DA2420 Manchester-Alicante), returned shortly after takeoff, when smoke entered the cabin. Fire and ambulance crews were on standby, but following safety checks only a minor fault was found and it eventually departed three hours later.

22nd   Bolkow 105 G-BCRG brought the Chairman of Rolls-Royce in to meet the Chairman of GKN, arriving on Islander G-AXXG. They were celebrating the 75th anniversary of Mr Rolls meeting Mr Royce in the Midland Hotel, Manchester, where they replicated the meeting!

25th   Air travel was greatly affected by the air disaster at Chicago O'Hare Airport, when American Airlines flight 191 from Chicago to Los Angeles crashed during takeoff, killing all 271 onboard and two people on the ground. The DC-10 was at takeoff rotation, when its No. 1 engine separated and flipped over the top of the left wing, causing damage resulting in the retraction of the slats. The left wing automatically stalled, but the right wing continued producing lift and the jet subsequently rolled to the left, reaching a bank angle of over 90° before impacting in an open field, near a trailer park at the end of the runway. It was discovered that the engine separation was due to a damaged pylon rigging structure holding the engine onto the wing. It was also found that the DC-

10 had design specification deficiencies, which made further problems very likely. Two weeks after the accident, the FAA grounded all DC-10s until the problems were rectified and banned them from flying into or within the USA. During this time, the airlines struggled to find replacements for the grounded aircraft. The ban was finally lifted on 13th July, although they were flying elsewhere in the world before this date.

25th RAF Devon WB533, arriving at 1658 (RR7533 from Wyton), night-stopped before its morning departure for Cambridge.

26th The ATC watch log recorded that Ontario World B.707 C-GRYN, departing at 1318 (OW508 to Montreal), burst a tyre, or tyres, at the point of crossing the ramps on the runway. A loud bang was heard by the Tower staff and large chunks of debris were seen on the runway. The Captain was informed immediately, but decided to continue to Montreal.

28th A near miss was reported by both Captains today, when Cessna 336 G-ASKS and British Airways BAC 1-11 G-AVMN (BA5032 from Heathrow), came within unacceptable distances of each other on the 24 final approach. Just for good measure the Captain of the BAC 1-11 complained about the runway's ramping as well!

28th British Airways commenced their summer B.747 transatlantic operations to Montreal and Toronto today, when G-AWNO operated Toronto/Prestwick and the return (BA080/1).

29th Eastern Airways DC-3 G-AMPO arrived at 1959, operating a crew training flight routing Cardiff-East Midlands.

30th The inbound diversion of Trident 3 G-AWZA at 1940 (BA4653 Belfast-Heathrow), was due to heavy thunderstorms on the final approach at Heathrow.

30th Transavia B.737 PH-TVC positioned in from Amsterdam at 1456 to operate Laker Airways flight GK247 to Tenerife, via Santiago. The return, GK248, operated into Liverpool due to the night-time runway closure.

31st First time visitor Sterling B.727 OY-SAU, operated Laker Airways flight GK214 from Heraklion, before positioning out later to Stockholm.

June 1979

Runway work is progressing well and the problems described last month regarding departures appears to be resolved. So far, 80,000 tonnes of asphalt has been laid, usually at a rate of 2,000 tonnes per night weather permitting. At a peak, 250-300 vehicles and pieces of equipment are parked on the runway during the night-time closures. The invasion takes place at 2300, when vehicles gather in large numbers on the Fairey Apron, waiting for clearance to proceed.

The weekly Cyprus Airways Manchester-Larnaca service, operating in conjunction with British Airways which recommenced in April after a five year absence, will become a year round operation.

The decline in freight should be partly halted by next month's commencement of freight services by Northwest Orient, to the USA and onwards to Japan. Operating twice-weekly, using B.747s capable of carrying up to 100 tonnes of freight, both flights will operate inbound from Amsterdam. Wednesday's flight will operate Amsterdam-Manchester-New York-Chicago-Seattle-Tokyo and Sundays flight will route Amsterdam-Manchester-New York-Detroit-Minneapolis.

Laker Airways were major losers from the DC-10 groundings. Their operating patterns were drastically changed when their transatlantic flights were either cancelled or sub-chartered to other operators. The B.707s used on IT flights were needed to maintain Laker's Skytrain flights out of Gatwick, so Manchester's IT flights had to be sub-chartered out. When the grounding order was released, DC-10s started operating IT flights and when DC-10 G-BBSZ departed to Tenerife on the 20th, it was the first DC-10 flight after the grounding. British Airways at Manchester were also affected by cancellations and aircraft downgrades when their B.747s were needed at Heathrow. Laker Airways sub-chartered the following aircraft for their European IT services: Sobelair B.707s OO-SBU (16th/17th) & OO-SBW (2nd/3rd/22nd); Sterling B.727 OY-SBD (5th/6th/7th), BMA DC-9s G-BFIH (8th/9th) & OH-LYB (8th/9th); TAE DC-8 EC-CDC (10th), Trans European B.707 OO-TED (13th) and Aeroamerica B.720 N730T (15th). Transatlantic sub-charters were operated by Aer Lingus B.707 EI-APG (13th) & B.747 EI-ASI (19th/20th) and Evergreen International DC-8s N800EV (25th), N801EV (25th/26th) & N810EV (19th).

Equipment changes on the European scheduled services were Air Malta (KM106): Transasian B.707s 9G-ACN (10th/17th/24th) & 9G-ACO (3rd); Lufthansa (LH074): B.727s D-ABIA (2nd) & D-ABKG (20th) and Swissair (SR842): DC-9-51 HB-ISS (22nd).

The only civil ILS traffic noted was British Island Airways Herald G-AYMG (7th). RAF ILS traffic identified included Hawks XX167 (28th), XX178 (25th), XX181 (27th), XX225 (18th), XX243 (1st), Bulldog XX547 (18th) and Vulcan XH537 (18th).

The Barton Air Show is now an annual event and the cause of a customary invasion of aircraft types rarely seen at Manchester. The military formed the largest proportion of types and a first visit was made by the Jaguar, as even though several have been seen over the years performing ILS approaches, none had actually landed. XX754 went tech with an engine problem after landing at Manchester prior to its display at Barton, so XX766 had to perform a solo display. Because XX754 was unable to return to Lossiemouth as scheduled on the 10th, spares and a maintenance crew came down on Shackleton WL790 on the 11th, which was a different Shackleton to the one arriving on the 10th for the display. Let us not forget these mighty aircraft were manufactured down the road at Woodford and affectionately referred to as 'ten-thousand rivets flying in formation'! The engine problem on XX754 was found to be more serious than first thought, so another Jaguar, XX828, was sent down on the 12th and again on the 14th, bringing in a pilot. The arrival of XX828 was interesting, as it caught up British Airways 1-11 G-AVMP (BA920) on the approach after it was slow to clear, due to the reduced number of exits caused by the runway work. The Jaguar had to overshoot and perform a high 'g' turn round the Tower. Jaguar XX754 finally left on the 14th, as did Jaguar XX828, which departed on a low level training flight to Lossiemouth.

The Red Arrows arrival on Saturday evening is likely to be their last with Gnats, as they are being replaced with Hawks. Their visit was not without incident, as shortly after Red 1-9 had departed to open the Barton display, Red 8 (XR993) lost his complete hydraulics system and returned to Manchester on a full emergency. Fortunately, it landed safely and was towed off the runway. While the Red Arrows were performing, resident Cessna 172 G-AZTS hit one of the runways edge lights, which left shattered glass on the side of the runway. When the Red Arrows reappeared, they decided to put on a mini-display and a BIA Herald being held on the runway after landing, had four Red Arrows with their trailing smoke passing either side of him! When they broke for landing, Red 3 (XR977) touched down on the left side of the edge of Runway 24, hit the broken glass and then shot off onto the fantail, sustaining minor damage. The incident forced the closure of the airport for an hour, during which time B-17 G-BEDF and a Vulcan from the air show were due in, but they were diverted away. Solo Jaguar XX766 had to depart from the northern edge of the runway, but as Shackleton WR963 had his departure to Barton delayed, the shows programme had to be reorganised. The two broken Gnats, XR993 & XR977, left for Kemble on the 12th in a cloud of smoke. Firefly WB271 requested to 'beat the field' up on its departure to Yeovilton on the 11th, but he was turned down by ATC. RAF C-130 XV177 was providing support on the 9th for the Red Arrows and C-130 XV290 was the support for the Falcons parachute team. For the record the aircraft involved with the Barton Air Show, on a very balmy weekend are as follows:

9th

1612/1428	XX766 Jaguar (ANO 17), Brize Norton/Barton, dep. 10th.
1613/1107	XX754 Jaguar (ANO 28/LGM143), Brize Norton/Lossiemouth, dep. 14th.
1824/1357	Gnat x 10 (Red Arrows), Binbrook/Barton, dep. 10th.
1836/1806	XV177 C-130 (RR5883), Binbrook/Manston, dep.10th (Red Arrows support).

10th

1102/1522	WR963 Shackleton (LTG66), Lossiemouth/Barton.
1232/1056	G-BESP Islander (Rothmans), Isle of Man/Lydd, dep. 11th.
1232/1634	Pitts x 5 (Rothmans), Isle of Man/Barton.
1314/1608	G-AWPH Provost, Reading/Barton.
1407/1132	XR993 Gnat (Red 8), Manchester/Kemble, dep. 12th (Full Emergency).
1420/1606	Gnat x 8 (Red Arrows), Barton/Manston.
1510/1625	G-BDFT Varsity, Leicester/Barton.
1519/1706	XX766 Jaguar (ANO 28), Barton/Lossiemouth.

1554/1041   WB271 Firefly, Barton/Yeovilton, dep. 11th.
1630/1839   G-AWPH Provost, Barton/Reading. .
1646/1659   G-BDFT Varsity, Barton/Leicester.
1705/1056   Pitts x 3, (Barton)/Lydd, dep. 11th (the other two dep. at 1410).
1717/1903   XV290 C-130 (RR5808), Manston/Brize Norton.
*Red 3 (XR977)   Dep. 1231 on 12th

1st   PA-44 Seminole PH-SYB, arriving at 0852 from/to Amsterdam, was a first visit of type.

2nd   Air France SE.210 F-BHRP made its last visit to Manchester, operating AF962/1. It was withdrawn in November and broken up the following year.

2nd   RAF VC-10 XV109 arriving at 1020 (RR2281 Brize Norton-Brussels), was operating an outbound trooping flight. The return flight on the 16th was operated by VC-10 XV107, arriving at 2029 as RR2287.

3rd   Early morning fog affecting Stansted, Luton & Birmingham produced the only visit of Swedish airline Linjeflyg. They diverted in two Fokker F.28s, originally bound for Stansted: SE-DGG at 1123 (LF089 from Stockholm) and SE-DGK at 1227 (LF063 from Stockholm). Also diverting from Stansted was Maersk Air B.720 OY-APY at 1056 (DM225 from Stockholm).

4th   The second Skyvan to visit this year was Shorts G-BGRY, arriving at 1143 in an all-white colour scheme. It stayed for just over an hour and was parked on the Freight Apron while the crew visited the CAA's Airworthiness division, based at the airport.

4th   First visit Aravco HS.125 G-BSAA arrived at 0802 from Stuttgart to clear customs. It departed at 0938 for Hawarden, returned at 1800 and departed again for Stuttgart at 1848.

4th June 1979 - Not a rare visitor, but the colour scheme was a little different! British Airtours B.707 G-APFD operated today's KT993/2 from/to Corfu. It's seen here having recently returned off lease from Air Mauritius, still in their basic colours. (Geoff Ball)

5th   The Fire Brigade was called to attend British Airways BAC 1-11 G-BBME, after a fire started inside the cabin as it was being prepared for departure to Paris (BA902). The problem was found to be a faulty radar box, which delayed its departure by more than two hours.

6th   RAE BAC 1-11 XX105, arriving at 1305 (Nugget 92 from Bedford) for attention at Dan-Air Engineering, was present until the 26th. Also today was RAE Andover XW750, arriving at 1519 (Nugget 93 from Bedford), acting as a crew ferry.

8th   Dan-Air Comet G-BDIV arrived at 1459 (DA2190 Gatwick-Faro) to pick up a number of Manchester passengers. It called again on the 24th, positioning up from Gatwick to operate DA4440 to Palma, but as the return flight was running too late to beat Manchester's curfew, it went to Liverpool instead. Unfortunately, these visits are all too rare nowadays, as probably for the first time since the 1960's, there are no Comet flights scheduled to operate from Manchester. The few still remaining in service are centred on Gatwick, although one is based at Edinburgh. An ATC conversation between a Comet heading south out of Edinburgh and Dan-Air ops at Gatwick, confirmed that 'Manchester was no longer a Comet base'.

8th BAE Dove G-ARHW operated daily until the 15th, in connection with the Paris Air Show.

9th Beech 76 G-BGHP was a first visit of type today, arriving from/to Barton.

10th Team Rothmans made a first visit with their five Pitts Specials, in connection with the Barton Air Show, with their Islander acting as a support aircraft. Their departure to Barton involved copious quantities of smoke and flick rolls, just after becoming airborne. They returned after their performance and departed the following day to Lydd.

11th Another new service began today, when Euroair started a six-times weekly newspaper flight from/to Luton (EZ581/2). The two Islanders currently being used are red/white G-BDWG and blue/white G-AWVY, which was formerly based at Liverpool. The flights are handled by NEA and they operated until 11th October.

12th Aeroamerica Boeing 720 N730T, arriving from Dubrovnik at 1828 today, operated BY423A/B to/from Palma the following day on behalf of Britannia Airways. It made six visits during the year, operating for Britannia, Laker Airways & Air Malta and was withdrawn from service in March 1982.

15th Today was the 30th anniversary of operations by Sabena from Ringway. They pioneered routes across the Atlantic from Manchester as far back as 1953 and started operations from Manchester on 15th June 1949 to Brussels, with Douglas DC-3s. They saw the possibilities of operating a route from the North of England to New York and did so for the first time on 28th October 1953, at a time when BOAC seemed less enthusiastic to put Manchester on the map! Later, the route was upgraded from Douglas DC-6s to DC-7s and then Boeing 707s, by which time BOAC was competing on the route. Originally, Sabena were given passenger rights at Manchester in exchange for BOAC being given access rights to the Congo, but Sabena's Manchester-New York rights were eventually withdrawn in March 1964, leaving the route clear for BOAC. Sabena were then confined to operating freight and passenger services between Brussels and Manchester, with a passenger service to Rotterdam being offered for a time during the summer months.

June 1979 – Two shots of two very different Sobelair Boeing 707s. OO-SBW (left) is shown having just positioned in from Brussels on 2nd June to operate GK225 to Palma. It also made numerous visits from 2nd-22nd June. It was sold in Zaire in 1985, withdrawn in 1988 and broken up by 1990. OO-SBU (right), seen in basic Air Algerie colours also positioned in to operate GK225, this time on the 16th June. This aircraft had previously visited Manchester in 1976 as N370WA with Korean Airlines Cargo and eventually saw service in the USAF. (Geoff Ball)

17th Pan American B.707s N408PA arriving at 1149 and N433PA at 1024, were both outbound Trans International sub-charters to New York.

17th RAF Pumas, XW231 & XW237, called in at 1216, en route from Leek to Odiham.

17th After much speculation, the South Side received a new and unusual resident in the form of vintage Harvard G-BDAM. Painted in Norwegian Air Force markings, it only carries its civil registration under the wing. The aircraft's pedigree reveals it's served with the Royal Air Force and its first trip as a Manchester resident was to the Greenham Common Air Show on the 22nd, before returning on the 25th. It has the same owner as Chipmunk G-BFAW, which was recently sold.

17th   The inbound diversion of Viscount G-AOHV, (BA5639 Inverness-Heathrow), was a full emergency due to smoke in the cockpit.

18th June 1979 – HZ-PCA was the 30th different Gulfstream 2 to visit Manchester. It's seen here on a hot afternoon from Jeddah/Corfu, on a fuel stop bound for Washington. It was carrying the badge of the 'Saudi Presidency of Civil Aviation' next to the door. (Geoff Ball)

19th   Due to the ongoing grounding of the Douglas DC-10, a transatlantic rescue has been underway, returning 1,400 delayed passengers to Manchester. Over the last week, Laker passengers destined for Manchester from Toronto and New York have returned to the UK via Heathrow, courtesy of Air Canada and TWA respectively. Today, Aer Lingus B.747 EI-ASI positioned in from Dublin to operate outbound GK093 to Toronto, before returning the following day as GK094. Also today, Evergreen DC-8 N810EV operated a Laker flight from/to New York.

19th June 1979 – Evergreen International made five visits to Manchester this year, all in June and with three different DC-8 aircraft; N800EV, N801EV & N810EV. These flights were covering for Laker Airways following the grounding of their Douglas DC-10's and N810EV is seen here operating an inbound flight from New York. (Geoff Ball)

20th   British Airways Helicopters Sikorsky S-61 G-ASNL called in for fuel, en route from Penzance to Aberdeen.

24th The final visit of a Pan American Boeing 707 took place today when N497PA operated a Trans International flight from New York at 0955, before positioning out to Dublin. The airline operated many transatlantic flights through Manchester, as well as making numerous appearances on diversion since their first aircraft, N758PA, arrived as 'Clipper 058' from Chicago as a Heathrow diversion on 25th January 1963.

24th Geminair Boeing 707 9G-ACK arrived at 1606, operating Britannia Airways flight BY977B from Mahon, before departing as BY077A to Munich.

25th Passengers were hit by major delays over the weekend and one flight was delayed over thirty-one hours! Some passengers were sent home and others spent an uncomfortable night on the airport's chairs! Around twenty-four inbound flights were delayed, some by as much as seventeen hours and twelve inbound due to land at Manchester, had to divert to Liverpool to avoid being stuck at Manchester due to the night-time curfew. The delays started on the 22nd, when British ATC staged a 24-hour stoppage. Flights were already running late due to the go-slow action by French and Spanish ATC, which extended the delays further!

25th Another new type to visit Manchester was the Brazilian EMB-121 Xingu. Newly registered G-BGIE, operated by CSE Aviation, undertook a demonstration flight for Air Kilroe.

25th Royal Saudi AF C-130H 1619 arrived at 1304 from Greenham Common, after taking part in a static collection of various Air Force C-130s, marking the Silver Jubilee of the Lockheed C-130 Hercules. A day-glo kangaroo was noted displayed near the crew door.

28th Clyden Airways DC-3 operation, which hadn't operated since February, finally started again when the Irish postal strike ended and the first flight was by EI-BDT today.

29th Passengers arriving at the airport to catch Laker flight GK243 to Corfu were told to return in the evening. It was normally operated by a Boeing 707, but it had been flown to Gatwick to operate a transatlantic flight, due to the continuing ban on DC-10s operating into the USA. The flight to Corfu could have been switched to the DC-10, but as Corfu was unable to accept them, the flight was delayed and then operated twice by the same BAC 1-11. After completing the first round trip, it returned to Corfu for the remaining passengers.

30th Long standing resident, NEA Islander G-AXXH, is due to be sold. Its titles have been removed and it's believed to be going to Lands End.

July 1979

Despite the current night-time runway closures, the airport recorded its highest ever passenger numbers. In June, 410,433 passed through, compared to 375,912 last June, an increase of 38% in IT/Charter flights alone.

The airport announced that Transasian Airways plan to operate charter flights to various European & US destinations next April, although they are likely to be operating under a different name by then. They considered Luton as their UK base, but chose Manchester after recognising its greater potential. They intend basing at least three Boeing 707s, operating a minimum of twenty-two flights per week. Included in their programme is a weekly flight to Miami, starting at £225 for a two week half-board holiday.

The revised date for British Airways to commence their Manchester-London shuttle service is now Sunday 28th October.

Tarom announced next year's summer programme from Manchester to Constanta. They intend operating two flights on Saturday mornings, four on Sundays (two in the morning and two in the evening) and one TU-154 flight on a Thursday. They are also planning a weekly ski charter to Bucharest from 23rd December with BAC 1-11s.

Northwest Orient deferred the start of their twice weekly cargo service to New York because of aircraft problems. It will now start in September and may increase to four-times weekly by the end of the year.

Equipment changes on the European scheduled services were Air Malta (KM106): Transasian B.707s G-TJAC (15th/29th) & 9G-ACN (1st/8th); KLM (KL155): NLM F.28 PH-CHB (18th/19th/30th), Lufthansa (LH074): B.727 D-ABFI (8th/21st), Condor D-ABIN (26th), D-ABLI (1st), D-ABKE (15th) & D-ABKM (14th); SAS (SAS539): DC-9-21 OY-KGF (21st) and Swissair (SR842): DC-9-51s HB-ISM (14th), HB-ISN (21st), HB-ISS (20th) & HB-ISU (23rd),

Civil ILS traffic noted were Bahamasair HS.748 C6-BED (3rd) & British Midland Viscount G-AZLT (10th). Military ILS traffic identified included Army Air Corps Beaver XV271 (2nd), RAF Hawks XX163 (12th), XX237 (3rd/12th), XX243 (3rd); RAF C-130s XV204 (4th), XV299 (6th), XV301 (10th) & XV306 (19th) and RAF Jetstream XX495 (20th).

2nd   Boeing 720 9H-AAL diverted into Manchester at 1733 (KM738 Malta-Glasgow), due to a hydraulic system warning light.

3rd   Amongst a mix of C-130s and Hawks performing ILS approaches this month, was Bahamasair HS.748 C6-BED, making two practice ILS approaches around 1125 today.

3rd   Laker continued sub-chartering aircraft this month. British Caledonian B.707 G-ATZC was utilised from/to New York today, operating as GK038X/037.

3rd   First-time visitor Balkan IL-18 LZ-BEO, arriving at 0759 (LZ1525 from Sofia), was transporting in a choir for a regional engagement. They returned to Bulgaria several days later from Gatwick.

4th   Islander G-AXXH operated its last flight for NEA, before carrying out numerous crew training flights for its new owners. It finally left for Lands End on the 13th.

5th   French Air Force Noratlas 181/64-KT arrived at 1513 from Evereux, bringing in French schoolchildren for an exchange visit. Noratlas 67/F-RBKA operated the return on the 18th.

6th   JAT used Boeing 727 YU-AKE on today's IT flights, JU206/219 & JU218/207, due to their Boeing 707s covering for banned DC-10 flights. B.727 YU-AKF was used the following week, but thereafter they reverted back to B.707 operations.

6th   Cessna 310 G-ATCR arrived by road from Liverpool today, for a complete rebuild by Air Kilroe and was still present by the end of the year.

8th   Beech 80 G-BDKG, which crash landed at Manchester on 15th December 1977 when its undercarriage collapsed, gave a repeat performance this time crash landing at Karachi! Previously owned by Vernair, it's now privately owned by an American individual, based in the Middle East.

12th   Having been mostly elusive to Manchester over several years, four RAF Bulldogs: XX545, XX616, XX622 & XX624, arrived at 1111 from Woodvale after the pilots were invited by one of the controllers to visit the CAA's air traffic control facilities. Another batch of four Bulldogs: XX545, XX620, XX621 & XX624, arrived on the 30th for the same reason.

13th   Falcon N1JN, arriving at 1450 to clear customs en route to Blackpool, was carrying golfer Jack Nicklaus and his party for the Open Golf Championship at Lytham St. Anne's.

13th   Transasian B.707 G-TJAA operated KM780/1, in full British Caledonian colours.

15th   Royal Saudi Air Force operated a rare C-130E flight when 453 routed Gander-Jeddah as RSF 818, before its departure on the 18th. The more regular variant these days is the C-130H.

19th   A 6,000 volt cable, cut by an excavator during the runway strengthening work, left several farms, hangars and the airport's flight catering centre blacked out for seven hours.

19th   KLM used NLM Fokker F.28 PH-CHB today, on the first of three flights during the month, all operating the lunchtime KLM155/6.

20th   First visit HS.125 G-BGGS operated by BAE, arrived at 0907 from Hatfield for customs clearance, prior to operating a return flight to Dublin. HS.125 9Q-CHD also called in at 1509 for customs clearance, after maintenance at Hawarden.

20th   Europe Air Service operated two further flights from/to Tarbes this month. SE.210 Caravelle F-BXOO operated as EY158/237 today and EY1234/5 on the 26th.

25th   Kar-Air DC-8 OH-KDM arrived at 1127 (KR3281 from Helsinki), with a party of schoolchildren.

25th   TAE DC-8 EC-EDC made its second visit to Manchester (GK248/7 from/to Tenerife), operating on behalf of Laker Airways.

25th   Private BAC 1-11 HZ-AMK arrived at 1621 from Luton for fitting out and modification with Dan-Air, cheekily for a more luxurious interior!

26th   Lufthansa used Condor 'short' B.727 D-ABIN on the evening LH074/5, which was the airlines first visit since September 1977.

27th   Finnair SE.210 OH-LSH, arriving at 1852 (KR3455 from Helsinki), was bringing in a party of delegates for a religious festival in Aberystwyth. The return flight took place on 11th August with SE.210 OH-LSD (KR3458).

27th   Mitsubishi MU-2 N325MA arrived at 1602 to clear customs, after crossing the Atlantic via the Faroe Islands. Based in Jacksonville, Florida, it was bound for Blackpool.

30th   TMA B.707 OD-AGN, arriving at 1702 from Heathrow, was transporting a cargo consignment ultimately bound for Jakarta, Indonesia.

August 1979

Finnair will increase their freight flight to three-times weekly from November. Iberia has applied to operate from Manchester again, with a four-times-weekly service to Madrid/Malaga next year. LOT will be adding Manchester to its scheduled network next year, with flights to Warsaw possibly operating twice-weekly.

Equipment changes on the European scheduled services were Air Malta (KM106): Transasian B.707s G-TJAB (5th/12th), G-TJAC (19th/26th) & Aeroamerica B.720 N730T (16th); Cyprus Airways (CY358): Kar-Air DC-8 OH-KDM (25th), KLM (KL155): NLM F.28 PH-CHB (2nd), Lufthansa (LH074): B.727s D-ABDI (3rd), D-ABFI (28th), D-ABKD (4th), D-ABKI (8th), D-ABKM (12th) & first visit D-ABKT (18th) and Swissair (SR842): DC-9-51 HB-ISO (19th).

Military ILS traffic identified included various RAF types: Hawks XX176 (2nd), XX237 (3rd/12th), XX243 (3rd); C-130s XV183 (17th), XV207 (1st), XV217 (6th), XV218 (17th), XV220 (20th), XV296 (3rd) and Dominie XS726 (15th).

2nd   Portuguese Air Force made their first visit to Manchester, on a grey and overcast day, when C-130 6803 arrived at 1145 to collect a consignment of guard dogs.

2nd   On the approach frequency at the same time as Portuguese C-130, was French Air Force Noratlas 148/64-BK as FM9920, on a training flight from Villacoublay to Moret.

3rd   Amongst a reasonably steady flow of ILS visitors throughout the month, was an unidentified RAF Jaguar, overshooting at 1107 as 'BUN32'.

3rd   Automobile Association Cessna 421 G-BBUJ, arriving from Auxerre, was carrying a number of passengers who'd been taken ill on holiday.

6th   Royal Saudi Air Force C-130H 1615 paid its first visit, routing Jeddah-Gander as RSF914. It was the last of their standard batch of Hercules C-130Hs to Manchester, apart from their tankers, which have yet to visit. It was also the month that saw the arrival of the 200th Saudi Air Force C-130 flight through Manchester, since the first on the 9th June 1972.

6th   A couple of French-bound light aircraft from Prestwick arrived to night-stop. 1971-vintage Beech 60 Duke N3984 landed at 2006 and PA-31 Navajo F-BRAS at 2023. They departed for St. Brieuc and Dinard respectively, the following day.

7th   Boeing 707 N473RN arrived at 2207 for storage. Operating until recently with Iran Air Cargo, it's in their basic colours, but with no titles. Owned by leasing company Atasco, it's expected to stay at Manchester for at least thirty days. Currently parked on the eastern end of the South Bay, the engines are regularly run by Dan-Air and its parking fees are paid by Pelican Cargo. Apparently, it's eventually bound for another Middle Eastern customer.

10th   Air Atlantique DC-6 G-SIXB was making it first visit, arriving at 1629 to operate the Air Bridge Carriers cattle freight flight to Milan. The new airline, in existence since 1977, operates charter flights with DC-3s and their sole DC-6, G-SIXB, which is ex-Greelandair. The airline purchased another DC-6, G-SIXA, later in the year.

10th   Citation 550 G-BFLY arrived at 1232 today from Reykjavik, on delivery to Northair Aviation, Leeds. It attempted to depart for Nice the following day, but returned with a technical problem, before leaving an hour later. It returned again on the 21st and remained inside the South Side hangars until its departure on the 25th. It was sold later in the year as HB-VGR.

13th   Air traffic controllers were clearing the backlog today, after one of the worst weekends of delays this year. Continuing action by Spanish controllers caused massive holdups for more than a thousand passengers over the two days. On Sunday alone, almost a hundred flights were hit by delays of around nine hours.

14th Worthy of mention was the arrival of Rockwell 690 G-BFGB, owned by the British Airport Authority. As Manchester is a council-run airport, there would normally be no need for this aircraft to visit, but its appearance was in connection with a group of BAA senior managers assessing the ongoing runway works.

14th There were no less than four LOT TU-134 charter flights from/to Warsaw during the day: SP-LHB LO4387/8 & LO4389/90, SP-LHE LO4385/6 and SP-LHG LO4391/2.

15th The ATC watch log recorded that a member of the public from the Northwich area called to report he'd seen an object falling from an aircraft. It was thought to be from departing Laker Airways B.707 G-BFBZ, (GK247 to Tenerife) and following an ATC conversation with operations at Gatwick, the aircraft rerouted there for an inspection.

17th US Army Beech C-12 77-22944, arrived at 1222 operating from/to Coleman Barracks, Germany and again on the 27th. The C-12 is the military equivalent of the Beech 200.

18th A second Aeroamerica B.720, N731T, made its one and only visit today operating extra Air Malta flight KM206/7. The airline established an overseas base in Berlin from 1974 to 1979, but ceased trading in 1982.

21st Cessna 172 N5342R, currently based in Switzerland, arrived at 1104 before departing for Luton on the 24th.

21st NEA's new Cessna 421, N2654X, arrived at 1833 from Keflavik. It's the direct replacement for Islander G-AXXH and although it performed a local flight the following day, it still hadn't moved by the end of the month. Reportedly, they have also ordered a Lear Jet, due for delivery in October. Harvard G-BDAM also remained firmly on the ground throughout the month, located at the back of the South Side hangars.

24th Inex-Adria DC-9 YU-AJP (JP563 to Pula) returned to Manchester nine minutes after departure, declaring a full emergency with an unsecure door.

25th August 1979 – Having made its first visit to Manchester in 1978, Kar-Air Douglas DC-8-51 OH-KDM was on a short-term lease to Cyprus Airways, due to the loss of Boeing 707 5B-DAM in a landing accident. It's seen here operating CY358/9 from/to Larnaca. (Geoff Ball)

28th First time visitor HS.125 G-EFPT arrived at 0725 from Heathrow, to operate a return flight to Geneva.

28th Air France SE.210 F-BHRM made its last visit to Manchester today, operating AF962/1. It was withdrawn in October 1979 and later preserved at Lyon.

31st Cardiff-based Beech 90 N60253 arrived at 0910 to operate an outbound flight to Munich.

September 1979

Although the Airport Committee has agreed to the 800ft extension of Runway 06/24, it's now subject to a public enquiry, which will look into the planning application for the extension and the compulsory purchase order of any land.

Tour operator Ellerman Sunflight, will be offering something different for the coming winter season. Due to rising prices and all the flight delays this summer, they have dropped mainland Spain for the winter and will introduce new direct flights to places such as Barbados and Miami, at very competitive prices.

British Airways have identified twenty-six domestic routes as chronically unprofitable, after making losses for some time and showing no sign of improvement in the foreseeable future. Co-incidentally they are operated by Viscounts and amongst them is Manchester to Jersey, Guernsey & Isle of Man. The scope of the cuts will be decided next month and if implemented in full would result in the closure of BA stations at Southampton, Cardiff, Leeds, Isle of Man & Guernsey. The withdrawal of all twenty-six routes would enable the airline to sell fifteen of their twenty Viscounts.

Equipment changes on the European scheduled services were Air Malta (KM106): Transasian B.707s G-TJAB (2nd/23rd) & G-TJAC (30th) and KLM (KL155): NLM F.28 PH-CHF first visit (27th).

Civil ILS traffic noted was HS.125 G-AYER (17th). Military ILS traffic identified included RAF Hawk XX170 (20th), RAF C-130s XV189 (10th), XV306 (18th), XV307 (7th) and RAF Jetstream XX497 (1st).

2nd   British Airways SVC-10 G-ASGG made its last visit today, (BA184 from New York/Prestwick), before positioning to Heathrow. Its last service was Amsterdam-Heathrow on 27th October, but it was reactivated and operated from 27th November 1979 - 26th September 1980, when it made another final service from Gutersloh-Heathrow.

3rd   Ferranti HS.125 G-AXDM is likely to be a regular visitor to Manchester. It arrived today at 1352 from Edinburgh, where it's now based.

3rd   Ontario World's summer programme came to a premature end today, due to the firemen's strike, when the last Toronto flight was operated by Boeing 707 C-GRYN. It was also their final visit as the airline didn't return in 1980 and it subsequently folded later that year.

5th   Royal Navy Wessex XT448 arrived at 1717 on a fuel stop, en route Plymouth-Woodvale.

5th   HS.125 EI-BGW, formerly G-BDYE, is the first of its type on the Irish register. The aircraft arrived from Dublin this evening on its only visit and night-stopped, before departing at 1045 for Cranfield the following morning.

5th September 1979 – The arrival of the very smart Douglas DC-3 HZ-TA3 was observed by the writer at 1345 on its descent into Manchester, en route from Houston to Riyadh. The aircraft, with its full VIP interior, appeared due to a shortage of the appropriate fuel at Prestwick. Purchased by a Saudi Sheik, it's seen here on delivery to Saudi Arabia. (Geoff Ball)

7th   The airport's firemen caused another total shutdown of Manchester operations, when the airport closed from 1200. It reopened an hour later, but closed again after Laker Airways BAC 1-11 G-AVBW landed at 1502 (GK212). The walkout, involving thirty-four fire officers from a ninety-strong brigade, was over pay differentials. They wanted written guarantees that the differential between themselves and ordinary firemen wouldn't drop below 12½%, from its current rate of 14%. After the management said they couldn't give the guarantee, the airport was closed again as it was unable to meet the fire cover regulations required by the operational licence. Aircraft used Liverpool Airport for the rest the day, which was quickly snowed-under with Manchester flights and passengers. After running short on fuel, several aircraft positioned back to Manchester to refuel, which is allowed under the rules, as long as there are no passengers onboard.

7th   This month's highlight to not actually land, was vintage bi-plane Beech 17 Staggerwing NC9885H, making two very low passes today, en route to Barton.

10th   Talks began with the firemen's union today, in a bid to end the dispute which was costing the airport up to £120,000 a day in lost revenue.

12th   The to-and-fro operations between Manchester and Liverpool were in full swing, with passengers being shuttled around by coach. Other airports, such as Birmingham, East Midlands, Blackpool, Leeds and even Gatwick, were all accommodating Manchester's diverted flights.

12th   Today saw the inaugural service of Northwest Orient's twice-weekly freight operation, when B.747 N616US operated the first flight as 'Northwest 923'. Although the firemen's strikes limited the use of passenger carrying aircraft, it didn't affect cargo flights, but even so the amount of freight carried was fairly low on the first few flights, as firms assumed the airfield was closed.

13th   Following the rejection of a pay offer by the union and striking firemen, the dispute became increasingly bitter, with both sides firmly entrenched in their positions.

13th   French Air Force Noratlas 179/64-BP, arriving at 1141, was operating another crew training flight (FM0402 Edinburgh-Lyneham).

16th   Cessna 150 Aerobat G-BCDY took full advantage of the lull in airport proceedings and was observed performing aerobatics during the afternoon!

17th   Whilst it was quiet, HS.125 G-AYER performed an ILS approach, en route from Heathrow to Blackpool.

19th   Fluor Corporation Boeing 727 N4002M arrived at 1312 from Luton, before departing to Bangor-Maine on the 21st.

20th   Dan-Air HS.748 G-AYYG arrived at 1625 (DA99'YG from Aberdeen) for pre-lease return maintenance, before departing back to Mount Cook on the 24th.

20th   With the firemen's dispute in its fourteenth day, a thousand manual workers employed at the airport realised their jobs would be under threat if the action continued and called a meeting urging the firemen to go to arbitration. They said they would, but only after the airport withdrew their threat of disciplinary action.

22nd   Operations finally resumed at 1121, with the arrival of Aviogenex TU-134 YU-AJV (JJ105 from Pula), but it was several days before the airport returned to normal. During the period of the closure, Liverpool was regularly breaking records by frequently handling flights carrying 450 passengers or more. Overall they handled forty wide-bodied aircraft in sixteen days and Birmingham alone took 73,000 passengers during this time.

23rd   Eagle Air B.720 TF VLB arrived in full colours, (BY230B from Malaga). It was covering for regular TF-VLC, which reappeared on the 30th.

23rd   The arrival of Cessna Citation 550 G-BMCL at 1823 was the first of two first visits of type this month. The second was N108WG (Birmingham-Luton) at 1246 on the 26th

26th   Spantax BX759/62 from/to Palma, normally operated by a Douglas DC-8, was operated by two Convair CV-990s today: EC-BJC (BX759B/762A) & EC-BZO (BX759A/762B).

27th   KLM Sikorsky SK-61s PH-NZD & PH-NZK are on charter to Irish Helicopters, assisting with the transportation of Pope John Paul II and his entourage to Ireland. They called in at 1025 on a fuel stop from Amsterdam to Dublin.

27th   RAF C-130 XV301, arriving at 1436 (RR3431 from Hanover), was on a trooping flight. Another military movement was Devon WB534 at 1321 as (RR7698 Wyton-Cranwell), making its last visit to Manchester, even though it operated with the RAF until 1984.

30th   Cessna 210 G-BGVX flew past the Tower prior to landing, after flying direct from Gander as part of a record breaking attempt.

October 1979

Last month was dominated by the fire officer's dispute, which closed the airport for fifteen days. The loss of revenue by the airport, British Airways and Servisair was nearly £1.7m. In addition, the airlines also faced the increasing costs of transporting passengers by road to other airports, after the demand for coaches' outstripped supply and prices rocketed. While the full cost may never be known, it's guaranteed to be recouped by higher package holidays prices and airline tickets next year. In the meantime, although the airport was operating normally again, arbitration to settle the dispute between fire officers and management continued.

If September had been trouble free, the monthly figures would have shown an increase of 13% in passengers and 33% in movements compared to last year. Freight figures showed a decrease of 41%, mainly due to the night-time closures. This meant the dispute had wiped out the years growth on passengers, as the figures to end of September were virtually identical to those for the same period last year.

Air UK was formed this month after the amalgamation of British Island Airways, Air Anglia & Air West.

Austrian Airlines announced a new service between Manchester and Vienna will commence next March, operating three-times weekly with Douglas DC-9 aircraft. British Airways confirmed the Manchester-Isle of Man and Manchester-Guernsey routes will terminate at the end of March next year.

Equipment changes on the European scheduled services were Air Malta (KM106): Transasian B.707s G-TJAA (28th) & G-TJAC (7th/21st); Finnair (AY032): DC-9F OH-LYI (31st), KLM (KL155): NLM F.28 PH-CHD (11th) and Lufthansa (LH074): B.727s D-ABKP (5th) & D-ABKC (12th).

Civil ILS traffic noted were BAe HS.748 G-BGJV (9th/12th/16th), HS.125 HZ-RC1 (18th) & Dove G-ARHW (29th). Military ILS traffic identified included Hawk XX179 (1st), C-130s XV193 (19th) & XV207 (3rd/22nd); Jetstreams XX493 (4th/12th) & XX497 (12th); RAF Nimrod XV241 (9th) and RAF Dominie XS710 (10th). British Midland DC-9 OH-LYB (9th) was operating a crew training flight from/to Liverpool.

1st Private HZ-AMK arrived at 1629 from Heathrow for further modification work at Dan-Air Engineering, before departing on the 4th.

2nd KLM Helicopters Sikorsky S-61s PH-NZD & PH-NZK called in again for fuel, whilst returning to Amsterdam after the Papal visit to Ireland.

2nd Two biz-jets made their first visits today. Gulfstream 2 N400J, arriving at 2059, night-stopped en route Gander-Le Bourget and Lear Jet 35 F-GBMB arrived at 1829 from/to Le Bourget, before departing on the 4th.

2nd British Airways (BE978/9) and Lufthansa (LH076/7) operated a daily service between Manchester and Hanover until the 11th, in connection with the Hanover Trade Fair.

3rd HS.125-700 HB-VGG, owned by Bosch, arrived at 1259 on a first visit operating a liaison flight for BAE. Their other aircraft, HS.125 HB-VBZ, which has been a regular visitor to Manchester over many years, is now likely to be sold. Another first visit HS.125 was G-AYIZ, arriving from Heathrow at 0815 to operate a return flight to Glasgow. This particular aircraft has been twice before in different guises as PJ-SLB & F-BSSL.

3rd Dan-Air's latest acquisition, Arkia BAC 1-11 4X-BAR, arrived at 1740 on a miserable Wednesday afternoon and went straight into the hangar. It was rolled out on the 10th, still in basic Arkia colours, but with new Dan-Air tail colours and titles. A test flight took place on the 11th and it was delivered to Gatwick the following day.

3rd British Airtours B.707 G-APFL made its last visit today, arriving at 1639 (KT991 from Corfu), before departing at 1837 (KT582 to Gerona). It was sold early in 1980 as 9Q-CRW.

5th PA-23 Aztec G-FOTO night-stopped while its owner lectured in Manchester. This particular aircraft is kitted out with sophisticated air-to-air photograph capability, including video cameras and remote controls.

5th The weekly cattle flights were operated exclusively by Invicta International's two Britannia's this month: G-ANCF (5th/10th/18th/26th/31st) and G-AOVF (15th/23rd). The crews of these flights tend to leave the freight doors open until the last possible moment prior to departure, due to the overpowering smell!

6th Since British Caledonian commenced operations in April 1978; their weekly Houston freight service has been erratic to say the least! It last operated on 14th June, but restarted today and now operates to Houston via Atlanta.

6th Dan-Air operated three Comet flights through Manchester this month, utilising G-BDIT for the first two, which flew from/to Gatwick as DA8338/9 today and again on the 17th (DA2193

Athens-Gatwick). Even though it continued operating up until November 1980, when it was withdrawn, the 17th was its last visit.

7th   Martinair DC-10 PH-MBT arrived at 0222, to operate a return flight to Palma on behalf of Laker Airways (GK227/8), whose B.707 had gone tech. During last month's firemen's strike another Martinair DC-10, PH-MBN, operated through Liverpool, also on behalf of Laker.

7th   Martinair Cessna 402 PH-MAZ arrived at 1320, ferrying a fresh crew to return DC-10 PH-MBT back to Amsterdam, as the original crew bringing in the DC-10 in from Palma had 'gone out of hours'.

7th   British Caledonian Boeing 707F G-BDEA was making its last visit to Manchester today, operating BR567 to Bangor/Atlanta. It operated for the airline for another three years, before being withdrawn in October 1982 and eventually sold.

10th   The first British Airways B.707 to visit so far this year was G-AYLT, arriving at 0910 as a Heathrow diversion (BA266 from Bermuda).

10th   Belgian Air Force HS.748 CS-01 arrived at 1012 to night-stop, from/to Brussels.

11th   The approaching winter season meant only one thing - the return of diversions to Manchester! The day saw ten wide-bodied aircraft, which is equal to the current record set on 16th December 1975. Pan American diverted into Manchester for the first time since August 1976, when B.747 N751PA arrived on a first visit at 1036 (PA106 from Washington), another first visit was Lufthansa Airbus A300 D-AIAA at 0951 (LH050 from Dusseldorf). Also worth noting were Air India B.747 VT-EDU at 1001 (AI106 from New York), the second visit of the year of Air New Zealand with first time visitor DC-10 ZK-NZM at 0931 (BA074 from Montreal) and LOT IL-62 SP-LAC at 0801 (LO4789 from Warsaw), which parked across two stands as the airport had no tow-bar for it!

11th   Lego's new corporate aircraft, Citation 550 OY-GKC, paid its first visit today replacing their older Citation OY-DVL.

11th   The next British Airways SVC-10 making its last visit to Manchester was G-ASGC (BA184 from New York/Prestwick) today. It made its final flight on the 22nd (Amsterdam-Heathrow) and was then stored before being flown to Cosford for preservation in April 1980.

12th   BIA BAC 1-11 G-AXBB operated from/to Gatwick as WD211/0, on behalf of Wardair. It also operated an outbound charter to Dusseldorf as UK3001 on the 17th.

14th   Four BIA Herald newspaper flights, originally destined for Blackpool, diverted into Manchester this morning due to fog: G-APWF, G-APWJ and G-APWE (twice).

14th   Having been a regular visitor on behalf of JAT last year, the only visit this year of Yugoslav Govt B.727 YU-AKD occurred today, operating JJ101/2 on behalf of Aviogenex.

15th   The airport was on standby for possible weather diversions from London and could accept up to eight narrow-bodied and eight wide-bodied aircraft. The writer saw HS.125 HB-VGG arrive at 0837, on its way for maintenance at Hawarden. It was followed by the first of eight wide-bodied diversions within an hour. British Caledonian DC-10 G-BGAT at 0840 (BR246 from Houston), Delta L.1011 Tristar N81028 at 0855 (DL010 from Atlanta), British Airways B.747 G-AWNH at 0905 (BA260 from Bermuda), South African Airways B.747 ZS-SAO at 0908 (SA234 from Abidjan), Air India B.747 VT-EBO at 0915 (AI116 from New York), British Airways B.747 G-BDPV at 0918 (BA020 from Dubai), British Airways B.747 G-AWNI at 0923 (BA278 from Miami) and TWA B.747 N93106 at 0940 (TW770 from Chicago). South African Airways were making their first visit since October 1978 and the record number of ten wide-bodied aircraft on the ground was equalled again, but there were no first visits amongst them.

16th   One of the last two remaining British Airways Merchantman, G-APET, arrived at 1806 on its final visit to Manchester, operating a freight flight from/to Heathrow.

17th   Spantax CV-990 EC-BJC made its last visit today, operating BX759A/762A from/to Palma, before being withdrawn the following month.

20th   British Caledonian Boeing 707F G-AYSI made its last visit to Manchester, operating BR567 to Bangor/Atlanta, before it was sold in January 1980 as N3751Y.

21st   British Airtours Boeing 707 G-APFD, operating in basic Air Mauritius colours throughout the summer, made its final visit to Manchester. It arrived at 0546 (KT597 from Malaga) and positioned to Gatwick as KT002P. After it was sold in January 1980 as N888NW, it left just the following Boeing 707s still in the airline's service going into 1980: G-APFF, G-APFG, G-APFJ, G-APFO, G-ARRA and G-ARRC.

22nd Tarom BAC 1-11 YR-BCM arrived at 1110 to take Leeds United to Romania for their UEFA Cup Second Round game with Universitata Craiova, taking place on the 24th. Leeds Utd was beaten 2-0 and again in the return leg two weeks later by the same score, meaning they were out of the UEFA Cup.

23rd The very last visit of a British Airways Vanguard/Merchantman took place today, when G-APEJ arrived at 2018, operating a cargo flight from/to Heathrow. By the end of the year, the remaining aircraft, G-APET, had been withdrawn, pending sale to Air Bridge Carriers. The very final British Airways Merchantman flight was 3rd December, when G-APEJ operated BA3763 from Stockholm/Gothenburg to Heathrow.

23rd Another British Airways SVC-10, G-ASGM, was making its last visit to Manchester today (BA184 from New York/Prestwick), before positioning to Heathrow. It was withdrawn in April 1980 and flown to Prestwick for storage on 7th May 1980, but on the 25th August 1980, it was flown back to Heathrow and returned to service until March 1981.

27th Air Europe began their winter programme from Manchester today when B.737 G-BMOR was used on 'w' pattern flight (KS1163/2 from/to Palma). On the 31st, B.737 G-BMOR positioned up from Gatwick in readiness for the first flight of their winter programme the following day (KS820 to Funchal).

27th The new Runway 24 fast turnoff was opened today and the first aircraft to use it was Tarom TU-154 YR-TPD (RO795).

27th The third Comet flight this month was G-BDIV, operating a 'w' pattern flight (DA1817/6 from/to Alicante), which was also its final visit and the very final visit of any Comet to Manchester. Its last flight was 12th November (DA3203 Frankfurt-Gatwick), before its departure to Lasham for storage two days later.

27th British Airways are using 1942-vintage Dragon Rapide G-AKOE to help promote the introduction of the airline's new shuttle service between Manchester and London. It arrived from Old Warden and performed several local flights the following day, providing a nostalgic flashback to the first BEA service between Manchester and London in 1947.

28th October 1979 – To promote British Airways new Shuttle Service between Manchester and London, Dragon Rapide G-AKOE was brought in to help with the publicity machine. (Manchester Airport Archive)

28th British Airways started shuttle operations between Manchester and London, complimenting their existing services between London-Glasgow/Edinburgh & Belfast. There's an hourly service at peak times and a two-hourly service at other times. The shuttle also reduces check-in time to ten minutes before departure and guarantees if the main flight is full, a back-up plane will be made available - even for just one passenger! The first outbound flight to Heathrow was operated by BAC 1-11 G-AVMV (BA4413) with Trident G-ARPK operating backup flight (BA4415) and the first inbound flight from Heathrow was operated by Trident 3 G-AWZB (BA4422), with Trident G-ARPK returning as backup flight (BA4424).

28th The ATC watch log recorded that due to fog, a general hold state was in force at Luton, Gatwick & Heathrow. Manchester could accept up to twenty narrow-bodied and six wide-bodied aircraft. However, the only diversions were two from Gatwick: Dan-Air BAC 1-11 G-AXCP at 0542 (DA2785 from Palma) and DC-10 G-BBSZ at 0641 (GK020 from New York).

29th After the first phase of strengthening work on Runway 06/24 was completed, night-flights were resumed for the first time since March. By the time the work starts again next March, it's hoped that planning permission will have been granted for lengthening the main runway by 800ft.

29th A major uplift of troops took place today, when the following C-130s arrived from Lyneham, operating out to Gutersloh: XV179 (RR5221), XV199 (RR5224), XV295 (RR5223) & XV305 (RR5222).

30th Yet another Air France SE.210 making its last visit to Manchester was F-BOHC operating AF962/1, before being withdrawn in February next year.

31st Air France SE.210 F-BHRT was another aircraft making its last visit to Manchester, also operating AF962/1, before being withdrawn the following month.

November 1979

£100m could be spent on the airport over the next fifteen years. The Government's made it clear that Manchester has been given the highest priority outside of London, for licensing and developing services. Included in the plan are extensions to the present terminal, five new surface car parks, improvements to aircraft facilities, extension of the existing main runway, updating the airports piers, new aircraft stands and improved cargo facilities. The biggest element of this blue-print is the building of two brand new passenger terminals and a second runway, scheduled for 1988.

The Airport Authority confirmed that a new remote apron, to be located at the west side next to Fairey and the fuel farm, will be large enough to handle up to six B.747s. Construction work will start next Autumn and some stands should be ready for use by summer 1981 and the rest by early 1982. The South Bay will also be extended eastwards in due course.

British Airways 'new' Manchester-London service showed a 17% increase in its first week, compared to the week before the shuttle commenced and they are hoping to carry 100,000 passengers in their first year. Next year's long-haul plans for Manchester involve operating the B.747 three-times weekly to New York, three-times weekly to Toronto and once-weekly to Montreal. From 1st April next year, they will not be operating any Viscount or SVC-10 flights from Manchester. The Viscount won't be required as services to Guernsey and the Isle of Man are withdrawn and Aberdeen services will change to the BAC 1-11.

Air Europe's first Manchester programme is well underway and all three aircraft had visited by the end of the month. An aircraft swap takes place each Thursday at Funchal between the outbound KS820 and the inbound KS821.

Air Transcontinental, who previously specialised in leasing aircraft, are moving their HQ from Windsor, Berks, to Manchester Airport. They intend using at least three of their four Boeing 707s on scheduled charter services, as their other aircraft is on lease to Air Malta. They expect to fly 250,000 passengers next year, in conjunction with various tour operators, with up to thirty flights a week in peak season. They are the first British airline to order the Douglas DC-9 Series 80 and the three on order are due for delivery in 1982, by which time they hope to have established an engineering facility at Manchester. Their summer operation is due to commence on Sunday 30th March 1980, with a flight to Palma on behalf of Horizon holidays.

Britannia Airways have adopted a new colour scheme and the first in the revised livery is B.737 G-AVRO. The word 'Airways' has been dropped, in favour of just 'Britannia', which is now in larger letters.

Northwest Orient is already carrying well above target and expects further frequency increases in the New Year. However, their flights have been regularly running late, due to crew scheduling problems and on two occasions this month, they operated inbound from Boston direct. Strong rumours are circulating that Flying Tigers are to commence a weekly cargo service between

Manchester and Detroit, following the growing success of Northwest Orient's Manchester operations.

Orion Airways, which is a new airline to be based at East Midlands, will begin operations next March and operate a summer programme from Manchester. They have three Boeing 737s on order and will be Horizon Holiday's in-house airline.

Pelican Cargo has completed their relocation to Gatwick, having operated just three flights through Manchester all year. Their original aircraft, G-BPAT, returned to the leasing company in June and was sold on to Zambia Airways as 9J-AEQ and their other, G-BEVN, is currently stuck in Entebbe, Uganda, due to an engine malfunction.

Direct holidays to Kenya and Sri Lanka, to be introduced next year, are the first direct flights offered to the East African or Indian subcontinent. The flights, operated by Laker Airways, are on behalf of OSL Holidays and Wings.

The following airlines made changes from this month: British Airways no longer operates to Montreal, while Toronto is served three-weekly via Prestwick (BA080/1) and New York (BA184/5) operates four-times weekly. British Island Airways terminated the twice weekday Rotterdam service at the end of the month. Finnair increased cargo flights to Helsinki up to three-weekly. After the summer's night-time runway closures the following cargo flights were restored: KLM four-weekly, Lufthansa five-weekly and Swissair five-weekly. SAS are operating a passenger flight six-weekly to Copenhagen, with three onward to Dublin and return. Sabena are still operating a Boeing 737 Combi on their SN617/8 passenger service. Winter IT flights are being operated by Air Europe, Air Malta, Britannia Airways, Dan-Air, Laker Airways & Monarch Airlines.

Equipment changes on the European scheduled services were Finnair (AY032): DC-9F OH-LYI (2nd/4th/7th/9th), KLM (KL155): NLM F.28 PH-CHD (11th), Lufthansa (LH074): B.727s D-ABKD (19h), D-ABKN (16th) plus first visit D-ABKT (23rd) & Swissair (SR842): DC-9-51 HB-ISP (21st).

Military ILS traffic identified included RAF Hawk XX179 (2nd), RAF C-130s XV183 (17th), XV207 (1st), XV220 (20th), XV217 (6th), XV218 (17th) &, XV296 (3rd); RAF Dominie XS726 (15th) and RAE Comet XS235 (21st).

2nd British Airways flights out of Manchester came to a halt at 0900, following a dispute in dispatches over 'who does what', but luckily it was resolved by the 4th.

3rd Boeing 707F G-BCAL was the third British Caledonian B.707 freighter to make its last visit to Manchester this year (BR567 to Bangor/Atlanta). It was sold during the month as LV-MZE. Following the removal of G-AYSI and G-BDEA from their fleet, the only pure Boeing 707 freighter operating is G-BDSJ.

4th British Airways B.747 G-BBPU, arriving at 1101 (BA9001 from Heathrow), was operating an outbound trooping flight to Gutersloh.

5th Britannia Airways Boeing 720 TF-VLC made its last visit today (BY238B Keflavik-Luton), after its summer lease to Britannia Airways. It was withdrawn at Stansted in 1980 and broken up the year after.

7th The entire nightshift of thirty baggage handlers and porters were sent home early due to a dispute sparked off by a supervisors good turn. It started after a duty officer gave a hand to short-staffed baggage loaders, during a shift-changeover. The trouble caused had been simmering since the weekend and last night, after the airport's porters and loaders refused to work with the officer concerned, they were suspended. This caused a number of flights to be delayed, including one that diverted to Liverpool. Talks held later in the day ultimately resolved the dispute.

8th RAF Andover XS644, arriving at 1026 (RR864), was on a crew training detail from Brize Norton to Leeds.

8th Bell 206 Jet Ranger N7845S, routing Stalybridge-Audenshaw and then onto Manchester, made a forced landing in a field near Stockport, due to engine trouble.

9th One that got away was an unidentified Cessna 414, routing Prestwick-Brussels as 'Floair 358'. It was diverting into Manchester around 0600 after losing power in one of its engines, possibly due to icing, but when the pilot managed to restart the engine around 8-miles from touchdown, he subsequently broke off the approach and continued to Brussels.

11th Beech 200 HB-GGO, arriving at 1114 from Geneva, was bound for the USA when it called into Manchester on a tech stop.

11th Dutch Air Force F.27 C-1 was carrying Prince Bernhardt, when it diverted in at 1906 en route from Northolt-Edinburgh, due to fog affecting the Scottish airports.

14th British Airways BAC 1-11 G-AVMX (BA5674 to Edinburgh) returned to Manchester shortly after takeoff, when an air conditioning fault caused smoke to enter the cabin.

15th RAF Hawk 'FOR 51' (registration unknown) was technically the first Hawk to land at Manchester, performing an actual touch-and-go rather than a standard ILS approach, which made it necessary for the airport to pursue a landing charge!

17th Based Skycabs PA-34 G-BFKO had great difficulty getting its engines started, on a very early morning kidney transportation flight from Manchester to Lee on Solent. It was aided by Dan-Air Engineering and a works vehicle, before finally departing at 0335, but that wasn't the end of the saga! The aircraft was reported missing at 0505, but it was confirmed later that both crew members were uninjured after making a forced landing in the New Forest!

17th Dense fog hitting many parts of England affected roads and caused delays and diversions, particularly at Heathrow. A morning diversion session produced six British Airways flights, one of which was another Air New Zealand DC-10 first visit, ZK-NZT at 0827 (BA270 from Boston) and 'endangered' SVC-10 G-ASGD at 0801 (BA058 from Larnaca). Apart from British Airways B.747s G-AWNC, G-AWNK & G-BDPZ, other B.747s were Air India VT-EBE at 0937 (AI110 from New York) and South African Airways ZS-SAN at 0905 (SA228 from Sal Island). The murk had blown away by lunchtime and was replaced with wet and windy weather.

18th Four RAF aircraft operated inbound trooping flights from Gutersloh today. C-130s XV293 (RR5302) & XV294 (RR5303) and VC-10s XV101 (RR2627) & XV109 (RR2628).

19th Today's movements were interrupted by fog, which became more persistent by the evening and there were no arrivals after Royal Saudi Air Force C-130H 467 landed at 2158.

20th The day was affected by dense freezing fog, with only four arrivals all day. Two were Dan-Air's early morning City-Link flights, G-BEBA DA052 & G-ATMJ DA053 and the others were Rockwell 690 D-IAFC & PA-34 Seneca G-BDUN, which arrived at 1029. The PA-34 was the last aircraft to land until Britannia Airways flight BY110B arrived twenty-three hours later. Heathrow was also affected by fog up until late morning and again from early evening, when Prestwick alone received eleven wide-bodied aircraft!

21st The first aircraft to land at Manchester today wasn't until 0953, but once the fog started to lift the airport was soon receiving fog diversions from Heathrow, which was affected until early evening. The first, British Airways BAC 1-11, G-AVMZ at 1105 (BA779 from Berlin), was followed by five more in quick succession: British Airways B.747 G-AWND at 1143 (BA278 from Miami), the second Braniff B.747 to visit, N602BN at 1200 (BN602 from Dallas); Air New Zealand DC-10 ZK-NZM at 1207 (BA270 from Boston) and British Airways B.747s G-AWNK at 1211 (BA190 from Washington) & G-AWNF at 1229 (BA174 from New York). There was a temporary lull before first visit Gulf Air Tristar L.1011 A40-TZ arrived in the fading light at 1504 (GF007 from Doha). After SVC-10 G-ASGJ arrived at 1601 (BA150 from Cairo), only nine diversions had been received, despite London's weather showing no improvement. By early evening, Liverpool had received two British Airways diversions: B.707 G-AXXZ (BA008 from Tokyo) and B.747 G-AWNP (BA012 from Prestwick), after having to divert there earlier in the day. One particularly interesting aircraft that tried to divert to Manchester, but was unable to, was Singapore Airlines DC-10 9V-SDE on delivery to the airline routing through Heathrow.

21st Lear Jet HB-VFB diverted into Manchester at 1132 to pick up a passenger from the diverted British Airways BA278 flight.

21st Air UK Herald G-BCZG, inbound from Rotterdam as UK855, declared a full emergency with a feathered engine.

21st Hapag-Lloyd BAC 1-11 D-AMOR arrived at 1448 from Frankfurt for routine maintenance with Dan-Air, before departing on the 7th December.

22nd   Two Heathrow diversions, arriving five hours apart, were both due to holding delays. First visitor Bangladesh Biman B.707 S2-ACE arrived at 0853 (BG003 from Dubai) and Pan American B747 N742PA at 1411 (PA124 from Los Angeles).

22nd   Cessna 402 N2614X was on its delivery flight from Reykjavik, when it diverted in at 1723 with technical trouble.

23rd   The first aircraft to operate the Rotterdam service in full Air UK colours was Herald G-BAZJ. The service had been reduced to a weekday evening flight, but from December it appeared to have been cancelled altogether.

24th   Air Anglia/Air UK F.27 G-BDVS, PA-31 G-FJGC and PA-34 G-GALE all arrived from Norwich in connection with the game between Manchester Utd and Norwich City at Old Trafford, which ended in a 5-0 defeat for the travellers!

25th   Having arrived from Torp at 1822 as WN467, Nor-Fly CV-440 LN-MAP was parked on disused Runway 20 due to the number of aircraft night-stopping these days, which is generally twenty to thirty aircraft!

27th   Ghana Airways VC-10 9G-ABO arrived at 0730 (GH702 from Rome), having diverted in from Heathrow due to low cloud.

28th   Royal Marines Gazelle XX372 made a fuel stop at Manchester at 1058, en route Mossend-Netheravon.

29th   Transavia B.737 PH-TVC operated today's cattle flight to Milan, positioning in from Amsterdam at 0858 as HV2125.

29th   There was a warm breeze for November and the high stratus cloud tinged with orange, looked rather strange and interesting to the writer. I understood why when the lunchtime weather forecast showed a high pressure system extending across the country, originating all the way from North Africa. It was also the reason for the strong reception on my aircraft radio and explained why I could pick up southerly frequencies not normally audible. The sunset was spectacular too, with a thick layer of cloud tinged with an amazing shade of orange. By the evening I was still enjoying listening to the new frequencies and two-way conversations for a change, rather than just the ATC controller, or the pilot. Two Heathrow diversions arrived during the evening, the first of which was the only visit this year of Concorde, when British Airways example G-BOAD arrived at 2052 (BA170 from New York), followed by British Airways L.1011 G-BBAJ at 2105 (BA639 from Copenhagen). Although both arrivals were due to fog at Heathrow, Stansted was the main recipient of the diversions on this particular evening. The following morning a thin layer of red sand, sent in by the Saharan wind, covered most surfaces and was especially noticeable on cars.

30th   Air Portugal Boeing 727 CS-TBV made its first visit today, operating an outbound charter to Oporto as TP9573.

December 1979

The weather was unremarkable to begin with, but the second half of the month was very cold, with occasional snow. Heathrow was fogbound for most of Christmas Day, but Manchester didn't receive any diversions, due to the lack of staff on duty.

Equipment changes on the European scheduled services were Air Malta (KM106): Austrian Airlines DC-9 OE-LDC (16th), KLM (KL153): DC-8 PH-DCT (1st), (KL155): Martinair F.28 PH-MAT (18th) and Lufthansa (LH074): B.727 first visit D-ABKS (27th).

The only civil ILS traffic noted was Dove G-ARHW (19th). Military ILS traffic identified included RAF Hawk XX250 (19th), RAF C-130s XV179 (17th), XV180 (3rd), XV217 (19th) and RAF Nimrod XV227 (14th).

2nd   British Airways B.707 G-ASZF arriving at 0322 (BA3678 from Toronto), was its last visit to Manchester, having made the first on 13th January 1966. It served for another two years, before being withdrawn from service in March 1982.

3rd   Royal Saudi Air Force C-130E 451 was making its first visit today, routing Jeddah-Gander as RSF834.

4th   Supplies of Shell aviation fuel dwindled rapidly, after tanker drivers walked out over the management's use of hire vehicles. Some flights operated from Liverpool for two days and supplies to petrol stations were affected, after thirty-three out of forty-six Shell depots were closed.

4ᵗʰ   Air Portugal B.727 CS-TBO (TP9570) arriving at 1643, was in the airlines new colour scheme, operating a charter from/to Lisbon.

4ᵗʰ   Air France SE.210 F-BHRI deployed its parachute brake on landing, which was observed blowing away before the aircraft made its high-speed fast turnoff! The SE.210 is the only jet airliner still possessing a parachute brake, which is rarely used nowadays.

4ᵗʰ   British Airways SVC-10 G-ASGB, made its last visit today (BA184 from New York/Prestwick), before positioning to Heathrow. Its final flight was September 1980 (Beirut-Heathrow), before being flown to Prestwick for storage on the 3ʳᵈ October 1980.

5ᵗʰ   PA-31 OE-FOP arrived at 1114, operating a freight charter from/to Vienna.

5ᵗʰ   Laker Airways BAC 1-11 G-AVBX (GK2843 to Munster) returned as a full emergency due to an engine failure. It was later ferried to Gatwick on one engine for further attention.

5ᵗʰ   Hapag-Lloyd BAC 1-11 D-AMUC, arriving at 1419 today for maintenance with Dan-Air Engineering, was in basic Bavaria-Germanair colours and Hapag-Lloyd titles.

6ᵗʰ   Alaskan International C-130 N106AK made its first visit today, arriving at 1603 from Las Palmas, with a 12 tonne generator.

11ᵗʰ December 1979 - British Airways SVC-10 G-ASGF made its last visit to Manchester today (BA184 from New York/Prestwick), before positioning to Heathrow. Withdrawn from service in 1981, it's seen here on 5ᵗʰ September 1979, operating New York service BA184/5. (Geoff Ball)

12ᵗʰ   British Airways increased frequency and capacity on their Prestwick/Toronto flights between the 12ᵗʰ and 23ʳᵈ. B.747 G-BDPZ, wearing a hybrid Aer Lingus/British Airways scheme, was the main aircraft used during this period, but B.747s G-AWNB (13ᵗʰ) and G-AWNL (19ᵗʰ) were also used.

13ᵗʰ   Transavia B.737 PH-TVD was used on the cattle flights twice during the month. Today as HV2134/5 from/to Milan and again on the 29ᵗʰ as IM913 Amsterdam-Milan.

14ᵗʰ   Citation YU-BIA arrived at 0742 on a flight from/to Le Bourget. It was the first YU-registered biz-jet to visit Manchester and the first of three biz-jet first visits this month. The others were HS.125 HB-VGF (17ᵗʰ) and Lear Jet 35 G-LEAR (22ⁿᵈ).

14ᵗʰ   Portuguese Air Force paid its second visit to Manchester, when C-130 6805 arrived at 1059, to collect another consignment of guard dogs!

16ᵗʰ   Austrian DC-9 OE-LDC, currently leased by Air Malta, made its first appearance operating KM106/7 in basic Austrian Airlines colours with Air Malta titles.

17ᵗʰ   New Dan-Air HS.748 G-BHCJ (ex-Philippine Airlines RP-C1030), made its first appearance today, operating DA050. It's currently all-white with Dan-Air titles, but in due course it will be painted in their new colours, similar to G-BEKA.

16th December 1979 - DC-8-63 N792FT, arriving from New York, was the second visit of US cargo airline Flying Tigers. It departed for Boston late-evening as 'Tiger 4046'. (Ian Barrie)

17th   Monarch acquired ex-Maersk B.720 OY-APY, which is now registered as G-BHGE. It made its first today and operated Manchester-Tel Aviv flight OM208 the following day. It's replacing B.707 G-BGCT, which was sold to Cyprus Airways as 5B-DAO.

19th   An unidentified RAF Jaguar 'JSV39' performed an overshoot this afternoon at 1627, as did RAF Jaguar 'LKI39', which overshot the following day at 1259.

21st   Air Transcontinental B.707 G-TJAB, in basic Air Malta colours with no titles, operated Britannia Airways BY429A/B to/from Tenerife after positioning up from Luton last evening. It positioned out to Cairo just before midnight as 'Egyptair 778'.

21st   LOT operated three TU-134 charter flights today, all from/to Warsaw: SP-LGA LO4867/8, SP-LHF LO4869/70 and SP-LHH LO4881/2.

22nd   NEA finally received their first Lear Jet, when G-LEAR arrived at 1525 from Gander and made a low approach and overshoot to Runway 06 before landing. Its first flight for NEA was on the 31st (Manchester-Heathrow-Rotterdam-Las Palmas).

25th   Resident Cessna 150 Aerobat G-BCDY was observed performing acrobatics again over the airfield, similar to the occasion of the strike last September.

27th   A Pan American B.747 ran off Runway 23 at Heathrow and onto the grass during the evening. Heathrow's main runways, 28L & 28R, were out of use due to severe crosswinds, but Runway 23 was open again around 2030. During the closure Manchester received four Heathrow diversions: British Airways Trident 3s G-AWZA at 1935 (BA4503 from Manchester), G-AWZL at 1945 (BA4963 from Glasgow) & G-AWZN at 2038 (BE627 from Geneva) and Lufthansa B.727 D-ABCI at 1956 (LH070 from Munich). There was also a Gatwick diversion due to high winds when British Caledonian B.707 G-ATZC arrived at 1914 (BR893 from Paris).

30th   Britannia Airways B.737 G-BECH (BY088A Leeds-Malaga) arrived at Manchester at 1554, having declared a full emergency with one engine shutdown.

First/Last Arrivals & Departures 1979

First arrival:	B.727 G-BAFZ/DA99'FZ from Glasgow at 0038
First departure:	B.727 G-BAFZ/DA1508 to Malta at 0838
Last arrival:	B.737 G-BMEC/KS809 from Palma at 2159
Last departure:	B.737 G-AWSY/BY019BF to Birmingham at 2109

(+/- % on Previous Year)		
Scheduled Passengers	1,769,000	-1.0%
I.T/Charter Passengers	1,675,000	+2.3%
Transit Passengers	76,000	+5.5%
Total	**3,520,000**	**+0.7%**
Freight & Mail (Tonnes)	25,300	-25.0%
Movements	75,000	-3.4%

5
Fairey Aviation 1970 – 1978

Fairey Aviation's roots can be traced back to 1918, when they acquired their first factory building for aircraft construction, in Heaton Chapel, Stockport. Their first hangar at Ringway was completed in June 1937, just prior to the opening of the airport itself. During the Second World War, as part of the massive expansion plan of aircraft manufacture, the Heaton Chapel plant built more than 1,200 Fairey Battles, which were transported to Ringway and re-assembled. Ringway itself was also used for the production, final assembly and test flights of a considerable number of Fairey Barracudas, Fairey Fulmars, Bristol Beaufighters & Handley-Page Halifaxes. After the war, aircraft production slowed down considerably and the final war design aircraft test-flown from Ringway was the Fairey Spearfish torpedo-dive bomber. Two were completed in late 1945, but orders for 152 more were cancelled.

Ringway then concentrated on the overhaul and modification of various military types, from a variety of air forces, which kept the facility busy for the next fifteen years. In 1959 the Government decided that UK aircraft production would be rationalised, which meant it would stop altogether as far as Fairey was concerned, although modification work on various military types continued, at least for short term. The last aircraft to leave Ringway after modification work was RAF Meteor VT340, in late 1960. Although Fairey had discontinued aircraft production in the UK, their involvement continued overseas, with one of the group's subsidiary companies, Fairey S.A at Gosselies. Fairey S.A. were involved in the production of F-104G Starfighters for NATO, when 578 aircraft were fully or jointly assembled at the plant. The Belgian plant also carried out an extensive overhaul and modification programme on F-84F, Pembroke & Hunter aircraft on behalf of the Belgian Air Force, as well as the Luftwaffe's F-104 Starfighter's.

The GAF Jindivik Mk-2, assembled at Fairey's Manchester facility, evolved at the Government's aircraft factories at Melbourne. Built to British specifications, it was designed as an unmanned target aircraft, under a joint programme between Britain and Australia. Powered by a Rolls-Royce Viper turbojet with Elliot avionics, it first flew in August 1952, but it suffered from protracted development. It's unique, as it operates in the UK with Royal Australian Air Force serials. Once imported into the UK, its final assembly was undertaken at the Fairey plant, before being used by establishments such as the RAE, Llanbedr, North Wales. (Fairey Aviation)

During the 1960's the UK Fairey group embarked on an expansion and diversification programme, with less emphasis on aviation, borne out of which was the creation of a subsidiary company, Fairey Surveys. Their aircraft, based at White Waltham, were used for ground surveying, air photography, aerial surveying and mapping work. They also undertook long-term projects on behalf of the Ministry of Defence. The wide extent of the company's operations could see these aircraft operating anywhere in the world.

As of 1970, Fairey's operating fleet consisted of DC-3s G-AHCT/ALWC/AMCA and Doves G-AKSS/AMKS/AWFM, but they were rarely seen at Manchester, except for liaison flights between Fairey plants or for maintenance. Dove G-AMKS was registered to the company until 1976, although it was actually withdrawn in 1971.

1972

The company's two Doves, G-ALWC & G-AWFM, passed through the hangar for maintenance during the year. On 12th January after eighteen years of service with the company, DC-3 G-AHCT flew into Manchester for the very last time, to what was ultimately its final resting place. Initially it was slowly stripped of parts, before the airport's fire service finally consumed it in a large fire in November 1975. They also took delivery of two Beech 65's this year, G-AZFS & G-AZOH, which were converted at Ringway to perform survey work.

Aircraft manufacturer Britten-Norman officially came under the ownership of the Fairey group in August; which meant they would be involved in UK aircraft production again for the first time since 1960, namely the Islander and Trislander, which were manufactured at Bembridge. The Ringway facility, comprising of 60,000sq ft of aircraft hangar space, would be brought into use to enable Britten-Norman to bring an extensive range of services including maintenance, checks, overhauls, Certificates of Airworthiness renewals, repairs, repainting and specialised modifications. Islander G-AWBZ, arriving on 23rd October, was the first aircraft for overhaul/maintenance at Fairey's recently converted repair facility, before it eventually departed on 6th March 1973.

1973

Islander G-AVKC was roaded to Fairey in March for a complete rebuild. It was the third production aircraft built and the second oldest flying. From 1967-1971 it was operated by Loganair, before being traded for a newer version. It was then used by Britten-Norman for the development of a crop-spraying variant. Whilst at Ringway, its wings and undercarriage were replaced, to help develop a higher-weight Islander. Specialised equipment was fitted including sliding pilot/co-pilot seats to allow full movement for camera operation, blister windows in the forward cabin area with an oxygen system, a dark room and comprehensive navigational and avionics for surveying. G-AVKC now had a large cabin volume with the capability of flight stability, low and slow flying and STOL ability for operating in remote, unprepared strips near work bases, with an altitude capability of over 20.000ft. Test flown on 23rd February 1975, it finally left for White Waltham on 6th March 1975.

A large number of Islanders passed through the hangar for maintenance, overhaul or modification work during the year, including G-BAKZ (12/01). It was re-engined and refitted for photo survey work, before being delivered to UK-company Helicopter Hire. G-BAJS (15/02) became PT-EFI and EI-AUL (24/03) departed as G-BAVT. G-AYXE (03/04) arriving in brown camouflage, was the prototype of the company's Defender, a military variant of the Islander, but it was converted for civilian use and departed on delivery to Aer Arran as EI-AWM. G-AVRA (12/04) arrived for a complete rebuild and G-BAYE (23/10) was the first BN-2 to be delivered direct from the Britten-Norman factory at Bucharest. Arriving via Gosselies, it was converted for aerial survey work for the Jamaica Defence Force. F-BUOQ (13/12) was formerly G-AVRA· and had only left in November after a seven-month rebuild. Finally G-BBFG (21/12), also arriving direct from Bucharest, via Gosselies, was eventually sold to Heli-Orient of Singapore.

1974

The number of Islanders arriving for modification work was much reduced this year, as according to Fairey officials 'it was far easier to carry out the fitting out work previously done at Ringway, at the company's Bembridge plant'. Aircraft passing through were Aer Arran EI-AWM (08/01), 5A-DEA (18/01) for installation of a camera was still carrying its former registration G-AWYW under its wing; N87JA (21/01) was in green primer, G-BBJF (14/02), Aer Arran EI-AWM (21/10) for maintenance/re-spray and G-AWNT (28/11). Trislander G-BBWP (03/04) arrived for special conversion to a survey aircraft for Questor Surveys, Canada. Upon departure for Bembridge (23/07), it was carrying two sensor beams 30ft long x 1ft square from the tail and nose, plus a ring aerial suspended from the fuselage and wing tips, which all formed part of the surveillance kit!

A local aviation society treated to a tour of Fairey's facilities on 9th April, noted the following: 'The main hangar contained two aircraft; BN-2A Islander G-AVKC was being totally rebuilt and awaiting wings as the ones intended for it were given to Islander G-AVRA. The other occupant was red Trislander G-BBWP, in immaculate condition and complete apart from engine cowlings. To the left of the main hangar is a smaller green hangar, divided into three sections inside. The middle section contained BN-2 Islander 5A-DEA, owned by Occidental Oil Co of Libya. It was ready for re-spray and interestingly, it's already had more than forty modifications carried out at Ringway. The second section was where the pilotless target-drones, the Jindiviks, were assembled and engineers were in the process of constructing and repairing various examples. The third and final section contains an area where Fairey constructs boats for export and the home market and those currently in production were for the Royal Navy'.

15th April 1974 - Fairey Survey Dove G-AKSS is seen here on a short visit to the hangar. It arrived for the final time on 28th February 1975 and was permanently withdrawn. It remaining parked outside the hangar until it was broken up and removed by road, early in 1976. Their second Dove G-AWFM, withdrawn in March 1975, was eventually sold to Fairflight Charter of Biggin Hill for spares. (Geoff Ball)

Company DC-3 G-AMCA arrived for a major overhaul in April. In May, Dove G-AWFM arriving on the 3rd and Beech 95 G-APUB, owned by World War II pilot Sir Douglas Bader, arriving on the 9th, were both renewing their Certificates of Airworthiness. July saw the first flight involved with the export of the company's portable bridge sections known as Bailey Bridges, when Transvalair CL-44 HB-IEN departed 27th July, bound for Tripoli.

11th May 1974 - Douglas DC-3 G-AMCA arrived for a major overhaul on 25th April, but as of this date, it still hadn't entered the hangar. Ex-RAF, it was operated by Fairey from 1949 - May 1976. (Geoff Ball)

Augusts announcement of the formation of Fairey Britten-Norman Air Services Ltd, brought together the flying, repair and overhaul facilities of the group. The aim of the centralisation was to bring greater efficiency and economy to its operations and build an aviation business by selling excess capacity and gradually acquiring additional aircraft as the market demanded. FBNAS aimed to have a fleet of twelve aircraft, a modern flying school and an aviation centre at Bembridge, after establishing a reputation for excellence with their geographic and geophysical survey operations at White Waltham. The Ringway plant offered overhaul, modification and complete rebuilds, as well as CAA approved engineers for C of A work.

1975
The following aircraft were owned and operated by the newly formed FBNAS group: DC-3s G-ALWC & G-AMCA; Doves G-AKSS & G-AWFM; Islander G-AWVY and Beech 65s G-AZFS & G-AZOH. These aircraft are based at White Waltham and rarely seen at Manchester, but due to the nature of their work, they spend most of their time on location. Islander G-AWVY exclusively operated a shuttle service between the factories at Bembridge and Gosselies and a second corporate liaison Islander, G-AVKC, was added in March.

The two Beech 65s were at Ringway in January for maintenance and again during the summer. They also undertook a variety of survey work in the area during July, but by the end of the year they had been sold.

Aircraft used during the year for exporting bridge sections to various destinations around the world were IAS CL-44 G-BCWJ, Tradewinds CL-44s G-AWGS, G-AWGT & G-AWOV; Transvalair CL-44 HB-IEN and Philippine Air Transport C-130s RP-C99, RP-C100 & RP-C101.

Islander G-BCSI, arriving on 7th February for the fitting of surveying equipment before its departure for onward sale in Belgium, was delivered on 30th April as OO-TOP. Islander TF-REH, arriving 23rd February, was for a complete overhaul and re-paint. Dove G-AKSS, arriving at the hangar on 28th February, was it final time. It was withdrawn from service and although it was officially up for sale, it remained outside throughout the year.

To help with vital disaster relief work during the country's monsoon season, the Government of the Republic of the Philippines placed an order worth £800.000 with the Fairey group in February, for the supply of medium girder bridges and ancillary equipment. These bridges were designed to be erected in just over an hour, with minimum manpower and preparation. Due to the imminence of the monsoon season, a series of flights between Manchester and Manila commenced on 23rd February, when the first set were flown out by C-130 RP-C100. The company's airport facility became a storage area for loading the bridges, rather than keeping them at the Heaton Chapel plant where they were manufactured.

Dove G-AWFM arrived at Ringway for the final time on the 6th March. It had operated for the company since 1968 and was last operational Fairey Dove. It was sold to Fairflight Charter and departed to Biggin Hill on 11th June but it never flew again, as it was used as a spares source for their other Dove's.

Islander G-AXRN, formerly owned by Humber Airways, arrived on the 10th March for maintenance, before its return to FBNAS. Used as a temporary liaison aircraft until November 1975, it made numerous visits. Islander G-AXRM, arriving 15th March, was the second Humber Airway's Islander for maintenance, prior to its return to FBNAS. It made numerous visits and also acted as a temporary corporate aircraft until October 1975. The third Islander passing through the hangar during March was Islander D-IHVH, arriving on the 31st.

Two arrivals on 13th May were company DC-3 G-AMCA for maintenance and Islander G-BCWU for an extra fuel tank. Royal Navy Sea Devon XJ350 was not strictly a hangar movement, but it diverted into Manchester on 23rd July with a serious oil leak and remained parked outside until its departure on the 30th. Islander G-AVCN arrived for a major overhaul on 30th July and August saw the arrival of Islander G-AWNT for minor work on the 27th. DC-3 G-AMCA also arrived for maintenance/overhaul on 29th August, before finally departing on 30th September.

Islanders G-AXRN on 23rd September and G-AXRM on 3rd October arrived for maintenance/overhaul. Defender G-BCVR, the military version of the Islander, made a brief visit on the morning of 6th October. It also made various other liaison visits during October and November, along with a second Defender, G-BCVS.

Islander G-AWVY made a rare visit to the Manchester facility on 31st October, as it's used exclusively as a shuttle aircraft between Bembridge and Gosselies. November saw Islander G-AXHE, operated by the Red Devils Parachute team, arrive for maintenance on the 10th and Defender G-BCVR on the 12th.

1976

Some of the niche work Fairey had specialised in for many years, mainly survey work, has ceased and as a result their Beech Queen Air and Dove aircraft were disposed of last year. However, they still own and operate two DC-3s, G-ALWC & G-AMCA, which remain infrequent visitors to Manchester. Islanders used for company business this year were G-AVKC, G-AVRC & G-AWVY and Trislander G-BDTS was added to the fleet in July. Company liaison Islander G-AWVY was sold as N48BN in November and replaced by another, G-BDRV. Long term stored Dove G-AKSS was removed from the Fairey hangar in January, after being stored there since February 1975. It was broken into sections and removed by road.

The export of bridge sections manufactured by the FBNAS Group continued throughout the year and aircraft used were IAS CL-44 G-BCWJ, Tradewinds CL-44s G-AWDK, G-AWGS, G-AWGT & G-AWOV and Cargolux CL-44 TF-LLI. Romanian built Islander G-BDMU arrived from Bembridge on 26th February, in primer, as did all subsequent aircraft. Islander G-BCWU, based in the Sudan, arrived for major overhaul on 27th February. Defender G-BCMY arrived for maintenance on 13th March and became the company's demonstrator of the type.

John Britten and Desmond Norman decided to leave the FBNAS group in April. When the group acquired Britten-Norman Ltd in 1972, they made an agreement that as soon as their company was fully integrated into the Fairey Company, they would leave their management posts, but still assist with specific design and development of prospective new aircraft.

April saw the arrival of Sir Douglas Bader's Beech 95 G-APUB on the 9th for maintenance and renewal of its Certificate of Airworthiness and Islander TZ-ACF arrived on the 13th, for the fitting of spray booms. Also during April, the company sold DC-3 G-AMCA. Having been built in 1945 and purchased by Fairey in 1949, it was an extremely low mileage airframe, having clocked up a mere 14,000 hours in thirty-one years. Red Devils Islander G-AXHE arrived for maintenance on 10th May. Also in May was the arrival of the first of nine Romanian built Islanders for attention/storage: G-BDMX (20th), G-BDMY (24th) and G-BDMZ (27th). Others for the same purpose were - June: G-BDNA (10th) & G-BDMU (24th); July: G-BDND (1st), G-BDRN (15th) & G-BDRO (22nd) and September: G-BDRV (14th). Islander D-IHVH (12/07) arrived for minor work and G-BDMY (05/08) & G-AVKC (30/09) both arrived for maintenance.

The sale of the company's last remaining DC-3, G-ALWC, in October ended a twenty-seven year association with the type. Also this month was the arrival of Islander LN-SAM on the 16th, for the fitting of de-icing equipment. After the influx of Islanders at Fairey for temporary storage, November saw the arrival of seven Romanian Trislanders: G-BDTO (1st), G-BDWR (3rd), G-BDWS (9th), G-BDWT (10th), G-BDWU (11th), G-BDWV (17th) & G-BEDM (26th). Two more arrived in December: G-BEDN (6th) and G-BEDP (19th). Islanders arriving for major overhauls were G-AXHE (23/11) and the Red Devils G-AXDH (15/12).

The Company suffered from industrial action in December, when no work was carried out, but noted outside the hangar at the end of the month were Trislanders G-BEDM & G-BEDN and Islanders G-AXDH & G-AXHE. The rest of the Trislanders were inside with Islander G-BDRW.

Full details of the Islanders involved in 1976 (1977) are as follows:

Reg.	First Flight	Del to the UK	Del To Ringway	Departed
G-BDMU	09/02	26/02	24/06	22/07
G-BDMX	27/02	12/03	20/05	15/07
G-BDMY	19/02	05/03	24/05	22/07
G-BDMZ	23/03	28/03	27/05	05/08
G-BDNA	29/03	03/04	10/06	14/09
G-BDND	10/04	23/04	01/07	31/08
G-BDRN	17/04	27/04	15/07	10/09
G-BDRO	26/04	16/05	22/07	20/09
G-BDRV	14/06	24/06	14/09	15/11
G-BDRW	25/06	05/06	15/11	26/01/77

Reg.	First Flight	Del to the UK	Del. To Ringway	Departed
G-BDTO	07/04	05/05	01/11	12/01/77
G-BDWR	24/06	30/06	03/11	06/12
G-BDWS	08/07	09/08	09/11	19/01/77
G-BDWT	12/08	18/08	10/11	08/03/77
G-BDWU	21/08	25/08	11/11	17/03/77
G-BDWV	09/09	15/09	17/11	23/03/77
G-BEDM	18/09	23/09	26/11	15/04/77
G-BEDN	05/10	11/10	06/12	29/04/77
G-BEDO	15/10	22/10	26/01/77	16/06/77
G-BEDP	29/10	05/11	19/12	14/09/77

1977

The FBNAS group used the following aircraft for company business during the year and all made regular visits to Manchester: Islanders G-AVRC, G-BDRV & G-BESE, Trislander G-BDTS and Manchester based PA-23 G-AZZA. Aircraft used for exporting bridge sections were IAS CL-44 G-BCWJ, Tradewinds CL-44s G-AWGS/G-AWOV and Transmeridian CL-44s G-AXUL/N447T.

In complete contrast to December 1976, when nothing moved due to industrial action, movements started up again in January with the following departures: Trislanders G-BDTO (12th), G-BDWS (19th) and Islander G-BDRW (26th). Islanders G-AXDH & G-AXHE disappeared inside and at one point during the month when aircraft were being rearranged; seven Trislanders were sat outside for a short time! The tenth and final Trislander for attention/storage was G-BEDO, arriving on the 26th. February saw little activity at the hangar. Trislanders G-BEDN & G-BEDO were outside all month and Islander G-AXHE undertook engine runs and then an air test on the 28th. After last month's inactivity, there were five departures in March: Islanders G-AXHE (5th) & G-AXDH (30th) and Trislanders G-BDWT (8th), G-BDWU (17th) and G-BDWV (23rd). Trislanders G-BEDN and G-BEDO went inside during the month. Further departures in April were Trislanders: G-BEDM (15th) & G-BEDN (29th) and Trislander G-BDTS operated numerous liaison flights from the 18th to the end of the month. In May, Islander G-AVKC arrived for minor work (4th) and Islander G-BEFK operated from/to Bembridge with a number of FBNAS management onboard (20th). Trislander G-BEDO, which had arrived 26th January, operated several test flights on 26th May before departing 16th June, only to return later in the day, before finally departing for Bembridge on 19th July.

Islander D-IHVH, arriving for maintenance on 1st July, was the last to be serviced at Manchester's FBNAS facility, before departing on 12th August. During the month the sole remaining Trislander, G-BEDP, was emptied out of the hangar and the only Fairey movements were liaison flights with Islander G-AVRC and Trislander G-BDTS. The hangar was then filled with prefabricated bridge sections. Due to uncertainty over the future of the company's aviation division, it's unclear whether the hangar will see any more Islanders or Trislanders. July was also the month the Fairey group signed a number of contracts to export bridges to the USA and Venezuela. September saw the final hangar-movement with the departure of Trislander G-BEDP on the 14th, as it was now full with prefabricated bridge sections, but PA-23 G-AZZA still operated from the hangar on a daily basis and there were two liaison flights on the 7th/28th with Trislander G-BDTS. Cessna 172 G-BAEO became a resident outside the hangar and was joined by PA-28 G-BBDB from Blackpool on the 29th September. Both of these aircraft were unconnected with the FBNAS group.

Aviation work had stopped completely by October and the arrival of Islander G-AVKC for maintenance with NEA on the 10th was a sign of the times, as it had previously been serviced by Fairey. The last company liaison flight took place on the 4th, when Islander G-AVRC operated from/to Bembridge. From October, PA-23 Aztec G-AZZA, Cessna 172 G-BAEO and PA-28 G-BBDB, all regularly parked on the apron outside the hangar. They were regularly flown and PA-28 G-BBDB departed back to Blackpool on 19th December.

1978

The Fairey hangar was full of bridge sections by now and several flights arrived to collect them in various quantities throughout the year. The apron outside was used for the parking and storage of various aircraft, mainly destined for Dan-Air engineering. The company's own PA-23 G-AZZA was sold in April to Air Charter Scotland. Cessna 172 G-BAEO was regularly parked until its landing accident in May. After being declared an insurance write-off, the fuselage was dumped outside. PA-28 Cherokee G-BBDB returned and was parked outside for long periods and seldom flew. PA-28 Cherokee G-BEZP, which arrived earlier in May, was parked outside occasionally when it wasn't flying and Cessna 150 G-BFRP, which had parked there since August 1978, was frequently active.

The Demise of Fairey

The Fairey group appeared stable, but alarm bells rang in July 1977, when a profit of £1.3m for the previous year was announced, a far cry from the £5m forecast! News of a special shareholders meeting to approve an increase in the board's borrowing powers sent the shares plummeting. As FBNAS had many interests outside aviation by then, the profit shortfall couldn't be solely contributed to their aviation activities, although it probably was the case.

The group manufactured the Islander, Trislander & Defender at their own Gosselies plant in Belgium and Bembridge had licence deals with Romania and the Philippines. As of July 1977, the production at Gosselies of eight aircraft per month had continued for longer than intended, due to delays in commencing production of F-16 fighter aircraft for NATO. At this point, Fairey had the expense of maintaining a 400-strong Belgian workforce. As their stock of Islanders stood at over £6m, they forced back the Gosselies output, stressing that production had been adjusted to reflect its selling rate. By this time sales of all versions of the Islander stood at 762.

In a statement issued on 19th August 1977, Shorts Brothers of Belfast announced their Managing Director was holding discussions with the Fairey Group's Chairman, Robert Holder, concerning acquisition of the Islander and Trislander aircraft business. Dealings in Fairey shares had been suspended on 16th August, when the group announced its detachment from Fairey Britten-Norman. This news and the groups concern over the excess unsold stock, estimated at one-hundred aircraft, caused further loss in confidence. During September, discussions on the Shorts Brothers takeover were underway and a declaration of intent was signed, with a view to the deal concluding on the 21st. Production at Fairey's Gosselies plant had already ceased in August, but one of the most difficult factors in the negotiations was compensation for the Belgian workforce and discussions on the transfer of jigs and tools from Belgium to Belfast were ongoing. The implications for Manchester meant the end of aircraft activity at the hangar and an uncertain future.

By October, there were still complications on the transfer of jigs and tools and the thirty unsold aircraft currently parked in Belgium were also stalling the final agreement. In the meantime a sit-in by Fairey workers at Gosselies was threatening the contract to build the F-16. In response to the action, Fairey threatened to close the plant and terminate the F-16 contract if they weren't allowed to transfer the civil aircraft production line without paying unacceptably high compensation. Shorts were unwilling to sign a firm agreement to take over the Islander and Trislander until the situation was resolved. By 11th October, the receivers had been called in and two parts of the Fairey group, Fairey Britten-Norman and Fairey SA (the Gosselies plant), were immediately liquidated. It was another story at Bembridge however, as it was business as usual for the three-hundred employees, involved in finishing, modifying, testing and selling the Islanders and Trislanders. High operating costs at Gosselies had emerged as the main reason for the group's financial difficulties, compounded by borrowings for the Belgian plant, guaranteed by the parent company. When the group's financial problems first came to light in the summer, great efforts were made to sell the design and manufacturing rights for the Islander and Trislander and had this have been successful, it would have relieved Fairey of a loss making operation and raised the capital to repay its debts.

Negotiations with Shorts advanced. The price and takeover of Britten-Norman had been agreed and would include the production jigs at Gosselies, but the Belgians decided the offer was too low and wouldn't compensate them adequately, so they forcibly prevented the removal of the jigs. At this point, Shorts still wanted to buy the Islander and Trislander part of the group and had the Government's approval to do so. Gosselies had been the primary manufacturer of these aircraft since Fairey bought the original Britten-Norman operation in August 1972. Bembridge had the design office and produced trial installations for modifications, fitted out primer aircraft and acted as a point of sale to the customer. Some of this work had been undertaken at Manchester, including major overhaul. The plan was for Britten-Norman (Bembridge) to buy the primer airframes from Gosselies and the Romanian production line. With regards to Shorts, their interest was likely to diminish if they couldn't obtain the equipment from Gosselies, to put the aircraft into production at Belfast.

By 5th November, hopes of Shorts purchasing the aviation side were receding and Fairey SA made independent efforts to sell Islanders, Trislanders and spare parts. It was even suggested they may apply for Belgian type certification. On 19th November, the receivers acting on behalf of Fairey's, rejected an offer from Shorts for both Britten-Norman and the Islander and Trislander interests of Fairey SA. Details weren't fully known, but Shorts negotiated jointly for the two sets of assets. Even though some rights, including the name Britten-Norman and the production and selling rights were understood to be held by Fairey SA, Shorts were still keen to acquire Britten-Norman, but they weren't prepared to resume negotiations as by then they were having difficulties raising enough funds from Northern Ireland to make a realistic offer. November also saw Britten-Norman amend its trading name to Britten-Norman (Aircraft) Ltd. By December, Britten-Norman was still going strong and appointing new dealers and Fairey SA at Gosselies were keen to continue marketing the aircraft, possibly in the USA. Negotiations with the Romanians on joint Islander production and sales ran into trouble when Fairey couldn't raise the funds. The Romanians were still keen on the venture, mainly because Fairey SA was the only organisation holding a complete set of Islander jigs and tools, as even the Romanian production line received the complete centre-sections from Gosselies, which was the only plant in the group capable of building and supplying the structures. By the close of 1977, the situation was not still fully resolved.

Fairey Holdings was formed in January 1978 to manage the non-aviation subsidiaries of the group, including Fairey Engineering. Production in Romania continued at the planned rate of four aircraft per month, which were delivered to Bembridge on completion. In February, after completion of the final assembly of twenty-two Islander and eleven Trislanders, production ceased at Gosselies, by which time the Belgian Government had effectively nationalised the Belgian plant to safeguard the countries commitment to the assembly of F-16 fighters.

Bembridge and Gosselies agreed terms for the delivery of the remaining aircraft to Britten-Norman in the UK. Belgium claimed they had the manufacturing and sales rights to the Islander and Trislander, but their claims were rejected by Britten-Norman. Another fifty Islanders, stored at Bembridge and Thorney Island, were mostly sold. In a final postscript to this story, in May the Fairey Group shareholders, who called in the receiver last October, were told they had lost their investment. Fairey tried for two months to sell the Britten-Norman part of the operation, citing the high cost of Islander and Trislander production at the Gosselies plant for the group's financial difficulties. At one time, Shorts seemed the likely buyer, but the extended negotiations had led to nothing. Britten-Norman continued to operate in receivership, but they no longer had the Belgian production line.

Afterword

WFEL Ltd, the world's leading tactical bridge manufacturer, is a successor company to the Fairey Aviation Company (FAC) and operates today (2011) from the same site in Heaton Chapel (National Aircraft Factory No 2), that was taken over in 1935 by FAC when it expanded its manufacturing base from Hayes, Middlesex.

Although not involved with aircraft manufacture WFEL Ltd is proud of its heritage and links with FAC and Ringway.

'Seventies Ringway' provides a detailed and fascinating account of not only the links FAC had with Ringway but also of some of its past history.

Mark Williams is to be congratulated on bringing a bygone age back to life that will remind aircraft lovers of the role the FAC played in the life of aviation in the UK and in the development of Ringway.

Max Houghton, Sales and Marketing Director, WFEL Ltd, Heaton Chapel

6

Airlines & Routes 1970-1979

Scheduled Passenger Routes

Aberdeen	British Airways	November 1974-October 1975, June 1976-1979
Amsterdam	BEA/British Airways	1970-1979
"	KLM	1970-1979
Antigua	BOAC	1970-1974 (Winter only)
Barcelona	Iberia	1970-1973 (Summer only)
Belfast	BEA/British Airways	1970-1979
Berlin	BEA/British Airways	1970-1979
Birmingham	BEA	1970-March 1971
"	Dan-Air	April 1972-1979
Bournemouth	Dan-Air	April 1972-1979
Bridgetown	BOAC	November 1970-April 1974 (Winter only)
Bristol	Dan-Air	July 1970-March 1979
Brussels	BEA/British Airways	1970-1979
"	Sabena	1970-March 1973, April 1975-1979
Copenhagen	Aer Lingus	1970-March 1978
"	BEA/British Airways	April 1970-1979
"	SAS	1970-1979
Cardiff	Dan-Air	July 1970-1979
Chicago	BOAC	1970-1971 (Summer only)
Cork	Aer Lingus	1970-1979
Dubrovnik	JAT	1973-1979 (Summer only)
Dublin	Aer Lingus	1970-1979
"	BEA/British Airways	1970-1979
Dusseldorf	Aer Lingus	1970-March 1974
"	BEA/British Airways	April 1970-1979
"	Lufthansa	April 1974-March 1975
Edinburgh	BEA/British Airways	1970-1979
Frankfurt	Aer Lingus	1970-March 1975
"	BEA/British Airways	April 1977-1979
"	Lufthansa	July 1970-1979
Geneva	BEA/British Airways	April 1972-1979
Glasgow	BEA/British Airways	1970-1979
Guernsey	BEA/British Airways	1970-1979 (Summer only)
Guyana	BOAC	1970-1974 (Winter only)
Jersey	British United	1970 (Summer only)
Larnaca	Cyprus Airways	1973 (Summer only), April 1979-December 1979
London-Gatwick	British Caledonian	November 1973-1979
London-Heathrow	BEA/British Airways	1970-1979
Madrid	Iberia	January 1970
Malta	Air Malta	April 1974-1979

"	BEA/British Airways	1970-November 1973, April 1974-October 1978, April 1979-October 1979
Milan	Alitalia	1970-October 1972
"	BEA/British Airways	April 1973-1979
Montreal	BOAC/British Airways	1970-October 1979
Munich	BEA/British Airways	April 1972-March 1976
Newquay	British Midland	1970/1972/1974 (Summer only)
New York	BOAC/British Airways	1970-1979
"	British Caledonian	June 1973-October 1973
Nice	British Airways	1976-1979 (Summer only)
Nicosia	Cyprus Airways	1973-1974 (Summer only)
Norwich	Air Anglia	November 1971-October 1972
Ostend	British Midland	1970/1972/1974 (Summer only)
Palma	BEA	1970
"	Iberia	1970-1971/1973 (Summer only)
Paris	Air France	1970-1979
"	BEA/British Airways	1970-1979
Port of Spain	BOAC	1970-1974 (Winter only)
Pula	JAT	1973/1975-1979 (Summer only)
Rome	Alitalia	1970-October 1972
"	British Airways	April 1974-1979
Ronaldsway	British Airways	April 1974-1979
"	Cambrian Airways	1970-March 1974
Rotterdam	British Air Ferries	June 1978-March 1979
"	British Island Airways	April 1979-December 1979
"	Swissair	1970-October 1971
Shannon	Aer Lingus	1970-March 1971
Teeside	Dan-Air	April 1973-March 1979
Tel Aviv	BOAC	January 1970-March 1970
Zurich	Aer Lingus	1970-March 1973
"	British Airways	April 1977-1979
"	Swissair	1970-1979

Scheduled Cargo Routes

Amsterdam	BEA/British Airways	April 1971-March 1978
Atlanta	British Caledonian	October 1979
Basle	Swissair	January-March 1970
Belfast	BEA	June 1970-October 1973
Boston	BOAC	May 1971-March 1972
"	British Airways	April 1974-March 1976
Brussels	BEA/British Airways	January 1975-April 1975
"	Sabena	1970-1979
Chicago	BOAC	November 1970-March 1973
"	Lufthansa	April 1972-October 1973
Copenhagen	SAS	November 1970-1979

Detroit	BOAC	November 1971-March 1972
"	BOAC	April 1973-April 1974
Dublin	Aer Lingus	1970-1979
"	Clyden Airways	September 1978-1979
Dusseldorf	BEA/British Airways	November 1971-April 1975
Frankfurt	BEA	1970-October 1971
"	Lufthansa	1970-1979
Helsinki	Finnair	April 1977-1979
Houston	British Caledonian	April 1978-1979
London-Heathrow	BEA/British Airways	1970-April 1975
Milan	Alitalia	April 1970-July 1977
Montreal	BOAC/British Airways	1970-August 1976
New York	BOAC/British Airways	1970-May 1977
"	Northwest Orient	September 1979
Oslo	SAS	April 1972-October 1972
Paris	BEA	September 1971-October 1971
Philadelphia	BOAC	January 1970-October 1970
Rome	Alitalia	April 1970-July 1977
Rotterdam	Sabena	November 1975-March 1979

Charter/IT Operators

Air Canada	Operated a summer programme on behalf of Jetsave using DC-8s in 1975.
Air Europe	From November 1979, served various IT destinations with a based Boeing 737.
Air Malta	Began scheduled services in April 1974, IT flights operated from Summer 1977.
Air Portugal	Faro (1979) Summer only.
Air Spain	June 1972-November 1974, a range of Spanish IT destinations were served all year round with DC-8s, before they ceased trading.
Aviaco	Alicante (1970-1971, 1975, 1977-1978), Barcelona (1973-1974), Gerona (1970-1971), Ibiza (1970, 1973, 1975), Malaga (1973-1974), Mahon (1979), Palma (1970-1978) and Tenerife (1978) also served as a winter destination (1976/77 & 1977/78).
Aviogenex	Summer only destinations: Dubrovnik (1970-1979), Ljubljana (1970-1971), Pula (1970-1979), Rijeka (1971-1975), Split (1970-1979) and Zadar (1971-1973).
Balair	Summer only destinations: Basle (1970-1973) with Douglas DC-6/Fokker F.27s (1970/1971) and Douglas DC-9s (1972/1973).
Balkan Bulgarian	Bourgas and Varna (1970-1979) Summer only.
Bavaria	Munich (1970-1972).
BEA/British Airways	As well as an extensive scheduled network, the airline also operated IT flights to various European destinations (1974-1979).
British Airtours	Various European IT destinations were served during the summer (1970-1979).
BIA	Jersey (1971/1973/1974/1977-1979) Summer only.
Braathens	Bergen (1971-1972) Summer only.
Britannia Airways	Throughout the decade, the airline operated an extensive IT network to various destinations.
British Caledonian	Operated to various IT destinations (1971-1976), as well as summer only charters to the USA & Canada (1972-1977).
British Midland	Operated to various IT destinations (1970-1973).

British United	Operated to various IT destinations (1970-1971).
Caledonian	Operated to various IT destinations (1970-1971), also numerous charters to the USA & Canada (1970-1971).
CP Air	From 1975, the airline operated a regular summer programme on behalf of North American tour operator, Jetsave, serving the following: Montreal (1977-1979), Toronto (1975-1979), Vancouver (1976-1979).
Channel Airways	Operated a summer programme to various IT destinations (1970-1971) and winter IT programme from November 1971 until 14th February 1972, when the airline went into liquidation.
Court Line	Operated IT flights to various destinations from 1970-1974, until the airline's collapse on 15th August 1974.
Dan-Air	Throughout the decade, the airline an operated an extensive IT network to various destinations.
Donaldson Intl	Munich (1971) Summer only. They went into liquidation in 1974.
Inex-Adria	Summer only destinations: Zadar (1971), Pula (1973-1979) and Dubrovnik (1973-1976, 1979).
Invicta Airlines	Munich (1972) and Basle (1973) Summer only.
Laker Airways	Operated to various IT destinations throughout the decade, as well as ABC charters to the USA & Canada, Los Angeles (1975-1979), New York (1974-1979) and Toronto (1973-1979).
LOT	Krakow (1976-1979) Summer only.
Monarch Airlines	In April/May 1971, they operated a series of flights to Rotterdam and Beauvais and an IT flight from/to Tenerife October 1976-April 1977. From the summer of 1979, they based a Boeing 720 to operate to various IT destinations.
Northeast Airlines	Paris Le Bourget (1973) Summer only.
Ontario World	Toronto (1979) Summer only.
Pan American	Although they never had any specific schedules through Manchester during the 1970s, they were regularly seen operating ad-hoc transatlantic charters.
Phoenix Aviation	Basle (1972-1973) Summer only.
SAM	Rimini (1971-1974) and Venice (1972). Summer only.
Spantax	Palma (1970, 1972-1976, 1978-1979) and Tenerife (1972) Summer only, also Tenerife (1971-1973 winter).
TAE	Alicante, Barcelona & Palma (1979) Summer only.
Tarom	Constanta (1970-1972 & 1974-1979) Summer only.
TEA	Lourdes (1978) Summer only.
TIA	Operated occasional transatlantic charters through Manchester during the decade, in 1979 operated a weekly summer Manchester-New York charter flight.
Trans Europa	Alicante (1977-1978), Gerona (1978), Ibiza (1978), Malaga (1979) and Palma (1976-1979) Summer only.
TWA	From 1970-1976, the airline operated regular transatlantic charters from Manchester. In 1978 a weekly summer transatlantic charter flight was operated from Manchester to New York, on behalf of Jetsave holidays.
Wardair	Began regular operations from Manchester in 1975, operating for North American tour operator Jetsave. Since then, the following destinations have been served: Calgary (1979), Edmonton (1979), Toronto (1975-1979) and Vancouver (1975-1979).
World Airways	From 1970-1973, the airline operated regular transatlantic charters from Manchester. In 1978 they operated a summer series of transatlantic charter flights from Manchester to New York and Los Angeles, on behalf of Jetsave.

7

Glossary of Aviation References

ADF	Automatic Directional Finder.
ATCC	Air Traffic Control Centre.
ATIS	Automatic Terminal Information Service.
BEL	BELFAST VOR.
BIG	BIGGIN HILL VOR/DME.
BPK	BROOKMANS PARK VOR/DME.
CAT I	Permits an aircraft to land with a decision height of not lower than 200ft and an RVR of not less than 550m.
CAT II	Permits an aircraft to land with a decision height of not lower than 100ft and an RVR of not less than 300m.
CAT III	Permits an aircraft to land with a decision height of not lower than 50ft and an RVR of not less than 200m.
CAT IIIB	Permits an aircraft to land with a decision height of between 50ft-0ft and an RVR of not less than 075m.
DCS	DEANS CROSS VOR/DME.
DME	Distance Measuring Equipment. A combination of ground and aircraft based equipment used to measure the line of sight distance of an aircraft from a navigational radio beacon in nautical miles.
Dogger	Waypoint on Airway Blue One, located in the North Sea.
DTY	DAVENTRY VOR/DME.
DVR	DOVER VOR/DME.
Exmoor	Waypoint on Airway Amber 25, located in South West England.
FIR	Flight Instrument Rules.
GCA	Ground Controlled Approach.
Glidepath	The final path followed by an aircraft as its landing.
HON	HONILEY VOR/DME.
ILS	Instrument Landing System.
KNI	KNIGHTON VOR.
LAM	LAMBOURNE VOR/DME.
LIC	LICHFIELD VOR/DME.
Low Level Corridor	Enables aircraft to transit the Manchester airspace complex without the need for a specific clearance and the carriage of radio equipment. It also ensures that aircraft flying within it will remain clear of the published instrument approach procedures for both Liverpool and Manchester.
MID	MIDHURST VOR/DME.
N/S	Night-stop.
PAR	Precision Approach Radar.
POL	POLE HILL VOR/DME.
RVR	Runway Visual Range.
Special VFR	Special Visual Flight Rules. Pilots may request an SVFR clearance to enter the airspace and fly visually. They need to be equipped with a transponder.
SRA	Surveillance Radar Approach.
STOL	Short Takeoff and Landing.
'W' Pattern	A flight originating from another airport, for example if an aircraft routes Gatwick-Palma-Manchester-Palma-Gatwick, therefore the aircraft operating into Manchester would be on a 'w' pattern.
VOR	VHF Omni-Directional Range. The VHF navigational signal transmitted from this ground based installation allows the pilot to determine a magnetic bearing from the VOR station to the aircraft. VOR's are used to mark the intersections along the airways. Navigational reference points can also be defined by the point at which two radials from different VOR stations intersect, or by a VOR radial and a DME distance.
WAL	WALLASEY VOR/DME.
WOD	WOODLEY VOR/DME.